The Journal of
Peter Horry
South Carolinian

For Matt & Elizabeth
Thanksgiving
2012
Dad

The Journal of

Peter Horry
South Carolinian

Recording the New Republic
1812–1814

Edited by

Roy Talbert Jr. and Meggan A. Farish

The University of South Carolina Press

© 2012 University of South Carolina

Published by the University of South Carolina Press
Columbia, South Carolina 29208

www.sc.edu/uscpress

Manufactured in the United States of America

21 20 19 18 17 16 15 14 13 12
10 9 8 7 6 5 4 3 2 1

Library of Congress Cataloging-in-Publication Data
Horry, P. (Peter)
The journal of Peter Horry, South Carolinian : recording the new republic,
1812–1814 / edited by Roy Talbert Jr. and Meggan A. Farish.
p. cm.
Includes bibliographical references and index.
ISBN 978-1-61117-104-4 (cloth)
1. Horry, P. (Peter)—Diaries. 2. South Carolina—History—1775–1865—
Sources. 3. South Carolina—History—Revolution, 1775–1783—Sources.
4. United States—History—Revolution, 1775–1783—Sources. 5. United States—
History—War of 1812—Sources. 6. Slavery—South Carolina—History—Sources.
7. Slavery—Southern States—History—Sources. 8. South Carolina—Biography.
I. Talbert, Roy. II. Farish, Meggan A. III. Title.
F273.H79A3 2012
975.7'03—dc23
2012021978

This book was printed on a recycled paper with
30 percent postconsumer waste content.

For our mothers,
Betty and Patricia

Contents

Illustrations

Acknowledgments

Peter Horry's journal is owned by the South Caroliniana Library of the University of South Carolina, a gift from his in-laws, the Guignard family. We are grateful to Caroliniana director Allen Stokes and his staff for the many kindnesses shown us. The publication of the journal was supported by the largess of the Caroliniana Society, to which we are deeply indebted. Summer research in Columbia was made possible by Walter Edgar's Institute for Southern Studies and the Lewis P. Jones Visiting Research Fellowship. Similarly the assistance of the specialists at the South Carolina Department of Archives and History proved invaluable. The librarians at our own Coastal Carolina University, as always, were stalwarts, particularly in expediting our numerous interlibrary loan requests. Significant aid for this project also came from private gifts to the Coastal Educational Foundation and from the Horry County Higher Education Commission. We also benefited significantly from the aid and encouragement from Eldred "Wink" Prince, director of the Waccamaw Center for Cultural and Historical Studies, and from Benjamin Burroughs, historian at the Burroughs and Chapin Center for Marine and Wetlands Studies. USC graduate student Rachel Love Monroy toiled diligently, helping identify individuals mentioned in Horry's journal, and Coastal Carolina undergraduate Isaac Dusenbury was also of considerable assistance. Stephanie Freeman, office manager of Coastal Carolina's Department of History, kept the project on track and on budget. The editors hope to produce a full biography of the elusive Horry, but for the moment we offer this edition of his journal.

Introduction

In early 1812 Peter Horry began writing again. It must have been the onset of hostilities that stirred the old warrior's heart and pen. During the Revolution he had commanded a regiment of the Continental Line before riding to glory with Francis Marion—in the 1950s television series *The Swamp Fox*, Myron Healey portrayed "Pete" Horry, Marion's loyal sidekick, and Leslie Nielsen starred as the Swamp Fox. After the war Horry performed a valuable service to American historiography by being one of the first to collect documents from the war.[*] He hoped to have all five volumes published, and in late 1803 offered his "history" to the Georgetown Historical Society, which delayed and finally decided the cost of printing it was prohibitive. Sometime during the next three years, Horry had the unfortunate privilege of meeting Mason Locke "Parson" Weems, one of the great scoundrels of the American biography. In 1800 Weems, an Episcopalian minister and traveling book salesman, had published his famous *Life and Memorable Actions of George Washington*. He was the writer who gave us many of the fabrications about Washington, including the cherry tree fable. Weems was looking for a new topic and Horry wanted a publisher, so the two struck a deal, and Weems put the finishing touches on the manuscript. In 1807 he wrote Horry: "Knowing the passion of the times for Novels, I have endeavoured to throw some Ideas and facts about General Marion into the Garb and Dress of a Military Romance."[†] Horry was appalled at the liberties taken by Weems and complained, "You have carved and mutilated it with so many erroneous statements that your embellishments, observations and remarks must necessarily be erroneous as proceeding

---

[*]Several versions of Horry's war documents have survived. The most complete eventually ended up in the Peter Force Papers in the Library of Congress. See also Wates, "Meanderings of a Manuscript." Some of these letters were also included in Gibbes, *Documentary History of the American Revolution*. See also Leary, *Book-Peddling Parson*.

[†]The Horry-Weems correspondence is included in the Force Papers.

from false grounds. Most certainly, 'tis not my history but your romance." The mythical Swamp Fox, that endures to this day, is a product of Weems's wild imagination.*

After the bitter experience with Weems, Horry was a tired old man. He had outlived most of his fellow Continentals and could seldom make the trip to Charleston to meet the survivors at the Society of the Cincinnati. In 1812 he tried once again to tell his story in an autobiography. He wrote 134 pages, 76 of which focused on the war. Today the pages describing the war are missing. It is believed they were on loan to someone in Columbia, possibly William Gilmore Simms, and were lost when the city burned in 1865. William Dobien James used them in his 1821 *A Sketch of the Life of Brig. Gen. Francis Marion,* and Simms used them as well in his 1844 *The Life of Francis Marion.*

Horry was now writing again, using a stack of composition books that he listed by number. Book 1 was his autobiography, less the missing pages containing stories of his manhood and the war and its aftermath. The book that survives contains mainly anecdotes of his youthful escapades and misfortunes, notably his miserable conditions as an apprentice to a Georgetown merchant. As he said, "Even now, tho 50 years have Past, I feel what I cannot describe." He might have run away if it had not been for Magdeline Horry Trapier, his aunt, who rescued him. In 1812 Horry reckoned that he was born on March 12, 1743 or 1744, in what is now Georgetown County. He came from Huguenot stock, a descendent of his grandfather Elias, the original Horry who fled France for religious freedom in colonial South Carolina. Peter always regretted that his family did not send him to the old country for an education. Instead what learning he did receive came from the free school established by the Winyaw Indigo Society. Peter's family developed rice plantations on the North, or "French," Santee and on Winyaw Bay. Eventually he possessed four plantations; Belle Isle, the most well-known of these, is now a marina and community south of Georgetown. Dover and Prospect Hill adjoined Belle Isle, and Cove was on the Santee. Briefly put, he was part of the well-to-do planter class, owning more than one hundred slaves.

At the outbreak of the Revolution, the two oldest Horry brothers, Peter and Hugh, were among the first to join the rebel cause. On June 12, 1775, a year before the Declaration of Independence, the state congress chose captains for the regiments being established. Out of twenty elected, Francis Marion tied for

---

*Despite Horry's condemnation of Weems, and it is full of material that Weems fabricated, there is nevertheless a core of truth in the work. The South Caroliniana Library has an original edition of the Weems book that contains marginal comments made by Horry. See Salley, "Horry's Notes."

third and Peter Horry was fifth. He rightly had, as he later insisted, considerable seniority. Horry and Marion were in the Second Regiment, which distinguished itself at Fort Moultrie in 1776. In late 1779 Horry gained his own command, the new Fifth Regiment, and the rank of lieutenant colonel in the regular Continental Army. He also held a full colonel's commission in the state militia.*

Perhaps his claim to fame was that Horry simply survived. When the British seemed triumphant in the South, he was one of the few senior officers left in the field. The surrender of the large army in Charleston was the greatest disaster of the war, but both Horry and Marion were out of the city at the time. Shortly thereafter a boat-destroying assignment spared them from the catastrophe at Camden. Their good fortune made Marion, Horry, and a handful of ragged guerrillas the only force left in the lower half of South Carolina to oppose the British during the dark days of 1780. Hiding out in the area's swamps, they perfected the tactics of hit, run, and ambush, and they played a valuable role in sealing Cornwallis's fate as he headed for Yorktown. Horry had his horse shot from under him, and he received minor wounds on other occasions. Involved in numerous firefights and dangerous missions near the end of the war, he commanded the Swamp Fox's brigade when Marion was away. After the war he held several official posts, some obviously given as rewards for his service, and a seat in the state legislature was his for the asking. In 1801 the state divided Liberty District into Horry and Marion Districts. Today Marion and Horry counties are side by side, a tribute to those great men who stood nearly alone against the British.

Behind this heroic portrait, however, is another, more human Horry. Like General Marion, Peter was afflicted with a thin skin and a brooding nature. Unlike Marion he was not a natural leader. After Charleston, Horry served basically as a volunteer in Marion's Brigade, a small, irregular organ of the state government. Consequently he never felt secure about his earlier commission in the Continental Army Establishment. He spelled out his problems in frequent letters to Marion, to Maj. Gen. Nathanael Greene commanding the Southern Army, and to South Carolina's governor, John Rutledge.†

The best-known incident in which Peter Horry was involved was a bitter quarrel with Hezikiah Maham. It was a petty, ugly, and not very patriotic fight over status. The basis for the feud, and the first downturn in Horry's career, came in early 1780, when the Continental Congress ordered the six undermanned

---

*For biographical sketches of Horry, see Bailey and Cooper, *Biographical Directory of the South Carolina House,* 346–48; Roy Talbert Jr., "Peter Horry," in Edgar, *South Carolina Encyclopedia,* 459–60; and Talbert, *So Fine a Beach.*

†These letters and those referred to below are in the Force Papers.

South Carolina regiments reduced to three. The reorganization created a surplus of officers, and Horry, who had gone to check on his plantations, was among those who did not get commands, were listed as supernumeraries, and retired. Horry may have understood that command was denied him because of his age—he was the youngest lieutenant colonel in the South Carolina line—and later he may have appreciated the fact that being sent away kept him from capture when Charleston surrendered. His supernumerary status, however, raised the question of whether or not he lost his early date of rank.

After Charleston, Horry fled to North Carolina, where Maj. Gen. Johann de Kalb took him on his staff, but only as an observer. In the summer of 1780, he came back to South Carolina with Marion, leading one of his cavalry units. Horry felt hurt about being relieved of his duties, and in his later writings, it was his habit to refer to himself as "an old supernumerary officer." In June 1781 he received what appeared to be a wonderful opportunity for command, but it instead started a dispute that came close to destroying Marion's Brigade. General Greene, with Marion's advice, created two new units, with the commander of each designated "Lieutenant Colonel Commandant of a Battalion of Light Dragoons for the State of South Carolina, to be employed in the Service of America." Each commander was to recruit his own men and to impress his own horses. Horry hesitated until he was assured that "the acceptance of the commission shall not invalidate any claim you may have to rank in the Federal Army," referring to his old Continental commission. The other command went to Hezikiah Maham, and both commissions bore the same date of rank. Friction between Horry and Maham developed from the beginning. Maham felt that only one battalion should have been authorized, and he was reckless in his criticism of Horry, who, he said, had been "throne out [of the army] as a supernumerary." When placed under Horry's direction in a plan of operation, Maham demanded to see his commission and refused to admit that Horry's older Continental rating gave him seniority. General Greene sided with Horry, but the damage was done. The plan designed to increase mobility in the South actually hampered operations. By late 1781 the tension led to the first of several breaks between Horry and Marion. "I used to submit to General Marion's Orders with pleasure," Horry wrote Greene, "but at present I assure you it is disagreeable to me and all my officers that have experienced his late usage." Greene responded gently that Marion "is a good Man, few of us are without faults. Let his virtues veil his, if he has any." Horry finally paid a visit to Marion's camp, where they were able to talk out their differences.

Even after Cornwallis's surrender at Yorktown on October 19, 1781, the situation remained tense in South Carolina. The British still held Charleston and the area surrounding it, and in the interior there were pockets under Tory control, such as that nasty piece of territory up the Little Pee Dee River where

Loyalists raided either side of the Carolina border. In South Carolina it was absolutely essential that the Patriot army remain in the field to subdue the Tories and to see that the British in Charleston did not attempt an offensive. It was also imperative that the state get its government organized.

Francis Marion was among those elected to the new state senate meeting at Jacksonborough, and when he departed for that place in January 1782, he left Horry in command of the brigade. The feud between Horry and Maham intensified, and the two came close to blows. Horry complained to Marion that "Maham interferes with my command so much I can scarcely act" and literally begged Marion to come back to camp. Marion actually asked for permission to leave, but with barely enough senators present for a quorum, he was needed at Jacksonborough. Initially Marion and Greene backed Horry, but actually both believed that Maham was the better cavalry leader. Maham and Horry finally departed company, Maham to take his seat in the legislature and Horry on sick leave, still suffering from an illness he had contracted in the swamps in the summer of 1780. Meanwhile the British heard of the turmoil in the brigade, and within hours of Horry's departure, they struck the camp on February 24–25, 1782, inflicting some of the worst punishment that Marion's men ever endured. Interestingly enough, both Horry and Maham blamed Marion for the disaster.

The British threat continued, and morale in the American forces was quite low, with enlistments running out and desertions increasing. Horry and Maham's battalions were considerably undermanned and the logical decision was to combine them, but who would get that single command? It never occurred to Horry that Marion would consider Maham. Yet the Swamp Fox gave him the nod because, as he wrote Greene, "it is the wish of most of Horry's officers to act with Col. Maham." First he gave Horry command of Georgetown, which at the time looked like a reward of easy duty but in fact had turned into a tough assignment, with privateers attacking and businessmen unhappy with continued military authority. Horry also learned that despite a recommendation from Marion, he had been turned down for promotion to brigadier general. He must have sensed that he was being had, and so he resisted the consolidation of units. The plan that had been concocted in mid-March 1782 hung fire for two months until Marion summarily stripped Horry of his horses, gear, and swords. The next month, after some angry letters to Greene about Marion, Horry relinquished command of the Georgetown garrison to Capt. William Allston and went home. He soon returned and made Georgetown a vital supply base for American forces in the South. In August he retired again, only to change his mind and ask General Greene for a command. By then the British were preparing to leave Charleston, signaling the real end of the war. Horry's help was no longer needed.

The relationship between Horry and Marion was too close not to overcome the damage done by the Maham feud, and within a few months after the war, the old comrades were reconciled. They both served in the state militia, and after Marion retired in 1794 and the system was reorganized, Horry commanded the Sixth Brigade, finally achieving his long-desired rank of general. He may have been the last of the old fighters to see the Swamp Fox alive when he made one of his frequent visits in February 1795, shortly before Marion died. Horry ran his militia effectively, most noticeably in 1798 when there were rumors that the French were about to invade, and again in 1802 against a possible slave revolt. He retired from the militia in 1806, when Robert Conway succeeded him. After the war Horry rebuilt his plantations and settled down to the life of rice planter. Sometime thereafter he married Sarah Baxter, a year or two younger than he. The couple had no children, and Sarah, his "amiable consort," died in 1791.* On February 9, 1793, Horry married Margaret Magdalen Guignard. Unfortunately that union also failed to produce heirs. Involved in numerous services to his state, Horry represented Prince George Winyah Parish in the South Carolina legislature in 1782 and again from 1792 to 1794. The same parish sent him to the state senate from 1785 to 1787.

In the last, surviving pages of his autobiography, book 1, Horry discusses his troubling economic situation. As a rice planter he was an exporter, and the European wars and self-imposed American trade restrictions of the mid 1790s had disrupted commerce. In the late 1790s, Horry attempted to dispose of much of his land holdings, and although he advertised frequently in the state newspapers, he found no buyers. That was Horry's condition when he began book 2, a journal of his daily activities. By this time he and his wife were an elderly couple who spent a great deal of time apart. She was often away visiting relatives in Stateburg and Columbia, while he lived in Georgetown managing his plantations. Georgetown was regarded as a sickly place in the summer months, so everyone who was able left during that season. The very rich were abroad or up north, while others, like Horry, removed to North Island just off the mainland. The journal begins in the spring of 1812, as he prepares to make the trip to the barrier island. It would be his last summer there, after which he moved to Columbia.

The journal becomes an account of the rest of his life—he died just two and a half months after the last entry. A good portion of Horry's journal appeared in print in the 1930s and 1940s thanks to Alexander S. Salley.† We

---

*City Gazette and Daily Advertiser, November 11, 1791.

†Salley published portions of Horry's journal in volumes 38 to 48 of the *South Carolina Historical and Genealogical Magazine.*

are pleased to present here the entire journal in one work. To be sure it has its share of mundane daily activities—the weather, the trips to collect firewood, and the names of numerous people he encountered. In that last regard, it is evident that Horry, retired brigadier general and state senator, ran with the elite. Because the same names appear so frequently, we provide biographical sketches in appendix C of all we could identify. We also give both Horry's version as well as the correct spelling of those names. Horry learned to write in the early 1750s, and his script is fairly difficult to decipher. In this regard we were aided considerably by Kip Sperry's *Reading Early American Handwriting*, and we have included a few pages from Horry's journal. We hope we have been gentle and faithful to Horry's work, and we have described in the editorial method section the protocol used. The manuscript itself is in fair shape, with generally the first and last pages of the books in the worst condition. There are then a number of places where we note that text is missing. We have omitted no material except a few obvious errors that Horry himself crossed out and corrected.

Apart from his association with his peers, several themes emerge over time. Horry spent most of his time in the company of his slaves, and his everyday life was shaped by his interactions with them. While Horry may have considered his domestic slaves as an extended part of his family, he had no reservations about the institution itself. Never once does he speak of the rising abolitionist movement or the contradictions of a democracy for whites only. Horry lived in a world he assumed would never change, even though questions of the morality of slavery were beginning to rock the political stability of the nation. To him slavery was not only necessary for his economic prosperity, but he also, clearly, viewed it as a "positive good." He considered it insulting and unfathomable that any of his slaves would dare abscond from the comforts and reliability of plantation and domestic life. We will never know the intimate details of the lives of Horry's slaves, but his journal provides a small glimpse of the changing nature of slavery during this era. In appendix A we have included the list of slaves Horry owned at the time of his death.*

Other significant themes presented by Horry include the sad state of the economy and the difficulties in transportation. His trips back and forth to Columbia and Georgetown are very revealing, particularly the fact that he had his household goods shipped to Columbia by boat up the Santee. Horry's interest in agriculture is evidenced by his concerns about storms destroying his rice fields, as well as his attempt to farm in Columbia. Equally obvious is

---

*Will of Peter Horry, Richland District, March 3, 1815, Book E, 296, South Carolina Department of Archives and History.

that he remained an ardent patriot, something of a war hawk, in the War of 1812. Politically he was a Federalist and an avid reader of whatever newspapers he could obtain. As an older man, Horry spoke often of his health and the remedies he applied. Similarly he attended church frequently and seems to have been equally satisfied in Baptist, Methodist, and Episcopalian services. His wife, Margaret, was a devout Methodist, who no doubt was converted during one of Francis Asbury's visits to Georgetown. Regarding alcohol, Horry may be an example of the emerging temperance movement. While he enjoyed wine on occasion, he was more likely to use brandy as a rub rather than a drink.

In 1813 Horry moved to Columbia to join his wife and her family. Much of the journal concerns his construction of his home, now known as the Horry-Guignard House. Located near the University of South Carolina (then South Carolina College), it is one of the few homes that survived destruction in 1865. He enjoyed the social life of the new town and state capital, especially the company of college students, and the journal at both North Island and Columbia clearly demonstrates the importance of visiting in those days. He also purchased a farm a few miles north of town, probably on Old Winnsboro Road, where he began growing crops, including cotton and rice. In very poor health after the summer of 1814, Horry died on February 28, 1815, and was buried in the Guignard plot at Trinity Church in Columbia. His personal property, including slaves but not real estate, was valued at slightly more than $38,000. To his wife he left Belle Isle Plantation, the Georgetown house, thirty-four slaves, and "my household and kitchen furniture, my riding chair, carriage horses, and mules." He divided the other plantations and slaves among relatives. Margaret died April 17, 1817, and was buried in Georgetown at Prince George Winyah.

Despite his lack of economic success and the self-pity that is evident in his journal, it is difficult to believe that Horry died feeling a failure. Until the last he hoped to find a publisher for his journal. His heart, it seems, was never focused on making money. If it had been, he would not have deserted his lands at great loss to fight the war, nor would he have spent so much energy on chronicling that conflict. Although not considered a legendary planter, Horry was certainly a patriot, devoted to public service.

Editorial Method

Journal entries are formatted as "day, month, year." Superscript numbers have been changed to arabic numerals. Horry's figures have not been converted to modern currency. Dollar and pound symbols have been placed before the numbers.

All names are capitalized, but other proper nouns follow Horry's style. Superscripts are spelled out in full. Charleston and Georgetown are spelled as written (George Town and Charles Ton or Charles Town). The first word of every sentence is capitalized, as is the first word of all journal entries. Journal entries end with a period unless the entry continues to the following day. Unless otherwise noted, Horry's capitalization and spelling have been left untouched.

In a series Horry customarily uses a mixture of periods, dashes, and commas. The periods and dashes have been changed to commas. Stray and multiple punctuation marks have been removed. Punctuation after abbreviated names has been removed, as has punctuation separating a person's first and last name. A period is used with currency and to separate initials and abbreviations. Ellipses have been deleted, except before or after *ditto*.

If correctly used, parentheses have been closed. Stray parentheses have been removed. Quotation marks have been completed and only one set of quotation marks is used per quotation.

Long dashes have been removed except when used correctly. If Horry used a long dash instead of a period, the dash has been replaced with a period.

Words underlined by Horry in the journal are also underlined in the text.

With the exception of *Co.,* all abbreviated words are spelled out in full. The following abbreviations and titles are standardized: A.M. and P.M.; Miss, Mrs., Mr., and Dr. (except when Doctor is superscripted); *N.B.* instead of *NB; Viz.* instead of *Viz*; pair* instead of *1/P; pound(s)* instead of *lb.;* and *etc.* instead of *&c^a.*

The following items are omitted from the published text: words and phrases Horry crossed out; marginal notes; newspaper articles found at the beginning of each book; Horry's militia rules and instructions and order book; and repeated words and phrases.

Where a page is broken off, "[text missing]" is inserted. When a word is not readable, "[illegible]" is used. Brackets are used to add letters to incomplete words when clarification is needed. Misspellings that could potentially confuse the reader have been corrected.

Blank spaces and blank lines inserted by Horry are included in the text. The following words are standardized: *today* instead of *to day; countrymen* instead of *country men; everything* instead of *every thing;* and *XCut* instead of *X Cut.*

The Journal of

Peter Horry
South Carolinian

BOOK TWO

June 10, 1812–June 21, 1812

Book 2nd. The Life of General Horry
[text missing] a Journal, daily Transactions
Enserted at George Town South Carolina.

*P*reface to the Reader. I Comonly say in this Book [that] my former or first Work, I found was too Laborious for me [to] Continue & therefore this mode of Amusing my mind thought best Suited my Present Situation, time will shew [text missing] if this or any other my Productions will be worth Reading by my Countrymen. I am free to write my Sentiments & they are not Oblidged to read them, unless they Chose so to do. I live a Painfull Life, 'tis not my Choice, but my Maker's I must Submit to his will, & as we all are Compelled to do.

The present times are Awfull & full of Doubts & fear. We have Enjoyed the fat of our Land & Lived Luxuriously but Lately many of us Live, or Rather but Breath & hunger [text missing] us in the face. We are not a happy People, whether the fault of Government, or ourselves is the question. Whether Internal Enemies are Praying on our Vitals, & whether 'tis not by our Manly Exertions, rid our Country of Such Vermin, to Cut [text missing] Throats, or Kick them from us. Some Say Let us have a Levelling Sistem, this is Prepostirous truly. None will then work & how are the world to Subsist. It must End in despair & Confusion. France once was for Such Government but Monsieur [text missing] This Great Minister wrote a book on it, & Convinced [text missing] it was only a Chemera or Dream. We are at this [text missing] root of all Evil, then Rouse my Country [text missing] You have all the Empliments of War Seize then this Juncture, & Step forward with your best foot & take the field your Leaders are Reader, then Courage (Americans) *only* are wanted & Surely you are not degenerated from your Ancestors. They have Conquered & so Can you.

Wednesday, June 10. I rose Early this morning & with Mrs. Helin went in my boat to my Dover plantation,* we dined thereat, our Servants Got us, huckelberries, Pumbs, black berries & Mullberries. We Embarked on Return & with a fair wind & flowing Tide Got home in half an hour. The dry weather I found was at Dover & as in Town, my Large Garden was nearly burnt up. I could not See my Overseer but directed my Chief Carpenter to Go with *his* hands to the North Inlet† to [text missing] my house there, for the Reception of Mr. [text missing] by the 16th Instant. I Soon went to bed [text missing] by this days Exurtion, only [text missing] Soon Left me. Before Going [text missing] The Militia was Ordered [text missing] companies had Volunteered their Services, & that he had also offerered the same at George Town. Note however fashionable Lately to Call for Volunteers. I have no Oppion of their Real Services. General Marion always Said it was a Sculking Position. Their Officers dare not fine the Men for fear of Loosing their Commissions. The Superior Subject to the Inferior is Contrary to all Military Rule, no People can war with success because all are Rulers or Nature Perverted Bonapart is Always Successful but he is dispotick, his will Governs France & his Army Surports his Will our Maker knows whats best for us. A Minister was Requested to pray for Rain, he said tis well, but he'll be dam'd if it Rained before the moon Changed. The same Minister at another time, said he [text missing] for Rain, Except the Planters Present were Unanimous [text missing] it in one field, but not in the one [text missing] their Corn & Cotton but not on [text missing] Suffering for want of Rain [text missing] Sullivans Island in 1776 said he did not pray, as Some of his Brother Officers had done Because his maker knew what was best for him, to Ask him for what he Already knew would be Insulting him. He was much Admired but this Officer was then a Lieutenant of mine, he rose to a Captaincy, took to Drinking & was found Dead in Charles Town Streets. General Moultrie Said a Good Officer must Run Risks, & that

---

*Dover plantation was one of Peter Horry's three Winyah Bay plantations. It had once been a part of the 12,000 acre grant known as Winyah Barony, and Elias Horry II acquired roughly 1,600 acres of the land through sale. Horry inherited the land from Elias and in 1801 divided it into his three plantations: Prospect Hill, Dover, and Belle Isle. At his death he willed the property to his niece Mary Horry, and the property eventually passed to Sarah Hall Horry Bay after Mary's ownership. Lachicotte, *Georgetown Rice Plantations,* 1.

†North Inlet is located about seven miles north of the Georgetown Lighthouse and connects to Winyah Bay through Town Creek and Jones Creek. In 1912 a second inlet broke through about a half mile south of the old inlet, each having a depth of roughly three feet at low tide on the sandbar. High sand dunes separate the two inlets. *United States Coast Pilot Atlantic Coast,* 66.

it was his Duty so to do, nor do any know whether he can be Successful for Events only Proves it.

Thursday, June 11. This morning I rode out in Company with Mrs. Elliot daughter of the Reverend Mr. Wayne. Saw in Town Miss Danford, Delesseline & one or two other Ladies, they were well & I talked Love Matters to them. In the Evening rode out with Colonel Huggins 2 Daughters.

Friday, June 12. This morning rode out with the Widow Davis & I wrote my Mrs. Horry a very long Letter, to be Sent to her at Columbia [text missing] Clouds but only a Little Rain fell, I am [text missing] Wench Tinah to Go to her Mistress up the [text missing].

Saturday, June 13. Rose very Early [text missing] Waggon. Then went to it my Self [text missing] the Sandpit Rode & on Returning met the waggon with Servants Baggage etc. A cool day for its Travelling. They went to the Gapeway* on Black River,[†] this night.

Sunday, June 14. This morning went to the Episcable Church[‡] heard a Sermon from Parson Halling. Returned to my house & Miss Francis Harvey Visited me. We taulked of Love & the Devil—no harm Surely in Either, wrote to my Overseer, by Servant Billy a fine Shower of Rain Last night, & Some today.

*Gapway Bay is a swampy region, slightly topographically depressed, that is located between the Pee Dee and Black Rivers near Winyah Bay. In November 1780 Francis Marion used Gapway Bay as a hiding place from the British, and it was from the Gapway camp that his nephew, Gabriel Marion, ventured out to his death. Rogers, *History of Georgetown County,* 166, 173.

[†]The Black River runs southeastward through Williamsburg County, South Carolina, entering the Waccamaw River about three miles from Georgetown. Nearly 150 miles long, the river drains parts of Sumter and Clarendon Counties and gives its name to a township in Georgetown. Thomas and Baldwin, *Complete Pronouncing Gazette,* 1:244.

[‡]While Prince George Winyah Parish was established in 1721, the cornerstone of the Prince George Winyah Espiscopal Church was not laid until 1745. The church was constructed with English brick used as ballast in ships on the corner of Broad and Highmarket Streets. The bell tower was added in 1824, and in 1873 a stained glass window was donated from St. Mary's Chapel for slaves on Hagley Plantation. Both the parish and the corresponding church take their name from George, Prince of Wales, later King George II of England. During the American Revolution, it is said that the British stabled their horses inside the church building during the occupation, a gesture that the Union Army repeated during the Civil War. Despite its multiple occupations, the church has never closed its doors for worship since its first service in 1747. Boyd and Clark, *Georgetown and Winyah Bay,* 44.

Excerpt from book 2 of Peter Horry's journal

Monday, June 15. This morning rose Early was Unwell rode out with Mrs. Davis, many Clouds. Some Rain, Saw Mr. Cheesborough & Smith. Gave him a Letter of Introduction to my Factors North & Web of Charles Ton & to Know their opinions of Rice.*

---

*North and Webb were rice and cotton factors in the city of Charleston who worked with Peter Horry. Factors operated in the city as agents able to store and hold their clients' crops and take advantage of the highest market prices. Factors charged

Tuesday, June 16. [text missing] out with Miss Delesseline & Miss Shields [text missing] Miss Delesseline & Miss [name not given] Visited [text missing] Unwell. Saw Mr. Cheesborough [text missing] to Go to the Inlet Tomorrow.

Wednesday, June 17. Rose very Early, & all my Servants & Getting Ready for Embarkation & Sent my Bedding Chain, bed Benches, boards etc. with Bread, Rice, buckwit etc. on boards with Some warm Cloaths. Breakfasted Early & all hands went on board about 8 OClock. A Promising Passage (a fine day) Stoped at Dover to take in 2 Oarsmen. Made our Passage from Dover to North Inlet in 3 hours & found my Carpenters forward Repairing my House etc. Captain Benjamin Trapier Visited me, & this Evening I Visited Mrs. Trapier at her House, Went to bed Early this Night. *I found my Room very Cold* Did Not Sleep well.

Thursday, June 18. Breakfasted with B. Trapier. Then Took Boat & went to Dr. Blythe, Dined with him & Mrs. Blythe, Miss Bowman & Mr. Pyatt Junior. Lodged with Mr. Michau. found him better.

Friday, June 19. Breakfasted with Mr. Michau & his two Sons. Took boat & Dined at home at Brown Town.* Mr. Croft Visited me. This Evening rode [text missing] & with Mr. Cheesborough.

Saturday, June 20. Rode out & Called on Doctor & Mrs. Helin. After breakfast at home Parson Norton Called on me & spent 2 hours with me. Not quite Recoved of my Excursion to the Island. This Evening Rode Alone but Mr. Cheesborough Called on me after night & Spent an hour or two with me. He wishes for a Lieutenants Commission in our Continental Army. He refused a 2nd Lieutenants Commission. I think he would Accept a Quarter Masters department. He is a worthy young man & none Pays me so much attention or has Rendered me more Services. I wish to make him happy. This thought made me Dream. I rose Early Sunday morning never more Satisfied with my Nights Performances.

Sunday, June 21. Rode out this Morning alone. Returned home. Breakfasted & Dressed. Shaved etc. etc.

---

a fee for their services and sold cotton and rice at the best possible price while keeping their clients informed of the status of their shipments. "James vs. Mayrant, Columbia, December, 1824," in *Reports of Equity Cases*, 181; Woodman, *King Cotton*, 10–11.

*Browntown was a section of Georgetown, South Carolina, given to the city by Charles Brown and Dr. Joseph Blyth. These ninety-one lots lay to the east of St. James Street and to the south of Market Street. Smith, "Georgetown," 94.

BOOK THREE

July 15, 1812–August 31, 1812

Book 3rd a daily Journal of the Life or Transactions
of Peter Horry, Late Brigadeir of the Militia of the
State of South Carolina. Commencd at North Island*
George Town district the 15th day of July 1812 & Ending
the 1st September 1812. Say 1 Month & 15 days.

To the Reader. Finding this Pursuit most Convenient & would not
Engage me but in Each days Transactions which would not tire My
Mind too much having Experienced the Same in Book Number 2 determined
my Continuation of the Same mode. I am at Liberty to write, so is the Reader,
to Read or not & if he finds it not worth his time, I Suppose he will read but
Little of this my Amusement for I write but to divert my thoughts from
myself, Perhaps amongst many things Related Some few may be beneficial to
my Countrymen. If so, my Purposes are fully Answered.

Tuesday, July 14. Just before Sun Set. I Got into My Sedan† & was Carried to the Sea beach & around to the Bason & Near to Mrs. Cogdells House

---

*Located ten miles southeast of Georgetown, North Island is a fifteen-mile-long
island at the mouth of Winyah Bay. The island consists primarily of marshland with
forested beach ridges reaching elevations of up to forty-two feet. During Horry's
stay there, a village called Lafayette, with approximately one hundred homes, existed
on the island. The 1822 hurricane swept away the entire town, and the island is now
a part of the Thomas Yawkey State Wildlife Refuge. Zepke, *Coastal South Carolina*,
66; Lennon, *Living with the South Carolina Coast*, 95.

†Originating in Italy in the late sixteenth century, sedan chairs were covered seats
carried with poles on the back and front. Prince Charles and the Duke of Bucking-
ham first introduced the chairs to England when they returned from Spain in 1623.
The name *sedan* was first adopted in England and probably came from the Latin
sedare (to sit). Although less likely, it may have also been connected with the French
town Sedan. Sometimes porches called sedan chair porches were constructed to
make getting in and out of the chairs more convenient. Groome, "Sedan Chair
Porches."

North Island in Georgetown

& Mr. Joseph Lessesne Butchers Pen & House & returned to my house, rather Uneasy that my flatt* with my Carriage, Mules & Cow & Calf etc. etc. had not made her appearance from George Town, yet I Slept this night uncommonly well, a fine Sea Air came into my Room till the Morning.

Wednesday, July 15 Awoke Early, felt much Refreshed, & as I arose the Appearance of the flat was announced to me, it was Good News Indeed, & I Saw my Carriage, Mules, Cow & Calf & Servants all well. Carpenters fell to work on my Carriage House, Kitchen, Stable, Steps, & Levelling Sand etc. etc. around my House, before night all was in Order & I rode out & Surveyed the Houses, beach & my old Situation for Getting fire wood & brought home a Small Load to my Kitchen Door, this Ride Enlivened me much I Saw Trapier today war was our Conversation, Paul Jones history he much Admired Trapier as an Officer Equals most at Winyaw. He is Captain of the George Town Light Infantry Company.

Thursday, July 16. Rose in Tolerable Spirits, arranged my Negroes to flat & boat Going up, the first to Dover, the other to George Town to my House to Mrs. Davis for Sundries wrote to her for. Isaac has directions to repair

---

*A flatboat is an old boat style that was popular throughout Europe and was later used in the rivers and inlets of the Carolinas. Flatboats have a flat bottom, sometimes slightly contoured toward the stern and bow, and flared sides that tapered into the bow. These boats are useful for their simple and economical construction as well as their adaptable design, good performance, stability, and ability to transport large loads in shallow, smooth, inshore waters. Constructed of a variety of woods, they can be rowed, poled, or sailed. Gilmore, "Flatboats," 414.

Immediately my Small boat at Dover to be brought me here to Catch fish, Clamps, Oysters, Crabs etc. Flat & boat Sot off from the Inlet about 9 OClock A.M. Rode as far as Collins road, pick up dry Wood Sufficient, & Loaded my Carrivan, & Landed it at My House Sussie, & Rachel, & Billy Zemo, London & Giddo are Left with me & Peggy & her Children & Abigal are Left with Mrs. Davis in my House at Brown Town. Yesterday Stopt at Major Wraggs & Captain B. Trapiers Houses, Saw their Ladies & themselves & Spoke to Trapiers Lady, & her Children. Wragg thinks no Enemy will Land on any part of South Carolina but at Sea we may Expect hard *fighting* Miss Maria Visited me Last Night for an hour, She was Inviting, & I felt myself but alass; the Thought of Sinning (Altho' the Devil Tempted me) prevailed & my better Sense Predominated.

Friday, July 17. Rose uncommonly well, having Last night Slept well, Rode the South Side of the Beach & on my way home took up Some Dry wood & Landed it at my Kitchen. A Cool Morning, it Rained Last night. Expect my boat today from Brown Town with Sundries from Mrs. Davis my friend at my house there. Saw but one Spot that a Sea Turtle had deposited its Eggs, it was already taken. I woke Soon enough but determined to rise in future by dawn of day for Several Reasons. I daily Kill flies when Setting at my Table; this morning being Clouddy & wet I Killed more than Usual, by Such means my House has not Superabundance of these Troublesome Insects. No flees as yet, & not many Musketoes at my house but near the woods, Southward of me & the marsh Road Leading to the Inlet are Great many. I have as yet Entered no House on North Island tho received many Invitations For Settlers thereon, as also from Dubourdieu* Side of the Inlet which is the North Side. Hope to Get News papers from George Town by Return of my boat today, I am as Eager after News as I ever was, tis Gratifying to hear how matters Goes on in the world altho' I can do but Little to benefit it. See In this human Nature Opperating on the mind which is never Satisfied. I fear I Moralize too much in my histories & tires the Readers therewith, I beg their Indulgences, for

*Located three miles north of Georgetown and six miles south of Pawleys Island, Debordieu Island has been called Yahany, Sandy Island, and finally Debordieu after the early, prominent citizen of Craven County, Joseph Debordieu. Variant spellings of the name include Dubordie and Debidue. Joseph Alston and Theodosia Burr, the daughter of Aaron Burr, spent many of their summers on the island at their residence "The Castle." A hurricane on September 27, 1822, destroyed most of the property on the island and killed a large number of residents. During the Civil War, Confederate soldiers successfully escaped to Debordieu Beach after their blockade-runner, the *Dan,* had been captured by the Federals. Zepke, *Coastal South Carolina,* 53–54.

The lighthouse on North Island in Georgetown

Certain I am my performances Requires, both Indulgences & Patience, my hours hangs heavy on me is my best Opoligy to my Readers & on their part may Equally press on them when they Read this my work. About 1 OClock P.M. Mrs. Cogdell, & Mrs. Croft & Mrs. Lessesnes Mother, arrived in Mrs. Crofts boat. Croft Stopt at her House near the Inlet, the two other Ladies came to their Houses near the Bason & not far distant from *my* House, On Enquery Mrs. Cogdell Sent me word That my boat was on her way but Called in at Dover so I Look for her this Afternoon. According to Expectation my boat arrived about 6 OClock P.M. with a Letter to me from Mrs. Davis & Sundry Articles that I had wrote her for, this Seasonable Supply Enabled me to Live more Comfortable. My Chief Carpenter Buddy also brought me a Dog a Cat & 10 pair Window Sashes which were Sufficient for my House up Stairs as well as below & now I Can Lodge a friend at any time, Yet I want a boat to Catch fish & Mr. Lessesne has not yet began to Butcher on the Inlet at his Pen & House. Saw Dr. Thomas for the first time Since my Arrival here. He Looks badly & Says Mrs. Thomas is very Sick at the Inlet House, formerly Occupied by Lieutenant Heriot & his Souldiers in Continental.

Saturday, July 18. Rose Early & rode out as far as Collins's Road which Leads to his house not far from Mrs. Martins house South Side of North Island. Returning home brought Some wood which Landed at Kitchen. Breakfasted & Prepared boat to Go up to Dover & Brown Town. Wrote Mrs. Davis & My

Overseer Each a Letter boat Sot off about 10 OClock A.M. After my boat Crew Embarked I found I was Left with only Susie & Rachel (I cannot say too much of these my two Servants, the former Acts towards me as a Mother & the Latter as a Sister, at All hours they attend to my Calls with Chearfulness & tenderness used towards me. I wish I may ever have it in my Power to Reward their Attention to me, few Negroes Possess a Sense of Gratitude, these were born on my Plantation & brought up by my hands—I will ever Acknowledge their Goodness to me) also Billy & two Little boys were now all my Domesticks—barely Sufficient to Raise & take me out of my bed. However Monday I Expect my boat to Return, which will Reinforce me with Addition of 3 more Servants, & yet more Supplies. High wind today & very Cloudy, made up another bed today in another Room below Stairs & went to bed for about 4 hours, at 1 OClock P.M. the Sun came into the South West Window, & Oblidged me to Get up & to write thus far of this my history, Dined at 2 OClock P.M. in the Evening rode out as Usual to North Side of my house & to Joseph Spoke to her & another Jew Lady. Not to mind their Cloaths being a Little Lifted for their Stockings were Clean Going onwards I came up with on the beach A Party of Islanders. B. Trapier Exercising them, these men Imbody here for their own protection against Maurauders of any kind. They are well Armed. Heavy Clouds appeared I made off & Rode home very fast, Soon after I Got home, it Rained a Little but in the Course of the Night a Great deal of Rain fell.

Sunday, July 19. Rode out (a Cool Morning). Today wrote to Mrs. P. Horry of my Removal to North Inlet & to our house from whence I now write. Also many particulars related to her & as I Usually do. Boat Arrived from Town & Dover, fowles from the former & from the Latter Ducks & Hogs the two Last Mentioned Support themselv[es] from Fidlers, Crabs etc. the produce of the Island, Got a news Paper which Contains Account of the British Government dismissing their Ministers & about Appointing others more favourable to America, they have also repealed their Order of Counsel, & tis Said the Russian & french have had a Severe battle in which Three french Regiments were Cut to Pieces. I say Soon there will be a General Peace, not only with America, but all Europe. Blessed End, worthy, the Interposition of the Sovereign of the world. Saw B. Trapier at his House in Company with, Hassell, Irvin Keith & John Man Taylor, all Drinking Good wine, I drank a Glass of it with them & Rode round to North Inlet & Returned home about dust of the Evening, & Soon was in Bed.

Monday, July 20. Rode out & discovered that a Sea Turtle had crawled up the beach & deposited its Egs but before we Could come up the hogs had Eat all the Eggs. Sent out & Got 3 Studs to fix in a Second Room to support a foot board to A bed therein, Sent Mrs. Trapier a Parcell of Water Mellions, also Mrs. Thompson. Last Evening Mr. Lessesnes Cattle arrived from Wacca-maw. About 30 head & appeared in Good Order & this Evening he will Kill a Beef from his Pen on the Bason for the first time, this Year. Mrs. Lessesne & Thompson Sent me a Messuage that they will Shortly Visit me with Joseph Lessesne Junior a Boy I Brought home this Morning a Load of fire wood. Susie is to feed the Hogs only at Night, to Cause them to Come home from the Woods & Marshes, where in the day they must find their own Sustenance. She also feeds Ducks & fowls as She finds Necessary. My Part is to See the Dog & Catts fed from my own Table twice a Day. Billy Says the dog also is fed by him from his own Allowance I now have a prospect of Much better Living & to See my Domestic Annimals in Good Condition.

Tuesday, July 21. Rose very Early & drove to the South Side of the Island. Saw Malitia Souldiers Encampment Near the Light House* about 160 in Num-bers, Spoke with Captains Hill & Gasqua & Visited Mrs. Martin, Saw there Windham Trapier & the Widow Wragg & her Youngest Son Dined with them & about dark Got home & went to bed.

Wednesday, July 22. My Cook Susie played me a Trick; for yesterday She did not go for beef & Rachael Sent for no Switches tho' She Knew none was here & that it was her duty to Say as Soon as She Got here, *there* was no Switches. So I Could Punish Neither of these Wenches. Words they Got, but words, from me to them without Switching are of no Avail. I Look hourly this forenoon for my boats Arrival from George Town & Dover. Got two Letters from my factors with Sales of 16 Barrels Rice at $2 ½ p Cents. I answered these Letters & Requested no further Sales without my Permission. This afternoon my boat Arrived with Sundries & Letters from Mrs. Davis & my Overseer, he has Given a Substitute Souldier to Captain Gasqua so he Remains on my Plantation. I Count myself fortunate if Mrs. Gasqua do Come & Stay with me all the Summer Season. It will Induce not only her husband to be with us frequently, but also Gasquas brother Officers, particularly if Madam is of a Fecacious & Agreeable turn of Mind. My Small boat also was brought me in Good Order so my fisherman Scipio fixed my hooks & Lines, ready Catching of Fish tomorrow. Rode out this Evening & brought to my Kitchen Door, a full Load of Dry wood. Have now Enough to Last Several days.

Thursday, July 23. Road out this morning but no marks of Sea Turtle Crawling out from the Sea tho' the Tide was very full & the moon near so.

---

*Built in 1801, the North Island Lighthouse, also known as the Georgetown Lighthouse, stands eighty-seven feet high on North Island. It has been rebuilt twice since its original construction, first in 1822 after a hurricane and again in 1867 to re-pair damage sustained during the Civil War. The lighthouse is the only structure on North Island that survived the hurricane of 1822. Zepke, *Coastal South Carolina*, 67.

Saw about 20 head of Lessesnes Cattle Lying on the beach they are Small but appeared fat. My boat went out to fish & I Got my Sow & pigs which were missing for two days. About 1 OClock A.M. John Cheesborough & John Murrell Visited me & Sot about an hour & went of[f]. I Shewed a Spare Room & bed for any friend that wished to tarry all Night, they both Said the[y] would accept the Offer & Soon would Come & tarry with me all Night, Tide very Low, no boat can come up the Bason with fish time Enough for Dinner. I must arrange this matter better. Myself however Eats Little or no fish Except Oyster Clams & Stone Crabs & Turpins which makes a Good Stew, or broth & their Eaggs are *mighty* Good Eating. A Clear day, wind at South East very hot. Disired my hogs may in future be drove towards the Horse Landing insteed of the Inlet, & that my Troughs may always have water for Poultry, hogs etc. etc. The Sun & Sand Causes Great Thirst & without fresh water Plenty Given these; They would Greatly Suffer if not absolutely die & here the Loss would be Irreparable. Saw Trapier, J. M. Taylor, Toomer & Cheesborough, & the Thomases. This Afternoon a Brig Seen in Chace of a Schooner, Night Came & they disappeared.

Friday, July 24. Boat men went Early to fish, having Clams, therefore only Shrimps wanting. Hogs, Mules & Cows daily in the Morning drove the South Side of the Bason, & in the Evening drove back Again. Trapier Sent me 6 News papers (the Courier of Charles ton) I wrote to Mrs. Davis & Sent her Some writing Paper. Wrote to my Overseer to Send me, Rice Tailings* for Poultry here which would Save Corn. Read Papers 13th July to 18th July 1812.

Saturday, July 25. Sent up my boat to Dover & Brown Town, Gave Passages to Mrs. Cogdells Sampson & Jamie, Sent Paper to Mrs. Davis also Seewee beans[†] & 16 fish. The Cat fish Gave to Scipio. Major Murray Gave me a plate of Shrimps which I Eat at Breakfast & he said Miss Shields was come, &

---

*Rice tailings are fine, strawlike particles from the leaf of the rice broken during the threshing process. They are separated through winnowing or fanning the grain clean to prepare it for pounding. Many planters grew both rice and potatoes in a rotation on their land using the rice tailings to place over the root potato crop. Allston, "On Sea Coast Crops," 226; Redmond, White, and Camak, *Southern Cultivator*, 25:142.

[†]A smaller and more slender version of the lima bean, the sewee bean or Carolina bean is South American in origin and was cultivated by Indians at the time of European settlement in Carolina. Because of its tropical origin, it has often been called a West Indian bean or saba after the West Indian island. The sewee bean plant is taller with larger leaflets and fewer pods than the lima bean. It is also more susceptible to cold and germinates later. The beans are small and flat, white or brown in color, and marked with red spots. Bailey, *Recent Apple Failures*, 89–90.

that Tuesday next Mrs. Murray & Miss Delesseline he would bring down to his House. Polly is very Poorly at George Town. I hope Sea Air will Soon Restore her. I pitty her, Oppressed as She is. Only a husband can Cure *all* her Complaints. Then She may Say Give me Children or I die. Boat carried up Conks & Sea Mud* & went off about 9 OClock A.M. with 3 Oarsmen & 2 Sails & was Soon out of Sight, Tide favourable Got 9 ½ pounds Beef this morning of Mr. Lessesne. Major Wragg Visited me this morning, he is a very Agreeable Gentleman & was always a favoright of mine, many years ago at Cambridge Colledge near Boston he shewed my Mrs. Horry & myself Great & Particular attention, Introduced into Several Colledge Rooms & Library Room & Shewed us Several Valuable Pictures belonging to the Colledge, had our Carriage & Horses taken Care of, & in Short was very Oblidging to us in all Respects. Several Young Carolinians Visited us at our Lodgings in Boston & dined with us at Different times in Cornhill Mrs. Greens boarding House. Wragg in particular drew the attention of about a Dozen Boston young Ladies they said this to me. Colonel Horry we have been in Company with all the young Carolinians Students of Cambridge Colledge even your Relations the Trapiers. Excuse us when we say Mr. Wragg far Excells them all, we are more than half in Love with him; So Smiling, handsome & agreeable in his Manners & Conversation, Sir we beleave in Carolinia you have but few Such as he is, Possessing so Sweet, & Mild Manners. We fear none of us Boston Girls will be fortunate Enough to Gain his heart (Note) I know of no Carolinians that Married in Masachusets.

Sunday, July 26. Rode out this morning (very Cool) Trapier Sent me 4 Charles Ton News Papers, which I read but tis plain 'tis a Federal Paper. Contains much in favour of the English but nothing in favour of France or America. A Republican Paper will just reverse this just Mentioned Recital. Pity Party Spirit Prevails So much in our Country. War ought to burry all distintions & all Combine in Union & harmony but different men will have different minds. If we are Invaded I doubt not all will be United under American Standard. I find Commodore Rogers[†] has taken no Part of the Jamaica Fleet, but

---

*Sea mud is a dark, fine, salt mud that resembles slime and is usually deposited in shoal waters along the sounds and estuaries of the Carolina coast. The mud forms when the silt brought down by the rivers mixes with the decaying seaweed or marsh grass and animal remains of fish, mollusks, or other marine creatures. Merrill, *Treatise on Rocks,* 340.

[†]John Rodgers was born July 11, 1771, in Harford County, Maryland. He entered the navy when it was organized in 1798 and became the second-in-command to Cdre. James Barron in the expedition against the Barbary pirates. When he returned to America, he was put in command as commodore of the USS *President.* During

has Injured a British Ship of War. Killed & Wounded Several of her Sailors. Halifax, must be taken. Yankees, this must be your Portion of Conquest. The Middle department will take Canady & the[n] we the Southern department will take the Floridas, & Mexico. No Account of Captain Gasqua & his Wife Coming to Reside with me. I hope he has Gone for her, is the Reason I hear nothing of them as yet nor of his Company coming to Encamp near to my House. I Looked for Return of my boat today, but in Vain.

Monday, July 27. Early this morning before I was up the arrival of my boat was Announced to me, & when I Returned from Riding I received Sundries Supplies; Chiefly Vegetables from Dovers Garden. I also Received a Letter from Mrs. Davis & a Letter from Mr. Williams (my Overseer) from the former I received a present of Apples, She Informs me of the Arrival of Captain Smith from the West Indies with Oranges, Limes etc. & that a Mrs. Cunningham & 2 Souldiers have Died in George Town Since her Last Letter to me. (Note) George Town must be now very hot, since I find it here very warm. My Overseer Sent me Several Bushels of Rice Tailings for my Poultry & he denies any knowledge of his Going to be Married to Miss Carville (a handsome Young Girl at George Town, that Lives with her Mother on the Bay) None Sick at Dover, or Brown Town house; Peggy's Youngest Child (a fine Little Girl) Mrs. Davis writes me Creeps about fast. I wish She may survive this fall. My Ducks here Thrives very much & is fat, I wish I could Say the same of my fowles & hogs, Mules, Cow & Calf. They decline in Looks tho' my Mules yet draws me along thro heavy sand twice a Day. But I feed them twice a Day with Corn, & fodder at Night, besides the marsh which they feed on. The Greatest part of the day dined on Apple Dumplins & a Pollow today.* Dont fare so well Every day tho' my Kind Little Relation Mrs. Trapier, Sends me many

---

the War of 1812, he commanded a squadron on the American coast and was wounded by a gun fired from the British ship *Belvedere*. Rodgers later became the president of the Board of Navy Commissioners from 1815 to 1824 and 1827 to 1837, and also served as secretary of the navy for a short period in 1823. He died in Philadelphia on August 1, 1838. Chisholm, *Encyclopedia Britannica*, 23:447.

*Originally a Persian dish, pilau, also know as pilaf, perlo, plaw, and perloo, is a rice casserole found in the southern coastal regions of the United States. In its simplest form, it consists of long-grain rice that has been washed and presoaked in a stock or broth. The rice is then cooked until the grains are juicy and plump, allowing them to separate easily from each other. Often times the rice is sautéed in fat prior to cooking in the stock for added flavor. Popular ingredients include okra, ham, chicken, and shrimp. Versions of the dish, usually accompanied by different spellings of its name, are found throughout the Middle East, Africa, Spain, France, Turkey, and India. McDaniel, *Irresistible History*, 65.

dainties by her handy house Maids. Poor Nemo, Ben's Right hand Man is
Quit[e] a Cripple with the Rhumatis. We live here in a Low damp & Wet
Country & a Warm one it is so Lyable to Colds, which brings on many Com-
plaints we Seem not aware off. Tho' Experience ought to Teach us Wisdom
but we follow the Good old book, which Says Sufficient is the Evil unto the
day thereof. Wind very high at North East for Sometime past & now tis heavy,
Drisligg Cloudy weather. I Look for a heavy Gale from the North East, or East
Quarter & directly from Sea. So Marriners on our Coasts be Vigilent on board
your Vessells Keep all Lights & Sails Close reefed & Bowlings all Clear, boats
Secured on Deck & Experienced men, at your helm & Good Night Watch,
& Lights in Benecles to See your Compass & then I & you will Expect to
Weather all. Sailors is Like Souldiers. Sometimes Lead Lazy Lives & Sometimes, hard times Overtakes them & dangers & difficulties Succeeds. But
hearts of Oak my brave Lads. Stand to it & trust to him that made you, we
must all Die but be Comforted for we Cant die before our times are Come.
'Tis Decreed & then we Go to a Land of Rest free from all Cares & Trouble
for Evermore amen. This afternoon about 2 OClock discovered a 3 Mast Vessell Standin for the Light House could discover that her Colors was hoisted
but could not discover of what Nation about 4 OClock P.M. She Stood of[f]
to the Eastward & Soon was out of Sight, I Suppose her of force & Cruising
on our Coast to Meet an Enemies Vessell. I hope She is an American.

Tuesday, July 28. Rode out South West & brought home a Load of wood.
Expect Captain Guasqua's Comp[an]y to Encamp near me today, Lessesne
beef very Good, Dined on Roast Beef & bake Pears etc. The Last sent me by
Mrs. Trapier who with her husband Visited me today with their Son Horry
Trapier, I would be bad off was it not for the friendship of this Family. In
return for the many things I Receive from them I am able only to send them
Watermelions Sometimes. Mrs. Lessesne has not yet Visited me as She Said
She would do. Today Major Murray & his family are Expected at their New
House here. We I hope will be Sociable Good Neighbours, they are next in my
Estimation to Trapiers family. Scipio Drawed Shrimps, Mullets & Crabs in the
Bason & with these Caught Whiting, Crocus & Catfishes in the Inlet. Hav-
ing now a Suitable Boat & Seine* I hope never to want fish of all Kinds when
tis Good Weather. (Note the weather for Several days Past very Cool, I Sup-
pose a Gale at Sea from the Eastward) I Sleep well at Nights. Go to bed a[t] 8

---

*South Carolinians often fished by pulling a seine or a circular net. Seines were
often used to fish for small creek shrimp in shallow, brackish waters that were considered sweeter than those caught further out in the ocean or rivers. Ben-Yami,
Purse-Seining with Small Boats, 1; Nathalie Dupree, "Shrimp," in Edgar, *South Carolina Encyclopedia,* 864–65; Cochrane, *Fishery Manager's Guidebook,* 35.

OClock P.M. & rise at 5 OClock. The Beach is now Low both Morning & Evenings fine & hard & Good Riding. My Tailings Saves me much Corn which my Ducks & fowls Used to Devour Greedily. This Evining Saw Major Murray, he told me all his family was in his House, that Miss Delesseline was so reduced I would not know her & Invited me to Breakfast with her tomorrow Morning Saw also Doctor Wragg, who Informed me That Captain Gasqua would not be Down before Thursday next.

Wednesday, July 29. I rode out & Got some wood. My Tailings very bad wrote Overseer for better, & Sent Mrs. Davis Some fish by boat which will Go up on Friday as my Servant Zemo appears better, & Says his bowel Complaint at Night is not so bad, as it has been. He Eats & walks about more than Usual during the day, Put on my Sundays apparel & went & breakfasted with Major Murray. Took Some buisket with me Least Murray Should have none very low Tide this morning. Tho' the wind is at the East tis almost a Calm, Scipio went with me to Major Murray to Assist my Getting out of my Carriage. About 10 OClock P.M. Returned Home. Had the Seine Drawed in the Bason, Caught only a few, very Small Mullets. Saw at Murrays Miss Delesseline She Looks better than I Expected, She is in Spirits & Taking Jesuits Bark* Manning is her Phisition. I jested her much of young Cockley (a Militia Officer Encampt near the Light house with a Number of men) & I find her Not averse to this Officers making Love to her. I Saw Also at Murrays, Charles Lessesne Quarter Master to Our Militia detachment on the Winyaw Islands. He has made Choice of a Spot of Encampment for Gasquas Company (which has 2 Subalterns under his Command) near the Inlet & to Major Wraggs house on the Point & just within the first Range of Hills nearest the Sea but says they cannot come there till his Supply of Provisions arrives from Charles Town by the first fair Wind. Lessesne, Peter Cuttino, & Murray all say they Know Mrs. Gasqua. That She is of a Cooper Family of the Irish Township. I say this Family I well Knew in the Revolutionary War & they are very Respectable; They further say She Mrs. G. is a well bred & Agreeable Woman so I Anticipate

---

*Jesuit's bark or cinchona is the dried bark of many species of the genus *cinchona*. It is named after the Countess of Cinchon, the wife of the viceroy of Peru, who supposedly brought the first bark of its kind back to Europe around 1640 to cure intermittent fever. It was used medicinally in the forms of quinine and cinchonine for fever, neuralgia, whooping cough, and similar ailments. The plant was harvested between May and November by felling the trees and completely stripping them of their bark. The bark was then dried quickly in the sun to be preserved for use. The medicine spread throughout Europe by way of the Jesuits, who acquired it from Peruvians and brought it to Spain. Ripley and Dana, *New American Cyclopúdia*, 5:248.

much pleasure in her Company & Of the Captain & his Officers; Lessesne & Cuttino took Leave of this Family about 1 OClock p.m. & went off as did Also myself. On my way home I met with Thomas R. Mitchell Esquire he was Engaged at Dinner but would a Little time hence Call At my House; I offered, him a Room & bed for Lodgings at any time; he said he would Make Use of Such a Privaledge Sometimes. I Saw the Spot designed for Gasquas Company; Mitchell I Saw again today & he then Said he would Call on me on the Morrow. Major Keith in his Carriage Visited Trapier who I Saw but did not See the Major.

Thursday, July 30. Rode out & Got Some wood & returned home found Mr. Mitchell at my house. He Stayed & Breakfasted with me, however before he did so; he A[s]ked for a Julop; my servant Rachal handed him, Brandy Sugar & water. I Soon found it 'fected his head, he Eat very Little at breakfast; a Decanter of Brandy, he Ordered to be placed on a Small Table Near to the One on which we were breakfasting on. He had frequently recourse to this decanter & Soon he realed to & fro. Laid down in a Room on a bed frequently, I found his Language, was Extreamely defective, he Stammered, & his Eyes half Closed. At this Instant he is Asleep on a Bed in a Spare Room. I Gave Rachael directions not to Wake him, As he Spoke of Swimming in the Sea. A Shark would soon Cutt him to pieces. I Sincerely Pity this Otherwise most Valuable Gentleman Planter & Attorney at Law but Alass he is Lost to himself, his friends & Country. Liquor, Oh Liquor what Mischief has thou Occasioned in the World. Scipio drew the Seine this Morning about 9 OClock a.m. & Caught only a few Small Mullets. I find Zemo No better. Sent him up to Dover in boat, The boat went off about 10 OClock a.m. Wrote Mr. Williams & Mrs. Davis. Scipio is Coxen. Sent Mrs. Davis 22 fish (Crocus). I hope Mitchell will be well Enough to Eat dinner with me. That his Sleep will Revive him Greatly. Went to my bed to Lay till 3 OClock p.m. & then to Eat my Dinner with Mitchell. He rose to Dinner but Eat Little, he drank a Tumbler of Brandy & Water. I suspect it was very Strong for it Soon put him to bed again, before which we Saw a Chair With two Officers & another Officer on horse back which passed us & along the beach from the South Side of the Island bound to the Inlet. Mitchell said they were Major General Thomas Pinckney & his two Aids, & an Engineer Swift. Aids were Lieutenant Morris & Swift Rank is Lieutenant Colonel. I could not Rely on Mitchells Report, for Soon he was fast a Sleep with a full Musqueto dose. I went to bed myself, till 6 OClock p.m. then rode in my Carriage towards the Inlet met John Withers formerly of Goose Creek, he said these Officers passed Mr. Shackelfords house where he was & he supposed I would find them at John Man Taylors house I went thither, but they were not there, but Mr. Cheesborough & J. M. Taylor Confirmed Mitchells Report who these Officers were. That they Travelled very fast. They arrived at George Town ferry & was met & Escorted by the Troop of that Place into George Town where the Artillery Company Received them under a Discharge of field pieces Say 18 Rounds. They without Loss of time proceeded to the fort at Dr. Blythes Point, where Lieutenant Commander Heriot with his Soldiers Compliment them also by being under Arms etc. Then they went to Visit Cat Island* where is Posted a Detachment Militia Soldiers then to the Light House on North Island where another Detachment of Militia Souldiers of about 160 were Encamped. Then they Passed the Inlet & my house as aforesaid, then a boat went to Colonel William Allstons house at Dubourdieus Island & Gave notice of these Gentle Officers coming to Visit him & his family & Returned across the Inlet in time & before Pinckneys arrival. There they Emparked & Soon arrived across the Inlet & proceeded by Land for Colonel Allstons Large House. N.B. Alstons Lady & Pinckney are very nearly Related. Thus far my Information Goes & no further Cheesborough told me Saturday he would Leave the Island & the day followed Set out from George Town for the upCountry & Requested that he might be the Bearer of my Letters to Mrs. Horry & Miss Bay. I now Grant his Request & are writing to these Ladies to Go by him before Tomorrow on which day he Leaves this. Thomas Pinckney was a Major & Aid to General Gates at the Unfortunate battle between him & Lord Cornwallis near Camden. I was also Aid at the same time to General DeKalb but Colonel Francis Marion & myself was ordered to Go Down the Country to Destroy all boats & Craft of any Kind which we found on Santee River in Order to prevent Cornwallis & his Troops Escaping him we Sot out from Camp about 3 OClock P.M. & by Night with about 10 young Carolinians Got but about 6 Miles from General G. Camp at Rugesley Mills to a Womans house, it Appeared afterwards this womans husband was a Tory & then with Cornwallis Army in full March

---

*Cat Island, separated from Georgetown County by the Inland Waterway Canal, was originally part of the Winyah Barony owned by Daniel LaRoche, an early Winyah resident. After LaRoche's death Thomas Lowndes (b. 1766), son of Rawlins Lowndes, acquired what is now Cat Island Plantation, a tract of land located closer to the North Santee River than to Winyah Bay. Thomas Lowndes married Sarah Bond I'On, and their son, Richard Henry Lowndes (b. 1815), eventually inherited the plantation. Richard built a shingle-sided home on the plantation that still stands today and with his wife, Susan Middleton Parker, settled as rice planters on the island. During the Civil War, the Union Army often used the rice mill and chimney on Cat Island for target practice. Richard Henry's son, Richard I'On Lowndes, inherited the plantation in 1905 but died in 1919, leaving the estate to heirs who eventually sold Cat Island and the adjoining Belle Isle. Lachicotte, *Georgetown Rice Plantations*, 162–63.

from Camden to Attack Gates Army. This woman appeared much frightned at our Regimentals, hid herself in a Room & would Give us nothing to Eat or Drink or Bedding to Lie on. Night took place & we could Go no further on Road we were Unaquainted with so we Lay down in the hall & Piazza on our blankets & Cloaks first Posting a Centinel or two to Prevent our being Surprized. Just at Dawn of day we were Greatly Alarmed with heavy firing heard at a Distance towards Camden Side & we could distinguish from field Pieces to those of Musketry. Marion was Certain it was General Sumpters Detatchment that had met the British Party from 96 on their rout to join Cornwallis. We Could have no Conception that it was an Engagement between Gates & Cornwallis, the former We had Left but a few Hours & no Expectation of Either Generals Advancing on Each other, however after Night, the night we Slept at the aforesaid Womans house, both Armies Advanced without the Expectation of meeting & at about 12 OClock their Advance Guard met when a Scirmish took place but Soon Ceased & both Armies Laid on their Arms, till dawn of day, both Armies were formed for Action. The British moved first & with Loud Cheers Charged Bayonets but at 100 yards Distance the American New Levies (North Carolinians & Virginians) broke & Run away most Shamefully, the old Continentals Chiefly of the Mary Land Line Stood & fought bravely under Command of DeKalb. He fell & was badly wounded in Several Places, with Balls & Bayonets & died the next day. Colonel Dubesany his Chief aid bravely defended his General, but he was Overpowered & taken with his General Prisoners of War. He received also Several wounds he Survived, DeKalb was buried at Camden by the Enemy with the honours of war. A Monument has been Lately Erected at Camden to his memory by Several Patriotic Gentlemen of that Place. Major Pinckney, as aforesaid was with General Gates in this Action he & Colonel Otho Williams, by desire of General Gates made the disposition for Action. History Gives a full Account of this fatal day for the Americans. I Lost Several Most Intimate Acquaintances of the Mary Land Line but General Smallwood* & Guest Escaped. Major Pinckney

---

*Gen. William Smallwood was born into a prominent and wealthy family of Charles County, Maryland, in 1732. Smallwood quickly distinguished himself both politically and militarily through his election to Maryland's lower house of assembly in 1761 and service in the provincial navy during the French and Indian War. On January 14, 1776, Smallwood joined the Continental Army, was commissioned a colonel, and charged with the task of assembling the First Maryland Regiment. In 1780 he went to South Carolina to serve under Brig. Gen. Baron Johann de Kalb and was placed in the reserve at the start of the Battle of Camden in August 1780. During the disastrous battle, Smallwood was separated from his brigade and swept to the rear by a stampede of fleeing American militiamen. Following the battle

was badly wounded in the Leg & taken Prisoner, & was a Long time Lame. Gates Escaped into North Carolina. Smallwood Saved about 70 Continental Souldiers. Colonel Ormonds Cavalry behaved Shamefully, they fell back & on Officers baggage, took the whole & With it joined the Enemy The historian beg Pardon for this Aggression, Occasioned by Speaking As Aforesaid of this Meritorious Man & Officer Major General Thomas Pinckney. I appreciate this appointment Greatly & time will Shew it a most Judicious one. I went to Mrs. Pryors house, Saw her & the young Ladies & was told by them that Mitchell, had Left my house & that they Saw him on horse back Coming this way. I Got home & found this Information was Correct, my Servant Rachael Said he woke before Sun Set & Asked for Brandy. She could Give him none & he Got his Horse & went off.

Friday, July 31. Rode out as Usual & Got wood as Usual, After breakfast Received A Present from my Neighbour Mrs. Lessesne (a Plate of very fine Malaga Grapes in Great Perfection). I Sent Mrs. Trapier a fine bunch of them. My boat arrived with 2 of my Carpenters Buddy & Isaac, to Caulk my Barge & Bathing Tub. Also with better Tailings & with a Barrell Pitch with 11 Water Melions & a Basket of Figs, Sent Mrs. Lessesne 3 Melions & a plate Figs, also Sent Mrs. Trapier 3 Melions & a plate figs.

Saturday, August 1. Rode to the Melitia Souldiers Encampment (near the Light House) They were drawn up on the beach & Officers took Post in Battalion. about 160 men on Parade. Captain Gasqua Exercising Officers Captain Bingham Captain Johnston & Captain Floyd & Eight Subaltern Officers, Mr. Davis Acting Adjutant for the day (Cuttino being Absent) Major Commandant Keith Acted the General. A Number of Manovres were made after the manuel was Gone threw & I was agreeable Surprizd to find these Country Melitia did so well. Gasqua Manoverd these men so well that tho' I was in my Carriage, & weeled about Continuall[y] the Battalion always faced me. I Supposed it was meant as a Compliment to me. I was more than two Hours viewing this Battalion which at Length Captain Gasqua dismisted to their Company tenths, Major Keith was in New & Compleat Uniform & on Horse back I never Saw him Look so well. I Lamented that very few men (Gasquas

---

Smallwood succeeded General de Kalb, who had been mortally wounded, as division commander. Shortly after Congress promoted Smallwood to major general. Smallwood continued serving through the war, working to requisition supplies from local farmers. He resigned his commission in November 1783 and in 1785 was elected governor of the state of Maryland, an office he held for three years. After his gubernatorial term, Smallwood served in the Maryland legislature's Upper House from 1791 until his death on February 14, 1792. Keith Mason, "William Smallwood," in Tucker, *U.S. Leadership in Wartime*, 83–84.

Company only) were Uniformed & several Officers were Likewise UnUniformed. Which Slouch'd Hats are Unbecoming a Souldier, which Should hold up his head & never Ashamed to Shew his face Unless Going to the funeral of a brother souldier. Keith Invited & we went & breakfasted with him, Say, *myself* & Captains Bingham & Gasqua which rode with me in my Carriage Keith Asked me then to Stay & Dinner with him, for as he found I Knew Not all these his Battalion Officers, he would Introduce me to them all. We repaired together just before Dinner & about 15 Officers were Introduced to me. Most of them honoured their Commissions Lieutenant Cockley of Camden is a fine young Officer, handsome & witty atracted my particular attention; I wish he was married to Miss Delesseline (who if I mistake not wish it also) but 'tis Said he is Engaged to Miss Hunter (Miss Bays handsome Cousin) who will be here January next I hope Miss Delesseline will however marry the Lieutenant Long before that time, & I told Miss Delesseline so. I passed the day at the Majors House quite Agreeable in the Company of these Military men & with Young Keith (Son of the Major), Ben Trapier & Windham Trapier. Gasqua said he hoped on Tuesday next to Introduce to me at my house here Mrs. Gasqua, Several Officers as Above said they then would Visit me on Said Day. The Supplies Expected for this detachment & Company of Gasquas (at least 50 Men) would be Stored in Major Savage Smiths Cellar, & for to be Served out in Camp. I drank more wine (say very Good) this day than I had Drank for a year Past. I was really merry for my head ached at Night, proved this Assertion. I Got home about 8 at Night & found my Bathing Tub Ready for me & my boat hauled up & Ready for Caulking & painting tomorrow. Keith Gave us an Eligent Dinner & we drank I Suppose about 2 dozen of wine in 2 hours Say from 3 to 5 OClock A.M. Today I heard General Pinckney & his Suit (as before mentioned) were already Gone for Charles Ton on Friday from George Town. He is in Activity a Second Bonapart, I wish he may meet his Success in war. Am Sure in merit he Equals any Officer whatever in *any* Country. I wrote to Mrs. Horry & Miss Bay & Sent their Letters to Mr. Cheesborough who Sets Off for Columbia & Stateburgh on This day.

Sunday, August 2. Rode out & went & Breakfasted with Mrs. Murray. Saw Polly Delesseline & Miss Shields & Mr. Hort (Machine Maker) I Jested much With Polly Delesseline of Lieutenant Cokley. Went to John Man Taylors House & Saw Mr. Cheesborough, Taylor, Hort, & Mr. Course Junior. Cheesborough Acknowed Receipt of Aforesaid Letters, I then wished him a Good Journey, & that he would Kiss Mrs. Horry & Miss Bay for me. The former he had no Objection in Obeying my request, but the Latter he Begged to be Excused from Doing. I Saw this morning also Mr. John Withers (of Goose Creek) & Mr. Dick Shackelford of George Town. I Got home about 10 A.M.

& about One OClock P.M. I wrote this days Journal & went to bed much fatigued with my two Last days Excurtions, dined at 6 OClock Past Meredian. Mrs. Lessesnes Soup was well Seasoned I Eat enough of it, & Gave my Maid Rachel of it. She is today better & Giddo is well. The boiled Beef & Broth therefrom; I Sent to the Kitchen for the Negro[s] I desired Susie to See that Rachal Received Nourishment Enough & was well Cloathed & warm: Last Night a heavy Rain fell & this day much more Rain fell near all day, the weather Stormy & very Thick (not Unlike Hurricane) Weather. The wind at South West. Missed a pig, which makes a Second that is Lost, Negroes Loves Pork & few Negroes are honest I dont Know one. When a fair Opportunity Offers & they think the Fact Cannot be Proved on them; they are all Liars & of Course are Thieves. I fear the bad Weather will deprive me of Mrs. Gasqua's Company Tuesday next. I went to Bed at 8 OClock P.M. No Company & Everything around me wet.

Monday, August 3. I rode out & Got wood & Saw & Conversed with Mrs. Wald[o] on the beach. Boat is Caulking & I bathed about 10 OClock A.M. for the first time, Rain again Last Night, Rachael this day attended me as Usual, Billy Cut his foot with his own Ax. Drawed the Seine but Got Nothing. Wind at North West very Thick Weather. Mr. Cheesborough not yet Gone from the Inlet.

Tuesday, August 4. Last Night it rained, also this morning so I Lost my Mornings Ride. Scipio drew the Seine, Caught only a few Small Mullet & Shrimps for bait. I Sent him with a Letter to Captain Gasqua Offering him & his Wife my boat at any time, they Chuse to Command her & to Convey him to George Town Tomorrow & to bring down from George Town his wife & Goods to the Inlet & to my house. 3 Rooms being prepared for their Reception Wind & Weather as Yesterday; my Carpenters work being finished here I mean them to Return by my boat to Dover tomorrow. I wrote by boat to My Overseer Williams & to my friend Mrs. Davis at my Brown Town House. I sent to the plantation for a Wench to Assist me as Susse is Cook. Sent for Paint from Mrs. Davis to paint my big boat. Rachael yet Sick in bed, Major Keith Introduced me to all the Officers Encampted at the Light House, I wrote Mrs. Davis to Give my best Respects to Mrs. Wayne & Lessesne & my best Love to Mrs. Elizabeth Elliot & to Francis Harvey. I Love Young Women & Girls, but I Cant Love old Women tho' I Venerate them. Captain Gasqua Wrote me he Expect to March his Company to my side of the Island Tomorrow but as Mrs. Gasqua's Daughter would very soon be Confined Cannot Leave her till that is over, so 'tis Uncertain when to Expect her Down. Note, This is a Disappointment to me but it Cannot be Avoided.

Wednesday, August 5. I Sent Mrs. Davis 70 Clams & 20 fish & wrote her to Send me Paint & Oil for my boat; Scipio went off in the boat with my 2

Carpenters & William & 2 Passengers. About 8 OClock A.M. S. Smiths boat Passed the Inlet also at 8 OClock A.M. I suppose She has on board Supplies Tents etc. etc. for Gasquas Company. Hourly Expec[t]ed at their Encamping Ground. About 10 OClock A.M. Gasquas Company passed my house along the beach with D[r]um & Fyfe. 'Tis now Raining. I bathed today. Dined at 3 OClock P.M. & Rode to Captain Gasquas Camp about 6 OClock P.M. Saw about 50 Men & 2 Officers. About dark Captain Gasqua rode to my house & Supped with me but would not Lodge at my House.

Thursday, August 6. Rode out a Little way. Rain & very thick Weather. A Small Sail appeared (Wind at South) She was Standing a South East. I Received a Letter Yesterday from my Mrs. Horry, my Factors & My friend Sam Smith at George Town, They are all Well. About 11 OClock A.M. Ben, Windham & Horry Trapiers Visited me for about an hour, They Read Some of my Daily history & Some Passages therein deverted them much. Miss Delesselines on the 4th of July Last the recital of which made Ben Trapier Laugh heartily & he said he would Frequently meet me at Captain Gasqua's Camp near to Man Taylors House. Ben is a Pleasing Chearful Man & a Good Officer who Loves his Country. I rode out about 6 OClock P.M. & Saw Captain Gasquas Company under Arms & his Centinal Posted. I Saw two men Supporting Mr. S. to my Landing & boat to Convey him on board S. Smiths Pitiauger Sloop* Lying of[f] the Horse Landing. Mr. S. was beastly Drunk. Note he is Seldom Sober when he Can Get Spirits of any kind. He or Thomas R. M. I dont Know which is the Greatest drunkard of the Two. The Sooner they are departed this world the better for their friends; & family Mr. Hemmingham Lodged at my house this Night.

Friday, August 7. Mr. Hemmingham Breakfasted with me this morning. Inquiring after Mrs. Horry I read to him Part of her Last Letter to me which Says "We are all in Great Spirits about the war, Several Methodist Preachers have turned out & Entered the Service of their Country, one of them joined John Ioors Troop of Horse. Another for Speaking disrespectfully of Congress & in favour of George will be dismissed the service. Sarah Bay is Truly fortunate She Gains the Affections of Every one that Knows her. I think you will now be without her till Christmas." Note Mrs. Horry is Living at Statesburgh† with Captain John Ioor of the Cavalry. I rode out & by Trapiers where I Saw

---

*Horry is referring to the French word *patauger,* which means to wade, flounder, splash about, or paddle. A pituager boat is a small rowboat used in shallow waters.

†In 1783 General Sumter drew up the plans for Stateburg, South Carolina, in hopes that it would become the next state capital. Instead when the capital was moved inland from Charleston, Columbia was chosen, and Stateburg remained an unincorporated village. The first residence in Stateburg, which actually preceded the

Mr. Hemming[ham] again. I went onward & Saw Captain Gasquas Camp & a Centinel Poasted. Liddy is Come down to me, as Zena is Sick at Dover. Susanna is Sick there also & Robert is very Sick at Brown Town House. Rice is Early at Dover & fields have Plenty of Water. It is now Raining. Examined my Paints & found I had but 3 Colours; Say White Yellow & Lead Colour & very Little Oil Perhaps not a quart Left in a Large Jugg. Desired my big Boat to be hauled up the next high water which will be Tonight about 8 OClock; Tomorrow & Sunday (if no Rain) She will be dry Enough to Paint. My Auning wants mending very much. When this is done I may Venture out to fish myself in Good Calm Weather Scipio must try Sometimes to fish for Bass, by Standing on the beach at Young flood & Cast out the Line as far as Possible even if in the Surf. Near the Inlet Bass Used to be Caught by Mr. Croft & others. Young Mullets are Good Bait.

Saturday, August 8. Bad Weather Could not ride out, my boat was hauled up to be painted Hemmingway went to Trapiers & they went in a boat to View Muddy bay & Some Creeks Contiguous thereto, they Got wet & Returned at Night I beleave without Satisfying themselves Wind at East & South East blows hard & Weather forebodes a heavy Gale if not a hurry Cane. Tide very high this Night. Rode out this Evening & with 2 Woemen Got Some wood, rain Increasing I hastened home & passed the hills with difficulty, Sea near running a Cross to the Bason. It Rained & blew hard all this Night. Boat Arrived with a Letter from my Overseer & Mrs. Davis. The former Says he has plenty of Water over his Rice & that Zemo is very Ill & the Latter Says Peggys Eldest Son Robert is very Ill. That a heavy Gale from the West, has blown down many Trees in George & Brown Town & that my Lot had Several Trees much Injured. Bad Weather Grows worse. Mr. Hemmingway & myself Confined all this day to the house It was almost a hurrycane. Archibald Taylors house on his Sandpit plantation was Struct with Lightling & burnt to the Ground.

Sunday, August 9. Wind & Weather as Yesterday. Hemmingway Got my history Books & Sot up to Read them Last Night but I went to Bed Early having Sot up the whole day. This morning Hemmingway Got my Book of War Letters & were Reading, them, My Cook Sick in Bed, so I directed that Liddy might be Sot to Cook in Place of Susie. I am uneasy about my Sick Negroes & fear the Last nights Tide Got over my River banks & Threw Salt Water on

---

town's establishment, was built in the 1750s and is known as the Borough House. It served as the headquarters for both British general Lord Cornwallis and American general Nathanael Greene during the American Revolution. Clark and Pierce, *Scenic Driving South Carolina,* 150.

my Rice fields, which but just Earing would Soften the Grain & in Pounding break very much in the hurrycane Some years ago. It was the Case & I only Got half Price for this Rice at Charles Ton Market. I wish I may not hear of Great Injury that Vessells on our Coast has Sustained as well as Vessells in Charles Ton harbour & Stores Suffering also by the Tide Getting into Cellar & damaging Country Produce. I have Rice in Some of them & may Suffer with others however I am Resigned to the will of Providence.

Monday, August 10. I rode out with Mr. Hemmingway & Saw a Centinal on his Post & Returned home with a few Conks. About 11 OClock A.M. my boat Sot out for George Town. I wrote to my Overseer & to Mrs. Davis & told Scipio to buy me Sundries & to Pay Davie for a Barrel Pitch two Dollars about 4 OClock P.M. a heavy Rain fell which Seemed to Clear the Weather. At 6 this afternoon I again rode out & Got Some wood. Wind at North & Sun Shine.

Tuesday, August 11. This morning Rode out with Mr. Hemmingway to Captain Gasquas Camp & along the Inlet & by the Centinal. Good Weather & Sun Shine. Beef day. I Got a Shank, Neck Beef, & a Steak, Piece. Lent my fishing boat to Davie, a fellow of Mr. Joe Lessesne. Saw a Schooner under Sail She appears Going to George Town. Benjamin Trapier went to his Brother W. Trapiers House South Side of the Island & were to Go together to George Town. Threw open every Part of my House to Air all doors & Windows & in order to dry after so much Wet Weather. Last Sunday Afternoon Mr. Waldo Called on me & with much difficulty Informed me that Mr. Grant was dead at his Plantation at Gueree Settlement on Santee River. That he died the 8th day of his arrival at His plantation there. Note Mr. Grant I think had 6 Small Children. I fear he has Left not much property to Maintain his Widow & Children. Mrs. & Miss Waldo is with the Widow & her Children. I Sincerely Pitty Orphans particularly if young. They must Suffer much & untill they are able to provide for themselves. I hope & doubt not That Waldo & others will be friendly in such a Case. Grant was much beloved by all that knew him.

Wednesday, August 12. Boat arrived from Town. Received a Letter from Mrs. Davis & my Overseer Williams at Dover. Sick all Getting better some has turned out. Got a Barrell Tailings & Vegetables from Dover. Rode round to the Bason, & Got Some Conks. Brought home a Good Turn of Wood in the Waggon. Plantation Received no Injury Sent Mrs. Trapier 3 Good Water Melions. Saw a boat Load of Water Melions at Joseph's Landing for Sale Price 7d Each. Received a George Town News Paper of 8 August. No very meterial News. The Order of Council Said to be Revoked. I wish this was a Fact. I bathed about 11 OClock A.M. & about 1 OClock P.M. Saw a Vessell Standing Easterly. She appeared to be a Topsail Vessell. My Boat is hauled up & Ready to Paint Tomorrow if no Rain in the Interim. This afternoon I rode out in

Company with Mr. Hemmingway. We met B. Trapier, Adjutant Cuttino & another Militia Officer On the beach Going towards the Inlet. Trapier said he had News Papers which he would Send me after he red them Scipio Examined Poles on the Bason to hang Seine *tomorrow.*

Thursday, August 13. Rode out on beach South Ward & dug up Several Stumps thereon brought them & other wood home. Scipio Cut a few More poles to hang the Seine at the bason. On my coming to breakfast I found Mr. Hemmingway Reading a Parcell of News Papers. He read to me as follows, "that Mobs had Prevailed at Baltimore, that many Persons were Massacraed, which the mob Supposed were Federalist, that General Henry Lee was Cruelly Murdered with one or two other Generals & many Gentlemen of the first Distinctions, That the Mayor of that City Shewed backwardness to quell the Mob.* That however many Principal Citizens were in Goal; in Short the days of Terror was in Baltimore. Many Citizens had fled the City & all was in Confusion." Note, Why Mobs in our Country, We have Laws Mild & Equitable, if Citizens do wrong punish them as by Law. Is our Government so weak as not to be able to Put her Laws in force I Say God forbid this Should be the Case. No my Countrymen we have Secret Enemies of Influence amongst us that have Great abilities, that Intriue & Impose on our Weak Citizens & bring forwards whatever will tend to the Advantage of the English Government. Nothing so Advantagious to Britain, as to foment & Keep up discord amongst us. To devide a Nation is Sure means of Conquering it. 'Tis Bonaparts maxims of Carrying on war in Europe. We Know this well, & yet will we Pursue it & be our own destroyers. Will we destroy our own Independence & become Slaves to Tyrants. Much blood have been Spilt in Putting us in our Present State. Do we Yet wish for more Blood Shed in Order to *undo* what has Cost us so much *to do* I have Long thought, I have lived too Long, I now again find Such thoughts not Eronious or Vain & Empty. If you will Murder Each other & become Slaves, then Oh! My Maker decree, That my Eyes behold it not. Death Welcome. I Embrace The[e] with joy & Gladness. No happiness, no Certainty for mankind here below. Major Murray with his Seine came to our bason & drew for fish but his Seine was not Long Enough, he Caught but 2 Mullets & returned home, telling me that the young Ladies in his family

---

*Horry is referring to an incident that occurred in Baltimore shortly after the United States declared war on Great Britain on June 18, 1812. Gen. Henry Lee, or "Light Horse Harry Lee" of Revolutionary fame, was injured but not killed in a riot. Lee's personal friend, the editor of the *Baltimore Federal Republican,* had his printing office destroyed because of his opposition to the war. Lee was seriously wounded in the attack and four years later died from complications. Hartley, *Life of Major General Henry Lee,* 294–99.

would Visit me, If I would Call for them in the forenoon they would Spend the day with me. I will do so with Great Pleasure. Mr. Skrine is arrived so Hemmingway & he will I Suppose Settle the boundary Line of the North Inlet, between Paul Trapier & Allston Michau, Frazer & Company when we Inlet Inhabitants will Know to whom we are Tenants. About 12 OClock a hard Shower of Rain fell I think it Rather too much & may Injure Crops. Major Keith Vis[ited] the Inlet Militia in a Review, of Captain Gasquas Company & returned home this Evening.

Friday, August 14. Rode out South Wardly & brought home Load of wood. Viewed the painting of my big boat, which is to my Liking; if no Rain today, the boat will be finished & be handsomely Painted, when I may form Parties of Ladies on fishing Matches & if they Carry beaus, may have also Courting Matches; the Latter will be mos[t] Agreeable to the bells. If *beau's* do not make Advances, *Bells* rather then Continue Scratching & biting, do *you* make Such, for when you are Married what Signifies which made the first Proposals—the Knot being once Tyed who can undo it. Then fall to work Night & day, untill the Kegg is Filled, thus will you my Good Girls answer the End of your Creation. I wish my Country to be Popolous to Repell attacks on us, by Sea; by Land come on Lads, we are Ready to meet you, & baist your hides, as General Green of Immortal Memory taught us to do. Samuel Smith Visited me this forenoon, from Dubourdieus Island. He Sot with me about an hour & returned from whence he came. Said the next Visit he made me he would Stay a day or two. I bathed about 10 OClock A.M. all at George Town was well when Smith Left it. In the Evening I rode out to the North Inlet & Saw Captain Gasqua Exercising his Company, he & Mrs. Gasqua came to my house & Lodged there this night.

Saturday, August 15. I rode out & Got wood, Saw a Small Sail Standing South East Suppose to be a Schooner, B. Trapier called on me but Soon went off. Gasqua Left me, Mrs. Gasqua Remain with me. Mrs. John Shackelford & Mrs. William Shackelford called at my House to See Mrs. Gasqua. I Saw on the Beach Mrs. Thompson, Mr. Hemmingway took Leave of me this morning for his home (Waccamaw). I find Mrs. Gasqua an Agreeable Woman. My boat went up for Dover & Brown Town I wrote to my Overseer Williams, & to Mrs. Davis (my friend) at Brown Town & Expect my boat to Return Tomorrow, Captain Gasqua about 11 OClock A.M. brought a Chair & took his wife to the Inlet Side of the Island. A fresh Breese of wind from the South at 2 OClock P.M. very Cloudy. North West Quarter, Thundered & Lightning very much. No Vessell in Sight; The Ladies here make much Enquiries after Mrs. Horry & Miss Bay, can I say they are Intended as Complimentary of me.

Sunday, August 16. Rode out South West Captain Gasqua & his wife did not Lodge here Last night, nor Breakfasted with me this morning (which I

attribute to Such Constant Rains). Now It is 9 OClock A.M. Such dark heavy
Clouds Southwest; I am afraid to ride & Enquire after the Captain & his wife,
but must wait the movements of the Elements; So much West Winds Causes
very Low tides, fine to Ride on the beach was it not for Rain so Constantly,
Scarce half an hour Enterval. Rode to Gasquas Camp & Parade this Evening,
Saw him Exercising his Company. Many Spectators of both Sexes. Amongst
them was General Joseph Allston who I had not Seen for years past, he was in
deep Mourning for the Loss of his Son, & only Child. Gasqua Spoke to the
General Brigade Major Carr, also Messrs. Meyers, & Quarter Master Lessesne
& other Officers. I had not Such honour. Perhaps Pride prevented. He was too
Proud to Advance towards me & I too Proud to Court his favour or Notice,
so we Remained as before, but Little Known to Each other. I think it best to
Remain so. I could Get no Knowledge of Mrs. Gasqua, in the Evening a Young
Lady Called at my house to See her & Left word when She was at home, She
would Call again. No appearance yet of my boat.

Monday, August 17. I rode out & Got wood. Spoke to Gasquas men on
the same Errand. One of these Men Informed me, that Mrs. Gasqua Stayed
at Mrs. Josephs house. I Suppose 'tis to be near her husbands Camp. I will
Send & Enquire after her health, now I have found her out, by Report to me
& as above. It Rained Last Night, & this morning is very Cloudy. The moon
fills next Saturday, which I hope, will End the Rain & Give us fair weather for
a While. I was Entroduced yesterday to a Mr. Ward of Philadelphia. He is Contractor of Supplies for our Militia Souldiers. Last Sunday appears here to be a
very public One. At 10 OClock A.M. Boat arrived. Received a Letter from my
Overseer; his Cart wants Tiring. Zemo is Returned, but Daniel Peggys Child
is come to me from Brown Town very Sick. Vegetables is sent me with Water
Mellions & Figs, Sent half of Each to Mrs. Trapier. Two Last George Town
News Papers I have Received. Trapier Called on me but being told I was
unwell & in bed he Immediately Retired. I Eat several Figgs which was very
Palatable & Cooled My Stomach. Also I found Tamarinds very beneficial in
this my feverish State of body & mind, it now Rains hard & has done so all
this morning, so much Rain & dark Cloudy weather (if in England) will make
Englishmen hang themselves, but I am in North America & am a french
desendant & I don't Seem disposed (at Present) to follow this English Rule, I
don't count myself a Coward, & tis Said none but Cowards Lay Violent hands
on themselves. Phylosiphers & men of Resolution, will wait the Event of time
& untill our Maker wills us to die, thus he Surmounts every difficulty & distress, by Persevereance & Resignation to the Will of heaven I fear reader I will
Moralize too much & tho' you may think I will not hang myself yet that this
bad Weather has deranged my Pennicranium. I hope however I am not far
Gone in this State.

Tuesday, August 18. I rode out & Got Some wood a fine Sun Shine Morning & but Little Clouds, bathed this morning. I took my Little Boy Daniel to ride with me, he came from Town much Swelled & very Poor, the Ride Gave him an Appetite & he Eat a hearty breakfast. I hope Exercise & Sea Air will Restore his health, In Town he Used to talk much with me, but now Scarce a word he utters. Mrs. Horry & Miss Bay thought much of this poor Ethiopean Little Boy, I must Endeavour not to drawn their Censure on me. I hear that George a Carpenter of the widow Croft is dead & buried at George Town. (Note) this is an Irrepairable Loss to Mrs. Croft who has very Little property & 2 Children to Support, I hope She is Resigned to fate & that which Can't be Cured must be Endured. I Saw Captain & Mrs. Gasqua today at Mrs. Pryors. She was just about Setting out to Go to her Daughter in the Country, but Expect to return Shortly with Horse & Chair to George Town, I Offered to bring these, or any thing Else *they* Chuse to the North Inlet drawed the Seine & Caught a few Shrimps, & Mullets. Butcher Joseph Lessesne Sent in his Account (only 23 days I had Beef of him) but he that Owes him money may Expect no Indulgence, he is as bad as a 3rd day fever & Augue. My boat went this Afternoon to Get fish, Oysters & Clams & Returned with only 7 Small fishes.

Wednesday, August 19. Rode out & Got a full Load of Wood. After breakfast Mrs. Thompson Visited me (for the first time). She has been very ill with fever & Augue but is now better, She Gave me Some Limes, & Sot about an hour, I will Give her a Ride in my Carriage Sometimes. Paid Lessesne $6 being amount of his Butchers Bill. Rachael Cut my hair today. In the Evening I rode round to Gasqua Camp which is Roved for more Air & Less Musquetoes nearer to the Beach & Sea. I Got Some Conks, Saw Waldo on the Beach. It being a fine Moon Light Night I Rode Past my House & Along the beach as far as Captain William Shackelfords House & Returned home about 9 OClock. I think the Moon fills Saturday next, when I hope for Less Rain. About 12 at Night Scipio was not to be found. On Questioning him I found he Greatly prevaricated, or Lyed & that he had taken up again his old Trade of Lying & Keeping Mr. William Shackelfords Wench in Spite of all my Endeavours to prevent it, & by my Express Orders to him to desist therefrom. About 2 OClock in the morning I Sent him off in my boat to Dover & wrote my Overseer to Keep him on the Plantation & to Send me Tailings & Carloes in place of Scipio.

Thursday, August 20. Rode out & Billy fell a Tree on the beach & Cut it up & the wood I brought home, Rachael went out with me as I took Daniel in my Carriage & when at the Tree that was fallen. I Sent Rachael to walk home with Daniel who Seemed to Get better for he Eat a very hearty Breakfast & talked much to me, & all abouts Eating & drinking of Tea. Boat went off with a fair Wind & Tide. Lieutenant Cokly of the Soldiers Encampt at the

Light House with a Mr. Taylor Visited me for about half an Hour they Informed me that Major Keith has Passed my house on his way to Review Captain Gasquas Company near the Inlet. That Lieutenant _____ the Deserter had his Sentence Read to him this morning which was that he was Cashered & dismissed the Service of his Country (note) a Sentence in my Oppinion Severe; he was but a Youth—the first time of desertion; a Militia Officer, & badly Advised by Tories. I doubt if any army Under Such Circumstances, would have Put Such a Sentence in Execution. He was Tryed by his Brother Officers on this Island. The Sentence was approved by Major General Thomas Pinckney & Ordered to be Put in Execution Two Sails appeared in the Offing this morning. Supposed to be Schooners one Standing Southwardly, The other Northwardly. Their Colours could not be discovered. Charming weather & high Tides. I returned Wench Liddy to my Overseer, as Zemo is now Well & here I wrote Overseer for Tailings for Poultry, the West Step to my House Scipio mended Yesterday. I feel myself Greatly dibilited today, & my appetite fails me & I can Get no Dainties here.

Friday, August 21. I rose Early to Avoid the heat of the Sun, & rode out & Got 4 Large dry Oak Logs. Met a Number of Souldiers Going for wood Some of them Always pulls off their hats to me & also Some of their Centinels Rest their firelocks to me as I pass their Post. I always Notice their Compliment, by my hatt, or hand. Some of them are very Conversable & well Educated, posseses Considerable Properties, they are many Militia men that have Volunteered Into their Countries Service, & are young men I hope of *Courage.* This however can never be Known till proved in *Action.* Lov[e] of Ones *Country* are Great *Virtue.* I think nothing can Excell it. *Family* Love is *amiable,* but Love of *Country* is on a Large & *Noble* Scale because it Encludes many we dont *Known,* & even have never *Seen.* Oh *once* happy *Rome,* thy Citizens have never been Excelled in any *Age* or *Country.* Would to *God* my Country*men* would Copy thy Valour & Patriotism & fight only in thy Countries Cause It & thy Personal honour defend at the risk of Life, for what is Life, if all we hold dear is Lost, do we wish then to Live. I answer no my Countrymen Embrace death, as a Welcome friend. Mr. Vareen (Son of the Widow Henderson) called on me & borrowed an Axe to Cut wood, he belongs to Captain Gasquas detachment Encamped near the Inlet. About 11 OClock A.M. B. Trapier Called on me & with my Spy Grass he Saw Two Sails—one Lying too just off George Town Bar. A Pilot boarded her & from her Rigging is Supposed to be a Gun Boat* one of 3 which is Expected to Guard our harbor. The other a Schooner

---

*Gunboats were most often small vessels with at least one heavy gun that could be fired forward or aft. Larger gunboats contained full broadside armament and were the size of brigs or schooners. Lavery and O'Brian, *Nelson's Navy,* 56.

from the North Wind bound in also & perhaps are the same Vessells, that we Saw yesterday. Today about 3 OClock p.m. Scipio Returned in the boat with a Barrell of Tailings, a News Paper of George Town dated August 19, 1812. A Note from my Overseer & one from Mrs. Davis. The Cart Wheels were Sent to the black Smith at George Town.

Saturday, August 22. Rode out & Got wood as Usual, Got Beef of Butcher as per Memorandum book. This Evening full Moon, but as the Wind is westward the Tides are not high. The night & full moon makes the beach delightfull to Ride or even to walk. My Little negro boy walks every time the Beach Allows & is Getting rid of his Swelled Stomach & he Eats hearty 3 Meals a Day & Sleeps well at Nights. His Aunt Rachael has the Care of him & She is very attentive to him, I Bathed Today about 11 OClock a.m. Last Night We heard a very Loud report of a Cannon from towards George Town bar, Supposed [to] be the Gun boat as mentioned Yesterday. I Expect to See Colonel Huggins here today if Vareens Report is Correct & I wish him to make my House his home while he Stays on the Inlet or Bason. He is my Town & Country Neighbour & a Good one he is, & he is much Respected by all who Knows him. This morning wrote Mrs. Horry & filled the Sheets of Paper as Usual with all the Winyaw News. Also wrote to Doctor Manning of George Town & to my Overseer Williams at my Plantation Called Belle Isle. I hope he has Embraced this fine dry weather & Gathered a Quantity of Corn Blades which my Mules & Horses will want much as fodder in the Winter, Straw must be Reserved if Possible till the new Year comes in & when there are Little or no Grass on the Ground, but what is Dry & no Moisture therein so it must be a Denier Resort. Alexander Campbell of Brown Town, Called on me nea[r] Sun Set, & Said he Stayed at John Man Taylors House; That Mr. Taylor was Gone to Meet the Legislature at Columbia. That he A. C. came to See after a Large Shell boat, that a Mr. Harrell Son of Old Harrell had taken the Deserted Ensign, & for his reward for So doing he was Given Command of a Company of Militia men. This Evening called at Captain Gasqua Camp, Saw him & his only Child (a Son) he told me that Mrs. Gasqua had Got Safe up to her Daughter which was as yet very hearty.

Sunday, August 23. Rode out with Daniel & took in Several Large Pieces of Sea Mud, Intended as Manure for our Brown Town Garden. It is very Salt[y] & Counted Excellent Manure Last Evening. At Camp I Saw Several Gentlemen, which agreed on the probability of Commodore Rogers & his Squadron having Gone to France, perhaps to Join a french Squadron & Proceed to the United State in force & to Act Together in our Seas Or Perhaps our Squadron has Arrived Safe in England. I would hope it Safe in the Former Port (Note) I am of Opinion our Ships of War ought to Act only on the American Coasts in Protection of our Trade & Guard our own Ships & harbours

The view of the marsh from present-day Dover Plantation

The English are too Powerfull for us in the Uropean Seas. On our own Coasts
we have many Advantages over them & their West Indies Trade is well worth
the attention of our Armed Vessells. The Produce of their Islands to us are of
Great Value & their Vessells are in our Power very often to Capture & Soon
are Safe in our harbours. This is the Game we ought to play with the British,
our Ships are well built for Sailing & our Seamen are Equal to any in the
world. In this way our brave Lads Let's have at them. Whither right or wrong
in declaring war I know not but having done so Unite together & Shew the
world we are not degenerated from our Ancestors. If we have Virtue we Can
fight without Money, only Arms & Courage are Necessary; I ask if we had
money to Carry on the Revolutionary War, *I know* we had not; yet a Determined Persevereance Gave us Independance; if our Enemy is more formadable
now so are we, in the Ratio of Perhaps Ten fould I cannot Allow that you are
degenerated. Then do *you* Prove that you are not, this morning a Perfect Calm
till 12 OClock I never felt it so hot & I Almost went Naked & do Pity the
Inhabitants of our Populous Towns. South of New England & which Lies on
the Sea Board. I Expect Soon to hear of men Dying in the Streets by Drinking Cold Water.

Monday, August 24. I rode out & Got my Waggon Load of Sea Mud. My boat went for Dover & Brown Town by Sun Rise She was under way. By her I Sent a Letter to My Factors to Go by Post to Charles Ton. Also (three others Letters) one to my Overseer at Dover one to Doctor Manning in George Town & one to Mrs. Horry at Statesburgh. Also Sent Conks & Sea Mud to my Garden at Brown Town I Got Information as follows. That my Cousin Sarah Belin was Dead at George Town, She is very Old & quite in her Dotage & as an Old Maid her Sister Belin Supported her for many years. I Also Got Information from Mrs. Samuel Wragg and Doctor Edward Thomas (by Letters to them from Charles Ton) That my Brother Jonah Horry was Dead (at Charles Ton of a Country Fever) he has Left a Widow, & two Daughters, one Married Captain Dent the other is yet single. His Estate are Negroes & Lands. About 15 Thousand Acres of the Latter & between 2 & 3 Hundred Slaves (mostly very Prime) It will now Soon be Known how far the Estate is In debt. I fear it will be found he owed much more than was Expected. He was too Penurious & Grasped at too much Say Spiculated on Negroes & Lands the Latter Inferior Inland Swamp? Poor fellow, he advised me by no means to Get in debt Yet he Got in debt himself tho' I made use of Every Argument to Prevent his doing it! Alass! How Common, do we advise our friends to that we do not follow ourselves but as to *my Brother* his Actions Shewed me That he relied on *my Extricating* him out of debts at any time. How mistaken or Infatuated, for I told him I was much in debt myself & by no means to depend on my helping him to Get out of Debt. He Seldom or Ever made Good Crops. He died about 66 years of Age. To his wife's Family he was Generous but to his own, he was not only the Contrary, but I may Say, Was unjust in many Particulars I have his Will at my house in Brown Town. About 11 OClock A.M. Major Wragg Called on & Sot with me about an houour, this Officer was my Brigade Major after Major Browns Resignation, then Major Capers, who Continued as Such untill my own Resignation, when Colonel Conway Succeeded me he Conway Resigned & the present Joseph Allston became Brigadeer Major Cambell & 6 Captains disputed the Propriety of his being a Brig[a]dier. A Court of Enquiry Sot thereon at Charles Ton, & *Allston* was Honourably Acquitted 'tis Supposed, *Cambell* will Prefer this matter to the Legislature (now Setting). Both Cambell & Allston are Members of the House. A Shower of rain has Somewhat abated the Extreme hot weather. I found the Souldiers were Carrying Ceader bows to Cover on poles Grated, & to Offord Shade over or in fronts of their Tents which being on dry Sand the men must Suffer much.

Tuesday, August 25. I rode out South Wardly & filled my Waggon with Cakes of Swamp Mud, the beach is now fine to Ride on both morning & Evening & the Inhabitants avail themselves of the Same. Major Wragg Informs

Lands for Sale,

THE fubfcriber's PLANTATIONS, viz DOVER, fituated on Winyaw Bay, about five miles below Georgetown, and not fubject to frefhes, contains above two thoufand acres, about three hundred acres tide land, below the upper refervoir, two hundred acres of which is cleared and under good banks; a faw mill works two faws; a pounding mill (built by Mr. Lucas) goes by water, grinds and beats with fourteen peftles; a threfhing barn and ftore houfe for rice; a new two ftory'd dwelling houfe, with every other neceffary building. The profpect, fituation and value of this plantation is fo well known, as to need no further defcription.

COVE PLANTATION, juft below the north brunch of Santee river; contains about 800 acres; about one hundred and fifty acres tide fwamp, twenty acres high fwamp, and feventy acres back fwamp and Savannah lands, fit for rice; under banks; the remainder pafturage and pine land. A dwelling houfe, kitchen, barn, pounding mill and negro houfes, are thereon. The fwamp foil of this plantation is equal to any in the country. For terms apply to Brian Cape, in Charlefton, Jonah Horry, at Combahee; Hugh Horry, at Georgetown or at Dover plantation, to   PETER HORRY.
November 2.

Peter Horry advertised the sale of Dover Plantation in the *City Gazette and Daily Advertiser* on December 7, 1793.

me Yesterday That General Hull with 1500 American[s] were 3 Times Repulsed by the Canadians under Command of General Provost* of the British. That the Cannadians had taken a Fort from the Americans. (Note) I much wonder at our Military Rulors to Send so few men in Canady appears as meant to Sacrifise them & have we more men than we know what to do with (there is a fault Somewhere) if General Hull[†] was Unpopular or they wished him, Killed,

*George Prévost was born May 19, 1767, in New Jersey, the oldest son of Augustin Prévost and Nanette Grand. Following an education in England and throughout the European continent, Prévost was commissioned an ensign in his father's regiment on May 3, 1779. He was promoted to captain in 1784 and in 1790 achieved the rank of major. He served in the West Indies during the war with France and was promoted to lieutenant colonel in 1794, colonel in 1798, and brigadier general in May 1798. He served for a short period as governor of St. Lucia but was forced to return to England for health reasons in 1802. On October 21, 1811, Prévost was commissioned governor-in-chief of British North America, and on July 4, 1811, he took command of British forces in North America. Spencer C. Tucker, "Lake Champlain and Plattsburgh, Battles of (September 11, 1814)," in Tucker, *U.S. Leadership in Wartime Clashes,* 123–26.

†Born in Derby, Connecticut, Isaac Hull began a career as a seaman on board a merchant vessel from 1783 to 1798. During the organization of the navy in 1798, he was appointed lieutenant and in May 1800 served as first lieutenant of the USS

as being Unfriendly to the Union, The Army (he commanded) could not merit his Punishment better have deferred the Expedition till a Strength Sufficient to Ensure Success could be Collected. If General Hulls Army is Lost Or he compelled to Retreat it will Greatly Encourage our Enemies, not only in Canady but throughout the Union & Maddisons Administration will yet more than ever be Condemned, & Perhaps he will not be Re Elected Pres[id]ent of the United States. Fine Weather, & Mullets runs finely I Saw this morning at Sea but near the beach two amasing Fish Large & almost Round, Swimmed near the Surface of the water. I knew it not, Perhaps It may be a Devil fish, Such I have heard Off. Many Persons both Whites & black Came to behold Such Monstrious Large fishes & we all Stared at Such Uncommon fishes. In the Evening had the pleasure of a Visit from Miss Delesseline & Miss Chees[borough] for the first time Since I arrived here. Met with Mrs. Allard Belin & Miss Mariah Belin on the Beach with the two Girls daughters of Mrs. Belin.

Wednesday, August 26. Rode out & Got a Load of Sea Mud. Last night my Boat Came from Dover & Brown Town. Received Letters from my Overseer & Mrs. Davis. She Says Peggy Continues very Poorly (I must Send for her here & Send Susie in her place). Mrs. Blunt of George Town is Dead Overseer Sent me 2 Axes & a Spade. He Got Cart Wheels from Rockeye full Tired & I Got a hook from R. for my Carriage Trace. I Got a George Town News Paper & Ben Trapier Sent me 6 Charles Town Papers Say the Times dated from the 13 to the 19 August 1812. I Received a fine Parcell of Okro, & I Sent them to my Good friend Mrs. B. Trapier. The Sea ran Ocross to the Bason near my House, tho' tis Past full Moon & no Storm, or high Wind, but fine Clear Weather. I fear the Rain a Little time Past, has Ruined the Up Country Crops & has brought down into Winyaw bay a Great Swell of Water the Sea Indeed appears of a Dark Colour, & as from Swamp Water. My Overseer write me one of my fields are Greatly Injured from back Water, which he could not Vend off fast Enough. The Afternoon a Sloop & Schooner appeared in the Offing. both Stood Eastwardly & was Soon ought of Sight.

Constitution. Given command of the *Argus,* he distinguished himself in the bombardment of Tripoli. He returned to the *Constitution* in 1806 as a captain and in 1812 narrowly escaped from a British squadron. Hull served as a captain in the US Navy for thirty-seven years and was unanimously awarded a gold medal by Congress for the capture of the British frigate *Gueriere* on August 19, 1812. Hull became a member of the Naval Board and served as a commander of the naval yards at Boston following the war. He died at his home in Philadelphia on February 13, 1843, at sixty-eight years of age. Morris, *Heroes of the Navy,* 153–65; Wyatt, *Memoirs of the Generals,* 206–13.

Thursday, August 27. I Rode out very Early & Got mud. Sent off my boat with a Load of Mud for my Town Garden. Wrote Mrs. Davis to send me Peggy, Robert & Little Susie, & I Sent her up Susie & Daniel. Tides very high Indeed, it Runs deep all round my House & the Creatures Cannot Get into the Marshes. I bathed today & took Physick as by Advice of Doctor Manning. My boat was under way by 8 OClock A.M. Susie, Coxen & 3 Oars. Say Scipio, Hardtime & William they had a favourable Tide & not much Wind. Major Commandant Keith & his family in their Carriage Paid Ben Trapier a Mornings Visit & Tarried with him & his family the day. This afternoon Mr. Coarse boat Run a race against Major Smith Boat & Co[a]r[se] won the Race.

Friday, August 28. I rode out this morning & Got a Load of Wood & Some Mud. Saw a Vessell in the Offing She appeared to be a Large Schooner Standing South East. The Winyaw Pilot boat was Seen Going out to her. By night I Shall Expect the arrival of my boat from Town. Tides not quite so high as they have been for Several days Past Cloudy Weather & Cool. Wind at North West. I Slept well Last Night. About 10 OClock A.M. a Brig Run Past my house in full Sail Going Southwardly appearantly bound Either to our bar or Charles Ton At dark my boat According to Expectation arrived with Peggy, & her two Children, She is however very Sick now in bed the Children are well.

Saturday, August 29. Last Night it Rained & this morning the Rain [illegible] Wind at North East (dark & Gloomy) not unlike a Gale at Sea. No Inhabitants out this morning. Peggy with a Hot fever & no Rest all Night. I am Sorry Scipio brought her from Town, (my Corn nearly out) I am uneasy about it & dont Know how I can Get more; Unless Dover can Spare me about 30 Bushels at George Town 'tis Cash & that Article & I are Unacquanted this Evening the Rain Ceased, Wind at West, Serene Sky that Quarter. Am in hopes Tomorrow will be a fair day. I rode to the Inlet & home before dark.

Sunday, August 30. This morning Wind & Weather as Yesterday Morning, but Peggy Seems better, by my Memorandum Book Dover can well Spare me 20 Bushels Corn from the old Stock. Yesterday I profesied this day would be fair weather, how am I disappointed, in this Life We are Sure of Nothing but Death, & it has not yet Called on me but I ought & I hope am Prepared to meet the Grim Tyrant, how many young & blooming Acquaintances are Gone before me. How many Relations are yet Left me (I mean those nearest & dearest to me) Mrs. Martin, my first Cousin (Infirm & near as Old as myself) remains, No Parents, No Brother, or Sister, Thomas Horry my first Cousin he promises to Live yet many years. All others are Distantly Related, Mrs. Martin Lives near to me & She only is my Comfort in all my distresses & I hope will Survive me I almost had forgot my Aunt Lynch Roberts who Lives in Charles Ton & I only See her once in many years. She was never very dear to me. I am in the hands of Negroes, & two of my house Wenches, Susie & Rachael are Kind to me. I may Say they are my Sisters & tends me as a Child (so helpless am I) they therefore are my Tryed friends, & they are found not wanting. My Maker only Knows why I am yet in this Terrestrial Globe & how much Longer I am to remain here.

Monday, August 31. I Rode On the beach South Ward. I bathed & my boat Sot out for Dover at 11 OClock A.M. Major Keith, W. Trapier & Mrs. Martin Visited B. Trapier & Returned before Night. At Gasqua's Parade in the Evening, I Saw Captain Irvin Keith & his Lieutenant Ford with a Number Spectators. (N.B.) I find more Spectators on Sunday Visiting Parad[e]s than Offering Prayers to their Maker. I wrote my Overseer for 20 Bushels Corn & my flat & to Put on board 2 Good Oarsmen to Assist bringing her down to me. Wrote him other Particulars Relative to the Plantation, None of my deceased Brothers Family (tho' he has been dead many Days) has Given me Notice of his Death nor do I find it Mentioned in any News Paper. No Sooner Dead than forgotten & as tho' we had never been, this is truly Scriptural & I Expect Such will be Verified in me.

End of Book Number 3 which Contains 1 Month & 15 days Transactions & to 1st September *1812* when Book Number 4 Commences.

BOOK FOUR

September 7, 1812–December 31, 1812

(first seven pages missing)

Monday, September 7. I think She is wrong, & I told her She must not have her way in this matter. Hort is Industrious & Miss D. is not Less so. Her Aunt is very Notable & deserves Great Credit in bringing up Several Young Girls which does her honour. I left Murrays house about 12 OClock, Sun at Maredian & Soon Got Safe home. Mrs. Murray Says the Married Couple (that is to be) must Live with her & the Major; but I say *no*. Do you & Hort, buy, or build a Good House in Brown Town (near to my House) & Let us Live in the Utmost harmony & as one family. Surely I am right in Wishing to Live (the few days which I may yet Live) in Sociability & Mirth & Slide down into my Grave, as tho' in Slumber & Repose. My Maker has been hitherto Extremely Kind to me. Will he not Receive me into his heavenly Mansions. To this Purpose in my bed Night & Morning in my Prayers & for my Country also to Continue his Past Blessings to take us at all times under his fatherly Protection.

Tuesday, September 8. I Sent off my flat to Dover plantation with Conks, Shells & Clams & wrote to my Overseer to detain the flat & her Crew. I Sent off at the Same time, by 8 OClock A.M. my big boat to George Town, with Mud & Some Oysters & Clams as a Present to Mrs. Davis & wrote her. Mrs. Thompson went passenger in my boat & 2 Wenches of Mrs. Cogdells a fine Wind & Tide, boat was Soon out of Sight. By Invitation I Visited John Man Taylor & breakfasted with him. Savage Smith came there, about 11 OClock A.M. I Left Taylors house & went home before 12 OClock. Taylor Says his father & Sister Allstons was at New Port, but Supposes them now on their way by Land for South Carolina. Dr. Futhy, Mr. B. Thomas, & Mr. Davis told me Last Evening at Gasquas Camp they would Visit me today but as yet have not made their appearance. Major Smith Says he Sent his boat to George Town to bring down Parson Botsworth today & he is accordingly Expected here in the Afternoon.

Wednesday, September 9. Rode out & Got Wood from Several Stumps, beach Look well I have Got many Stumps Cut out therefrom, the Ladies of the Island ought to thank me to Give their Carriages so fine a beach as Soon they will have, quite from the Inlet & Round the Point to Major Keith House the South Side of the Inlet so their will Remain no Obstruction whatever. Wind being Eastwardly The Tide has fell Very Little, which Prevents my Getting much Sea Mud which is Excellent for my Garden as yet very Little Gravel appears on the beach, next Month there are Generally more than I can take away before I Leave the Island. I have not heard if Parson Botsworth is Arrived. Tomorrow Evening dicides Miss P. D. Maidenhead. Pray Reader what must be her feelings today, *I Say* not Equal to their Going to bed Together. Fear & joy Alternately Prevails. My boat about 1 OClock P.M. arrived from George Town & Scipio brings me welcome news & Letters from Mrs. Horry & others & which I have been Expecting for Sometime past. All my friends & Relations are well, & Mrs. Davies Sent me Sundries which I wrote to her for. Two Samples of broad Cloth Scipio brought me from Mr. Whitehurst of George Town to Look at for Coats for myself & my man Billy. Gave Zemo a New homespun Jacket this morning, & he has Mounted it. I will not Relate all that Mrs. Horry writes me & of Miss Bay also as a Sheet of Paper would not Contain it.

Thursday, September 10. I rode out & Got Some wood, Last Evening before Gasquas Camp I met with Mr. Hort. He Said Tomorrow Evening you are Expected at Major Murray House, I Answered, I will Obeyed Orders. He Said the Reverend Mr. Botsworth was but a Little distance from us & was Viewing the men Exercising. That Tomorrow After breakfast he would Call on me, which he did with young Mr. Cuttino & he Gave me Several News papers Sent me by Mr. Whitehurst. He & Cuttino Staid about an hour & took their Leaves of me. I went to Murrays house about Sundown, about 7 OClock P.M. I Saw Mr. Hort married to Miss Polly Delesseline about 20 Persons were Present (Males & Females) a very Agreeable Party in Deed. The Bride Looked beautifull. The Brides Maid was Miss Hort. About 9 I Got home.

Friday, September 11. I Rode out & brought home wood & went & breakfasted with Ben Trapiers Family, about 10 OClock A.M. Major Savage Smith & young Cuttino came in & Staid about an hour & departed, I Got home about 12 Sun on the Marodian, I Received a Letter from my friend Mrs. Helin, & am Sorry She is much Afflicted with the fever she rites me her Son James is on a Cruise in Hudsons bay, I fear General Hulls Army is Captured as Report Says. Also that Captain Wilson of the Winyaw Cavalry has (in a Duel) Killed Keating Simmons of Charles Ton. Mrs. Helin writes me that Francis Kinlochs only Son is Dead or Past Recovery & that I Speak disrespectfully of the Devil that he is a King & will Pinch me with Thum screws whenever he Gets hold of me. About 8 OClock this morning I Sent off my boat to Dover & George Town & Sent Mrs. Horry Letter to be forwarded to her by Mr. Samuel Smith Also wrote to my Overseer, Mr. Whitehurst & Mrs. Davis.

Saturday, September 12. I rode out & Met Ben Trapier on the beach. He Informed Me that Altho General *Hull* was taken & all his men Say about 2500 in Canady. Yet his Nephew Captain *Hull,* who Commands the Constitution Frigate, had fought a *British* Frigate Killed & wounded Great Number of her men & *Sunk* her. That however Captain *Hull* Lost a *Leg* in the Engagement. Alass how *fickle* is fortune, no dependance on her *Smiles* or *Frowns.* I Rode to Major Murrays to Enquire after the welfare of his Family Particularly the Bride & Bridegroom, Mrs. Hort & her husband Mr. Hort, found all well. Rode Round & Called at B. Trapiers House & Got two Boston Papers, one of which Give an Account of the Action fought at Sea by Captain Hull & other Particulars as above mentioned were Correct as by my Information, these Papers I Returned to Major Wragg by a Servant.

Sunday, September 13. I rode out & Met Major Murray & Benjamin Trapier. He Said he would Go to my house after he had breakfasted, he Breakfasted, & met Major Keith & they both came to me when I Shewed him one of Captain Dents Letter to me, which said if I Qualify as an Executor on my Brothers Estate that I do appoint him, my Agent but as Mrs. Horry will Qualify on the Estate, Keith & myself thought it best; that I do not qualify, & that Mrs. Horry ought to Appoint Dent her Agent Heyward, Pringle, & Elias Horry, declines Acting as Executors on the will. Keith will in a day or two deliver me a Copy of my Brothers will which he thinks I delivered him, when I was Going to the Virginia Springs. Dent & the Widow Acting on this Estate will I think be most Advantageous to it & I hope will Soon Extricate It out of Debt, Particularly If Peace takes place Soon, If no peace Soon I Sincerely Pitty the heirs of the Estate about 11 OClock A.M. I went to Major S. Smiths House where a full Congregation was Gathered together & we heard a Sermon from the Reverend Mr. Botsworth. Ben Huger, A [illegible], Cuttinoes, Heriots, Irvin Keith, Ensign Coker & many others my Intimate Acquaintances were Pre[s]ent also many Ladies honoured me by Shaking hands with me. About 1 OClock P.M. I Got home. On my Evening Ride I met Lieutenant Coker & Mr. McGregor. The Lieutenant Said about 1st Next month he would be in the Neighbourhood of Statesbourgh & Offered me to Carry any Letters for Mrs. Horry & Miss Bay.

Monday, September 14. Rose Early & Gathered Gravil on the beach with all hands. Filled therewith at the Landing 6 Barrels Saw Mr. Thurston on the Beach on Horse back. He has been very Ill, Look Shocking. His fever however has Left him & also has Left His Daughter Caroline, these are Valuable Citizens.

Tuesday, September 15. Gathered Gravil & wrote Several Letters in Answer to those Received. Also bathed, & Rachel bathed Daniel & Giddo (two of Negro boys) I called on B. Trapier & he told me that a frigate of ours The Essex had Captured an English frigate & Carried her into Boston (*Note*) I wish this may be so. As it will Convince the Maritime Powers; That American Seamen, Can fight Equal to the English or any Nation.

Wednesday, September 16. Rode out & Got a Little Mud, It blew a Storm Yesterday & all Last Night the wind blew very hard from the North East Loaded my boat with Mud Shells & Gravil & Sent Scipio with her up to Brown Town. Wrote also Several more Letters, which he Carried up in all 10 Letters—five of which Goes by Post. I Expect Mrs. Whitehurst & Children will return in my boat. Spoke with Major Murray near his House. He said the Present Report was that General Hull did fight the British in Canady & Lost 500 Men before he Surrendered himself, Officers & men of 2000. The British had 8 Thousand men besides Officers. I thought no Officer would Surrender without Some fighting. If General Hull had done the Contrary, he must have Lived with the Enemy our Government I hope would never have Exchanged him being a New Englander. That Country would have hanged him but Reader youll say Catch him first. Arnold is Dead, or Hull might have Lived with him in Halifax & be pointed at (Even by the British) as a Traytor & Scoundrel, often the Act is approved of but the Traytor is dispised, this was Arnolds Case. He Lived in Continual fear of being KidNapped by the Bostonians who Sent him word they would do so & deliver him to his Countrymen.

Thursday, September 17. I rode out & Got wood. Discovered a Sloop in the Offing. Steering a South East Course, Last night Captain Gasqua & his wife Lodged at my House in the Straingers Room & She breakfasted this morning with me. Mrs. Gasqua had the birth of a Grand Son. I Expect She will now Stay with me while I Remain on the Island, High wind from North East high Tides & very Cloudy weather. Mrs. Gasqua (in the Evening) rode out with me to Captain Gasquas Camp & he returned with us to my House this night my boat returned & brought me Sundries from Dover & Several Letters from George Town.

Friday, September 18. I Rode out, & Got wood. Now fine Clear & Cool Weather. 4 Corps in George Town in one day as Mrs. Davis Informs me. Not a Well Person in Mr. Whitehurst family, as his Letter Informs me, my boat went off about 9 OClock A.M. for George Town, Captain Gasqua Lieutenant McCollough & the Captains Son dined with me. I wrote to my Overseer by Boat & Expect She will Return Tomorrow with Captain Gasquas Supplies from his Plantation & with Mr. Whitehurst & his family to Spend Several days with me. In the afternoon Miss Henderson, called on Mrs. Gasqua. Doctor Futhy Called on me but Soon Left me. When the Two Ladies rode with me to Gasqua's Camp & Miss H. Returned with me & Mrs. G. round about

& as far as Ben Trapier house, where She Lives. Captain Gasqua did not Meet us as we Expected, however he came to my House Late at Night & Lodged thereat. Beautiful Moon Light Night.

Saturday, September 19. I Rose Early this morning & found Mrs. Gasqua up She Said her husband was Sick all Night with a Fever & She Sent to Camp for his Son & Negro boy. I Got some wood & a few Shells, & on my Return home I found the Said Negro boy & Son & also two of Gasqua's Officers with his Wife Setting in Gasquas Room. We all Breakfasted Together Except Captain Gasqua who was in bed. The Obstinacy of boy London, had nearly Overset My Carriage & Mules. The Activity of my Servants Billy & Zemo Saved me. On my Getting to the House London was Punished. I hope he will in future be more Careful & on his Guard. Gasqua is in Bed & Sweating with drinking hot Garden Tea. Wednesday next the Sun Cross the Line, or Meredian, the day & Night therefore must be Equal in duration. I Sent Rachael to Mr. Ben Trapier with my Watch to Set & Wind up & to Look if the Hour & Minuit hand do not Entercept Each Other. He sot her & Said no more was wanted I hope Captain Gasquas fever Will Leave him by the afternoon & so as he can Go to his Parade. Tis very Cool Weather & I begin to think of Returning to Brown Town with my bag & baggage & I purpose setting out however from thence by the 16th October, now but 26 days to Come. About 1 OClock P.M. Doctor Wragg Called & Saw Captain Gasqua. Said he was Sweating & his fever Going off. We discovered a Vessell Standing South East. A Light breese from the North. I Look for my boat Return before Dark. Only Mrs. Gasqua & his Son dined with me. A Bright Sun Shine day. Gasqua's fever did Go off by night but he did not go the Parade Miss Joseph's & Several other young Ladies Visited Mrs. Gasqua this day I Saw on the beach Mr. Waldo & his Assistant Mr. the most Gaughky man on the Island, but he is a Great Scholar & good School Master.

Sunday, September 20. I rode out, tis very Cold. Wind at due North. No appearance of my boat even at Breakfast time, Some disappointment has happened at George Town. Saw Two Schooners Standing Southwardly. Not far from Major Murrays. I Got Compleatly bogged both Mules Sunk in the Sand, broke my Traces & I Thought one of the Mules had a Leg broke, I Sent my Servant to Murray's for Assistance, he was Kind Enough to Come himself with four fellows & all hands at Length drew out the Carrage & Mules to hard Sand, Traces being mended, & Mules fixed thereto. When I found I was fortunate in received but Little Injury the Mules drew me home very well. I was told Reverend Mr. Frazer preached today at Dubourdieus Island & next sunday Reverend Mr. Botsworth will Preach at the House of Major Savage Smith on this our Side of the Island. I Saw Mr. Hort & his Bride riding out Together for the first time about 11 OClock A.M. 2 More Small Vessells appeared Standing also South Wardly. Dr. Wragg Called to See Captain Gasqua. My boat arrived at my Landing about 3 OClock P.M. Passengers Mr. & Mrs. Whithurst, their two Sons & a Prentice Boy & a Negro Girl Boat Also brought Sundries for Gasquas & Whitehurst families & a Wench for Gasquas family with Ockro Rice & Snap Beans.

Monday, September 21. I Rode out (with Mr. Whitehurst Son James) Got some Wood & a few Clam-Shells. Whitehurst went with Captain Gasqua to his Camp, Scipio went with 2 Oarsmen to fish & Get Oysters & Clams, drew first the Seine in the Bason, Caught a very few Shrimps, & Small fishes fit only for Bait, Sent Billy to Major Murrays to know if he would Lend me his Seine to Stop the Bason tomorrow about breakfast time, fish is now Running many in Schools at Sea near the beach & many Seen within the Inlet. Fish for my Present Family would be very Co'venient. Ben Trapier called on me to Give a Negro a passage to George Town, I Saw an Order which my Overseer drew on me in a favour of a Mr. Johnson for about $30 Dollars I had not so much money. Johnson Said he would Leave the Orders with Messrs. Taylors Merchants in George Town as most Convenient for my taking up the same.

Tuesday, September 22. I Rode out & Got Wood Murray Came to the Bason, but would not fix his Seine he then said he would draw at his own Landing the two Ladies with myself & a Child rode to his Landing, when [illegible] he declined Drawing there, also. We then passed by Gasquas Camp, & returned home. I bathed about 11 OClock A.M. & James & Daniel Whitehouse bathed also with Giddo & Daniel—two Small Negro Boys. Mr. Ward (Deputy General Quarter Master for the States of South & North Carolina & Georgia), honoured Mrs. Gasqua & Whitehurst & myself with his Company At Dinner today. I found him, an Agreeable well Informed Gentleman. He Says Charles Ton is his home. He Left us near Sun down, & Rode off for Mrs. Charles Lessesne house on the South side of this Island.

Wednesday, September 23. Last night I was very Sick with a Violent Cold, Slept none. I Eat Crabs at Supper & I ride out too Late at Night. These Imprudencies I must Rectify in future, I Sent off my boat with Gravil Early this Morning for my Lot in Brown Town & I wrote to my Overseer for a Barrell of Ruff Rice & of my Sick Negroes. Mrs. Whitehurst went for George Town in Major Murrays boat & is to return tomorrow in Mr. Wards boat on the South Side of the Island. Mrs. Gasqua very Unwell, could not breakfast with us. About 11 OClock A.M. Mrs. Gasqua, & Mrs. Whitehurst with her two Children Entered my Room & bathed themselves in my bathing Tub, while I Sot in the Hall & wrote in this my History or daily Journal. Beautiful Weather Clear & dry, Planters I hope are Embracing the Same. A fine quantity of wood Lies before my Kitchen. I must Cease bringing more & Get Gravil at my Landing & put it into barrells, & Ready to Go into my boat whenever She is

Going to my Town Garden, Wind this day at North East & Light Air. Boats Goes to Sea & Catch fish near the Surf or beach. Yesterday was Caught upwards of 300 Sizable Mullets. I Saw this morning Sharks in a School of them & the fishes Even jumped out of the Sea to avoid their Great Enemy.

Thursday, September 24. I Rode out & took out from the Beach two Very Large Stumps, Got a few Shells & a Little Sea Mud. Major Murray drew in a haul Mullets Sufficient to Make 3 barrels. Our Family are Getting better of their Colds. Changing Cloaths & Coverings to Beds are particularly dangerous at this Season of the year Mrs. Cogdell, Sent her boat to Town this morning with a fine Tide & Wind. Saw a Vessell Standing South East Apparently making for George Town bar. She came to Anchor. Wind North East a fresh breese about Sundown my boat Arrived. Got a Letter from My Overseer & Mrs. Davis. Received a Barrell Ruff Rice from Dover to feed my Mules. Having but Little Corn, only for my House Negro.

Friday, September 25. Rode out & took up 2 Stumps from the Beach & Cut half of 3 Other Stumps. Major Keith & Adjutant Cuttino Passed my House in Compleat Uniform, to Review Captain Gasqua's Company. Sent Mrs. Trapier a Parcell of Ockro & See Wee Beans. Major Keith Sent me word he would Call on me this Morning & Inform me Respecting my Brothers Will. Miss Henserson called this morning to See Mrs. Gasqua. I Sent Scipio, to fish & Get Oysters & Clams. He Got Oysters & Clams but no Fish. Mr. Whitehurst Returned from Town with Mr. Ward (Deputy Quarter Master General) before Night Ward returned to Mr. Charles Lessesnes house at North Island where he Lodged, $3000 is arrived at George Town to Pay our Militia Souldiers, at the Inlet.

Saturday, September 26. I rode out & Got Wood & Sea Mud. Captain Gasqua & Mr. Whitehurst went to fish near Dubourdieus Island. After breakfasting with us I Got a Set of Cows feet to boil for Oil for My Carriage Traces. Very Cold Morning. High Wind at North. "Whip up Old England or America will win the Race, We fight at Sea, better than in our Revolutionary War & worse on Land than we did then. Noble Captain Hull & Ignoble General Hull they are Nephew & Unkle But no Relation in War. The above fish Party Sent home Some fish for Dinner. Mr. Dozer & Mr. Goutier Called me & Sot an hour. Goutier & McCollough dined with us. I rote today to Mrs. Horry & Miss Sarah Bay. Dozer & Gasqua are very near Neighbours & Lives near black Mingo.

Sunday, September 27. Rode round & to Savage Smiths House & found Mr. Botsworth too Sick to Preach today. Rode out in the Evening with Mrs. Whitehurst & her Childrin, Lieutenant Cockley Called on me & I delivered him a Letter for Mrs. Horry, & also a Letter for Miss Bay, to be Sent to her at Columbia he will Propable See Mrs. Horry at the high Hills of Santee. I delivered Mr. Whitehurst a Letter to be Put in the Post Office at George Town, & a Letter to be delivered to John Shackelford & Son Merchants in George Town.

Monday, September 28. I rode out & Got Gravel & Wood, Mr. Whitehurst went for George Town this morning with a fine wind & Tide, he is to return tomorrow. Rode out in the Evening & Got Gravel & wood. Joseph Lessesne Butcher sent me his Accounts with a receipt thereto. I Returned it Immediately saying to the Bearer I will Pay when it suited me.

Tuesday, September 29. I rode out & Got wood which I sent by boat to Town. Boat went to Dover & Town. Put therein Gravel & Shells, & Sea Mud, 2 Books & Crab Shells. Wrote My Overseer & Mrs. Davis, for a quart Salt & from Dover, ½ B.C. Rice. Captain Gasqua dine's today with Major Murrays Family. I commissioned him to Kiss the Bride & Bride's Maid for me fine dry weather, Cool Evenings & Mornings, my Cruel Cough Continues tho' I take a good Deal of Honey (Given me by Mrs. Gasqua) my Brandy is out, tomorrow I Expect more by Scipio from George Town.

Wednesday, September 30. I rode out & Got 8 fine Strait Logs (Ceader) to be Sent to my Town House, I mean to Get no more Shells or Gravil while I tarry here, but only Mud & fire wood. I Visited Captain Gasquas Camp this morning & Saw his men Exercise. The Captain Complains of Mr. Ward not Supplying his Company with Rations, Captain Bethia's Company at Cat Island is dismissed to their Respective homes. It Seems all our Militia Souldiers will Soon be discharged & Regulars Succeed them or Peace will Soon take Place; when no Souldiers Of any description will be wanted, Every Citizen will then Set under his own fig Tree in happiness.

Thursday, October 1. I Rode out & Got Wood & Gravel my Boat Arrived with a Supply of Brandy, ½ Bushel Clean Rice Salt, & Vegitables from Dover, I Sent Scipio & Hard time (by request of Ben Trapier) to Carry the Chain for Mr. Hemmingway the Surveyor to Survey from the Bason to the Inlet. He called on me & I Saw him Yesterday on Captain Gasqua's Parade.

Friday, October 2. I Rode out & Got wood, Saw Major Wragg on the Beach, he said young Bay of Charles Ton was Killed in a Deuel. I Sent up my boat to George Town with Gravil & Wood & Sundry household firniture, all the Inhabitants are preparing to Go to a General Review Tomorrow, Mr. Whitehurst & Mr. Ward Returned from George Town today.

Saturday, October 3. I rode out & Got a Little wood, a Storm arose with rain & I hurried home & waited Captain Gasquas Company Passed by on the beach. I rode (with Mrs. Whitehurst) to Captain Gasqua & then we found that Major Commandant Keith had Countermanded his Orders of Yesterday; so there was no Review Today. On my way home I took in a Load of Gravil or Shells & Put it in Barrells at my Landing. Gloomy Cold Weather. I Expect when the weather Clears there will be a Frost. Surely then no Risk Can be apprehended by Going to George Town.

Sunday, October 4. I Rode out & Got a few Chips. Billy & his Dogs Caught a fat Raccoon & I Gave him a quart of Rice to Eat with it for his Dinner. I Received from George Town a Letter from North & Web of Charles Town, they Sent me a Barrell Sugar & Informed me they had sold my Rice. By Accounts Rice now Sells at Charles Ton for $3. Mr. Ward Dined with us.

Monday, October 5. I rose Early & Got all on board, also Whitehurst & his Family & Goods, & the boat Sot out for George Town about 7 OClock A.M. with a Good Wind, & 'tis a fine Morning, I hope all will Soon be Safe in Town. Tomorrow I Expect my flatt from Dover. About 8 OClock A.M. I Sot out with Mrs. Gasqua to See a General Review on the Island of our Militia Souldiers—about 150 in Number. The North Island division of 2 Companies & the North Inlet Division of Captain Gasquas Company met halfway, say about Mr. Collins turn off. Road to his House. Many were Present as Spectators, Major Commandant Keith Superintended the whole. Captain Gasqua on the Right Wing & Captain Bingham on the Left Wing. I with Mrs. Gasqua & Miss Henderson went to See the Light House, the Pilot Conducted these Ladies to the Glasses or Lamps which Gives Light at Night, no wood about the Light House all is brick or Stone & the Invention is admirable & well Executed. We went round the South Point of the Island & Got home about 4 OClock P.M. Appetites for Dinner were very Good.

Tuesday, October 6. I Got up about 8 OClock A.M. when my Carriage had Conveyd two Loads of Gravil to my Landing. Yesterday I was Informed Mr. Evans of George Town was dead, he was a partner of Mr. Cogshell. He has left a young Widow to Lament his Loss. After Breakfast I rode out & Got wood & Mud, & began to Get Ready; for Tomorrow my Flat & boat arrive I shall Go for George Town, after taking & Early breakfast.

Wednesday, October 7. I rose Early & Loaded flat & boats & at 9 OClock A.M. Sot out with them with Mules & Cattle for George Town & arrived all Safe by Night. Mr. Whitehurste & Mr. Samuel Smith Called on me. I found Mrs. Davis & her Children well, & houses firniture, Garden etc. etc. in Good Order.

Thursday, October 8. I rode out & Visited Mr. Whitehurst & rode out with his Children to Mrs. Helins, Mrs. James Belin & Mrs. Cheesborough's Senior & Sent off to Dover my flat for Corn, Horses & Riding Chair to Go for Mrs. Bay. Mrs. Horry, Miss Hunter & two Elder Miss Bays from Columbia, & High Hills Santee. I Also Visited Mrs. Wayne Senior & I Saw at her house Mrs. (the widow) Shackelford.

Friday, October 9. My Chair, Mule & Horse, with Some Corn arrived from Dover, Scipio & William Getting Ready for the up Country. My boat

Returned to Dover. Scipio has money for Mrs. Horry & I have wrote to her, Colonel Huggins called on me & he & Miss Hannah Shackelford Sent me Letters for the up Country. Cheesboro' is Expected tomorrow here.

Saturday, October 10. I Rose Early & at 6 OClock A.M. My Carriage & Chair Sot off for the high Hills of Santee, with Scipio & William, Mrs. Cambell Sent me a Letter for her Son at Columbia. Mrs. Whitehurst Sent me Some Nice Venison for Stakes, Samuel Smith Visited me this Evening. He thinks (as I do) that Dr. Blythe Ben Huger, John Man Taylor, & Thomas R. Mitchell will be Elected.

Sunday, October 11. I requested Airon to hire me a Negro Man this morning to Assist Zemo to Carry me in my Sedan to Church & I wrote R. Shackelford for freight of 46 Barrels Rice to Charles Ton. I Received a New Coat from Mr. Whitehurst 'tis not Altogether to my Liking. I went to the Methodist Church* Mr. Norton preached. I dined in Company with Captain Gasqua at Mr. Whitehurst House, he promised me a bottle of honey in a few days & when he returned from his home, I Engaged freight of Rice by Captain Marsh for Charles Ton he commands a Sloop. I sent Bill to bring me tomorrow 3 Negro men in my big boat to Cooper & Put my 46 Barrells Rice on board of the Said Sloop.

Monday, October 12. Yesterday I Received a Letter from Mrs. Horry it has no date & Came by Mr. John Murrell from its Contents it is of an Old date. I could not Answer it by Scipio who went off Yesterday, today I Received a Letter from Miss Bay. It was very pleasing to me. I wrote my Factors for sundry Family, Supplies & for money to buy Corn & Sent the Letter to the Post Office Last Evening I Supped with Mrs. Davis in Company with her Son & Daughter, Mr. & Mrs. Croft & Miss Deshamps & I Voted for a Senator to Congress & 4 State Representatives. My Overseer Visited me with 3 hands to Assist Packing & Trimming my Rice in Store.

Tuesday, October 13. My Negroes drawing hoops. I borrowed 2 [illegible] for Packing Rice. Lost 9 barrell in the 1st Store so there are but 18 Barrels there,

---

*Methodism first came to South Carolina through the missionary efforts of Francis Asbury and Rev. Woolman Hickson, Rev. Jesse Lee, and Rev. Henry Willis, who traveled through the state as itinerant ministers. On February 23, 1785, they arrived in Georgetown and stayed at the home of William Wayne. Wayne was converted to Methodism during their stay, becoming the first recorded South Carolina Methodist. Hickson remained in Georgetown and established the Georgetown Methodist Church in 1785. He eventually received a license to preach and in 1791 was ordained a deacon. Côté, "South Carolina Methodist Records," 51; *Methodist Magazine* 1 (1818): 455–59.

Mr. John Cheesborough Returned Last Evening & Called on me at 1 OClock P.M. He is very well. Whitehurst Lent me Twenty Dollars.

Wednesday, October 14. Finished Packing my Rice there are   Barrells in 2 stores. I defer Puting it on board of Captain Marsh & have Sent off my flat to Dover with Shells. Whitehurst & Croft Called on me Mrs. Cambell Called on me also Mr. Croft & the Reverend Mr. Botsworth Major Murray, one of the Managers of Election for Representatives Reported to me that these four following Persons were the fortunate ones Viz. John Wilson had 150 Votes, Joseph Blythe 140 Votes, Nathan Huggins 135 Votes & Thomas R. Mitchell 122 Votes.

Thursday, October 15. I rose & found it Raining hard & as it did all the Night, my Garden & yard are afloat. Last Evening Captain Gasqua Sent me a Bottle honey & Some Comb. My bowell Complaint Continues tho' I have taken a Dose of Physick from Dr. Manning & Used other means. I wish this heavy rain might not be a Impediment to Mrs. Horrys Coming down the Country to me. By the Road, etc. being full of Water. I Expect a frost Soon after so heavy a Rain, when my Overseer must dig Potatoes for I find his harvest near over & fear tis a very Short Crop. Sent my boat to Dover & sent some Barley & Sent for Ducks & wood the Sun appears to be Getting out of the Clouds about 1 OClock P.M. John Harvey is very Sick.

Friday, October 16. It did not Rain Last night, it Grows Cool & is windy & Cloudy. Wind at West. I wrote by Captain R. Shackelford to North & Webb & put on board 3 Dimy Johns for Rum, Brandy & Molasses I Received a Letter from Mrs. Horry & I Expect to See her & S. Bay very Shortly Miss Hannah Shackelford Visited me this forenoon also Mr. Whitehurst who says a Number of Small Vessells Pr[i]vateers briggs have taken 8 of Our Coasting Vessells, these Privateers belong to New Providence. Charles Ton is Compleatly blockaded. General Pinckneys Vessells taken Loaded. Allston Lost more than 100 barrels Rice. Almost all of our George Town Merchants have Suffered in Goods Coming to them. Some near $2000 in Value it has proved fortunate that I could not have Shipped my Rice. Our Cannon at the Magazine is today Mounting to be fixed on Fort Winyaw.*

---

*In 1776 the South Carolina militia and volunteers of Georgetown built an earthwork on the Sampit River east of Georgetown, eventually known as Fort Winyah. In June 1782 Col. Christian Senf, the senior state engineer, began fortification of Fort Winyah with the use of slave carpenters and other artisans from confiscated Tory estates. The fort was located on the southwest tip of Waties' Point on the left bank of the Sampit as it flowed into Winyah Bay. The fort never met battle during the American Revolution, and work continued under the direction of engineer Paul Hyacinth Perrault. Peaceful relations with Britain brought an abrupt end

Saturday, October 17. I had all the Chimneys in the Lot Swept & white washed the Sides of the Chimneys, & blacked their backs. Removed the bed Stead from the hall into the back Room, for Mrs. Horry. Cleaned the Fenders, Shovels & Tongs & fire Dogs & prepaired for the Reception of Mrs. Horry. My disordered Seems somewhat abaited this morning, Cleaned the yard this morning in a Particular manner, Yesterday Planted a Bed of English Pease Mrs. Whitehurst & Mrs. Croft Visit me Also Mrs. Wayne. No Allarm of Privateers this morning however Captain Davis is not yet Arrived only Captain Tarbox is come from Charles Ton, all other Accounts or Reports Relative to Vessells taken appears doubtfull. Time only can put us on a Certainty. Mr. Samuel Smith & Mr. Whitehurst Visited Me this Evening.

Sunday, October 18. Fine Clear Weather Wind at North West. Mr. William Cheesborough died Yesterday Evening, he has Left a Widow & 3 or 4 young Children, a Mother & a Brother. I went to the Methodist Church & Mr. Norton Preached. I Visited Mr. Whithurst Family, after Church. 'Tis now said Captain Davis is actually taken, his Vessell was Seen in Possession of one of the Privateers.

Monday, October 19. Last Evening Mr. Whitehurst, Mr. Samuel Smith & Captain Marsh Visited me, I had all by broken Conks taken from my yard & Established Good Ones, & took up a Dead Tree at the Corner of Stable, Got my Cow in Mr. Mitchels field for the first time this Season. My barley is Coming up very well. Beautiful Weather wind at North, I Expect Mrs. Horry tomorrow, Mr. Whitehurst Sot with me an hour after night.

Tuesday, October 20. Sent to Dover a Basket Salt & all my broken Conks. Sent for Tom & for a Basket Potatoes, & for Rose for Wood & for Swamp Mud. I Expect the boat to Return by night. Sent my Coat to Whitehurst to be Altered. Captain Tarbox Sailed this Morning for Charles Town.

Wednesday, October 21. Captain Keith yesterday Returned my Sword by My Servant, he, his Lieutenant Ford & Mr. Cheesborough Visited me in the Evening they said that General Hull had Shot himself, That General Harrison had stormed Fort Malden in upper Cannady & taken it with the Loss of 500

---

to the construction in 1795. On May 21, 1798, the citizens of Georgetown appointed Peter Horry to head a committee on the defense of the town. The fort was built on the site of the old earthwork during the summer and fall of 1798. Nine years later it had fallen into decay but was reconstructed in 1809. Lt. Benjamin D. Heriot and the Third Infantry established the first garrison at Fort Winyah in February 1810. Following the War of 1812, the fort once again fell into ruin, and the former location of the fort has now been transformed into East Bay Park. Wade, "Fort Winyah at Georgetown."

men, that the Enemy Lost 1100 Men. The Americans were mostly Caintuck-
eans, That the Privateers Brigs on our Coast was Gone, with only 3 of our
Coasters, they were Pursued by Some Charles Ton Vessells.* I Got a Fat Pig
from Dover Yesterday. Mr. Whitehurst Visited me this morning, as did Also
Mrs. Whitehurst. I Sent my boat to Dover for my flat to be ready to Put my
Rice on board of Captain Marsh whenever he Called for it & I wrote my Factors for a half Barrell Crackers & a Jug of Venegar to be Sent me as Soon as
Possible. I Sent Mrs. Whitehurst Some Ockro & See Wee beans, I Saw Roses
breast, & found it So bad, that I Sent her Immediately to Doctor Manning
who prescribed for her Cure.

Thursday, October 22. Last Evening Miss Carville & Miss Frances Har-
vey Visited me & after night Mr. Ward (Contractor for our Army) with Mr.
Whitehurst Also Visited me. This morning my flat arrived from Dover with
wood & Cabbage plants. My Barley Shows very well in rows & my Pease is
Sprouted in the Ground, Yesterday I Gave Mrs. Wayne Some pease, I planted
out 136 Plants about 11 OClock this morning Mrs. Horry & the two Eldest
Miss Bay Arrived here in Good health I Received a Letter from Mrs. Bay & I
Returned all Mrs. Horry & Miss S. Bay Letters which I had Received from
them while up the Country.

Friday, October 23. Last Evening Mrs. Horrys & S. Bays Acquaintances
Visited them, Mrs. Helin is very Sick in Bed. I turned out all my Rice 44 Bar-
rels & Put on board Captain Marsh Sloop for Charles Ton, Consigned to
North & Web Factors there Bars markt P.H. Mrs. Croft & Miss Godfrey
Visited Mrs. Horry this afternoon & at Night Doctor Futhy Mr. Murrell, Mr.
S. Smith & Mr. Cheesborough drank Tea & Coffee with us.

Saturday, October 24. Rode out & Gathered flowers & Trumpits a
Detachment of Militia Souldiers from Captain Gasqua's Company at North
Inlet under Command of Lieutenant McCollough arrived here & marched to
Fort Winyaw on Blythe's Point. He is to Succeed Lieutenant Heriot (of the
Continentals) in command of said Fort. All the Continentals at Winyaw are
Ordered to Go to Georgia. Boat Arrived from Dover with 2 pair Turkies &
other Family Supplies.

Sunday, October 25. Last Eve'ing Rachael Runaway. This morning I wrote
my Overseer to Endeavour to apprehend her. Mrs. Horry & the two Miss
Bays went with me to the Methodist Meeting & we heard a Sermon preached
by the Reverend Mr. Norton & Returned home to Dinner, Miss Coursay &

---

*While Horry seems to be referring to Gen. William Henry Harrison's success at
the Battle of the Thames, the news he received was premature and incorrect. Harrison's victory did not occur until the fall of 1813. Ingersoll, "Battle of the Thames."

Miss Mary Smith Visited the Miss Bays. In the Evening Mr. Cheesborough &
Mr. Rouse visited us.

Monday, October 26. I Rose very Unwell, it Rained Last Evening the
Wind now at South, w'ether fine for Gardening. Billy brought Cabbage plants
from Dover which were Immediately Planted while it Rained. In the Afternoon Reverend Mr. Norton Visited us, It Rained Last Night.

Tuesday, October 27. Garden Looks Lively after being Watered Mrs.
Horry unwell. Wind at South. I Rode out with Miss Bay & Mrs. Helin, She
came with us & found Mrs. Wayne at our House. Captain Roger Shackelford
arrived this morning from Charles Ton, brought a Letter, Also Sundry Go[o]ds
for me. Captain Ma[r]sh not yet Sailed. Powder & Shot is come & I will in a
Day or two carry them to Dover, & the Overseer I hope will Supply us with
Ducks & Turkeys. Miss Bays will Go with me to Dover & Perhaps Mrs. Helin.
A Vessell Arrived from New Orleans. Say a Gun Boat with Perhaps 100 Men,
a hopefull Crew of Negroes & Molattos & a very few white men.

Wednesday, October 28. Mrs. Horrys Rumatis so bad Last Night She nor
no One Else could Sleep. Sent my Boat to Dover with Powder, Shot & 8 Bun-
dles Homespun for Negroes as by Cloathes Book. I desired Potatoes may be
Used at Dover for Allowances & I wrote the Overseer so to do. I Received a
Letter from North & Webb with an Account Current & $200. Also received
2 Letters from Captain Dent Informing me of the Death of my Aunt Lynch
Roberts. I Saw about 30 Artillery men under Captain Ben Huger & Lieutenant Wragg, Parade with a field Piece. Their Uniform is Elegant.

Thursday, October 29. Last Night my boat Returned from Dover with
Supplies Potatoes etc. Samuel Smith Esquire Called to see us & Dr. Manning
to See Mrs. Horry who is much better this morning & did not disterb the
House Last Night. I rode out & with Mrs. Helin, met Delesseline just from
the up Country he is very hearty. The Privateer Sailed for Charles Ton. Several
Coasters took his Convoy. I bought Some Cheese & Gave Scipio my old Blue
Coat. I paid Mr. Whitehurst $20 which I borrow of him. Mr. Cheesborough
Visited us this Night.

Friday, October 30. I Sent Scipio, William & 3 field Negroes from Dover
to the North Inlet for Clams Oysters & Some things Lent Mrs. Gasqua. She
has left my House at the Island. I rode out with Miss Ann Bay & I paid Mr.
Cooper my Account, also my Overseers Order on me to Messrs. Taylors Mer-
chants. We rode to Mr. Cassells's Gate & to Mrs. Martin's House, Saw her, &
Miss Ann Lighted & Viewed her Garden, Windham Trapier was not at home.
We Returned home about 12 OClock & found Mrs. James Belin & her
Daughter Maria with Mrs. Horry.

Saturday, October 31. Gave Zemo my old Coat, a Straw Hat, 1 pair Overalls & a pair Shoes, & Shoes to Susie & London Rode out & Got Lightwood,

& as I did Last Evening Saw Judge Knot, Mrs. Whitehurst Captain Burdout Mr. Cuttino & Windham Trapier, paid Mrs. Elliot for 4 pair Negro Shoes, Captain Marsh Sailed this Morning for his Vessell which Lies below, Miss Myers,' Visited us today & at Night Doctor Futhy Visited us. Met Parson Halling On the Road from Wilmington.

Sunday, November 1. Scipio returned from my Island House but no part of what I Lent Captain Gasqua was to be found (so much for Lending to Oblidge) we Got Clamps & Oysters by Scipio, & Sent to Dover the 3 hands borrowed Whitehurst informed me Gasqua left my Things at Joseph's The 2 Miss Bay's Accompanied me this Morning to the Episcoval Church where we heard a Sermon from Reverend Mr. Halling Elias Horry I saw at Church, he Says he'll Call & See me Tomorrow before the Court Sitts. At Night Mr. Samuel Smith & Cheesborough drank Tea with us.

Monday, November 2. Rachel Returned Yesterday Evening, & Begged my Pardon for her Ill behavior; so I forgave her. I Got 2 pair Window Glasses Which I Lent Captain Gasqua. The Court Sot today. I went to it & found many of my Acquaintances. E. Horry, Trapiers, Young Mayrant, Attorney General John S. Richardson, Captain Keith Delesseline, T. R. Mitchell, McGregor, Joseph Lawyers Many, Gadsden Esquire a Session Sermon was d[el]ivered in the Court House from Mr. Halling.

Tuesday, November 3. Harvey, Futhy & Mr. Scott (Lawyer) from Columbia Spent the Last Evening with us. Dr. Futhy was Uncommonly Agreeable. I rode out with Doctor Halling & returning I met Mr. Hassell & Windham Trapier. I wrote to Captain Dent by Elias Horry John Smith Richardson Called on us this Evening, also Mr. Cheesborough.

Wednesday, November 4. Cloudy weather I with the Miss Bays & Cheesborough Visited Belle Isle Plantation* & we dined there, I saw my Pounding Mill, 'tis near finished I Saw our Garden & Barnyard & Potatoe Houses. I Saw

---

*Belle Isle Plantation was one of the three Winyah Bay plantations owned by Peter Horry. Once part of the Winyah Barony, a tract of 12,000 acres granted to Robert Daniell in 1711, Elias Horry II acquired around 1,600 acres of the land and bequeathed the property to Horry. In 1801 Horry designated 640 acres as Belle Isle Plantation. In his will he gave it to his wife, Margaret Mayrant Horry, who willed the plantation to Sarah Hall Horry Bay. Sarah's grandson, William Mayrant Richardson, inherited the property from his grandmother in 1868, and upon his death in 1894, the property passed to Gardner B. Penniman, whose wife began the famous plantation gardens in 1895. During the Civil War, the plantation served as the location of Battery White, which guarded the entrance to Georgetown Harbor. Lachicotte, *Georgetown Rice Plantations,* 143–48; Barefoot, *Touring South Carolina's Revolutionary War Sites,* 31.

my Driver* & I delivered out 28 pair Shoes to my Negroes. I fear my Crop will be a very Small One. I hear'd that my Rice Sent by Captain Marsh had Arrived Safe at Charles Ton. We returned home about Sun Set.

Thursday, November 5. Mr. William Richardson, Dr. Beaufort, Mr. Andrew Bay, Mr. William Mayrant & his Son, Visited us Last Night, I have Paid Mr. Thurston's Account. Mr. William Richardson & young Mayrant Lodged in our House Last night, I rode out with Miss Bays, & Saw Andrew Bay, Samuel Smith, & Doctor [illegible], Major Wragg, Ben & Windham Trapier, & Doctor Hillin is Set at Liberty by the Court. Mr. Mayrant & William Richardson Dined with us today as did also Mr. Mayrant Son.

Friday, November 6. Mr. Samuel Smith, Mr. Harvey & Mr. Cuttino Visited us Last Night. Dry & warm weather, tho' the wind is at North, Rode out with Mrs. Helin, & brought her & her Grand Son to Diner with us. This Evening no Person Visited us. Mr. Whitehurst Changed me One Hundred Dollars in paper Bills, Mr. Ioor require Dollars or American Gold or Silver to Travill in our back Country say to the Mississicy. I must Therefore Give 5 per Cent premium If Mr. William Richardson approves of the Same.

Saturday, November 7. I rose before day, & Sent to my Landing but found my boat aground. I wrote to my Overseer for 2 boatman & for Sundry family Supplies. I rode out with Miss Ann Bay. Saw Mr. Cheesborough, & Whitehurst, Mayrant & John Smythe Richardson & Mr. Collins, Gave him Joy of his Marriage.

Sunday, November 8. I rode Early, Dark Gloomy weather, wind at North Expect my boat hourly as 'tis flood Tide, John Smythe Richardson Left Town.

---

*Slave drivers played an integral role in the organization of the plantation economy. The different managerial levels included the head driver or overdriver, the underdriver, and the foreman. Most drivers were black men, although some slave women worked as drivers, supervising "trash gangs" of young children, superannuated slaves, and women in the late stages of pregnancy. Most were between thirty and forty years old and distinguished for their intelligence, forceful personalities, and leadership skills. The job of a driver was to maintain a disciplined and efficient agricultural slave force. Often called "whipping men" for their power to punish field hands, the drivers monitored production and reported to the overseer. In the absence of an overseer, slave drivers scheduled production and planned the use of plantation resources. As a symbol of their status above regular field hands, drivers were usually given high-top leather boots, greatcoats, and top hats, as well as better housing and food. Some drivers were given extra land for personal use and the right to force other slaves to work for them. The resulting produce was sold at market for cash. Some drivers received wages and bonuses for their work. Katz-Hyman and Rice, *World of a Slave*, 443–44.

Yesterday, a French Minister is to Preach at the Baptist Meeting this morning I went with the two Miss Bays to the Episcopal Church, my boat Returned about one OClock P.M. with Rice, Corn & 3 Turkeys also with 2 boat Negroes. I sent Inclosed by Mr. William Richardson to John Ioor $100. Mr. William Mayrant & Son Charles & Colonel Huggins & two of his Daughters all Spent the Evening with us. The Mayrants Lodged at our House.

Monday, November 9. Rose, Early & found the weather so thick & drifting as Induced me to dicline Going to the Inlet this morning. Therefore Sent off to Dover the two Boatmen belonging thereto Mr. Mayrant & Son breakfasted with us. I Rode out about 11 OClock A.M. as far as Francis Kinloch's Avineau, & Met Benjamin Trapier Coming down to Town to Train his Volunteers. Last Evening Mr. William Mayrant & Son Charles, Mr. Cheesborough & Samuel Smith Spent the Evening with us.

Tuesday, November 10. This morning Mr. Mayrant & Son breakfasted with us. My Cincinata Gold Eagle* Mrs. Horry Gave & Sent Inclosed in a Letter to John Ioor (with my consent & Sent the Letter by Charles Mayrant today) 'tis a handsome present & it Cost me 8 Guineas being beautifully Enameld in Gold. I rode out to Mr. Francis Kinloch Avineau, near to it I Saw Major Wragg. It now Rains hard & is fine for my Garden. I Got home dry about 11 OClock A.M. The president Address to Congress will be out in Baxters Paper Tomorrow at this Crisis it will be particularly Interesting.

Wednesday, November 11. My Garden plants etc. etc. Look well this Morning after so fine a Rain. Weather very Clear & Moderate William Mayrant & Son Charles went off this Morning for their Home at High Hills Santee. Wind at North West (but not very Cold) I rode out with Miss Bay as far as Kinlochs Avineau & Got Some Lightwood. Saw thereat Doctor Wragg Returning Home we meet thereat Doctor Norton & Colonel Huggins who agreed to Go with us tomorrow Morning to the North Inlet. Received a Letter from my Factors, My Rice is Sold a[t] $5 1/16 p Cents & my Goods is on board Captain Marsh Sloop which is windbound in Charleston. My factors

*The Society of the Cincinnati was a fraternal organization formed to commemorate the patriotism engendered during the years of the American Revolution. It was founded in the summer of 1783 with George Washington as president general, and all officers with three years of service in the war were eligible for membership. The Roman Cincinnatus was chosen to represent the society because of his fame as a warrior, his distinction as a republican citizen, and his selflessness in retiring and returning to the plow. The society met early opposition, most famously from the pen of Aedanus Burke, from those who feared the society was an attempt to establish hereditary aristocracy. Hunemorder, *Society of the Cincinnati*, 5–21.

thinks Rice will Soon fall. I have however none pounded to Partake of the Present Good Price. S. Smith Spent the Evening with us.

Thursday, November 12. Rose Early & Prepared to Go to the North Island. Fine Weather & a fair wind at West. Got to the Light House about 2 OClock p.m. Colonel Huggins & his Daughter Sharlotte, Miss Bays, & Adjutant Cuttino assended to the Lights & Viewed the Sea & Land Side. About Sun Set Arrived at Major Smiths House Near the Inlet & there we Lodged.

Friday, November 13. About 9 OClock a.m. Sot out for Brown Town & Arrived There about Sundown, wind very high at West & Truly very Cold we Crossed the bay & with hard Rowing Got into George Town Creek, all hands near frosed. Took Refreshment & Retired to Bed.

Saturday, November 14. A Large White Frost. Fair Weather Wind at South West Susie Sick. Got my Goods by Captain Marsh. Received a Letter from my Factors, Sent my boat to Dover with Negro Shoes, wrote for Mud & wood. Boat went off about 9 OClock a.m. Rode out & Saw Cheesborough Irvin Keith, Whitehurst & Joseph Lessesne & the Meyers, Young Shackelford & his Sister Luptan & Windham Trapier. Returned home & found 2 Mr. Warings & Doctor Blythe I drove Mrs. Hellen home.

Sunday, November 15. Heard a Sermon from Mr. Norton in the Methodist Meeting. Severly Cold Mrs. Helin Dined with us. Mr. & Mrs. Whitehurst, Mr. Cuttino & Young Shackelford Spent the Evening with us. Also Miss Courser, Miss Mary Smith, & Miss Boone.

Monday, November 16. I was very Sick Last Night. Rode out & Got Some Lightwood, Saw Mr. Cowen Mr. Solomon, Mr. Hort, Mr. Car & Talmash.

Tuesday, November 17. I Rode out with John Harvey & Got Wood. Saw Mr. Archibald Taylor & Mr. Cassells, had Some Political Conversation with them. No Tinman in Town. My Carpenter Altered the Spout to my Stove in my Hall Mr. Wise (formerly a Dragoon in my Continental Regiment) Applied to me for Appraisment of a Horse taken into Service. I Examined all my Papers but found no Such. Saw Mr. Singletary & Mr. Ward Quarter Master General to our Militia Souldiers he, Mr. Whitehurst, & Lieutenant Thomas Heriot Spent the Evening with us.

Wednesday, November 18. Wind at South West. Cloudy, Small, Drissle Rain, I rode out & Got Some Lightwood; Made fire in my Stove, Moon fills this Evening, Mr. Cheesborough Spent the Evening with us. I rote to Mrs. Bay, that I would Spend Next Summer with her & Sent the Letter by Mr. Waring.

Thursday, November 19. Wind as Yesterday. Dry weather. I rode out & Got Lightwood. Gave London, a New Homespun Jacket & Overall, bought 7 ½ yards Homespun for Walls to my Carriage the following Gentlemen Spent the Evening with us—Young Mr. William Shackelford, 2 Mr. Cuttinoe's,

Captain Irvin Keith, Lieutenants Thomas Heriot & McCollough. Yesterday Mrs. Wayne rode out with Mrs. Horry for her Health, I Saw Mrs. Mariah Elliot She Seems much worsted.

Friday, November 20. Last Night I was very Sick Rose from my Bed 3 Times before day, & drank Mint Tea with Loaf Sugar rode out as Usual for Lightwood, Sent Zemo & William off therefor[e] 3 Hours before I went, Lighted Stove this Morning in the Hall & breakfasted thereat. It now Groes very Cold. Received a Letter from Captain Dent, I will Get very Little from my Aunts Estate Colonel Chase of McDaniel & Burdout. Bought Hummuers of Soloman. Parson Halling & Mr. Cheesborough Dined with us today. I Sent my boat to Dover for Sundries. She is to return tomorro[w] flood Tide with Wood & Straw, Mr. Helin & the Doctor Drank Tea with us.

Saturday, November 21. Rode out & Got wood, Saw Ben Trapier, Captain Counott Mrs. Eliby, the two Last I think were Going to the Cheraws at 11 OClock A.M. My boat has not made her appearance. At about 3 OClock P.M. The flatt Arrived with Straw, Wood; Potatoe Allowances for Family & Vegitables.

Sunday, November 22. Served Allowances. Sent the flat to Dover took a Dose of Castor Oil, Expect my boat to return Tomorrow from Dover. Large Frost Last Night (but no Ice) weather continues yet Dry. My family went to the Methodist Meeting to hear Mr. Asberry Reverend Mr. Botsworth of the Baptist Church is Gone to Charles Ton to have a Second Attropfia on his Eye. He Suffers Greatly, his Affliction nearly Equals my own which however is not So long Standing as mine. Sam Smith not yet returned from Charles Ton. I wish much for his Arrival, with Answers to my two Letters wrote to Captain Dent & North & Webb. The Latter I hope will Send me Some money which I very much want to Enable my paying Some of my debts. I think they must be in Cash for my Last Parcell of Rice. I am told Rice yet Continues to Sell well but my Pounding Mill is not yet Ready. In one year my Stock has diminished one hundred per Cent, Overseer & Cattle Minder Certainly do not attend to their Duties. I rode out in the afternoon round the George Town Race Course. Met Robert Heriot Esquire & his Lady near this Course, met in George Town near the House of Mr. Waldo Lieutenants Ben & Tom Heriot. Saw Mr. Ward Contracter for our Militia Souldiers on Duty at North Island, Also Mr. Whitehurst Taylor near our Market house, they inform me that our Said Souldiers will in a Day or two all be discharged to their homes one Company only Excepted which will take Charge of Fort Winyaw for a Little time when they will be Relieved by North Carolinians, William Shackelford Junior & Mr. Rouse Spent the evening with us.

Monday, November 23. I rode out & Got some Lightwood, Saw Ben Trapier Coming to Muster. My boat Arrived about 11 OClock A.M. with Mud for my Garden. It rained towards night & in the Night Rained & blew a Storm from the North West, five Pannels of my Garden Fence was found Down in the morning The Miss Bays were Alarmed & removed down Stairs.

Tuesday, November 24. Wind at South West. Billy & Scipio mending Garden fence & Setting down 3 New Posts, Some nails wanted & a few boards. Put near a flat Load of Mud Last Evening in the Garden. Bought a Curry Comb. Rode out & Got Lightwood Mended my Curtain to my Carriage.

Wednesday, November 25. Wind at North West Cold & piercing. A frost fell last night. I Rode out & Got Wood. Captain Lieutenant Heriot & his Company Left George Town today for Fort Hawkins in the Creek Nation, the Militia Souldiers all Left North Island & went into Fort Winyaw. Saw Mr. Ward Saw Doctor Ford. Mr. Cheesborough & William Shackelford Junior Spent the Evening with us. Got a Letter from John Ioor & from Captain Dent. Never had I a Greater Cold. Could Get no Sleep Last night.

Thursday, November 26. Rose very Unwell. Finished my Carriage walls with Homespun & blackened them, by Scipio my Painter. Rode out & Got Lightwood, passed by opposite Priors House Captain Gasqua's Company overtook a Number of Militia Souldiers on the road & found a Number of Them Encampt in Tents near Pinckneys Turn off to his House. Saw Lieutenant Thomas Heriot in George Town. Also Francis Kinloch on the road Galloping in the Rain to his home. I rode through a Small Drissle for Several Miles before I Got home.

Friday, November 27. I rose very Early & Rode out & Got a Load of Wood. Saw Militia Souldiers under Captain Bingham Encampment as Yesterday near Pinckneys Road. 'Tis Said they wait till next Monday to Receive their Pay. It has Rained all the Morning & till 12 OClock.

Saturday, November 28. I rode out & Got a Load of Lightwood Saw Militia Camp as before mentioned, Left $100 with Mr. Whitehurst to Pay my Account of $7 ½ to Mr. Joe Lessesne. Saw Major Keith & he Invited me to Attend a Review this Evening near the Court House of about 170 Militia Souldiers under Captains Bingham & Canty, (no men Remains at North Island) Captain Gasquas Company is Posted at Fort Winyaw till further Orders. A Party of North Carolinians is Expected Soon to Relieve Captain Gasquas Company. I Saw Mr. Hort at his House he Informed me he & his Lady would move from Major Murray in 10 days. That he would Buy a House adjoining Captain Wilson of the Cavalry. I received Yesterday by Post $300 from North & Web my Factors in Charles Ton. Mr. Course will Receive my Order on Mr. Collins & my Factors for what I owe him. Mr. Soloman Offers me Bed Tick to Cloathe my House Servants. Mr. Cheesborough Spent the Eve[n]ing with us.

Sunday, November 29. It rained hard Last Night, Wind at South very Windy but Clear Weather. I rode out as far as Mrs. Martins Rod, Rain Came & I Returned, William Shackelford Junior Called on us in the Evening Cheesborough & S. Smith were with us. Also Miss Catharine Boone.

Monday, November 30. I Rode out & Got Lightwood, Wind at North East. Clear & not Cold, Saw Whitehurst he Settled with Joe Lessesne for me Say Paid him $7 ½. I Received $50 of Whit[e]hurst I Saw Mrs. Gasqua, Major Keith, Dr. Wragg & W. W. Trapier. Received a Letter from Captain Dent. A Daughter is born to him. Saw Frank Huger & Cleland Kinloch, Thomas Heriot & Mr. Cohen & Richard Shackelford. In the Evening I rode out & returning after dark my Mules took fright on George Town bay, tore off their Traces & broke their Collars etc. & went off. Fortunately the Carriage did not Overset, & Negroes drew it home with me therein, Neither Mules or myself were hurted. I am determined to ride no more at Night, for I risk my Life Eminently by so doing tho my Life is of Little Value.

Tuesday, December 1. Examined my Carriage & Tackling, the Latter found to be much Injured; Billy & Scipio fell to Repairing the Damages, No Company Last Evening. I Saw Major Keith Exercising our Militia Souldiers near the Court House. At Night two Mr. Cuttinoes Spent Several Hours with us.

Wednesday, December 2. Rode out & Got Wood Saw Major Keith & Lieutenant Ford. Also Whitehurst & Captain Johnson & Mr. Anderson also Lieutenant [illegible] of the Militia Camp Still as before. Most of the men however attend Mr. Ward at Mr. Whitehurst to Receive their pay, fine weather wind blows fresh at West Saw Lieutenant Thomas Heriot. Mr. Samuel Smith, Dr. Futhey, & Mr. Phillips Spent the Evening with us. Also Mrs. Croft & Miss Godfrey.

Thursday, December 3. Rode out & Got Wood. Saw Lieutenant Thomas Heriot & Robert Heriot Esquire Mr. Hort & Mr. Samuel Smith. Boat returned Last Night from Dover. Brought a Pig & 6 Wild Ducks (Killed) Vegitables The Miss Bays Went with Miss James to Mrs. Ford House Black River. Mr. Whitehurst & Wife & Sons Dined with us today. Also Doctor & Mrs. Helin, & Samuel Smith. Wrote by Captain R. Shackelford for Sundries from North & Webb of Charles Ton.

Friday, December 4. It rain's hard before Breakfast & Lodged Some Water in the Garden, wrote my Overseer & Sent Scipio in boat to Dover, Wind at South East. Miss Bays Returned home, boat Returned. I rode out & Got Some wood. I Received a Letter from Mr. Osburn with a Barrel Salt. Ben Huger, Cheesborough, & Samuel Smith Spent the Evening with us.

Saturday, December 5. I Sent Scipio to Overseer & wrote him for a Barrel Ruff Rice, Some Clean Rice & Potatoe Allowance. Wind very high at South West. Could not ride out but Sent Billy who brought home a Load of

Wood, Mr. Ward is to Dine with us Tomorrow it Rained today. Cleared before night, & Grew Cold. My head Acked much Last Night I beleave I have frequently a fever.

Sunday, December 6. I wrote North & Webb by G. Mitchell, for [illegible] & Ax & Shaul & Gown for Mrs. Horry. Tis' so Cold this morning that I could not go to the Mithodist Meeting House, but Mrs. Horry & the Miss Bays went & heard Mr. Norton, No Services at Either of the other Churches, William Shackelford Junior Called on us Mr. Ward Dined with us. he, Cheesborough & Samuel Smith Spent the Evening with us.

Monday, December 7. I rode out & Got Wood. Sent Billy in my boat to Dover & wrote the Overseer Saw him today & his Account of Rice etc. are Extremily disagreeable I wish I had never Seen him, he is Either a Nave or a Fool.

Tuesday, December 8. I rode out & Got wood Billy Returned in boat from Dover brought a ½ Bushel Clean Rice Some Potatoes & Greens & a Barrell Ruff Rice Wood & Straw. It Rained a Little towards night our Dogs Got under the house, & barked so much that I was not able to Sleep All Night.

Wednesday, December 9. Clear & very Cold. Wind at Northwest. I rode out & Got wood. Saw Ben Trapier Exercising the George Town Volunteers near the Court House bought 3 Yards Plains for William & a pair Shoes for Billy Overseer sent me 4 Ducks by Jumper & wrote the Mill would beat as tomorrow Say Friday. Weather Clear & Cold.

Thursday, December 10. Ice Last Night, I rode out & Got wood with four Axes, 3 House Servants & one from the plantation Miss Cogdell & Hannah Shackelford Dined with us today I fell very Sick before night.

Friday, December 11. A Cold Night. In the morning it Sleeted & Snowed, I Sent Waggon for wood & Corn of Mr. Course & Sent Jumper Home with a Letter to Overseer & with 2 Rice Seives & 3 Blankets. Mr. Cheesborough Ward & Whitehurst Spent the Evening with us.

Saturday, December 12. Wind at South West. Frose very hard Last Night. I Sent my Carriage this Morning for wood. William Shackelford & House Spent this Evening with us.

Sunday, December 13. Excessive Cold. Myself & family went to the Methodist Meeting house & heard a Sermon from Mr. Norton. On his Shacking hands with me (Perhaps for the Last time) I Shed Tears in the Meeting House, before the Congregation. I Saw Mr. Mitchell at the Meeting House & at my House brown Town. Kept my bed the Remainder of the day was very Sick & Untill.

Monday, December 14. I Got better & Sent for wood, Got a Barber to Shave me & went to the Episcopal Church about 11 OClock A.M. & Gave my

Vote for a Member of Assembly, Saw a Number of my Acquaintances Electioneering. Dr. Futhy & Sam Smith Spent the Evening with us.

Tuesday, December 15. Large White frost, Clear Wether Sent for Wood Sent my boat to Dover for Wood. A hog Straw, Ducks & Greens Mr. Norton, Mr. Cuttino, my Overseer, Doctor & Mrs. Helin, Mrs. Simons, Miss Boone, Miss Smith & Shackelford. Sent my Boat to Dover.

Wednesday, December 16. White Frost Wind at South West. Clear Sunshine Ann Bay Sick this Morning, I was very Sick Last Night, yet I Rose & breakfasted. I Received a Letter from Office from my Factors Inclosing me $300, Betsey Wayne Called on us.

Thursday, December 17. Rode out & Got Some wood. Miss Mary Smith dined & Spent the Evening with us also Mr. Cuttino Visited us, Miss Ann Bay Sick.

Friday, December 18. I went to Dover, & Lodged there. Saw my Mill Pound. Saw my Overseer & Paid him $100. Gave my Driver up the plantation with full directions for its Man[a]giment & returned to my House Brown Town.

Saturday, December 19. Mr. McClinchy Offered himself to me as an Overseer, Mr. S. Smith Called on me, also Mr. & Mrs.

Sunday, December 20. Miss Meyrs, S. Smith & Mr. Thomas R. Mitchell called on us. H. Shackelford, Mr. Chesboro' & Mr. Cuttino Spent the Evening with us.

Monday, December 21. Saw Mr. Harrell who breakfasted with us. I rode out & Got wood Saw Mrs. Helin & Mrs. Gasqua. Saw Colonel Huggins & brought home young Shackelford with me. Sent William to Dover.

Tuesday, December 22. Had a Beef yesterday of Mr. Harrell, Cost $. Borrowed a Seine & Sent my boat with it to Dover to Draw fish. Rode out & Got wood fine Weather Robert Paisley died Last night.

Wednesday, December 23. Rode out & Got wood. Gave Liddy 5 Yards Plains, & Billy 6 yards homespun. Gave 4 ½ Yards Plains to Peggys Children, Gave Rachel a Shift of Homespun Say 3 ½ Yards. Boat Returned with Fish, Wood & Straw Vegitables, Potatoes, but no Ducks. Saw Ben Trapier & his Wife, Saw Lieutenant McCollough, Mr. Meyers & Doctor Allston. Bottled Currans, Raisons & Dryed figgs for Christmass & also Whiskey for the Negroes, Gave them Rice & a Bull Dandy came to me & Received his Orders for Christmass.

Thursday, December 24. Fine dry Weather wind at South West. Rode out & Got wood, bottled 1 Gallon Peach Brandy, Mr. Shackelford Junior Mr. Cheesboro & Mr. Mitchell Spent the Evening with us Mr. Bay returnd home.

Friday, December 25. Rose Early. Miss Boone Mr. Delesselin J. Cheesborough S. Smith, & Shackelford breakfased with us & Drank Egg Nog & Also dined with us as did Mr. Ward & Mrs. Helin.

Saturday, December 26. I rode out & Got Wood, a White frost Clear Weather Wind North West. Doctor Blythe Called on us.

Sunday, December 27. Clear Weather, Wind at North West. Black Frost Last Night an Alarm of Fire. It was found to be Doctor Allstons House Chimney, fortunately it was a Calm & Shingles were very wet. Engine was out, but found Unuessary to be Employed. Too Cold for me to Go to Church or Meeting House but Mrs. Horry & Sarah Bay went in the Afternoon to Meeting Mr. Wayne Senior Preached, in the forenoon Mr. Paul & Windham Trapier Mr. Mitchell & Smith Visited us. Paul is in Great Health.

Monday, December 28. Last night a Severe Black frost fell. A Clear SunShine day. Wind at North. Before breakfast Sent Scipio for wood. Sent William to Dover with Mr. Bays Horse. Billy Returned from Dover with 16 Ducks & Vegitables, I Rode out & Saw Captain B. Huger & Cleland Kinloch also Mr. Whitehurst Got his Account against me, Saw Mrs. Hort & Miss Sally Delesseline, & Windham Trapier. Sent Mrs. Davis an Armfull of Pine Wood. Hugers day of Training at the Court House. Miss Hannah Shackelford Dined, Supped & Lodged at our House.

Tuesday, December 29. Wind at South West. A Large White Frost, Sent Scipio [to] Dover for flatt, wood & Straw & 2 Hogs, received 13 Ducks from Dover. Mrs. Cample Visited us yesterday also Miss Hardwick. Mr. William Shackelford Junior Visited us *today* Mrs. Hellin dined with us. Miss Ann Bay with a Severe Cold Mr. Cheesboro, Smith, & Vareen, Spent the Evening with us.

Wednesday, December 30. Fine Weather, Wind at South, Billy borrowed Mr. Cambells Cart & Got Corn of Mr. Lartigue Say 30 Bushells at half Dollar. Miss Hort & Delessline Dined with us. Scipio Returned with 2 Shotes, the Carriage Wheel mended & Delivered [it] to Rockey said Wheel Tire to be mended, Wood & Straw & Vegitables. Doctor Helin Left Town to Live on Black River.

Thursday, December 31. Yet fine Weather Carriage mended & ready, Sent my boat to Lartigue for Corn received 75 Bushells which I Sent by Billy to Dover. Rode out & Got wood. Doctor Blythe Spent the Evening with us, on my Ride I Saw Dr. Blythe, Samuel Smith, & John Shackelford Junior a Letter for Charles Ton, Saw Whitehurst & Francis Kinloch also Mrs. Helin.

End of Book Number 4 & to 31st December 1812.

BOOK FIVE

June 10, 1813–July 31, 1813

*T*hursday, June 10, Continued. I Received Titles for my half Acre Land of Mr. James Guignard who has it to Record in his Office (1814) I am to Give $ payable.

Friday, June 11. Clear dry & hot Weather. Last Evening Mr. Lance (of the Hospital) Visited us, as did (in the Morning) Mr. Ward, of this place (Attorney at Law) I rode out & was Introduced to Colonel Pickins (of the Continental forces) a Son of General Pickens. I Got Draughts of my buildings of Guignard & Secured to him payment of Said Lands by Mortgage of the Same. Mrs. Davis & her Daughter Visited us also Mrs. Tom Taylor. I Saw Mr. Robert Waring in Guignards Office, they are on Monday to begin to Get me Lumber, Lieutenant   Called on me about 12 OClock Mid Day. A Columbia Paper Extra Announced that in Candady we have been Successful by Land & had beaten an Enemies Squddron. Judge DeSassure Sot out on his Curcuit down the Country Say black River & Colonel Hutchison & his Wife Visited us in the Afternoon also Mr. Taylor, who is to furnish me with Lumber from his Mill. James Guignard & his Lady also Visited us today A heavy Storm Come on, about dark, it Rained Thundered & Lightened.

Saturday, June 12. Cloudy & Cool wind South West, I rode out to Colonel John Taylors House & Saw him well & his Son Franklin also. Major Clifton & his wife Called on us this Morning. Mrs. Guignard Senior & Junior Called on us also. Saw Lieutenant Hampton & on the Road, they are Going to Virginia & to Canady.

Sunday, June 13. Clear & Cool this morning. Wind as Yesterday I Received Titles for my half Acre Land, & Bill of Scantling with the Cost [illegible] of Same from Mr. James Guignard & to be Got by Mr. Thomas Taylor. I Received a Letter from Windham Trapier, a Washington Paper from Mr. Gourdine Senator at Congress now at Washington The Presedent Speech to the Nation is very pleasing. I went to the State house* & heard Mr. Lance a

---

*Religious services were often held on the grounds of the State House in the early 1800s. In 1802 Rev. John Dunlap, a Presbyterian minister, and Rev. John Harper, a Methodist minister, alternated holding services on the grounds of the State House.

Young Student at this Colledge. A Mr. Hails Spent the day with us. Misses Gaillard's Spent the day with us.

Monday, June 14. Full Moon Last Evening, this Morning fair. Wind at South. I rode with Mr. James Guignard to the House of his Father, we Breakfasted and Returned home to Dinner. Began to dig holes for Posts in my uper Lot. Saw Dr. Green near his House, Miss Georgiana Blackburn & Misses Dinkins Spent the Evening with us. Mr. Lynch I Saw at Night at Dr. Greens, he said his Sisters & Aunt might be Expected Daily in this Town, That he Lived in a house 6 Miles out of Town, & Soon after the arrival of these Said Ladies, they would all Visit us together at Mrs. Bays, Mr. Guignard Senior Visited us.

Tuesday, June 15. Clear Morning began to haul up & Trim the banks around my Garden Grounds. Every day now is hot & many Clouds daily Threaten Rain I rode out to my Lot & Garden, to Guignards Office, & Saw Colonel Hutchinson, & Mr. Taylor. Our Ladies went to a Party at Mr. Blackburns, Mr. Robert Waring Called on me & agreed to begin Waggoning Lumber Tomorrow.

Wednesday, June 16. Calm Morning, fair weather, I Rose Early & Collected Carpenters Tools, Mr. Taylors Waggon made a Turn of Lumber by Night Say 25 boards & 20 pieces Scantling wrote to Samuel Smith to forward my Carpenters to me Spoke to Mrs. Waring Carpenter Nero to work for me he & his Son at   Dollars per day.

Thursday, June 17. Fair Morning & Cool, I went Early to my Lot, Paid for 5 ½ pounds Sorted Nails $1. Raised a Shade of boards Mr. R. Waring waggon* brought forty Eight Boards first Turn today, Mr. Harbamond Called on me at my Lot & Offered to Supply me with Cut Nails from his Nail Manufactory. Received 17 Posts by Mr. James Guignard Waggon Laid off 2 Walks Garden. Bought a Jack Plain Mrs. Davis Called on us in the Evening.

In the summer of 1812, a missionary for the Society for the Advancement of Christianity in South Carolina, Andrew Fowler, renewed the tradition and held the first Protestant Episcopal service in Columbia at the South Carolina State House. From his efforts came Trinity Episcopal Church, founded on August 8, 1812. Chreitzberg, *Early Methodism,* 83; Moore, *Columbia and Richland County,* 84.

*Horry is likely referring to a wagon belonging to the Waring family. A contemporary of Horry, Benjamin Waring V was the son of Benjamin Waring, a planter and member of the South Carolina House of Representatives who had served as a captain in General Marion's brigade. Edgar and Taylor, *Biographical Directory of the South Carolina House,* 698–99.

Friday, June 18. Wind South, Clear Weather Sent my Carriage to be mended. Went to my Lot & 2 Men began to Plain Posts. Mr. Taylor Waggon brought 38 fetheredge* & 30 Scantlings Received from Mr. James Guignard *Waggon* 18 Posts first Load, 18 ditto 2nd Load Mr. Waring Waggon brought a Second Load Say 67 Fetherage, 35 Ruffage boards by Waring Waggon Saw Mr. Benjamin Waring at my Lot. Mr. Robert Waring Called on us, Miss Maria Davis, & Miss Goodwin Spent the Evening with us. Goddard, & Savage Smith Son Arrived here from George Town, Goddards Negro fellow Gave us very pleasing Intelligence. Viz. that all was well at George Town, & that Miss Smith & Miss Botsworth were Married, that a Detatchment of Militia had arrived at Fort Winyaw, to Garrison it, that Major Wragg & his family was Gone to the North Inlet & many other Inhabitants were on the move to the Said Island. That my 3 Negro Carpenters were on Last Monday Setting out with their Tools for Columbia & that they were very heavy Loaded with baggage. The Extreme heat today over Came me. Thomas Waties Called on me. Mrs. Horry & Rachael Rote to George Town by Said Negro Man Goddard.

Saturday, June 19. Fair day, Moderately Cool for the Season Wind at South West. My Carriage Got to me this Morning from Mr. James Guignards black Smith. Mr.   Cuttino from George Town Called on us, he Sets out for Charles Town Monday next I Received 7 Posts from Mr. Waring Waggon, I Saw James Guignard his Lady & Miss Hughs at my Lot, I Visited today Major Ward & Major Clifton.

Sunday, June 20. A fair Morning, a Thunder Gust Last Evening, but no Rain fell, 'tis Greatly wanted, I went with Mrs. Horry to the Methodist Church† & heard a sermon delivered by Reverend Mr.   Greene (Son of the Major) Mr. James Guignard Visited me in the Evening, Saw Major Savage

---

*A featheredge is formed by beveling of one or both sides of a board or slab so that the sides meet in a sharp arris. It can also refer to the edge on a knife or sharp instrument and is usually a very fine, sharp, and fragile edge. Sturgis, *Dictionary of Architecture*, 2:29.

†Methodism was first brought to Columbia through the efforts of Rev. Isaac Smith, who occasionally preached at the home of Thomas Taylor when passing through Columbia along the Santee Circuit. In 1802 John Harper alternated services with a Presbyterian minister at the South Carolina State House. Harper was the first Methodist to obtain a considerable following in the city, and he also donated the property on which Washington Street United Methodist Church now stands. In 1803 the first house of worship was built around a congregation of six members. Chreitzberg, *Early Methodism*, 83.

Smith (of George Town) his Son Received a Letter from Gabriel Guignard Relative to his Carpenters & to my buildings on my Lot. Saw Doctor Fisher this Morning at Mrs. Bays.

Monday, June 21. Cloudy & Cool, Sot a Plow to work up my Garden Ground, this Morning. Wind at South East, Obscure Sun Shine, I Rode to my Lot & Garden, Called on Major Ward. Saw Colonel Hutchison Introduced to Reverend Mr. Smith of Camden, Called on Mrs. Davis in Company with Miss Martha & Ann Bay. Called on Mr. Douglas. I could not Get his Carpenter. Wrote to Mr. Guignard Senior & Answered his Letter of Yesterdays date. Mr. James Guignard went this morning to his Plantation. His Plow (Lent me) do not Answer my Purpose. Mrs. Waring Called on us, Also Doctor Hughs & Doctor Fisher. I went to Mr. James Guignard by Invitation, a Methodist meeting took place there, & the Reverend Mr. Smith at Night held forth, Reverend Mr. Green was Present, also Mr. Lance & many Respectable Ladies & Gentlemen were there.

Tuesday, June 22. A Cloudy Morning, wind at south I rode out to my Lot & Garden Ground, Scipio went to Mr. James Gignards plantation for a Coulter plow. From his Overseer I received a plow, Budy his Son & Grigs Arrived here from Dover with their Tools as per Memorandum Book. Myself with Mrs. Bays Family Visited Mrs. Davis's Family, met there her Sons & Several other Gentlemen Passed an Agreeable Evening with them returned home & found Mr. Simons in Bed with a fever.

Wednesday, June 23. I rose Early a Cool Morning, wind at North West, Scipio better, Directed budy to take Charge of all my Carpenters & to apply to Mr. James Guignard & Mrs. Bay for whatever he may want, Rode out to my Lot Garden Ground & as far as the Market Saw Mr. Ward & Major Clifton & Miss Hughs; Mr. Simons is better today. Mr. James Guignard went this morning to his Fathers. Received 2 Large Posts for a Gate from Mr. James Guignard Waggon & 30 Posts; Mrs. Horry bought homespun to Cloath Cugjo & Grigs about $5 Value. Received 10 & 20 Nails of Mr. Hobermount amounting to $16 Say 56s. 10d. & 50s. 20d. ditto.

Thursday, June 24. Cloudy & Cool, Wind at South West. I Rode out to my Lands. Sent to prepare Slabs, & began to Ditch again around my Garden Ground, went to the Market, Saw Dr. Greene; Mr. Lance went with me this Morning to the Methodist Church & we heard Major Clifton Preach a Sermon. Saw young Desaussure, Mr. Green Colonel Hutchison & others Paid for 20 Bushels Corn a 2/4. 500 weight Blades $5 Paid Johnathan for mending my Carriage $3 ½. Miss Davis & a young Lady Miss Goodwin Called on us as did also young Savage Smith &.

Friday, June 25. Cloudy & Warm, wind at South. Went to the Market, Rode with James Guignard to Lot & Garden. Received yesterday 31 Inch boards from Wades Mill* by Warings Waggon & a Sell & plate, put down Gate Posts to Garden & also to House Lot Received 31 Slabs, Rode to Mrs. Davis, Saw her & her Family.

Saturday, June 26. Warm & Cloudy Wind at South East. Rode to my Garden & Lot & began to Nail Slaps on my Garden Posts Received a Letter from Mrs. Helin of George Town, all are well there. Put on all the Slabs on Garden fence & Sot down Pots to the house Lot, Answered per Post Mrs. Helins Letter. Judge Gaillard Visited me this Morning. Mr. Davis Visited us in the Evening also Mr. Robert Waring, Sot down Posts in house Lot & finished a Pannell thereof Mrs. James Gignard & Miss Hughs Visited us at the house Lot about Sun Set.

Sunday, June 27. Some Rain fell Last Night, Cloudy morning & pleasant weather. Mrs. Bays family & myself went to the State House & heard Mr. Lance Officiate, Read, Sung, etc. etc. to an Episcopal Congregation there Assembled, Wind at North West. Judge Desasure arrived Last Evening, Mr. Lance dined with us, as also Mr. Thomas Waties.

Monday, June 28. I rode to My Lots & Put the Carpenters to Work on Ditch & to Put on Pailings† on my house Lots, Calm & warm, I went with Mrs. Horry & Mrs. Bays Family to the House of Mr. Simon Taylor & Spent the day with his Family; his Wife is an Old Acquaintance of mine & is the daughter of General Henderson, an Acquaintance & Brother Officer in the Revolutionary war.

Tuesday, June 29. A fair morning Wind at North West. I rode to my Lot, 2 pannells pallings were finished, I Received yesterday 1 Long Cill & 2 Short ditto & 4 plates for my Kitchen. I directed Buddy to begin the Gates on both Lots. I Saw Captain Wade & Mr. James Guignard Engaged Some Lumber from him for me. I Rode with Mrs. Horry to Gabriel Guignard Esquire. We dined with him & returned home in the Evening. I began A Memorandum Book to be Left with James Gugnard Esquirer for his Guidance after I Leave Columbia. A Party of Ladies & Gentlemen Spent this Evening at Mrs. Bay, it was a Social & Agreeable Party Mrs. Gilliard & Mrs. Davis were Present.

Wednesday, June 30. I went to my Lots. Yesterday I Received 15 Posts. Buddy at making Gates, & Grigs Putting down Posts. A fair day wind at

---

*The mill probably belonged to George Wade (1747–1823), a successful planter and statesman from Richland County. Bailey and Cooper, *Biographical Directory of the South Carolina House*, 733–34.

†Palings are subordinate or temporary fences made of small strips of wood. The horizontal paling is mostly used for agricultural purposes, while the vertical paling often takes on a more ornamental purpose in gardens. Brown, *Forester*, 2:86–87.

South, Mr. Habbermont Visited me at my house Lot, Laid off the North East Side of my Garden Ground in order to ditch of the Same, 'tis the only side now Ramaing to be Ditched. Received Yesterday a Letter from George Town from Mr. James Ward of Said Town, & today I Answered it.

Thursday, July 1. I rode to my Lotts, Posts & Gates of my house Lot put up, Got 4 pair Small Hinges of Mr. Harmamount, Colonel Taylor Called to See me at my Lodgings, Several Ladies (unknown to me) Called on Mrs. Horry this morning James Guignard Rode out to Send Waggons for Lumber. Captain Hart with Justice Goodwin & Mr. Motte, Son of Major Motte deceased of the Continental Army, Called on me, & I Vouched by Oath that Major Motte was Killed before Savanna & that I beleave Said Motte to be the Majors Son, I Received 15 Posts & 16 by Warrings Waggon Mr. Habermount Called on us. I received 3 pair Small hinges weighing 9 pounds from Mr. Habermont Reverend Mr. Greene Called on us, I Rode to & Saw Mrs. Dinkins & Miss Lynch & Bowmans.

Friday, July 2. I Rode to my Lot. I returned Mrs. James Guignard Pavillion, Wind at South East. Clear & Warm weather. Received a Load of Scantlin by Warings Waggon. Received 2 Loads of Slab's by Green Waggon.

Saturday, July 3. Yesterday at Night I Received (by Post) a Letter from Captain Dent & two from Gourdine, a Member of Congress. I Rode out today & Put my Carpenters to work on Railing & Slabing my Lots. Saw Mr. James Gignard. Called on & took Leave of the following Persons. Miss Lynch, Mrs. Simon & Mrs. William Taylor I Rote to the following Persons. Captain Dent & John Cheesboro & Samuel Smith, Doctor Blythe & Mrs. Blythe arrived here this Morning Doctor Tucker declines Selling his Land at Present, his friend is John Woddrop Esquire of Charles Ton. Received a Load of Slabs from Wades Mill by Greens Waggon. Received a Load of Posts by Warings Waggon from Joe Brown Say 17 Posts. Mr. Goddard, Mr. Allston Junior, Mr. McGill, In the Evening I rode out, Reverend Mr. Green called on us. I Saw Doctor Blythe he Says all was well at George & Brown Towns & at Dover plantation. I Received another Load of Slabs by Greens Waggon from Wades Mill. I Received a Load of Posts by Warings Waggon.

Sunday, July 4. A fair day, Calm Morning, very hot Weather wind South, my House Lot is Inclosed by Railings, & my Garden half Inclosed by Slabs. Colegians McGill, Allston & Goddard Spent the Last Evening with us. I took my Leave Last Evening of Major Ward. I went to the Methodist Church & heard a Sermon delivered by Reverend Mr. Greene. This day American Liberty was declared it has been preserved 38 Years & now again we are fighting with Great Britain for the freedom of the Seas. May God Grant us Success & Long bless us as a Nation. The above mentioned Colegians Dined with us. Miss Davis, Goodwin & Georgiana Blackburn Spent the Afternoon with us.

Monday, July 5. Clear day & Calm weather. Resigned all my Concerns at Columbia to James Guignard as my Attorney. Delivered Gignard a Book of what Lumber I had for my Lots, & what Ironwork I had of Mr. Hermormont. Drum & fife beat before Day. I took my Leave of Major Clifton, & judge Desausure. Dr. Blythe Called on us, Saw Colonel Hutchinson at Doctor Greens. I went to Colledge & heard an Oration delivered by Mr. McDuffee a Student. Saw many Acquaintances there, went to the State house, & dined with the Citizens Paid $2 ¼ for a Seat thereat. Was Chosen President Colonel Taylor Vice President. The Military & Citizens dined together amidst Guns firing, Drums & fifes Played, & Colours displayed many Patriotic Toasts were drank, Songs & hizzas's Noise & Mirth Prevailed, all Ended in Confusion by Sun down.

Tuesday, July 6. Wind at South Clear day I rode to my Lots, Carpenters Slabbing Garden; Saw Drs. Blythe & Green. Received a George Town News Paper. Judge Desasure, Called on me about 2 OClock A.M. also Mr. Read of the Coledge, Mrs. Horry Dined with Mrs. James Guignard, Saw young Allston & McGill.

Wednesday, July 7. Calm Morning, Clear day, I Rode to my Lots, Carpenters Ditching, Dined with James Gignard & Left him $27.75 Cents & took my Leave of his & Mrs. Bays Family. Bound to William Mayrant high Hills santee Left 3 Carpenters Lodged at Meyers's Tavern.* Took my Leave of Dr. Hughs Mr. Lance Mr. Bowman Lynch & Mr. McGill (Paid Drum & fife 1/2 for 5th July). Gave Mr. James Guignard my Note of this date for $55.15 Cents. Also Paid for Lumber & hauling as per Account $93 ¼. James Gignard Rode with me about 2 miles to Shew me the Road I Got to Meyers about 8 at Night Past Meredian & Supped there.

Thursday, July 8. I Rose very Early & rode to Mr. Bell my Carriage wheel Broke down I was detained Several Hours to Mend it I owe Mr. Bell 3 1/4 6. I Got to Mr.   at the ferry $1 ½ I owe him. I Gave a Due Bill to ferry man 7/7d.

Friday, July 9. I Got to William Mayrant Esquire about 11 OClock A.M. & there I met Mrs. Horry Dined in Company with Miss Eveligh & Miss Richardson Rode to Benjamin Ioor house, the family was absent, Mayrants family went to Visit Cleland Kinlock & Lodged at his House.

---

*David Myers operated a tavern and general store on Garner's Ferry Road in the Richland District of South Carolina. A planter, tavern keeper, and merchant in the lower Richland District, he served in the South Carolina House of Representatives from 1818 to 1823 and 1830 to 1831. Moore, *Biographical Directory of the South Carolina House*, 192–93.

Saturday, July 10. I Rode to Judge James & breakfasted with him. Mrs. Rees Junior came there I Rode home to W. Mayrants & found himself & Family was Got home. Thomas Eveleigh & Rufus Mayrant (Son of John) came to our house about 12 OClock Maredian. Mrs. Ioor Senior Visited us with her Neice. Mrs. Waties & 3 of her Daughters Visited us & Took Tea with us. Benjamin Ioor & his Family dined with us. Rufus Mayrant Visited us, I Lent him a Book of War Letters.

Sunday, July 11. I rose as Usual (Early) a Cloudy Morning a Little Rain fell Yesterday. Samuel Mayrant Rose Early & came to me in my Room. I wrote to Sarah Bay at Columbia. Mrs. Horry, Mrs. Betsey Ioor & Rufus Mayrant went to Manchester & heard a Sermon from Reverend Mr. Capers, returned to Ben Ioor & Dined & in the Evening returned home to William Mayrants, found there Mr. Rees & his Lady. Miss Rees & Miss Waters also Mr. Potts heard of Major Brown & Colonel Huggins & his Son; received a Letter from my Overseer Mr. Blunt all Well but my Corn is Lost. My Carriage broke down, Tire & a Fellows broke, by Ropes Tied made Shift to Get home. I see no Ladies on the Hills Equal to the Miss Mayrants, say Francis & Placedia. I wish they were happyly Married.

Monday, July 12. A fair Morning. Mrs. Elizabeth Ioor & her Neice arrived here this morning from Ben Ioors. Yesterday I met William Richardson on the Road near Manchester. This morning Mrs. Horry went home with her Sister Ioor. I Sent my Carriage to Mrs. Rees for her B. Smith to mend it as Soon as Possible. I wrote to Ann Bay at Columbia & Sent it to the Burrough to Go by Post. I Got my Carriage before night John Mayrant Esquire his Lady & 2 daughters with Miss Leonora Davis Spent the Evening with us, Reverend Mr.   dined & Spent the Evening with us, & went off with Mayrants Family.

Tuesday, July 13. Cool & Clear Morning, Yesterday I Got 4 Papers (Last to 2nd July) from Gourdine Esquire at Congress. I rode out this Morning & breakfasted with General Sumpter. Took with me Scipio & Zemo (Isaac is with Mrs. Horry) from G. S. I rode to Cleland Kinloch & Dined with him in Company of his Daughters his House & firniture very fine & his Plantation very highly Emproved, I was highly Entertained by this Gentleman & before night I Got home, at Post Office (Statesboro) I Left a Letter for Miss Ann Bay at Columbia.

Wednesday, July 14. Clear & Cool Morning. Yesterday Miss Francis Mayrant bought a Hatt at the Burrough for Rachael, Cost half a Dollar. I this morning rode out in Company with Francis Mayrant to Mr. John Mayrants. Rote my Overseer & Sent it to Stateburgh Dined with John Mayrants family. Francis M. Returned home before Dinner & I Returned before Sun Set. Received from Columbia a Letter for Mrs. Horry.

Thursday, July 15. Cool & Clear Morning, Calm; wrote a Letter to James Guignard at Columbia & Sent it by Statesburgh Post I rode out & Visited Judge Waties dined with his 3 sons & Daughters & the Reverend Mr. Strebeck an Episcoparian Minister. It Rained after Dinner, happy Rain Mr. Strebeck after Supper Read a Chapter in the Bible, Said Prayers & Sung a Psalm, the Family then dispersed & I went to my Room & Bed.

Friday, July 16. Cool & Clear, I breakfasted, took Leave of the Judges Family & Rode off to William Mayrants N.B. The Judes Family are very Amiable & must be very happy. I knew him a Child & his Present Situation Afford me Great Satisfaction. I this day also Rode to Ben Ioors, where I met Mrs. Horry.

Saturday, July 17. Clear & Cool Morning I Sent Rachael & Isaac to William Mayrants for my Cloaths, I rode to William Richardson & Saw there John S. Richardson & his Family. Changed $10 at Manchester Mr. Brown did me this favour. Mr. Thomas Eveleigh Visited us this Afternoon, Mr. William Richardson came home Last night.

Sunday, July 18. Cloudy & warm Morning; Wind South, No Rain, Corn will be all Lost. I breakfasted with Eveligh Family & went off about One OClock P.M. & Lodged at The Widow Thomas Johnson It Rained Last Night. I was well Received by the widow & her Daughter.

Monday, July 19. Cloudy Morning, warm; wind a South. Tire Got broke Yesterday. Rode to the Governor James Richardson after Breakfast, Saw there Colonel Boone Mitchell & his Lady. Got Acquainted with Mr. Maurice Power a School Master (a Learned man) Got Spokes from Mr. Charles Richardson for my Carriage, Colonel James Richardson went to the Mill It Rained very hard today which prevented his returning home to Dinner.

Tuesday, July 20. I rose Early, & Sent my Carriage to the black Smith (of Colonel Richardson) to be Tired etc. No Wind this morning, Mrs. Mitchell Sick today. My Carriage finished & came home.

Wednesday, July 21. I was Unwell Last Night. Was Introduced to Mr. Charles Richardson this Morning. Got a Early breakfast it Rained Last night & today. I went Onward & Got to Young Cantys House & Dined with him, & by Night I Got to Captain Lessesnes House where I took a Bed, Saw his Son William.

Thursday, July 22. Left Captain Lessesne this morning after Breakfast. Got to Captain Samuel Perdriau, dined with him & his Wife, Lodged at his house at Night. It Rained about 12 OClock Midday.

Friday, July 23. It Rained all Night, & is very heavy weather this Morning, I breakfasted & Sot out for George Town where I with difficulty Arrived at 7 OClock P.M. at my House at Brown Town. After Dining with Mr. Greene & family, Called on Mr. & Mrs. Cheesboro & Got the Key of my House from

Mrs. Wayne who I saw, found Billy at my house all the Negroes there well, Mrs. Cheesboro Sent me Some Coffee & Bread which I Eat & Went to Bed, It Rained all this day.

Saturday, July 24. It Rained all Night & this Morning. Very heavy Weather & no prospect of its Clearing up. Gave 12 quarts Corn out for Mules. About half Barrell Corn found in Store Room, I wrote to Mrs. Horry & James Guignard, Gave out a Weeks Provisions to Negroes here Say 6 Allowances. Mr. Blunt Senior Called on me at 11 OClock A.M. Also Mr. Cheesboro at about 3 OClock P.M. & Mr. Whithurst in the Evening.

Sunday, July 25. It Rained all Last night & this Morning also. Calm & no appearance of Clear Weather. I fear for Dovers Reserve, & that so much Rain will Inundate the Country. The Enemy has it is said taken 3 Towns in North Carolina, so we ought to be prepared for Self defence. Our Militia requires time for their Manovres, Mrs. Helin & my Overseer Called on me this Morning. I went to the Methodist Church. Mr. Chevis Preached.

Monday, July 26. Dined yesterday with Mr. Whithurst, his Wife & Mr. Ward Contractor for the Troops here, Saw the following Persons Today, Mr. Cheesboro, Mr. John Smith, Captain Britton & Gasqua & his Wife, Mrs. Helin breakfasted with me, yesterday Saw Mrs. Belin, Wigfall Mrs. Davis & her Daughter a fair Morning. Wind at North West, Isaac & two Boys Come to me from Dover also Dandy who returned Sot my Negroes here to Clean out my Garden. Billy came from Dover in boat with Grass. Saw Mrs. Cambell & Croft. Saw Dr. Wragg. Saw Mr. John Taylor brick Layer & John Taylor Senior Saw Whitehurst & Mrs. Thomas (of Kingstree) Saw Mr. Pawley & Mr. Marvin Senior. Went to the Governour House & Conversed with him on the Defence of Winyaw, he Miss Hannah Shackelford & Mr. Cheeseboro is to Call on me this Evening. Bought for Cash 5 Bushels Corn at $1 a Bushel. Saw Mr. Croft (School Master & Auditor) & Mr. Phillips the Governours Secretary, & Mr. Isaac Carr (Lawyer).

Tuesday, July 27. Last Evening I wrote to Mrs. Horry & Sent the Letter to Mrs. Francis Shackelford to be forwarded. Mr. Samuel Smith Called on me after night as did Mr. Ward. A fair morning & a Calm one. I rode out & Saw Mr. Whithurst Mr. Soloman, his Excellency the Governour, & Breakfasted with Mr. Cheeseboro & his family & returned home; about 11 OClock A.M. I went to the Court house & met the Citizens Assembled. The Business was over Isaac went for Wheels from Dover for my Carriage, I bought 10 ¼ Yards homespun from Soloman at 3/ per yard. See Solomans Book; In the Afternoon Mrs. Helin Called on me, & at Night S. Smith Supped with me.

Wednesday, July 28. Cool & Clear Morning, Wind at North East. I rode to Mr. Whithurst & breakfasted with his Family, I went to the Town Meeting

& Gave in my Plan of defence which was Read & I was appointed one of a Committe to make defence at propper Places, Say Brest Works etc. I Saw the Governor at his House.

Thursday, July 29. A Clear Morning, wind at South East Cool The Committe I am on are Ben Huger, Gasqua, Major Keith & Thomas Chapman I went & Breakfasted with S. Smith, his Mother, Brother & Sister. Mr. Course boat Came up from the North Inlet himself a Daughter of his, & his Wife & Mrs. Allard Belin came Passengers, I saw these. My flat with my Driver Arrived from Dover with 11 barrels Rice which was delivered to Mr. James Whithurst to be Sold on my Account for Ready money, I saw Captain Gasqua, Mr. Cheesboro, & his Mother & the Governour I Received also by my flat, Some Figs, Water Melions, Green Corn Tomatis, Ockro, & Squashes, I wrote Major Keith to come to Town to meet Commissioners, on Fortifications, I Saw Mrs. Helin, Mr. McFarlin & Mr. Collins, Mr. Whithouse called on me with a Sample of my Rice. I wrote by Post to North & Webb my Factors Charles Ton. Whitehurst delivered my 11 Barrels Rice to C. & Marvin at $2 ¾ a Hundred, S. Smith Dined with me Dandy with my flat went off before Dinner a Storm & Rain fell before S. Smith Came to me.

Friday, July 30. Clear Morning, Wind at South East. I rode out & Breakfasted with Mr. Whithurst. Sent to Mr. T. R. Mitchell for Potatoe Slips. Settled for my Rice with Mr. Marvin received 50 Dollars of him, Saw Mrs. Scott, & Captain Lawson, & Mr. Anderson Planter on black River, Saw Mr. Ward (Contractor) Gave Course & Marvin my Note of hand for £37.9/. with Interest. Drank Tea this Evening with Hannah Shackelford Dined with Mr. Ward & Whithurst, Saw Mr. Blunt Senior & Mrs. Cambell & one of her Daughters Hardwick. Saw Mrs. Scott who Lives On Major Wraggs Plantation.

Saturday, July 31. Thick Morning & Cool, wind at North East. I went & breakfasted with the Reverend Mr. Halling & his Family, Served out 10 Allowances to House Negroes, Saw Mr. Blunt Senior, Major Keith & William W. Trapier, & with Mr. Thomas Chapman, met at my House about 11 OClock on Public Business. Fresh Alarm is Circulated this Morning Relative to the Enemy at North Carolina, we the above 3 Commissioners agreed to write to Captains Huger & Gasqua Informing them to meet us on Tuesday next at my House. This is therefore But a Partial Meeting. I wrote to Captain Huger & to Mrs. Bay at Columbia; bought a Hambro Line & 2 pounds Coffee of Marsh also 2 Bushels Corn, about 5 OClock P.M. It Came on to blow & Rain, a Perfect Storm, I wrote to Captain Thomas Hall & Sent the Letter by Post to Charles Ton. At Night Mr. Samuel Smith Visited me.

BOOK SIX

August 1, 1813–September 25, 1813

P. Horrys History Continued

*S*unday, August 1. Cloudy & Cool Morning, Wind at North West. I rode out but declined Going to Church as it Rained I Got in Carriage & went & Dined with Mr. Whithurst, Ward & Mrs. Whithurst I Rote a Letter to Major Clifford of Columbia & also a Letter to Theodore Gourdine Member of Congress at the Federal City. I Saw at Whithurst Captain Irvin Keith & James Grier, they dined with us & Spent the Evening. I Returned to my House after Supper.

Monday, August 2. A fine Sun Shine Morning wind at North East I began to be Impatient of my Long Stay here, & must if Possible Get a Pituager boat & Mend or Buy Wheels for my Carriage I could Get no beef at Market today, I rode out in my Carriage with Miss Hardwick, & Saw Mrs. Helin, Ward & Whitehurst Saw also Mr. Blunt Senior & wrote to his Son. Saw Mr. Green, Grier, John M. Taylor & Washington Heriot Dandy Come from Dover & brought me fellows figs, Water Melions & Ockro etc. I Gave him Some Tallow & 6 Yards Homespun I wrote to Mr. Robert Carr for a boat & for Lime, I Refused paying Estate Grants Demand of £3.10/ for making my Will as I Consider it Unjust. I dined with Mr. Whithursts Family, I Saw Captain Irvin Keith, & Captain Gasqua, at Night Mr. McGregor Junior & Mr. Fleming Senior Called on me.

Tuesday, August 3. A fine Sun Shine Morning, wind at North East My Flat came from Dover with Spokes & Grass & returned with Ox Cart. We the Commissioners for fortifications, met today & Entered into Resolves On that Subject & Reported According to the Citizens. Mrs. Helin, & S. Smith. Received a Note from Mr. Skine & Replied that I would not pay an Unjust demand & would plead the Limitation Law. Mr. Blunt Senior Called on me. I rode out & Saw the following Persons Mr. & Mrs. Whithurst, Mr. S. Smith, Hazzle, McGreor, Flemming & Captain   of Fort Winyaw. Ensign Logan of Said Fort was buried on Sunday Last with the honours of War. He was a Native of North Carolina. About 11 OClock A.M. Captain Benjamin Huger of the Artillery Called on me, & the other 3 Commissioners also; when we

Entered into Resolves Calling on our Brother Citizens of George Town to meet on Friday next to receive our Oppinion on defence which Mr. Chapman took with him to make a fair Copy. Therefrom when we desolved ourselves. Justice Skrine as Such waited on me. Mrs. Helin & Samuel Smith called on me.

Wednesday, August 4. A fair & Sun Shine Morning wind at North west. Isaac & Carlos went to Mitchells to Mr. Blunt to make Wheels for my Carriage, I rode Out after Breakfast to Mr. Whithurst, Saw his wife & Children, Called for S. Smith & we went to Justice Skrine, where I made my defence against the Account brought against me the Justice required time to Consider the Case I rote to Mr. Habermount here at Columbia & Gave him an historical Account of my Journey Since I Saw him, I received a Letter from my Overseer & Returned an Answer thereto. I rode to Whitehurst & Dined with his family. Saw Mr. Pawley, Dr. Wragg, B. Huger Hazle, Man Taylors & Parson Hawling & Travis & T. Carr of the Methodists Church. I Received a Letter from North & Webb.

Thursday, August 5. Cloudy Morning & warm wind at North West. Very Early I Sent Scipio with a Letter to Robert Carr at Sandpit. I Sent London to Whithurst to Know if his Family meant to Go to North Island this morning. Answer No. I wrote to North & Webb to Send me $70. I rode out to Mr. Blunt Senior. Saw him & Justice Skrine about 10 OClock A.M. it Rained & blowed very hard, Saw Mr. Robert Carr I can have his boat & 300 Bushels Shells.

Friday, August 6. I Rose Early, a Wet morning, wind at North East, I & my Negroes, removed everything from above Stairs, I wrote to Robert Car & my Oversseer, Sent Isaac, Carlos & William for Pitiauger boat I wrote to Mrs. Horry & to Windham Trapier. Paid for 2 pounds Powder 7/ for Dover in the afternoon Captain Irvin Keith, Mr. Ward, Mr. W. Trapier & Mr. Hawling. Mrs. Wayne & her Daughter Betsey also Visited me.

Saturday, August 7. Fair morning wind at North East. Gave out Provisions for Zemo, William, Billy, Abijah, London, (for boat People, Isaac L. Stephen, Carlos, Lot people Peggy, Rachael, Children,) Matthias, Mercury Scipio, Pembroke, Susie, bought 5 Bushels Corn of Cooper rode out to Whithurst, and Ward Saw S. Smith Gasqua, Dr. Wragg Thurston, Grier & Blunt Senior. Mrs. Helin Called on me this morning, wrote to Judge Waties. Mr. Cuttino Called on me with an Account due Savage Smith. I went & Dined with Mr. Ward Saw Irvin Keith, My flat Arrived from Dover with 8 barrels Rice. Two Barrells I Sent to Columbia & 6 Sent to Whitehurst for Sale. Mr. Cuttino & Fleming Called on me after Dark.

Sunday, August 8. Clear & Cool Morning wind at North West. I rose Early & went to Whithurst & Ward, Saw Young blunt at a Distance. Took Coffee & we all went in Mr. Wards boat to Dover dined there & Returned by Night to Town.

Monday, August 9. Cloudy Morning, Calm, Young Blunt not to be found, Pittiauger Loaded to the hatches, As by Scipios Report. Mr. Blunt Senior went to the boat, Sun Came out before breakfast Yesterday Received a Letter from Ann Bay & one from James S. Guignard Columbia. Wrote to Sarah Bay & put in Post Office. Saw Mr. Robert Carr, & Mr. Watts, Wrote to my Overseer & Sent down the boat with Shells to Unload at Dover & return to me, To Put Iron on board of her. Went & Dined with Whithurst Family. Saw Mr. Munnerlin Senior & Samuel Smith & Cheesborow. Dandy came & returned to Dover. I wrote a 2nd Letter to my Overseer. Carrs boat went to Dover. Joe Hugguns Called on me with a Letter from Mrs. Huggins (his wife) which I replied to by him, Bought 6 yards homespun & Sent it to Mirah by Dandy. Saw Mrs. Lessesne & Helin. They Called on me.

Tuesday, August 10. Fair Morning; very hot Last night & this morning. Wind at South West. I wrote a Letter to Miss Anna Bay at Columbia. I Removed to a Room, right wing of our House I went to Dinner with Mrs. Whithurst Family, I Saw Mr. Hassell, It Rained about 3 OClock P.M. Sun Scaulding it must Rain again before night it did so, my Pitiague[r] boat came from Dover with Iron. My two Wheels carried to Mr. Blunt my Small boat also came up. Mr. Croft called on me, It Rained very much Last night.

Wednesday, August 11. Verry Cloudy Morning, wind South West. Began to Load Pitiauger boat (as by Memorandum book) Mrs. Wayne delivered me some Silverware (Spoons etc.). My Overseer came to me. Blunt Senior Called on me, about 12 OClock I went to Mrs. Whithurst & Dined with her & her Family, saw there Captain Marsh. At Night Returned to my Quarters.

Thursday, August 12. Cool & Cloudy morning wind at North West Pituager near Loaded Sent a boat to Dover for a Mule & Horse by flat & for wood, Ruff Rice, & Some Clean Rice, Gave my Overseer a Memorandum of Sundries by Boat & Inclosed one Also to James Guignard. Sent Mrs. Helin a Picture (Tompson Summer). She Visited me I Visited my boat found all my furniture in her, & no more at my house. Received $065 from my Factor Charles Ton. Received a Letter from Mrs. Horry Answered it This Evening & Sent Letter per Post. Saw Rockeye & bespoke a Broad & felling Axe also that he do begin to tire my Carriage Wheels. Mr. Blunt Senior being Sick Can't work on my Wheels today I dined today with Whitehurst & his family & got home about five OClock P.M. Mrs. Wayne Visited me, I Saw Reverend Mr. Wayne on the Bay. Now Clear & fine Sun Shine.

Friday, August 13. Clear Sun Shine Morning. Wind at South West. Mr. Ward, (Contractor) Breakfasted with me. Sent J. S. Guignard Letter per Post. Billy with Flatt & boat returned from Dover with Mule & Horse & Sundries. (Paid Blunt $10) Say 20 Ducks, 4 Jars Butter, 1 ½ Bushels Rice, 1 Bushel Rough Rice, 1 Shote. Boatmen are Scipio, Carlos, Matthias, Mercury & Ponnae 5.

Carriage People, Billy driver 1 Susie, & Abigal & William Chair 3. London behind Carriage 1 Isaac Chair Rains 1. Zemo Blunts Horse 1 I dined with Whithurst Family I had of Rocky a New Axe (del. Scipio) $2 Cost. Saw Received Mr. Halling & Captain Hazzle. Had of Rockey 2 Iron hooks & 2 Forks (these for Poles).

Saturday, August 14. Pitiague boat went off Last Night for Dover (Scipio) Commander about an hour before day with my household furniture, 10 Ducks & a Shoat. A fair Sun Shine Morning wind at North East. Dandy came to me with my Overseers horse. I wrote him a Note; & Dandy Immediately returned to Dover on foot; I Received a Letter from his Excellency, in Charles Ton (by Mr. Lynn Express), & Returned an Answer thereto, by Said Express. I wrote a Letter to Hannah Shackelford. I went to Mr. Whitehurst & dined with him & his Family. I Saw Captain Gasqua Mr. Fleming, Mr. Smith (Cassell's Overseer) Samuel Smith, Ben Huger & Burrington Thomas. Received a Letter from Justice Skrine in my favour Saw Charles Lessesne, & talked to him of our Arsenal, of which he is the Keeper & about 4 OClock P.M. I Got home Sick & went to Bed.

Sunday, August 15. Cloudy morning, Cool & wind at South East Mr. Ward Called on me it Rained, we went & Dined with Mr. Whithurst family & I Returned in the Afternoon & went to Bed.

Monday, August 16. Cloudy Morning wind at South East yesterday I wrote to William Bay & Put the Letter in the Post Office, I Received from Dover, Vegitables & Some Ruff Rice, it Got wet. Bought 3 yards homespun of Soloman for Giddo, Sent Mr. Wards boat to Dover for Ruff Rice, & Grass & Giddo & Sam, This morning I wrote to Rufus Mayrant near Statesburgh & Put the Letter in the Post Office. Fine Weather & bracing to my Limbs. Boat went off with Billy, Zemo & William about 12 OClock. It Rained, Light Showers all day Doctor Allston Called on me, Also Mr. Whithurst I wrote to Windham Trapier & Sent the Letter by John.

Tuesday, August 17. Clear & Sun Shine Morning (very Pleasant weather) wind at South. Billy came from Dover this morning with Ruff Rice, Grass, Some butter & Sam & Giddo, Gave Sam a Jacket & Overalls, wrote to Hannah Shackelford also to Aron Marvin I Let Giddo remain at Dover to take Care of his mothers Child. They all three Returned to Dover this morning, I Rode to Whithurst & Dined with himself & family, Saw the following Persons this day Mrs. Rockey, Captain Ben Huger, Mr. Chapman & Returned home. Wheels done this day & Prepare to Set off next Thursday very Early. Whithurst paid me for a Barrel Rice a[t] 2 ¾ $100 Say $18. Gave Rockey an Order on Mr. Whithurst for $27.86 Amo[un]t of his black Smiths Bill for Tiring my Wheels.

Wednesday, August 18. I breakfasted with Whitehurst & his family Saw Blunt Senior. Took my Leave of George Town & went on the Sandpit Road for Columbia, & before night Arrived at Mr. Osburns Pine Land Settle. Found himself & Family well Saw on the Road Mr. Glass.

Thursday, August 19. A Cool Morning & a Clear Sun Shine. Calm Morning, breakfasted with Osburn & his family & went to his Plantation with him, & his family & dined with them at his Pine Land here & Suped with them also.

Friday, August 20. Cool Morning but Clear Sun Shine My Horses Mules & Negroes came from the Plantation of Mr. Osburns We breakfasted & Sot off, for Captain Lessesnes House. I was much Gratified with Seeing my two Cousins Mrs. Osburn & Henretta Glover, they appeared happy & being now Acquainted with Mr. Osburn, I hope for a happy Intercou[r]se with his family & that they will Visit us at Columbia. Sot off about 9 OClock A.M. & dined at Captain Lessesne. Saw his Son & a Mr. Martin, Got to Mr. Davis's, Supped there & went to Bed.

Saturday, August 21. Cool, Clear Morning, Left Mr. Davis's House Early, They are very Agreeable People. A Lady & a Gentleman composes' it, everything here appears in Plenty & fashionable furniture etc. etc. I beleave they are Rich. Sot out about Sun Rise Say 6 OClock A.M. & proceeded on our Journey; breakfasted at Mr. George Canteys house near Nelson ferry. From thence I went to Governor James Richardson.

Sunday, August 22. Yesterday I rode up to the House of Governour Richardson, but on being Informed he had a very Sick Family, I declined Staying & went on to the House of Mrs. Johnson & was very friendly Received by her & her daughter; I Supped with them & after much Agreeable Conversation I Retired to Bed. N.B. They must be happy, That are Intimate with this Family & I hope & wish to Cultivate their Acquaintance, & That they will Visit us at Columbia. I Shall Ever Retain a Gratefull Remembra[n]ce of their Politeness to me! I breakfasted & Sot off for Mr. William Mayrants plantation, where I hope to Arrive Safe, before Sun Set, & to meet this Family in health. Francis & Placedia Mayrant are Charming young Ladies, Indeed I Greatly Value this Family & I have Experianced many favours which they have from time to time Conferred on me. I Got to this House about 5 OClock P.M. found a Letter from Mrs. Horry wrote to her Mrs. Mayrant Send her Horse & Chair for her.

Monday, August 23. Cloudy, Cool & Calm Morning I, rested badly Last night, was over fatigued & too much Anxiety to See Mrs. Horry Occasioned this; I rode out a Little way for Exercise & went to the burrow, & Receved from Post Office 7 Letters one from Captain Dent, one from Mr. Cheesboro, one from Mrs. Dent, one from James Guignard, one from Sarah Bay one from

Thomas Blunt, one from North & Webb, Rufus Mayrant Called on me. A Dance at Mrs. Rutledge this Night. Young Mayrants went to it also William Mayrant Esquire.

Tuesday, August 24. It Rained Last Night & this Morning. I Got Sick in the Night & Kept my Bed this Morning. I found myself very Costive & drank Butter Milk without the desired Effect. I Left William Mayrants house, & Mrs. Horry there after Dinner & went on to Judge James, where I Lodged.

Wednesday, August 25. A Cloudy Morning. I breakfasted with the Judge & his Family & about 8 Oclock A.M. Sot off for Columbia. Was Overtaken by Young Desausure in a Chair with his sister also Young Mayrant with *his* Sister in a Chair Going for Columbia, I arrived at Mr. Meyers about 4 OClock P.M. Dined, & Lodged thereat.

Thursday, August 26. Left Mr. Meyers House about day light & arrived at Columbia about 10 OClock A.M. Rode to my Lots & to Doctor Greens Saw there Captain Keith, Lieutenant Freeman, Colonel Warren, Mr. Goodwin Mr. Davises, & Mr. Glen. Saw Major Clifton, Mr. Gignard Junior Mrs. Guignard & Miss Hughs. Dined at Mrs. Bay, & her family 39 Bushels Corn of Mr. Guignard, Allowances of a Peck to Each of my Negroes—Say 11 Allowances.

Friday, August 27. Yesterday Served out Allowances A Thick Cloudy Morning & warm. Wrote to Samuel Smith & James Whitehurst, both of George Town. It Rained after Breakfast & I went over & Dined with James Guignard. Was Present his wife & Children, Miss Hughs & Robert Waring. I wrote a Letter also to Captain Dent at Charles Ton. Paid for 38 ½ Bushels Corn a[t] 2/4 is $19.25 Cents.

Saturday, August 28. A Storm Last night, it Thundered very much also rained & Continued after day Light, bad Weather Prevents my Carpenters work very much; wind at West, & very Cloudy. This morning I wrote to Mr. Thomas Blunt who Lives near Brown Town at Thomas Mitchell Esquire Plantation. I also wrote to John Cheesborow of George Town & Put his & 4 other Letters In Post Office. I rode out to Dr. Greens Office & to my Lotts, I rode to Mr. Gabriel Gignard House & Saw him & Mr. McCleland, Sot a Plow to work in my Garden. Isaac & Grigs went to Flooring my Kitchen, I Sent William to Assist them. A Waggon of boards arrived at my Lot. Captain Benjamin Waring Artillery Company Turned out to Exircise. I wrote to Mrs. Helin.

Sunday, August 29. Fair & Sun Shine Morning I moved from Mrs. Bay to my Kitchen in Lot. A Calm Morning, Sarah & Margaret Bay Visited me this Morning. I rode to the State House & heard a Sermon Read, prayers & Singing. Saw many of my Acquaintances, & Dined with James Guignard & his Family & Miss Hughs.

Monday, August 30. Fair Morning, wind at South West began to Settle my House & make Conveniencies therein, Plow Goes on Received 12 pair Hinges

The Horry-Guignard House in Columbia, South Carolina

from James Guignard. I wrote to Mrs. Horry & to James Ward at George Town & Putt his Letters in the Post Office, Saw Mr. Cassells at his Lodgings, also Dr. Green Mr. Davis & Judge & Senator Gaillard Dined today with Mrs. Bay, & her Family, before night finished flooring my House over head & Cleaning my yard of Chips, Shavings etc. etc. Received a Load of Scantling from Wade's Mill, Received also a Load of Shingles from James Guignard. After Night a Waggon Load of Fether Ridge boards came from Wades Mill, a Heavy Storm of Wind, Rain, Thunder & Lightning.

Tuesday, August 31. Fair Sun Shine Morning, but Calm, Land very Wet. Saw James Guignard & Captain Wade, opened a Door on the North Side of my Room. Partitioned between two Rooms, Miss Bays Called on me as did Also Mr. Habermont, Simons, Goddard & Mr. McGill. Received a Load of Joice by Warings Waggon, Put a Step to my front Door South West. Received another Load of Joice by Warings Waggon Miss Martha Davis & Miss Gooden Called on me in the Evening I rode out & Supped with Mrs. Guignard.

Wednesday, September 1. Now very hot weather Clear Sun Shine Morning. Wind at South West. Put a Step to the North Side of my house, Measured my Garden Ground & Laid out Some walks, Enemy has Landed at Hilton head, near Beaufort. Miss Ann, Martha & Margaret Bay Visited me before breakfast Received a Load of Joice by Mr. Waring Waggon. Sarah Bay Visited me, I wrote to Cleland Kinloch for his Brick Layer. I saw Mr. Sparks. Pettiager boat Saild 12th August from George Town for Columbia, I wrote John Ioor at the Missipicy Territory.

Thursday, September 2. A Cloudy Morning wind at East finished Plowing Garden, I wrote to Mrs. Horry & I rode out to my Garden & fell 3 Trees near the Collage to make Blocks for my House, It drissles & I fear today will be a Rainy day which will Backen my work as I have no Shelter for my People to work Under I borrowed a XCut Saw of Mr. Douglass, Saw Mrs. Bay at my House Mrs. Gignard Senior & Junior called on me this morning, as did Sarah & Margaret Bay. Cut down & Trimmed Trees in my Neighbourhood. It Rained today. Received a Load of Refage Boards from Wades Mill by Warings Waggon, Received Also a Load of Inch boards by Mr. Wades Waggon.

Friday, September 3. It Rained Last Night, a Cloudy morning, wind at South, bought 6 yards homespun 3 broad Hoes & some Waifors. Sarah & Martha Bay Visited me this morning, also Ann & Margaret Bay, Simons Gallant, the Last & Mr. Hannah is Ann Bays Gallant. I rode out to Garden Lot, & to Sawing of blocks & around the Colledges. Got home this Evening 2 more blocks, about 12 OClock I felt Sick. Laid down & Slept an hour Mr. Rufus Mayrant & Warren Davis (Son of Ransom Davis) Called on me, a Waggon Load of Shingles was Received after dark.

Saturday, September 4. A Clear morning wind at North I felt Unwell this morning & kept my Bed till Breakfast time, Sarah & Margaret Bay Visited me this Morning I rode to the Post Office. Mr. Gabriel Guignard made me a present of Five Pegeons which Mrs. James Guignard Received for me as I have no house for them. Got a Letter from Mrs. Blunt Senior. My Plantation has Suffered by the Late Storm & Tide & also the North Island & George Town & its Neighbourhood. Saw Mr. Cassetts Miss Davis's & Miss Goodwin, Mr. Goddard & McGill. I wrote to Mrs. Horry & to Thomas Blunt by Mr. Cassells. I Received at Night by Wades Waggon from his Mill a Load of Boards & Scantling.

Sunday, September 5. A fair morning wind at North East. 2 Blocks brought home Last Night Paid for 3 pair Shoes $3 for Abigal, London & William. Sent a Letter to Captain Wade about Lumber. I went to the State House & heard Service Performed by an Episcoparian Lance. Early this morning Miss Margaret Bay Visited me; also Gabriel Gu'gnard Junior & his two Sisters. I am Uneasy, my boat is not yet Arrived, Messrs. Bay, Simons, Tatum, Hannah & McGill Visited me about 10 OClock A.M. I dined today with Mrs. Bay & her Family. Mr. Tatum was bled Yesterday. Sarah Bay is Got well but her Mother is Poorly. Near Sun Set the 3 Miss Gailliards (daughters of Judge Gailliard) Visited me. This family's Acquaintance I shall Endeavour to Cultivate. They as well as myself are from the old french refugees that Emigrated from Paris in Lewis the 14th Time & Settled on Lower Part of South Santee. Long may they live to Enjoy this Soil of Liberty, which they now so honourably Possess. Hereafter their Country will Sing their Pra[i]ses & write their Names in Letters of Gold. After dark Mrs. Goddard & McGill Set with me about an hour & retired to Mrs. Bays house where they Lodge.

Monday, September 6. I was very Sick Last night with a Cholic & Pain in my Back. Took Warm Tea & Brandy before day & the same after day, Grew better & arose at Late breakfast time fair Weather but Uncommonly Cold. Wind at North. Part of James Guignard Family are Sick this Morning, Saw Mr. Tatum at the frame, Negroes Piling Shingles, Sawing Blocks, & Framing this *Morning.* After Breakfast Miss Sarah & Margaret Bay called on me also Mr. Simons, made Shelve in my Room, wrote a Long Letter to my friend Ben F. Trapier. Setting up Rafters to my dwelling House. William Sick, Guignards Waggon from Taylors Mill* a Load Inch boards, Received at Night a Waggon Load from Wades Mill, Braices, Scantling & Ruffage boards. Finished Getting Blocks.

Tuesday, September 7. A fair Morning, wind Westward, fine Moon Light Nights, Yesterday Gabriel Guignard Senior Visited me, also Doctor Hughs. Isaac & Grigs went to the Garden walks. Returned Mr. Douglas his XCut Saw which he Lent me. Got a News paper from George Town, Sarah Martha & Margaret Bay Visited me before breakfast. Opened a Path from my House to my Garden Gate. I rode to the Post Office this morning. Opened a Path to Mrs. Bays House; Ann & Martha Bay Visited me after Breakfast, as Did Sanders & Elizabeth Guignard. Mrs. Bay Sent me a Columbia News Paper. I Got 10 pounds 20 dozen Nails from Mr. Habermont Shop. Left B. Trapiers Letter at the Post Office this morning; Saw Lieutenant Freeman at Doctor Greens, Mr. Lance Called on me, Mrs. Bay Sent me Carrot seed Cabbage ditto, & Turnup ditto, Mustard ditto, Lettece ditto, Onion ditto. Mrs. Davis (Widow of Ransom Davis deceased) with Ann Bay Called on me dug up a Squ[a]re in Garden near the Gate, Wades Waggon after dark brought a Load of boards.

Wednesday, September 8. Fair morning but very Cool Wind at South West. Isaac & Grigs joined the Carpenters this morning. Two more Blocks brought home Last night, Last Evening Martha Bay, Mr. Taitum & Gabriel Guignard Junior & Taitums Son Visited me. I rode out & Got from Post Office 3 Letters Sarah & Margaret Bay Visited me this Morning. Saw Mr. Wade, he Offers me Slabs & Bricks if I can fetch them, wrote to Samuel Smith of George

---

*Horry is likely referring to a mill belonging to Col. Thomas Taylor in Richland County. Taylor owned a home on Taylor's Hill with a surrounding plantation called the Plains. Bailey and Cooper, *Biographical Directory of the South Carolina House,* 1586–87.

Town. By Post Received a Letter from Mrs. Horry I Received a Letter from
Mrs. Helin & from W. W. Trapier, Gives a Full Account of the Late Hurri-
cane. Boat has been out 25 days, Miss Blackburns, Miss Goodin, Miss Dinkin
& Lieutenant Stark, Simons McGill & Taitum Visited me about Sun Set.

Thursday, September 9. Cloudy & very warm. Wind at South. Got 200
Bricks (by my own Waggon from Wade) Piled them up. Got 24 pounds Nails
from Habermont. Shingled my Kitchen. Wrote to Mrs. Horry in Answer to her
Letter & that She do Give up Going to George Town. Saw Mr. Wade; James
Guignard, Ann & Margaret Bay, this morning. Today is fasting & humiliation
for our Sins (as by Order of President Maddison) Miss Bay's Eats nothing
today & Mr. Lance holds forth in the State House, on this So Solomn Occasion. Drew all the Slabs about my house Lot, into the Garden Ready to Build
a House therein, I rote to Mrs. Helin in Answer to her Letter Received Yesterday & Sent it to the Post Office. I saw Lieutenant Spark, & James S. Guignard & Sanders Guignard, his Son & wife Called on me, all Mrs. Bays Family
Visited me today (also Taitum & Hannah) after Night I Received a Letter from
Mrs. Horry by Mrs. Desausure.

Friday, September 10. Warm & Cloudy morning, Wind at South West.
Framing Goes on, blocks etc. etc. moved from around the frame & Piled up
out of the way thereof. James & Gabriel Guignard, & Sarah Martha & Margaret Bay Visited me this morning. Borrowed Major Clifton Waggon & today
brought 400 & 200 Bricks from Wade. Mr. Habermont, & Mr. Cassells Visited me, also Mr. Taitum.

Saturday, September 11. Fine Moon Light Nights, fair beautiful & warm
weather, Wind at South, Saw Captain Wade & James Guignard, Sarah Bay
Visited me this morning Received by my Waggon 250 Bricks & 200. Mrs. Bay
also Visited me, & Master Hunter, Also James Guignards two Daughters,
Mrs. James Gugnard Visited me this forenoon. Received from Mr. Greens
Waggon 500 Bricks, 400 ditto Mr. Warings ditto, 400 ditto, 500 ditto, 500
ditto. I had a Hogshead Tar by Warings Waggon. Put it in the yard on Skids
Sarah Bay dined with me today, I wrote a Letter to James Ward to Get Susie's
money for Washing. A very hot day, & many Clouds appears, took down Par-
tition, buried a Hogshead of Tar. S. Pier Shaved my Beard, Tomorrow being
Sunday at Evening Miss Blackburns Visited me.

Sunday, September 12. Clear Sun Shine Morning wind at South, Expect
to Raise my House on Wednesday next & to begin my Kitchen Chimney
Tomorrow. I rode out this morning to the State House & towards Granby
Wednesday next the Legislature meets here the 15th Instant & on that day my
Pittiauger Boat with my household furniture from George Town will be a
Month out This morning Gabriel & Elizabeth Guignard Visited me. I Saw
Simons & McGill Going to my Garden. They Called on me I wrote a Note

to Mr. Habermont & he Called on me in Consiquence thereof, Sarah & Margaret Bay Called on me; as did James S. Guignard, I dined with J. S. Guinard & his Family, Saw Miss Hughs after Dinner & Miss Martha Bay.

Monday, September 13. Last night very warm, also this morning Wind at South, Cloudy. Last Evening Judge Desausure Spent an hour with me, Sent Billy for a Load of Bricks to Captain Wades Kiln, he Refuses me any more & untill I want for the Great house Chimneys. Saw James Guignard. Returned Major Clifford his Waggon. Brick layer began to work on Kitchen Chimney, Margaret Bay Visited me this morning also Ann & Sarah Bay, Mr. Lance Called on me with a Subscripion Paper for building an Episcopal Church* in Columbia; I Subscribed $100 & hope Mrs. Horry will do the Same. Mrs. Bay Called on me about 2 OClock p.m. Major Cambell of Williamsburgh Township came here Last Evening. He is a Continental Officer.

Tuesday, September 14. Cloudy & Cool Morning; wind at North. Chimney Continued, Mr. James Guignard Called on me, Sarah & Margaret Bay also Called on me. Wrote a Note to Mr. Chapple. Matthias (from Boat) brought me a Letter from Blunt who Informed me the boat was Sunk above the Canal & that he wished for a boat to bring away the Goods which is at Mr. Palmer. I Received by Mr. Guignards Waggon a Load of Inch Boards from Mr. Taylors Mill.

Wednesday, September 15. Cool Morning North Wind, but very foggy I was very Sick Last Night, I Sent off this morning a Boat to Blunts Assistance & added two more Negroes Cuggo & Zemo to his former Number of five. Both myself & James Guignard wrote to Mr. Blunt, Relative to his Coming up in the boat Sent him for the Goods Saved. Saw Mr. James Guignard before Breakfast. Mr. John Smith Richardson Ann & Martha Bay Called on me. It Rained today & I had Planted in my Garden Some Seeds Gave me by Mrs. Bay, I Yesterday wrote a Long Letter to Mrs. Horry. Drew Today Ten Pecks Corn for my Negroes. Received by Warings Waggon 500 Bricks, 500 ditto & 500 ditto wrote a Long Letter to Thomas Mitchell of George Town Received

---

*Trinity Episcopal Cathedral in Columbia was founded through the efforts of Rev. Andrew Fowler, a missionary for the Protestant Episcopal Society who began preaching on the grounds of the State House in 1812. With the generosity of members such as Wade Hampton, Charles Cotesworth Pinckney, and Elias Horry, the church incorporated on August 12, 1813, and the wooden structure was consecrated by Bishop Dehon in 1814. The Protestant Episcopal Society funded the church for the first three years, and their minister, the Reverend Christian Hancknell, was appointed on November 29, 1815, and eventually resigned his professorship of mathematics at South Carolina College to be pastor of the church. Dalcho, *Historical Account of the Protestant Episcopal Church*, 394–95.

by Guignard's Waggon flooring boards from Taylors Mill. A House was formed this Morning & business Commenced, The Governor has Arrived. Received by Major Smith Son Savage $231.37 Cents for 13 Barrels Rice sold by Thomas Blunt 9 September 1813. Colonel Huggins is Arrived here. Received a Waggon Load of Scantling & Fitheredge from Wades Mill by his Waggon.

Thursday, September 16. Received Last night by Mr. Guignard's Waggon 25 flooring Boards. Colonel Huggins & his Son Called on me Last Night. This morning James Guignard, Doctor Blythe, Mrs. Bay & her Daughter Ann Called on me. I Sent my Strong Negroes to Get off the boat which we failed in Getting off Yesterday. A Thick Foggy Morning. Wind at North, Sarah & Margaret Bay Called on me before breakfast. I wrote a Letter to Thomas Blunt (at George Town) & Sent it by Mail. Received a Letter from Mr. Chapple & Answered it Immediately. John Smith Richardson Called on me, Received by James Guignard Waggon, from Taylors Mill boards. Wrote a letter to Joseph Manigaunt at Charles Ton & Sent it by Post. Today about 12 OClock the hired Boat with 4 hands Sot out from Granby to Go to Mr. Blunt, at Mr. Palmers Plantation, about this time fell a Shower of Rain. After night wrote a few Lines to Mrs. Horry, Sent her two Letters by Guignards boy who went the 17 Instant. Goddard Simons & McGill Visited me.

Friday, September 17. Cloudy Morning wind at North began to Raise Blocks & Cills to my Dwelling House & will Raise the House I hope today, Ann, Sarah & Margaret Bay Called on me a Columbia News Paper of Today gives the Governors Message, tis very Lengthly & contains Great Patriotism & Energy in defence of his Country, his abilities has never been doubted & I have no doubt of the goodness of his heart, his Property & Family must bind him If no other motives are Necessary. Bought Bacon, Whisky & Rice for Negroes Raising the House. Mrs. James Guignard Called on me, we Conversed on the Subject of my Getting Lands for my Gang of Negroes, Mrs. Bay called on me, about Mid Day it Rained very hard, the wind being Southerly, sills & Lower Joices being fixed, Riceived a Letter from Cleland Kinloch, & Answered it Immediately, Simons & McGill Visited me also John Smith Richardson, Agreed with a Methodist Man to finish my Chimney by Wednesday next for $20. Saw the Huggines Father & Son. Raised 2 sides of the Lower Story of my House. Lieutenant Allston, McGill & Goddard Visited me after night.

Saturday, September 18. Very Cloudy, & warm, Wind at West, It rained all Last night. (Billy Sick) I wrote to Mr. Palmer who resides near the Santee Canal To Save my Effects that may be found in Pittiauger boat After my Overseer had Left her & to write me thereof. Entervals it yet Rains. Mr. Willey Brick Layer this Morning Got to Work on the Chimney. This Morning John Waties & young Desausure Called on me about 10 OClock the weather Cleared &

Sun came out, Ann & Margaret Bay Visited me this forenoon, Bought 2 Baskets & 1 ounce Assoefaeta.

Sunday, September 19. Sick Last night, Cloudy Weather & warm. Wind Eastwardly. Ann & Sarah Bay Visited me before breakfast, I rode out to the State House, & heard Mr. Lance Officiate to a full Audiance, many Members of the House were Present. This morning Saw Mr. Cassells & Sanders Guignard & Doctor Blythe. Saw at the State House, Judge Gaillard & his family & Sundry Gentlemen as follows Daniel Elliot Huger, Ben Huger, Mr. Cokley, Mr. McGill, Mr. Habermont Junior Doctor Fisher, Mr. James Guignard, Mr. Andrew Bay & Ladies Mrs. Bay & her Daughters, Mrs. Blythe Mrs. Habermount, Mrs. Chapple, Miss Lynch & 3 Miss Bowmans, Lieutenants Allston & Spark, Major Chapple, Mr. Thomas R. Mitchell, Mr. Goddard, Mr. Daniel, Mr. Goodin, Miss Goodwin Mrs. Guignards Senior & Junior, Mr. Youngblood & Shingleton called on me. This afternoon I wrote a Letter to Miss Frances Mayrant & Mrs. Blythe & Withers called on me before Sun Set.

Monday, September 20. Clear Sun Shine Morning. Wind at West. Both Carpenter & brick Layer at Work The following Persons Visited me before Breakfast to Say Mrs. & Martha Bay, James Guignard, also his 2 sons, also William Bay & Mr. Jenkins, Ann, Sarah & Margaret Bay. After Breakfast Margaret Bay Visited me & After Dinner, Mr. Taitum, Simons & McGill. I bought Rice and Bacon for Carpenters. Received by Guignards Waggon broad Lathing for Pailing about Sundown, Benjamin Ioors with Mrs. Horry Arrived from the high Hills Santee & Immediately, Mrs. James Guignard & Mrs. Bay with their Families Visited her.

Tuesday, September 21. Clear Sun Shine Morning, wind North West, Today we Shall Attempt House Keeping with Such means as we have in our Power. Before Dinner the following Persons Visited us—Ann & Sarah Bay, Mr. Willey (no Bricks this morning) Mrs. Bay & Margaret Bay, James Guignard & his Daughters, Mr. Bay Jenkins & Simons, Martha Bay & John Waties. I rode out & Got 4 pounds Large Nails from Mr. Habermont Shop, Mrs. James Gigniard Visited us this Morning finished Raising our Dwelling House, Mrs. Horry unwell today Wrote a Note to Mr. Willey, Brick Layer, to Get me Bricks. Saw Mr. Spark. Betsey Ioor Sent me Some beans & dried Pears. Bought Sundries towards house Keeping, as per Bill After Dinner the following Persons Called on us, Ann Sarah & Margaret Bay & their Mother, William Bay, & James Guignard Also Colonel Huggins & Thomas R. Mitchell Esquire. I Received a Letter from Thomas Blunt.

Wednesday, September 22. Clear & warm Morning, wind at South. Today Dwelling House was finished Raising; bought Beef & Bacon before breakfast was Visited by (Drew 10 Pecks Corn for to Grind) the following Persons (Nero is Sick) Mrs. Bay, Sarah Bay, Margaret Bay, Elizabeth & Sarah

Guignard Mrs. Guignard & Ben Ioor Visited me before Dinner; & after Dinner was Visited by Sarah, & Martha Bay & Guignards 2 Children, I rode out & Viewed our Garden & Houses around Mr. Taitum & Hanah Visited us.

Thursday, September 23. Cloudy & warm morning. Wind South West. Made Alterations in the Kitchen to Receive our Household furniture Expected by Pittiauger Boat next Sunday. Nero & his Son absent today. Visited us before Dinner Sarah Bay, Huggins's (Father & Son) Charles Mayrant, Ben Ioor, Gignards 2 daughters & Mrs. James Gignard. Received Last Night by Wades Waggon 20:2 Inch plank. The following Persons Visited us After Dinner— Martha & Margaret Bay, James Gignard, Mr. Willey, Opened two doors in Gable End up Stairs of our Kitchen, & Raised a House in the Garden. Saw Robert Waring. I rode out to my Garden & to Colledge & Supped with Mrs. Bay & her family, Saw there Miss Blackburns etc.

Friday, September 24. Clear Sun Shine Morning Wind at South West. Made a Small Lader & floored the Kitchen up Stairs, Garden House Continued & finished today. (Buddy Sick) Persons Visited us before Dinner as follows. (Paid James Gignard for Nero & Son framing our House balance $31). Mr. Hill (a Souldier) Sarah Bay, Doctor Hughs, Doctor Blythe, Ann Martha & Margaret Bay, Elzabeth & Sarah Gignard. Bought 10 pounds 5 dozen Nails of Habermont. Received by Guignards Waggon 2000 Shingles. I Supped with James Gignard & his family bought 2 Baskets 3/.

Saturday, September 25. Clear & Cool Morning Wind at South. Floored above the house & made Shelves in Rooms Persons Visited us before Dinner are Sarah Bay, & Margaret & Ann Bay. Raised floor of Garden House, with Ground & ditched around the said House. All Ready to receive my boat Negroes & Household Firniture. Gourdine Esquire & Judge Gaillard Called on me about Dark.

Reader—Thus far has P. Horry's Life been Continued & as he finds this mode of writing, diverts his mind & time Passes without Pain, & diverts him from himself, he thinks to Continue so doing till his Desolution, he has now Changed his Scines of Life; Left the Low Country, for Columbia; where no Relation of his own Resides. Time only will Shew if he has Changed for the better & if he will have any *Real friends* by Such a Change. Fortune have not hetherto favoured him tho' She Protected him in the Revolutionary War, She has Left him to fell much distress Since.

BOOK SEVEN

September 26, 1813–December 31, 1813

Peter Horrys Life, Continued from
27 Septembr 1813 to [illegible] January 1814.

*S*unday, **September 26.** A Cloudy, warm Morning Legislature Adjourned the Night before Last, & now very few (if any) Members remain here. I walked out before breakfast to Garden House & returned to my Quarters, wind at North. I rode to the State house & heard Service Performed by Mr. Lance. Saw thereat a Number of my Acquaintances, Ann, Sarah, Martha & Margaret Bay Visited us after Church. Mrs. Guignard Senior Called on us. I wrote a Letter to Thomas Blunt. I rode to Granby Landing & John Withers, Lieutenant Allston, Goddard & James Guignard & his Wife Called on us, also Huggins Father & Son.

Monday, September 27. Warm & Cloudy Weather, I Saw Mr. Willey. This morning he is to Get Bricks Stopped under both Chim'y hearth, & Laid them with Bricks. Began to Inclose for my Horses & Mules. The following Persons Visited us before Dinner, Sarah Bay, Ann, & Margaret Bay. Elizabeth & Sarah Guignard, Visited us this morning. Received a Letter from James Ward at George Town. Paid Mr. Burrows for 200 Bricks 7/. Borrowed 200 Bricks from Mr. Mulder of the College. Colonel Huggins, & John Withers took Leave of me (for a time) Mrs. Horry dined today with Mrs. Simon Taylor. I Received 50 Fethiridge Boards by Wades Waggon from his Mill.

Tuesday, September 28. I was Unwell Last Night, a Cloudy, Cold Morning Wind at North, it Drissles, began to Pail in the front Side of our House yard. No more bricks to Continue our Chimney. Was Visited by the following Persons before Dinner (Put 10 Posts on Desaussure Line) Sarah Bay, Thomas Simons, Margaret Bay wrote to the Reverend Mr. Halling at George Town. Doctor & Mrs. Blythe Visited us after Night also Mrs. Bay's Daughters, & Mr. Simons, Edwards James Gignard & [illegible]. My yard (Contracted) is Inclosed & Last night my Mules were Confined therein.

Wednesday, September 29. It rained Last Night. This Morning Cold & very Cloudy. Drew 9 Allowances Corn & Got it Ground at Tool Mill for

Two miniatures of Peter Horry donated to the
South Caroliniana Library by the Guignard family in 2001

Negroes here, Pailing Continued on South West Side of our House Lot The
following Visited us before Dinner Margaret Bay, Sarah Bay Elizabeth & Sarah
S. Guignard, & Mrs. Guignard, Gabriel Guignard I wrote to James Ward in
Answer to his Letter of the 10th Instant. Sent Mr. Halling & Wards Letters to
the Post Office. I Received a Letter from Mr. Blunt & another from James
Ward dated at Charles Ton. Visits received after dinner Viz. James S. Guignard, Mrs. Bays Daughters & a Number of young Gentlemen three of which
were Continental Officers. On account of a Naval Victory Obtained Over the
Enemy the Artillery of Columbia were fired as Rejoicing for the Same.

Thursday, September 30. Clear & Cold Morning, wind at North. Pailing
Continued, drove up the flooring of my Room. London Sick. Boat Daily
Expected, Visitors before Dinner are as follows—James Gignards 2 Daughters,
Martha Bay, & Sarah Bay, & Margaret Mrs. James Guignard. Bought Sundries
as by Expence book of this date, I rode out for Exercise Mr. Guignards Wag-
gon brought a Load of Shingles after Night.

Friday, October 1. I was very Ill Last Night & this Morning Mrs. Horry
& myself Kept our Beds till Late. Cool & Clear Weather, no wind. Miss Ann
& Sarah Bay & James Guignard Called on us. Drove up my Room floor &
Lined it with featheridge Pailing Continued on Yesterdays Line & to Desaus-
sures Fence. Margaret Bay Visited me this Morning. Paid for 5 Bushels Oats

at 1/9 & for Forty Six Bushels Corn a[t] 2/4. My boat is Arrived at Granby Received a Note from my Overseer Blunt & Sent him his Horse. Bought 75 fetheridge 1000 feet for $10. Mr. Taitum & Hannah Visited me this Morning.

Saturday, October 2. A fair warm morning. Wind at South, The Miss Bays Visited us, also Mr. James Gignards family. Fitted up Mrs. Horrys & my Chamber. Received 50 Fitheridge by Wades Waggon from his Mill. Received a Letter from Mrs. Helin. Sent Sundries to Mrs. Bay, Guignard & Habermont Houses. Mrs. Fuzle & Mrs. Simon Taylor & her Children Visited us in the Evening.

Sunday, October 3. Mr. Blunt Junior Lodged at our House, a fair Sun Shine Morning, Blunt Breakfasted with us. By him I wrote to Mr. Thomas R. Mitchell & Judge James, James Guignard 2 Sons Visited us this Morning also Elizabeth Guignard Visited us. I went to the Methodist Meeting & heard a Sermon from Reverend Mr. Green Gabriel Guignard Junior breakfasted with us. Paid Mr. Blunt Junior Ten Dollars, & Gave him Written directions as to the Roads & Stages he should Travel to George Town. Used my Sedan to Carry me to Meeting house & home again. After Dinner, Ann Martha & Margaret Bay Visited us. Colonel Huggins & John Withers Called on us as did James Guignard & his wife.

Monday, October 4. Fair Sun Shine Weather, wind North East. Sent James Guignard all my Old Iron. Brought from him all my Corn Got a Barrell Damaged Rice & put it in house Loft. Pailings Continued on upper Line & finished today & bigan pailings on Lower Line. Visited us before Dinner Viz. Ann, Martha & Margaret Bay & Mr. James Guignard & his Family, I Got 12 pounds 10 dozen Nails from Mr. Habermont. Today the Coledgions Conveine, or Meet Together at the Colledge to recommence their Respective Studies. Paid for Clock 7/. Received from Captain Taylor a Mill boards & Laths by James Gignards Waggon.

Tuesday, October 5. Cool & Cloudy Morning, wind at North West, Pailing on Last Line, Continued, Sent my Carriage for Bricks from Taylors Brick yard, Received 300 by my own Waggon. Clock has Stopped Going, Mr. James Guignard Visited us this Morning also the following Persons before Dinner to Say, Mr. Lightfoot of Virginia Mrs. Guignard & her Daughters, Miss Margaret Bay & her Mother Got 20 pounds 10 dozen Nails from Habermont, In the Evening the Miss Bays, Mr. Ford, Mr. Rees Junior and a Number of Colegian's Visited us.

Wednesday, October 6. Cool & Clear Sun Shine Morning, finished all our Inclosures. Sarah Bay Lodged at our House Last Night. We Shall now Consider her as one of our Family. Last Night Mr. Willie Visited me. Before Dinner the following Persons Visited us Viz. Mr. James S. Guignard Margaret Bay, & after Dinner Mrs. Bay, Martha. Bought & paid for 2 Spades of Mr. Purvis as by his receipt $2. Isaac went out to Get Posts & Rafters for a Shed to Shelter my Carriage. About 1100 Iron Sold Mr. James S. Guignard Came by boat from Dover. Received 500 Bricks from Taylors Yard in Davis Waggon ditto . . . 500 . . . ditto . . . ditto . . . ditto. Got of Habermont 1 plain Iron 3/1d Received by Guignard Waggon 450 Bricks from Colonel Taylors ditto . . . 460 . . . ditto.

Thursday, October 7. Cool & Clear Sun Shine Morning, Chimney Continued, Carpenters preparing to begin a Shed to the Kitchen. This morning James S. Gignard & his Son Saunders Visited us. Two Spade men Opening Drains out Side fences. Mr. Willey came to Lay bricks & I hope the Chimney will tonight admit of our making a fire therein. Miss Martha Davis, Miss Martha & Margaret Bay Visited me this forenoon. Received by James Guignard Waggon 450 Bricks from Colonel Taylors Brick yard. Mrs. Horry & S. Bay went to Mr. Ion funeral. Sot up Plate & Rafters. After Dinner the following Visited us to Say Margaret Bay. I wrote a Letter to Mrs. Elizabeth Ioor & Sent it by Isaac. After Night Miss Blackburn, & Miss Davis & Goodin Mr. McGill & Mr. Trazevant Visited me.

Friday, October 8. I was very Sick Last Night Clear Sun Shine Morning, wind at South, Isaac went off for the high [Hills] Santee [to] fetch winch Tirah, Chimney finished today also Shed finished. The following Persons Visited us before Dinner *to Say* Mrs. Bay & James S. Guignard (Paid Mr. Davis $4 ½ for Waggoning Bricks) also Visited us Elizabeth Guignard, Margaret Bay, & Martha her Sister had a fire made in Chimney it did not Smoke.

Saturday, October 9. I was truly Sick Last night, with Bowel Complaint Susie went this morning to Market, (8 ½ Beef) filled up all holes on the North Side of the Kitchen, fine weather, Every Morning Clear Sun Shine but Cool, fire in Chimney very Comfortable, boarded up the Street Side of the Shed. Paid Mr. Willey $20 for buil[d]ing a Chimney in Kitchen all bricks Carried under the New House to Under pin the Same. The following Persons Visited us before Dinner to Say Mr. Willie, Margaret Bay, James S. Guignard (who made us a Present of a Hog) Mr. Habermont, Mrs. Bay made us a Present of a young Sow Pigg. Also Mrs. James Guignard Visited us this Morning & also this Evening. I wrote to Doctor Green for Twelve Thousand Bricks to be delivered in my yard. Ann Bay Visited me [at] Sun Set, also Martha Bay, Mrs. Branthwait Mr. Trezevant Mr. Ford & Sanders Guenard.

Sunday, October 10. Again I was Sick Last Night & Got no Sleep, a Sun Shine Morning, Hogs turned out into the yard. Visited today by Ann & Margaret Bay also by Martha & Ann Bay & their Mother, Also James S. Guignard & Son Gabriel. I Received a Letter by Isaac & Tinah from Mrs. Elizabeth Ioor. I Kept to My bed all day, Rose 4 OClock P.M. & walked as far as my Kitchen, Mr. Ford & Simons Visited us.

Monday, October 11. Raw Weather & Cloudy, wind at West. Hogs Got out of yard & Gone, put Locks on Gates, Got from Habermont Shop 20 pounds 10 dozen Nails & 20 pounds 20 dozen Nails, Recovered our Hogs. Visited us Today Ann & Margaret Bay Mr. Willey, Also Martha Bay Susie & William Sick. Mrs. Bay Visited us. Received by Doctor Greens Waggon 600 Bricks, a Pellar of House began this Morning from Wades Mill Fetheredge Gave 14 pair Shoes to Negroes here, Fowl House Finished, 600 more Bricks from Doctor Green & 600 More. Visitors, Elizabeth & Sarah Guinard. Mrs. James Guinard Visited us. Finished 2 Brick Pillars under Dwelling. House Mrs. Brathwait Visited us after night.

Tuesday, October 12. Clear Sun Shine Morning, a Large White Frost had of James Guignard 2 Bushels Ric[e]. Brick Pillars Continued by Mr. Willie. Received Loads of Bricks by Doctor Greens Waggons as follows 600, 600, 600, 600. Visited Today by the following Persons to Say Margaret, Ann, & Martha Bay & Miss Blackburns drew 18 Allowances today, Rice out & ballances of Corn made the Said Allowances full, Sot up a Grinding Mill in Garden House for Corn. Windy Morning at South west. Begun a Stair Case to the Gable End of our Kitchen to go aloft, paid for 2 Chains for Gates. Paid for 14 pair Shoes for our Negroes.

Wednesday, October 13. Cloudy Morning, Wind at North West Received a Letter from Mr. John Palmer. Brick Pillars Continued. Visiters Today as follows Margaret & Mrs. Bay James S. Guignard & his 2 Daughters. Paid Mr. John Willey Twenty Dollars. Sent my Carriage & Rains etc. etc. to be Repaired, Mrs. Guignard Sent us 3 Muscovy Ducks, Boy William Sick, Mr. Jethro Raiford agreed with me to do my Carriage work well for forty five Dollars in about Ten days. Mercury Sick.

Thursday, October 14. Cool & Clear Morning wind at West Brick Pillars Continued, but no Bricks brought Yesterday Visiters are as follows (Troft done & Sot down near Kitchen) James S. Gignard (Stairs finished) Miss Lynch, Miss Bowman Sanders Guignard, Elizabeth Guignard & Mr. Taitum. Received 600 Bricks by Doctor Greens Waggon, 600, 600, 600. Mr. Goddard & Simons Visited me at Night.

Friday, October 15. Cloudy Morning Columns of Brick Continued. All blocks taken out from Under the New House, Sent out for Lightwood Posts Visiters today Mr. Willey, Margaret Bay, The two Mrs. Guignards, Martha Bay, Mr. Baxter of George Town Received from Greens Waggon 600, 600, 600, 600, Finished Pillars under the New House William was Bled, Wrote a Letter to Mr. Blunt Senior of George Town Respecting Mr. Carrs boat. Small Drissle Rain. Martha Bay & Martha Davis Visited us this Afternoon also Gabriel & Elizabeth Guinard, & Mrs. Davis, also Ann Bay.

Saturday, October 16. Warm & Cloudy Morning Settled my Room, No wind this morning, Prepaired Post for 4 Rooms under New House. Visiters today are as follows Ann, Margaret & Martha Bay, Mr. Trezevant & McGill Sot down Posts for two Rooms It Rained today.

Sunday, October 17. Warm & Windy Morning also Cloudy It Rained Last Night, Visiters today are as follows Margaret, Martha Bay. I went to James S. Guinard & Saw his Family. A Remarkable fine Evening, Young Bossard, Huggins & Goddard Visited us after Night.

Monday, October 18. A Clear Sun Shine Morning I Sent Greens Waggon to Hamptons Mill for a Load of Slabs, began to board up Rooms under our New House & finished digging the Same. Visiters Today are as follows—Ann, Margaret Mrs. Fisher, Mrs. James Guignard. Boy Sam is Sick, Received a Letter from Frances Mayrant. Fry, (my former Drumer) Called on me he is 60 years of Age & is blind, he was always an honest man & Lives now on Saludy about 10 Miles from here, he has a wife & 4 Children Paid Mr. Raiford $15th On Account. I wrote Mr. Palmer for my firniture at his house. Made to Mr. Stanly my Return of Males to work on Streets Say 3. Received a Load of Slabs 22 by Dr. Greens Waggon from Taylors Mill. Elizabeth & Sarah Guignard Visited us also. Received by Greens Waggon 30 Slabs from Hamptons Mill.

Tuesday, October 19. Warm Morning, no Wind. Two Waggons Gone for Slabs, Going on with Rooms under new House & removing Earth therefrom, Negroes Drew Corn Allowance. Sam Sick again today, & William is Sent to Doctor Fisher, Got beef from Market, Visiters Margaret, & Ann Bay & their Mother & Ann Bay, Guignards 2 daughters, Paid for Hinges & Staples 7/. Received by Greens Waggon from Taylors Mill 30 Slabs & 30 More ditto by Desausures ditto . . . ditto . . . 14 ditto. 13.

Wednesday, October 20. Cool & Clear Weather Wind at South West. Rooms under New House Continued & Ground Removed finished both Today & began Stairs up to New House. Visiters today are as follows Ann, Sarah, Martha & Margaret Bay, Paid Patton Junior & Company for Sundries $3.87. Paid Mr. Harisons Beef Bill 22/. Received by Desausures Waggon 13 Slabs. News is just Arrived *Glorious News,* Commodore Chancey defeated the Enemy on the Lakes & took 4 of their Armed Vessells & a Number of their men prisoners with Little Loss on our Side, The Artill[ery] fired many field Pieces & at Night this City was Illuminated.

Thursday, October 21. A Cold frosty Morning Last Night, field Pieces was fired till 10 OClock, Drums beat & Military Music Sounded, with Loud huzzas etc. Many Citizens Complimented me by Calling at our House & Gave me joy on our Late Victory, Emblimatic works was beautifully displayed, with Names of our Naval Heroes, my old friend Colonel Taylor also came & Gave me Great Joy. I wish we had many as Good Patriots as he. Britons would

Soon be brought to Reason & Peace Restored to this our Country of Freedoms. Visiters today are as follows—Sarah Bay Miss Hughs & Elizabeth & Sarah Guignard & Martha & Margaret Bay. Wrote to my Overseer & to Windham Trapier. Bought Loaf Sugar 2/11 dozen Locks & Keys to two Doors under Cellars Number 1 & 2.

Friday, October 22. Cold Raw & Cloudy Weather. Wind at North West. Began to fence on Desausures Line. Visiters today are as follows. Mrs. Horry dined today with Mrs. James Guignard, at Night Inglisby, Bossard & McGill called on me & Miss Hughs Lodged at our House.

Saturday, October 23. Warm & very Cloudy, no wind, finished Fence on Desausure Line, & floured new House first Story, Visiters as follows, James S. Guignard, Sarah Bay, & Sarah Guignard, Martha Bay, & Elizabeth Guignard. Paid for 2 hand Saw files 1/2. Made 2 Little Houses in home Lott. Sent William again to Doctor Fisher, who has Ordered a Blister on his head Mr. & Mrs. Simon Taylor & a Daughter of hers Also Visited us, in the Afternoon also Doctor Hughs Visited us & Mrs. Guignard & Willey Received at Sun Set my Carriage from Mr. Rayford.

Sunday, October 24. Warm & Smokey Morning. No Wind I rode out before Breakfast. Mercury Sick. Mrs. Horry went to Methodist Meeting, Mr. Dalton (a Coledgion) Buried. Visiters today as follows—Ann Bay, Mr. Bossard, McCord, Huggins, Inglisby Mrs. Robert Waring, Mrs. Davis.

Monday, October 25. Rain Last Night & this Morning, 'tis Cloudy & warm, Sent Scipio & Zemo to Work on the Streets in Columbia, & Susie to Market, wind at South. Sent Waggon for Wood, finished 2 Little Houses in yard & a Cow House therein. Sent Grigs with 2 hands to Get a Cill & Plate Removed Sundries out of Loft into our Room Number 1. Visiters today are Sarah Bay, Mrs. Guignard Junior & her two Daughters & Andrew Burnet Margaret Bay & two Sisters. Corn removed to Store Number 1. Say a Barrel Corn. I wrote to North & Webb of Charles Ton. Harrisons Cannon fires here, the News is that General Harrison has taken Upper Cannady. I Gave James S. Guignard my Noted 26 October 1813 for amount of his Account delivered me Say $176.77 payable 1st January next.

Tuesday, October 26. Cloudy morning fog & wind at South made Shelves in outer Rooms. Paid James S. Guignard forty five Dollars to Pay Mr. Rayford for new harnesses to my Carriage. Floored over two Store Houses under New House, Put Shelves in the said Rums. Served out Negroes Allowances, Saw Mr. Willey about Getting me more bricks. Found a Letter of Judge Waties & Inclosed it to him & Sent per Post. Visiters today are as follows Sarah Margaret & Martha Bays J. Gugnards 2 Daughters (Getting a Cill & plates in the woods) Mr. Habermont, Doctor Fisher, began Window Frames, & plaining Fether Edge boards.

Wednesday, October 27. It Rained Last Night & this Morning. A Plate Left in Woods. Window frames Continued, & fether Edging new House began. Visiters Today are as follows—Sarah Bay & Mr. & Mrs. Habermont. Wind fresh at South, Rode to woods Saw Cill & plate. Neither could my Carriage bring.

Thursday, October 28. Cool & Clear Morning wind at South West. Brought in a Plate & half a Cill, Saw Willey & James Guignard. Fither Edge North East Gable End of New House Continued, Rode out with Mrs. Horry. Visiters today are as follows, Mr. Trezevant, Miss Hughs Mrs. Guignard Saw Mrs. Bays family & Mrs. Guignard Junior & her daughters, & Mr. Habermont, Got of him 20 pounds 10 dozen Nails.

Friday, October 29. Sun Shine, & warm Morning wind South West, Fetheridge Continued. Fell a Pine Tree near Habermont, Visiters today are James S. Guignard, Sarah Bay, Mr. Taitum, Miss Millin, & Gabriel Guignard, Sent to Market & Got Beef & a Shank. Finished boarding North side of New House. Sent Mrs. Horrys Chair to be fitted up. Zemo is Runaway & I have wrote to Mr. Blunt Senior at George Town to have him apprehended. Put Lock on My back Room Door & Front Room Door.

Saturday, October 30. Cold & Clear Morning. I Wrote to Mrs. E. Ioor & Sent it by Ned to her at her plantation on black River. Began to board up the East Side of New House. Visiters today are Sarah & Martha Bay, Colonel Hutchison & Elizabeth & Mary Guignard Received a Letter from Mr. Blunt & another from Ben Trapier Brought a Waggon Load of Wood. Wind at West, at Night James S. Guignard Visited us.

Sunday, October 31. A Frosty Sun Shine Morning. Sent Mrs. Horrys Horse & Mule to Mr. James Guignards Cornfield & 6 Negroes, to his Plantation to Pick Pease I wrote a Letter to Ben Trapier in Answer to one of his received, I found it too Cold to go to Church, I kept 5 Negroes in Lot as Carpenters. Tinah is Sick today & Took Physick. Mrs. Horry went to *her* Church. Mrs. Ioors Letter went this Morning by Ben Ioors Servant Ned. 'Tis very Cold Indeed. Visiters today are as follows Mr. & Mrs. James S. Guignard & Nancy their Daughter. I wrote to Mr. Samuel Prioleau Junior of Charles Ton, Near Night, Ann, & Martha Bay Visited us also at Night Major Clifton & Mr. Welch with 2 Ladies also Mr. Bossard, Johnson, McGill & Goddard.

Monday, November 1. Much Ice Last Night, Clear Sun Shine Morning, Sent our Horse & Mules to Guignards Cornfield. Chair Wheel brought home. Visiters today are Sarah, & Margaret Bay, Caroline Guignard I wrote to my Overseer by Charles Huggins. Fether Edge broading Side New House to 2nd Story. William appears better today. Tinah is yet Poorly, Visited Us after Dark James S. Guinard & his wife & Daughters.

Tuesday, November 2. Clear Frosty Morning. We rode out to Whilst & Company & bought Negro Cloths Blankets & Coffee Mended Mrs. Horry Chair & Harnesses. Visiters Today are Sarah Bay & her Sisters, James Guignard & his family and Charles Huggins. Served Blankets & N. Cloth to Negros.

Wednesday, November 3. Cold & Clear Morning, Mr. Willey Visited us, also today (Wrote to John N. Taylor), for Mr. Willey. We are Invited to attend the Funeral of Mrs. Ben Waring Junior this afternoon at 3 OClock. Bought a Gallon Whisky 3/6 Gave Mrs. Horry $4 ¾. Sarah Bay, Martha & Margaret, & Gabriel & Sanders Guignard Visited us today.

Thursday, November 4. Fair Morning wind at North East. Mr. Goddard & Sarah Bay Breakfasted with us. Martha & Margaret Bay Visited us Immediately after Breakfast, Mrs. Horry in her Chair Sot out for George Town about 10 OClock A.M. Sent to James Guignards Plantation for my Negroes, wheat & Pease. Paid for Bread 4/8. Mr. Bossard Lodged at our house, & Mr. James Guignard Visited me after Night.

Friday, November 5. Clear Morning. Received Pease Last Night & this Morning Served out five half Allowances. Sarah & Margaret Bay Breakfasted With me. Carpenters began to board up South End of New House. Sent for Remainder of Pease from Guignard Plantation. Got Some Pumkins 23 from Said Plantation. Visiters are James S. Guignard, the Miss Bays & Lieutenant Spark. Ovan for first time Baked Potatoes. Wrote Captain Wade for Lumber, Sent a Note to Mr. Willey. Got a Peck Wheat from James S. Guignard plantation & planted it in our Garden.

Saturday, November 6. Clear Morning & a White Frost. Carried Bricks to House in Garden & to Kitchen to Make Chamneys. Visiters today are James S. Guignard, Sarah & Margaret Bay. Planted Wheat in our Garden. Drumer fry Called on me. I Gave him a Dollar for Apples he brought me. I wrote Mrs. Horry at George Town. I Received a Letter from Joseph Manigault. At Night William Bay & Tom Simons Visited me.

Sunday, November 7. Sick Last Night. Clear & Warm Weather, could not go to Church, Sarah Bay & Gabriel & Sanders Guignard Visited me (Sent Mrs. Horrys Letter by Post) also the following Mr. McGill, Mr. Bossard Rutledge, & Goddard, & Ann & Martha Bay & Martha Davis. Bossard & Inglisby Lodged in Mrs. Horry Room.

Monday, November 8. Hazy Morning & warm. No wind boarding up New House Continued & fixing blocks Cills & plates to New House. Visiters today are as follows Got in 4 Cills (Short ones) Zemo returned Yesterday absent 10 days. Visiters Sarah & Margaret Bay, Mr. Trezevant, Mr. McGill, Broughton, & Bossard. I rode out & Called at Guignards Office, at Messrs.

Whitz & Company in front Street, on Harris (a black Smith) in front Street & borrowed a Broad Axe of him, Saw James S. Guignard Near Corn field, Called on Mrs. Bay, Saw my Garden. Got 20 pounds 20 dozen Nails from Herbemont Shop.* Borrowed a XCut Saw from Mr. Douglass to Saw a Tree Cut down near Judge Desausures House. From it I Got 3 Short Cills for New House. Finished Carrying Bricks to Garden House Visited further by Miss Blackburn Dinkins, & Mr. Scott, Mr. James Guignard & his Sons.

Tuesday, November 9. Fair Morning wind at North West. Last night received by wades Waggon 5 1 ½ boards, 9 Ruffage ditto, 1 dozen Fether Edge. Sent 2 hands to Hamptons Mill for Slabs. Also Guignards Waggon went for Slabs Received from Market 9 Beef Built a Chimney to Kitchens, Continued boarding up new House, Served out full Allowances to Negroes of Corn. Mr. Willie Visited me also. Sarah & Margaret Bay & their Sister Ann. Received 18 pounds 10 dozen Nails from Habermont Shop, Mr. Lance came to me Received from Hamptons Mill by J. Guignards Waggon 22 & 28 Slabs.

Wednesday, November 10. Warm & Cloudy received from Muldroes Kiln 500 Bricks 500, 500 Got 2 pair door Hinges from James S. Guignard at [text missing] pair finished Slabing Cow House, [text missing] 10 feet Large posts into 4 Small Studs [text missing] today are Mr. Willy, James S. Guignard, Sarah Margaret, Ann & Martha Bay.

Thursday, November 11. Weather as Yesterday, began Chimney in Garden House, Visiters. Received Bricks from Muldro this day 300 & 550, 550 & 400 I rode with James S. Guignard to his Plantation, around it, I rode up John Taylors Junior house on a high Emenence & about 12 OClock Mid Day Got home to my house, Removed Corn & Oats from Loft to Store under New House & otherwise Settled said Store, Visiters—The Miss Bays, Colegians Mr. Rutledge, Bossard, McGill, Simons, Broughton, McCord, etc. etc. My Room filled with them. Received 3000 Shingles James Guignard.

Friday, November 12. Cold & Clear, wind at West [text missing] Garden Chimney finished [text missing] Continue; to fether Edge Last Side of New House [text missing] Got Beef from Market Say 7 ½ pounds [text missing] breakfasted with me. I Received 300 Bricks from Muldro, by Waggon & 400, & 400. Got of Habermont 10 pounds 10 dozen Nails, Visiters Mr. Laurens Junior Gabriel Guignard Junior. Received 25 Ruffage boards 20 feet long from

---

*In 1813 the vintner Nicholas Habermont opened a cut nail factory in Columbia meant to complement Guignard's brick manufactory. His cut nail shop played an important role in the building boom that developed the city. The store continued in operation for at least three years but probably closed soon after transatlantic trade revived following the War of 1812. Herbemont, *Pioneering American Wine*, 9.

Wade Mill Messrs. Bossard, Simons, Inglisby, Johnson & McGill Visited me after night.

Saturday, November 13. Clear & very Cold wind [text missing] North, I was very Sick Last Night, & Susie is Sick [text missing] Morning finished boarding new House. Sent [text missing] for wood by my Waggon. Visiters, Sarah, Margaret. Fortunately my Kitchen & Garden House, both have [text missing] Chimneys, which will be very Comfortable to my [text missing] Received from Muldro, 400 Bricks & 500. Cleaning Garden & Cleaning Squares therein.

Sunday, November 14. Cold & Cloudy, wind at North East. Mr. Bossard Junior Lodged here Last night. Sarah & Margaret Bay Breakfasted with me I rode out to the woods but was not well Enough to go to Church. I dined with Mrs. Bay & her Family Mr. James Guignard & Mrs. Guignard Visited me also Martha Bay Bossard, Smith, Cudworth, & Inglisby.

Monday, November 15. Clear & Cold wind at North West [text missing] 3 hands Sawing ruffage boards for Lathing New House the rest Gone to the woods to Get poles for Shingle [text missing] Scaffold Sarah & Margaret Bay breakfasted with [text missing] Bossard & Inglisby Slept in Mrs. Horrys Room Last Night. Visiters are Ann & Martha Bay. Billy in Waggon went for wood. Brought [text missing] 18 Long Poles today, Susie is better this morning [text missing] Visiters after Night Mr. Simons, Johnson, Goddard [text missing] Rutledge, McGill & Inglisby & Rees Junior [text missing].

Tuesday, November 16. Cold & Cloudy, drew Allowances. Got Beef from Market, Sawing for laths & putting up Scaffold for Shingling. Got Oak Wood. Got [illegible] 9 dozen Shingling Nails from Habermont. Received Last Eveing from James Guignard by his Waggon 2500 Shingles Received this Morning from Muldro 500 Bricks [text missing] 500 ditto, ditto, ditto. Susie took Physick I Received 3 Letters Say one from Windham Trapier, one from North & Webb [text missing] one from Thomas Blunt Junior. After night Gabriel Sanders Guignard Visited me.

Wednesday, November 17. A Rainy Morning, no Wind. Received & Flatted Poles for Rafters. Sent out to [text missing] Poles more, Cleaned the yard. Yesterday Planted 2 Rows English Pease in our Garden. Grigs is Sick, & took Physick. Susie is better Visiters are James Guignard after Night. Wrote to North & Webb for Paints, Oil & Glass as per Memorandum Book. Paid for 30 Fowls 25/, wrote to Windham Trapier & to Mrs. Horry at George Town. It Rained all Day.

Thursday, November 18. Cloudy, Raw & Cold Weather Sarah & Margaret Bay, Breakfasted with me. Lathing New House, Sent out for Wood. Got 10 pounds 10 dozen Nails from Habermont. Susie no better. William Recovering Fast. At 2 OClock P.M. finished Lathing House (a fine Dinner) Mrs. Bay & Mrs. Guignard both Sent me a plate full & the Latter Sent her two Daughters to See me. 500 Bricks from Muldro. At Night Mr. James S. Guignard, Rutledge & Goddard Visited me.

Friday, November 19. Fine Clear Morrining [text missing] began to Shingle New House, Susie yet Sick. Visiters Sarah Bay & her Sister Margaret. William is nearly well. Received 20 pounds 10 dozen Nails of Habermont Shop. Hoed in Garden Received 2 hatchetts from Mr. Prescot & Company Price $3. Received 500 Bricks from Muldro. Elizabeth & Mary Guignard Visited me this morning & their Brother this After noon. House but half faced above Second Story. After Night Mr. Bossard Visited me.

Saturday, November 20. Cold frosty Morning, Sun Shine, Shingling Goes on. Mr. James S. Guignard Sarah & Margaret Bay Visited me, also the following persons—Elizabeth Guignard Mr. Savage Smith Junior [text missing] is much better & walks about & to the Garden [text missing] Bossard, & Mr. Inglisby. [text missing] by 3 Waggons from Muldro's 1500 Bricks [text missing] by 2 ditto . . . ditto . . . 1000 ditto [text missing] Went out in my Waggon for a Load of wood [text missing] Giugnard Gave me 9 Quarts of Rice. Also [text missing] Bricks more of Mr. Muldro & 1000 more after Night. Mr. Rutledge after Night Visited me.

Sunday, November 21. I was very Sick Last night. A Cloudy Morning, Sarah & Margaret Bay Breakfasted here. I could not go to Church. I wrote to Cleland Kinloch to Get me made, a Rolling Chair & I put the Letter in the hands of his Son, who Goes to George Town. Mr. Willie Visited me also Mr. Rutledge, I dined with James Guignard and & his Family & at Night Messrs. Bossard & McGill Called on me.

Monday, November 22. Warm & Cloudy, Sarah & Margaret Bay Breakfasted with me, Pomro is Sick, Shingling Continued & jointing Shingles & boards, The Legislature Meets here today, Thomas R. Mitchell a [text missing] is arrived here. Major Clifton & Mr. [text missing] Called on me. Mrs. Horry with Colonel [text missing] Expected here today, as by Report of Sarah Bay to me. I gave a Certificate to William Smart for his Father who was a Militia Man in General Marions Brigade at George Town in the Revolutionary War. Received a Long Sill & plate from Mr. James Guignard by his Waggon.

Tuesday, November 23. Warm & Cloudy, Continue Shingling began to plane poles for Rafters, Sarah & Margaret Bay breakfasted with me, Served Negroes Allowances Yesterday both Houses (Senate & Representatives) made a Coram to do business, the Governour is arrived. Goddard, McGill, Lance & Eveleigh, Called on me I received a Letter from W. W. Trapier. I Received a Long Cill by James Guignard Waggon. I Received a Letter from Justice Skrine.

Wednesday, November 24. This morning the Weather as Yesterday, Yet Shingling & hoeing etc. in the Garden. Got 60 pounds 5 dozen Nails of Habermont Visiters are James S. Guignards Daughters & Sons & the Miss Bays.

Thursday, November 25. Warm disagreeable Weather, Cloudy & high Wind, workmen as Yesterday. James Guignard, Mr. Muldro (with his Account) & the Miss Bays Called on me this morning about 12 OClock till 2 it Rained, so much, work Lost however by Night the Shingling was finished. After night Colonel Huggins & Doctor Blythe Called on me.

Friday, November 26. Cold & Clear Day. Sarah & Margaret Bay Breakfasted with me. James S. Guignard Called on me before breakfast. Mr. Willie began a Chimney to our New House. Piling up Shingles that are Left Removing Bricks, Making Mortar & tending on brick Layers etc. etc. Visiters today Elizabeth & Sarah Guignard, Miss Bays, Bossard & Inglisby, Mr. James Guignard & his Wife & Mr. Hebermont.

Saturday, November 27. Cloudy & Cold, Carpenters Making doors, Chimneys Goes on. Visiters the Miss Bays, Doctor Blythe & Judge Grimkie. About Mid Day Sun came out & a fine Moderate day. Further Visiters are the 2 Miss Guignard.

Sunday, November 28. Last night Mrs. Horry arrived with Lydia. This morning Cloudy & it Rains, Visiters Sarah & Margaret Bay, James Guignard & Caroline & Sanders & Gabriel Guignard. I cannot go to Church today, I Received a Letter from James Whithurst & John Davis both of George Town, which I Answered also Dr. Blythe, Mrs. Guignard Senior & Elizabeth & Sarah Guignard Visited us this Morning. Answe[re]d Justice Skrine Letter & wrote to W. W. Trapier my Attorney at George Town & to my Overseer. Judge Waties Called on me, also Young Frazer & Bay. A Most disagreeable day. After dinner the following Visited us, Miss Bays, Mr. Trezevant, Ben Huger Rutledge, & a Number more Gentlemen.

Monday, November 29. Monday Morning. Cold & Clear, Sent off for Dover Matthias & Pomroe with Several Letters. House Chimney Continued by Mr. Willie, Sent Waggon for Wood [text missing] Carpenters making doors & Scaffold to Go into the Passage way. Visiters today are Ann & Sarah Bay. Gave 7 plane to Buddy which Came from Dover. Further Visiters Mrs. James Guignard & her Daughters & Sanders Guignard & Colonel Huggins.

Tuesday, November 30. Cold Frosty Morning, wind at North, Chimney Goes on by Mr. Willy, Served out 17 Allowances to Negroes. Received from James S. Guignard $10. Paid to Antonio $6.75 Cents for 9 pair But Hinges, per Receipt S. Henderson. Visiters Sarah Bay (paid for Screws 8/9) James Guignard at Night Visited by Miss Bays & James Guignards Family & Mr. Trezevant & McGill.

Wednesday, December 1. Cold & Clear, Mr. Fry, my Continental Drimmer & his Son Yesterday Visited us, I Gave him   Dollars & Recommended him to the Governour & Legislature for Charity, he & Son Lodged here Last Night. Visiters are James Guignard, Mr. Willie, Doctor Blythe & Sarah Bay.

Glazed 4 pair Window Sashes which is a Room & began framing Shed
Rooms. Received a Load of wood by our Waggon. Baked a Basket Potatoes,
Mr. Fry received about $Ten Dollars from the Governour & other Gentlemen
& was Assured he would be put on the List of Pentioners which is a Certain
Annuity during Life. I am happy in having it in my Power to render Service
to this Poor man & his Family.

Thursday, December 2. Cold & Clear Morning Mr. Fry took Leave of me
this morning for his home, I Received Last Night a Load of Ruffage boards by
Wades Waggon from his Mill Say 20 boards 18 feet Long. I was verry Sick Last
Night with my Old Complaint. Removed Sundries to East side of Store
Room, Judge Drayton & Doctor Blythe Called on me. Chimney Continued
& framing Shed Rooms, Paid Postage 2/4. Visitors today are Sarah, Martha
& Margaret Bay & Goddard Received Yesterday a Letter from Samuel Prioleau & one from my Overseer. Wrote a Letter to Elias Horry. Visited my Gar-
dens & Store Room. Mrs. Horry dined today with Mrs. Waring, Received by
J. Gignards 2 Waggons from Wades brick yard 5000 bricks which appears to
be Good.

Friday, December 3. Clear & Cold, Mr. Willy Chimney Goes on & framing of Shed Rooms. Received by James Guignards Waggon from Wades brick
yard 450 Bricks. Doctor Blythe Visited us before Breakfast & others after as
follows Sarah Bay. I wrote to my Factors & to Mrs. Fields, Received 2 Waggons more Guignards with 400 & 450 Bricks from Wade made a fire Screene
450 & 450 Bricks Received from Wades Mill 23 ruffage boards.

Saturday, December 4. Cold & Cloudy, Colonel Huggins breakfasted
with us. Saw Young Frazer. Sent off Grigs & Mercury to Dover 10 3/4 bought
Bushels Corn at 2/4 dozen, 20 Bushels Oats at 1/9 which James Guignard paid
for amounting to $12.89 Cents. Agreed with Huggins to Manage Dover for
10 per Cents, & [illegible] pay an Overseer $128 per year, Dover to Maintain
his horse & himself in Bread Kind Such as Straw & Rice flour for his
Horse. Received by Dr. Greens 2 Waggons 900 Bricks from Wade Sent for
Wood, by my Carriage. Began 2nd House Chimney & Glazed a Room in
New House. The 2 fellows Sot off after 12 OClock Mid Day for Dover Plantation By Dr. Gree[n]s Waggons (2). 800 Bricks Wades Yard ditto . . . ditto.
Ditto 800 . . . ditto. Sarah Bay Sot our Clock & Dined with us bought 10 ½
pounds Bacon for $2. In the Afternoon Reverend Mr. Sebeck & Lance drank
Tea with us.

Sunday, December 5. Cold, Cloudy & it Rains, I could not go to Church,
but Mrs. Horry went, Mr. Sebeck Preached at the State house. Doctor Blythe
Called on us before Breakfast. Other Visiters today are Mr. Sebeck, Major
Campbell, Colonel Huggins & his Son, James Guignard & his Sons & young
Mayrant (Son of William).

Monday, December 6. Rain, warm & Cloudy. Sent a Horse & Mule by Scipio to James Guignards Plantation Brick work & Carpenters work Goes on. I went on a Review & their was about 1200 Men under Arms, I Saw on Parade Colonel Huggins, his Son, the young man Bays, Governor Charles Pinckney Mr. Daniel, McGill, Rutledge, Johnston, & Goddard & many others, returned & Dined with Mrs. Horry about 3 OClock Past Maredian. Wrote a Letter to Miss Eliza Smythe of Charles Ton & Sent it by her man Anthony Saw also the Miss Bays & James S. Guignard, Cheesborow drank Coffee with us.

Tuesday, December 7. Cloudy Rainey Morning, Sent Carriage for wood. Wind South West. I wrote a Letter to my Overseer & another Letter to my Factors Charles Ton This morning the following Persons Visited us Placedia Mayrant & one of her Brothers. Mr. Willy brick Layers Goes on & my Carpenters with flooring South West Room. Paid for 15 Fowls $1 3/4. Sarah & Margaret Bay Visited us. Served out to Negroes a Weeks Allowance. Paid Mr. Rees for Mending my Carriage 150 Cents. At Night James S. Guignard Called on me.

Wednesday, December 8. This Morning as Yesterday Morning & work as Yesterday Glazed Windows & Door frames. Visiters today are Doctor Blythe, Mayrant, Willy, Sarah & Margaret Bay, Mr. Solica, Habermont, Trizevant, & Player Mary Fields is Come to Live with us. Paid Willie for 3 bars Iron for Brick Chimney $2. Shackelford & Withers came after night also Frazer & Masters Guignards.

Thursday, December 9. Cool & Clear Morning Sent a Letter to North & Web by Post. House Chimney Continued & began to put up Shed Rooms. Visiters today are Sarah Bay, Mr. Cheesborow (who received my Letter to my Overseer) Mr. Sebeck, Mr. Willey, Miss Bays. Received by Dr. Greens 2 Waggons Scantling & Inch & fetheridge Boards. After night Came Mr. Johnson, McGill Goddard, John Huger & Rutledge.

Friday, December 10. Cold & Cloudy wind at West. Chimney Goes on. Raised Shed Rooms, & began Sawing Ruffage boards for Laths. Visiters today are Mr. Willey, E. & M. Guignard (at Night) Mr. Cheesborow & Mr. Trezevant.

Saturday, December 11. Cloudy, Raw Morning, Chimney Goes on; Rafters to Shed Rooms began to be Put on. Visiters, Mr. Willey, Mrs. John Mayrant Miss Davis & Miss Bays, Leonory Mayrant, Mr. Brown Rote to Thomas Hall of Charles Ton & Sent it by Mr. Trezvant Cut   panes of Glass to 8 by 10. Paid them after night Mr. James S. Guignard, Trezevant, Johnson, Gibbs Goddard, McGill, etc. Visited me.

Sunday, December 12. Cloudy & Rainey so I could not go to Church & hear the Bishop Of the Episcoparians. Visiters today are as follows—Miss Mayrant, Davis, Martha & Margaret Bay, & Simons & Inglisby.

Monday, December 13. Cold & Clear, brick work Goes on Carpenters fin[ish]ing Rafters over Shed Room, Visiters today are Doctor Blythe, Miss Bays, to Say Sarah Bay, Mrs. Guignard & her Daughters Miss Hughs, Received from James Guignard Pains Glass 15 & 65 Say 80 a[t] 10 ½ Received by Dr. Greens Waggon from Mulder Bricks 400, & 500, 500. Mr. John Mayrant Visited us, also, Mr. Rutledge, Goddard, Inglisby & McGill.

Tuesday, December 14. Cold, & Clear frosty weather, Served out a Weeks Allowance wrote Captain Wade for Boards. Carpenters & Blick Layers at Work Solely to Get a Room, ready by this day Week. I rode out. Visiters today are Sarah Bay. Received by Doctor Greens Waggon 550 Bricks from Mulder & 550, in my Ride I Saw General Jacob Reid, General Fishburn, James S. Guignard Edward Croft, Doctor Green & others my Aquaintances, I brought home Some wood, Received of Habermont 14 pounds 5 dozen Nails. Miss Waring Visited us also Doctor Welch & his two Daughters at Night Mr. Simons & Trezvant, Received by Greens waggon from Mulders Yard 500 Bricks.

Wednesday, December 15. Cold & Cloudy Workers Employed as Yesterday. Received Bricks as follows by Dr. Greens Waggon 500, 500, Visiters today are Mr. Willie, Sarah & Margaret Bay James Guignard. James Guignard Lint me Ten Dollars & $25. Gave my Note for $125.58 with Interest. At Night Mr. Goddard & McGill.

Thursday, December 16. Rain & very Cloudy Sent Billy with Waggon in Search of Corn, Also Sent for wood. Work as Yesterday, Visiters are Sarah Bay & James Guignard Paid for 8 Yards Homespun & 4 Bushels Corn $5.

Friday, December 17. Cloudy & Warm with Small Rain wind Southwest. I was Very Sick Last night, Carpenters Setting up Rafters over Shed Rooms & boarding up outside & above Rafters, & Getting Laths. Visters are Sanders Guignard, Mrs. James, Fry & his Son. These 2 Last Lodged at our House Last night.

Saturday, December 18. Cold & Clear Chimney finished & Carpenters Lathing the Shed Rooms. Visiters today Are Sarah & Margaret Bay & Elizabeth & Sarah Guignard. A Bitch pupt Last Night & a Sow also Pigged. Glaze Sashes Continued Mr. Willy came & hearth was Laid after Night Bremar, Colonel Huggins Doctor Blythe & many others Called on us. The Legislature broke up this Night.

Sunday, December 19. Cold but Sun Shine Morning, Sick Last night, no Church for me today, President Savage Smith, Colonel Huggins & Doctor Blythe Sot out this morning for George Town. Many other Members also Sot out for their homes. Our Calf died Last night. Visiters today are Sarah Bay Bossard, Rutledge & Bossard. I wrote to my Overseer & to Windham Trapier Last Night Received from Wades Mill 53 flooring Boards by a Waggon. I Rode out to Captain Wades House & about Round my Garden, after dining with James Guignard & his Family. A very dark & Gloomy Afternoon.

Monday, December 20. Warm & Rainey Morning, burying all the Grass in our Garden. Putting in Glasses & flooring New House. Visiters are Mr. Willey. Moory Fields went home to Spend the Christmas Holy days.

Tuesday, December 21. A fine Sun Shine Morning. I yesterday Received by Post a Letter from Cleland Kinloch, Blunt Senior & North & Web. Removed Cills. Billy & Carlos Sot off for Winyaw about 10 in the Morning. I rode with Martha Bay to Granby & to Pinckneys plantation. Saw two Large boats Coming up & I Suppose one, has my Goods on board, tomorrow I mean to Send to Granby for them. I Got home to dinner, Roads very Wet even by the way of General Hamptons, I resolved never to Go again the River way. Visiters Sarah Bay, Ann Bay & Margaret Bay.

Wednesday, December 22. Sun Shine but very Cold, Sent my Waggon to Granby for Paint Glass & Oil. Glazing Continued. Visiters today are Sarah & Margaret Bay, Mr. McIver & Gabriel Guignard.

Thursday, December 23. Cloudy Morning Buddy, Cuggo & Isaac Sot out for Dover Plantation. Got a Hog from James Guignard Cost $8.76 Cents which 146 had of Mr. Harrison 1 Quarter Beef, a Tongue & a Tripe. Visiters today Mr. Harrison, Mr. James Guignard Sarah Bay & Mrs. J. Guignard & her Daughters. Received from J. Guignard by his Waggon 3,000 Shingles Visiters at Night Mr. Goddard, McGill, & McIver.

Friday, December 24. Warm & Cloudy Morning wind South West. Paid for 25 ¼ Bushels Corn at 2/8 is $14.25 Cents. Visiters today are Sarah, Ann Martha & Margaret Bay, Taylor & Amus a Tripe of Harrison. William Bay came to me, Got a Turn of Wood Prepared for Tomorrow.

Saturday, December 25. Christmas day, Warm & Rain Morning, Guignard Junior & Sons with Miss Bays & Several Colegians drank Egg Nog with us & 3 Miss Bays & Miss Emmer Taylor Breakfasted with us. Visiters are as follows (a Drunken Party with a Drummer, Entered our House & Complemented us with Martial Musick, Hazzas etc. etc.) At Dinner 5 Ladies & 10 Young men Dined with us. Toasts were Given & after Sun Set Pawn plays Ended Christmas when all Retired to their Respective homes.

Sunday, December 26. Cold but fair Sun Shine, Yesterday I received a Letter from Daniel G. Williams (my former Overseer) I went to Church & heard Mr. Lance, & took Dinner with Mrs. Bay & her Family Present Also Mr. Lance, Williams & Porcher & at 3 OClock P.M. returned to my House Mrs. Horry went to the Methodist Church both Morning & Evening.

Monday, December 27. A very Rainey day, wind at South, I wrote a Letter to Mr. Williams & to Mrs. Cheesborow at George Town. Visiters today are Sarah & Margaret Bay, Gabriel & Sanders Guignard.

Tuesday, December 28. Warm & Cloudy wind at West, Sarah Bay Served out Allowances to Negroes. Yesterday Planted Pease in Garden. Sent Carriage for wood. Visiters today are Mrs. Davis & Miss Bays, & James Guignard Family I rode out to Wicht & Company & bought Sundries as per Bill Parcells. In the Afternoon was Visited by Parson Green & his Wife & Parson Rasberry.

Wednesday, December 29. Warm & Clear, wind at South, Sent for wood & for my Goods at Columbia by Greens waggon. Lent him my Carriage Visiters Sarah, Ann & Margaret Bay. Received my Goods Right.

Thursday, December 30. Fine Sun Shine Morning, wind at North West. Sent Waggon to Mr. Mulders plantation for Trees to Plant in our Garden. Got 21 Trees & Sot them out around Garden, the Inner Side of the bank. Puppies & Piggs Grows finely. Visiters today are as follows Mr. Willie, Mr. J. Guignards family, Mr. Goddard & Mr. Bossard & Sarah & Margaret Bay.

Friday, December 31. Sun Shine Morning & a white Frost & very Cold. I sot out the above Trees in my Garden. Mrs. Guignard Gave us 3 Muscovy Ducks. Drew an Order on James S. Guignard in favour of B. Harrison for Amount of his Beef Bill to this Day Twelve Dollars. Visiters Sarah Bay &c.

BOOK EIGHT

March 13, 1814–July 11, 1814

Peter Horry's Life from
13th March 1814 to 16th March 1814
Included & to the 8th of July 1814.

*H*istory or Daily Journal of the Life of the Late Brigadier General
Peter Horry.

Commencing with his 72 year, being this 13 day of March 1814.

Sunday, March 13. Fine Spring Weather warm Sun. Ann Chivers break-fasted with us, I rode out & went to the Chapple* & heard the Reverend Mr. Montgomery. I dined with Mrs. Bays Family, Mrs. Guignard Visited Mrs. Horry & Mrs. Ioor. Also 2 Miss Warings & 2 Miss Hughs.

Monday, March 14. Fine Sun Shine Morning, Carpenters Laying boards in the Passage, wind at West, Zemo Gone to Trim Slabs at Wades Mill, Tinah Sick. Visiters today are as follows, Sarah Bay, who Paisted my fire Scrine over again with New Paper. Doctor Hughs Visited us today. Mrs. Ioor Removed into New House a Shed Chamber, Cleared out Room below, took up its hearth, flooring below & up Stairs, & took down the Stairs, which Lead to the upper flooring. Before night it Grew very warm & Cloudy, after night Mr. McIver's Visited me.

*Rutledge Chapel is part of the first structure on the South Carolina College campus. Built in 1805 to house close to fifty students and faculty, it consisted of the chapel, the hall of the Clariosophic Society, the library, the old laboratory of chemistry and physics, and the lecture rooms. Located in the center of the campus, it was known as South Building and Old South Building until 1848, when it was named after the eighteenth-century statesmen and brothers John and Edward Rutledge. The structure was destroyed by a fire in 1855 but rebuilt immediately. The original chapel consisted of a six-foot stage with a narrow pulpit allowing the preacher to be at the same level as the galleries. Clark and Horn, *University of South Carolina*, 6; *Catalogue of the University of South Carolina*, 10; Green, *History of the University*, 149.

Tuesday, March 15. Much Rain fell Last night & Continues this morning, warm & Cloudy, Isaac finishing flooring Passage. Taking fether Edge from Wash Room. Visiters Doctor Hughs, Sarah Bay, James S. Guignard & his Wife a Heavy Storm came on. Blew down pair Sashes & Several Pannells fence in our Garden. Mary Fields fell from up Stairs into the Celler & hurted herself. Storm Continued about an hour & Ended about 2 OClock P.M. Paid for Mending my Clock & for a Goose 50 Cents & for Fish 50 Cents.

Wednesday, March 16. Cold & very Cloudy, Put up a pair Sashes & a Window which fell from 2nd Story. Paid Robinson for 938 pounds Hay at 100 Cents & 12 Bushels Corn at 60 Cents total $16.88. Took down my Camp Bed Stead & Sot up in my Room a Bed Stead, Visiters today Sarah Bay. Mary Fields went home with her Brother. Got 60 Bushels Corn of Mr. OHenlin, Received by Dr. Greens Waggon 42 Slabs from Wades Mill, Carriage brought a Load of Wood. Paid A. Hall for 20 yards Rope 50 Cents. Sent into our Gardin & Put up fallen Trees which fell in the Late Storm, At Night Several Bells & Beaus visited us.

Thursday, March 17. Cold but Sun Shine Morning. Sent by Omy to farm 6 Pecks Corn & Salt & XCut Saw, Visited this Morning Judge Bay at Mrs. Bays. Sarah Bay Sick, Visiters today are James S. Guignard. Carpenters finishing Passage; boarding & making Stair Case. Got from Habermont Shop 20 pounds 10 dozen Nails. Received by Dr. Greens Waggon, from Wades Mill 40 Ruffage boards. Received a Letter from James Ward, a Letter from Windham Trapier Paid therefor 32 Cents.

Friday, March 18. Fine Frosty Morning wind at North. Scipio brought 60 Bushels Corn more from OHenlin making in all 180 Bushels at 60 Cents which I paid as by Receipt, Yesterday Sent the Printer Form of Advertisement to Publish my history. Answered W. Windham Trapiers Letter, & James Ward's Visiters today are Sarah Bay & Mrs. Caroline Guignard, Sophia Hugh's & Mr. Willey Nothing to be had at Market. Judge Bay went off this Morning for the Upper districts, Paid for a Box Waifers 7 dozen. Paid $102 for 70 Bushels Corn as by Mr. OHenly receipt Miss Hughs Dined with us, After Night Ann Bay Came.

Saturday, March 19. A fine Morning Paid for Beef 100 Cents & for Eggs ½. Wrote to Gabriel Guignard for Garden Seeds etc. Mr. Lance is Returned to Columbia, I Rode out & Saw Mr. Douglass, Mr. Intendant, Mr. Brathwait, Mr. Prescot, & Mr. Gabriel Guignard, Sarah Bay, Miss Chevis & Mrs. Mulenot. Dined with us in the Afternoon Lieutenants Smith's & Lieutenant Reynolds. Called on me after night Mrs. Barksdale & Ann Bay Called on me as did Mr. Gibs & Simons 2 Colegians, Miss Waring & Millen also.

Sunday, March 20. Fair day, Billy came to me from the Farm, Visiters today Sarah Bay, I went to & heard Mr. Lance read a Sermon in the State

House & about four OClock P.M. returned home to Mrs. Horry & her Sister Mrs. Ioor, Saw Habermonts, Mr. Cambell, McGill, Simons, Rutledge, John Waties Mr. Stark Senior & McCords at the State house this Morning, I dined with James S. Guignard & his Family, after Night a Number of Bells & Beau's Called on us.

Monday, March 21. Rainy Morning, finished Stairs to the 2nd Story & boarded under the Corn House. Visiters today are Sarah Bay, Ann, & Margaret I Sent Mr. Faust (the Printer) my History to 12 day of March Last After night Mr. Winstan & Bossard Called on us.

Tuesday, March 22. Fine Spring Morning, but Cool & Windy Sent Carriage for Wood. Received a Quantity of Garden Seeds & Shrubery from Gabriel Guignard, Served out a Weeks allowance. Visiters today are Sarah Bay Ann Chivers. Finished Lining my bed Room floored a Room in 2nd Story, above the Parlour, Court of Sessions meets today, & Colegians to be Tryed for their Late Riot in the Colledge. Andrew Burnet is Said to be Dead Mr. Cambell & Bossard after night Visited me. I Received a Letter from John Ioor of Mississicy & from Windham Trapier of Winyaw.

Wednesday, March 23. Spring Weather Visiters today Mr. & Mrs. James Guignard, Sarah Bay. Got half Bushel Potatoe seed from Said Guignard. Rode out to Farm & brought home a Hog. Visited Miss Smythe & Miss Hughs. Dined at home. Laid hearth in a Room up Stairs Got a Hook & Eye from Prescot & Company. Received a Letter from Dr. Brownfield a Letter from Windham Trapier & Another from Major Keith. Answered Trapiers Letters by Keiths Servant man Adam.

Thursday, March 24. Began to Plain & Jount flooring Boards of the Hall finished a Closet under Stairs Leading to 2nd Story Visiters today are Sarah Bay, James Guignard & his Wife & Mr. Mulder. Paid for Milk 100 Cents, Paid for Butter 100 Cents, for Table Salt 50 Cents. Wrote to John Ioor Bought of Wicht & Company 2 ½ yards homespun for Sam's Shirt, Got of Glaze & Prescot* 7 Setts hasps & Staples. Anything may now be Planted without fear of being Killed by the Frost. Buddy mended Mr. James Guignards Cart, after Night Mr. McIver Visited me. Also Ann Bay at Sun Set.

Friday, March 25. Fine Weather I rode out to Farm I Saw Mr. Bostick & Mr. Witch & Company had 4 Handkerchiefs of them Cost $2 Visiters today

---

*Glaze and Prescott operated a blacksmith shop in Columbia where they made a number of tools as well as guns, swords, and pistols to supply the state militia troops. The Shields Foundary, present in Columbia during the Civil War, was a lineal descendant of the Glaze and Prescott firm. Salley, "Journal of General Peter Horry" (1946), 121–23.

are Sarah Bay, Frank Bremar & Several Colegians & the Miss Bays. I received 27 Slabs by Doctor Greens Waggon from Captain Wades Mill.

Saturday, March 26. Fine Morning Scipio & Carlos went off for George Town & Dover at Sun Rise, Gave Scipio 150 Cents to Travil with, Rote to Dovers Overseer Debose, to Windham Trapier & to Peggy & Rachel, & Windham to Give Scipio money Visiters today are Sarah Bay, Mrs. Guignard & Mr. Lance Got 2 ½ Bushels Potatoe Seed from James Guignard & Yesterday Got from his Plantation 8 Bushels ditto. At Night Sarah & Margaret Bay & Bossard & Waties Called on us.

Sunday, March 27. Thick Morning it Rained Last Night, Billy & Stephen Came from the Farm, before Breakfast, Sarah Bay Visited me. I rode to the State House & heard Devine Service Performed by Mr. Lance. I dined today with Mrs. Bay & her Family & Saw a Number of Colegians.

Monday, March 28. Thick & Misty It Rained very much Last Night, Lodged water in our house yard. Yesterday I Got Acquainted with Mr. Mulleger (Son of Major Muller of Marions Brigade & with Mr. Boykin of Camden). Visiters today Sarah Bay, Mrs. James Guignard & Elizabeth her Daughter Saturday Last I Received by Dr. Greens Waggon from Wades Mill 27 Slabs. I planted in Garden Corn & potatoes. At Night Miss Bays, Simons, Johnston & Winstan Called on us.

Tuesday, March 29. Raw, damp & Cloudy Morning. Omy came for Corn for the Farm & Got 4 Allowances for Negroes there; those here also drew Allowances, put Steps to Corn House, I rode out to Post Office & Received a Letter from James Ward of North Carolina. Postage 17 Cents. I Got of Witch & Company 1 yard black Silk, ½ pound salt Petre 2 Knives 100 Cents. wrote to North & Webb by Mr. Witch for a hand Saw a Grind Stone & a Grits Mill. At Night Sarah & Margaret Bay Called on us. I Visited Doctor Hansworth at his Lodgings.

Wednesday, March 30. Cloudy Morning, raw Weather. I Got buried 2 Poplar Trees before my bed Room Windows. Closet under Stair Case in Passage Leading to 2nd Story finished I rode to our Farm with Sarah Bay and Sophia Hughs & Returned about 2 OClock P.M. Brought home a Pigg & 2 Holly Trees. Put up a Shelf & a Picture Say of the State House of this Place, in my Farm House. Mrs. Ioor returned to our House.

Thursday, March 31. Cool Cloudy Morning wind at North Removed Everything from Celler into Closets above Steers say, Passage Hall & Parlour Closets. Settled with Mulder & Gave him my Note payable at 60 days for $162.90 Cents. I rode to our Farm & put in the House a Picture & Several Crab backs, Billy filling up there an Old Well, brought home 3 Piggs & 2 Poplar Trees brought home Omy & his Coopers Tools. Dined at home today Mrs. Guignard & Elizabeth their Daughters Visited us. Glaze & Prescot done a Small Job of work to my Carriage, Stair Case bannisters finished about 4 OClock P.M. a heavy wind Came on but no Rain fell. At Night Several Colegians Called on us. This Morning my Negro man Carpenter Buddy fell into a most Violent Passion with me about his Cloaths that he would not Submit to my Ill Treatment any Longer, & would have Satisfaction or die, he did not Value his Life, Mrs. Ioor & Horry Saw him & his Treatment to me. I think he means to do me Injury & perhaps to take my Life. I am determined to have Recourse to a Magistrate.

Friday, April 1. A fine Morning Received Last Evening from Prescot & Company 2 plain Irons, a Mill Picker & a round Shave & a Small Crow. Sent a Carriage to be mended by Glaze & prescot, James S. Guignard Visited me. I made Oath before him of Buddys Treatment to me, & he went away Saying he would Soon have him Secured in Goal. Buddy has Escaped Justice & Ran off. I Saw Mr. Prescot & Taylor & Miss Ferguson & had much Conversation with her. I Sent Zemo & London to the Farm, with a Large Iron bound Chest. About 5 OClock P.M. they Returned with a Pigg & note from Mr. Miller. Sent Zemo & London in our Garden to plant Windsor Beans & Water Mellon Seed. Mr. Bossard Sent me word, That *Tomorrow,* he will Breakfast with us & go with me to Horrys Farm at Night Wainslaw & Huggins called on me.

Saturday, April 2. I wrote to Cheesboro, Windham Trapier & my Overseer about Buddy, I with Mr. Bossard went this Morning to my farm. Sent Isaac to Mr. Prescot to fit up a Waggon. We returned to Dinner. Guignards Mill came to my farm. Huggins Dined with us also Sarah Bay. I brought Home a Pig. Paid for 6 Bushels Potatoe Seed.

Sunday, April 3. Warm & Hasey Morning, Sarah Bay Visited us I rode to the State House, & heard Mr. Lance, & dined with James S. Guignard & his Family & at Night was Visited by Several Lads & Lasses.

Monday, April 4. It Rained all Night & Continues this morning. Cuggoe & Omy have runaway Inticed so to do by Buddy. I wrote of these ranaways to Mr. Cheesboro & Mr. Debose & Sent the Letters to the Post Office. Visitors today James S. Guignard, Sarah Bay. I wrote Also to North & Webb. I rode to Gabriel Guignard Senior & Dined with him & his wife & Returned home about 4 OClock P.M. Today a very Rainey day.

Tuesday, April 5. Very Rainey it now Rains & did so all Last night. Isaac Finished a Cubbard for my Farm, I Sent for Wood. I wrote a Note to James Guignard of my disturbed Mind & begged him to Assist me. William Came from the Farm for Allowances. Rain Seems not over. Visitors today are Sarah Bay, Mrs. James Guignard, Doctor Haynsworth Mrs. Ioor rode out with Mrs. Horry. Planted in Garden Corn, Pumkin Seed, Ockro Seed & Beans, & other Seeds Removed Corn Mill from Garden House into our Wash Room, Picked

Excerpt from book 8 of Peter Horry's journal

the Stones thereof Sent to Farm by William 3 Allowances, 1 Beaufet with Lock. About 2 OClock P.M. Mrs. Ioor & Mrs. Horry Returned Home from Mrs. Waring.

    Wednesday, April 6. Truly fine Morning. Sarah Bay Visited us, I rode to the Farm with Martha Bay & Davis. Took Eggs & ham & Bacon with us also Corn for our Mules Received a Platt of Waccamaw Borroney Cost $ We Visited Mr. Burks Family Dined at the Farm & Returned home about 5

OClock P.M. Saw Mrs. Davis & Mrs. Parault at Columbia, also Mr. Barsdale, & Smith & Miss Smith, & Miss Ann Bay.

Thursday, April 7. Clear Morning. I rode out to our Farm in Company with Mr. Barksdale we Viewed all the Land of the Farm, Isaac will finish a Large double Gate to Admit my Carriage up to the House. On Return Gathered sarssafrax blossoms & brought home Some Split Wood. Found Sarah Bay at our House Saw my Neighbou[r]s Mr. & Mrs. Birk, we Got home about 4 OClock P.M. Being much fatiqued I went to my Bed Mrs. Horry went to Mrs. Bay, on a Visit to the Widow Roger Smith, I Saw Mr. Prescot at his black Smith Ship, he said my Saw was done & on Saturday Mr.   Said my Waggon would be done. At Night the 2 Mr. Chisholms Visited me.

Friday, April 8. A good Morning. Settled with Mr. Willey & Gave him my Note of hand for $ payable   Visiters today Sarah Bay. Mrs. Elizabeth Ioor (at our house) appears in a Low dejected state of mind & Cannot Sleep. Visited us before Dinner the two Mrs. Guignard an Excessive hot day my Room in the Afternoon is Intollerable at Night Mr. McGill, Scot & Gaillard called on me.

Saturday, April 9. Last Night Traces, Collars & Bridles for my Waggon came home from Mr. Davis. Also my Waggon came home. Bought 2 pounds Cheese for 7/ I rode to our Farm Accompanied by 2 Mr. Chisholm's. Visiters are Sarah Bay, Last Evening the Miss Bays Visited us, field Pieces fired for Good News General Jackson of Georgia has Killed & wounded a Thousand Enemy Indians (chiefly Creeks) I with Mr. Chisholm Visited my Neighbour Burke & Returned to Columbia before Dinner much fatigued, Afternoon Mrs. Faus (wife of Major Faus) Visited us also Mrs. James Guignard & her husband, at Night Mrs. McGill & Cambell Visited me. I delivered McGill Inclosed to Windham Trapier, a Survey of the Waccamaw Barrony in dispute, to be delivered to George Smith, Going to George Town.

Sunday, April 10. It Rained all Last night very hard & this morning very heavy & Promises much more Rain. All our yard afloat & I suppose our Garden the Same, Visiters today Sarah Bay, Ann Chivers & Gabriel Guignard Junior I Visited State House, Mr. Lance Officiated. I dined with Mrs. Bay & her Family also Major Player dined with us & other Gentlemen also. At Night Mr. Muller, Bonneau, McGill & others Visited me.

Monday, April 11. Rainy, Cloudy Morning. I Packed up my Bedding, Cloaths, & went to our Farm to Stay till Saturday Next in Order to finish my fencing & to begin Planting Corn. I Got to the farm & Planted Irish Potatoes in the Orchard & Carriage in any Rails, Dined on Cheese Bread & Eggs.

Tuesday, April 12. It Rained very much Last Night & now is very warm & Cloudy Sent Mules to Columbia for Waggon, which did not Come a Mule being Sick. Nothing but Rain, Cleared Passage between House & Gate.

Wednesday, April 13. Cloudy & warm, Sent London to Columbia. He & Zemo returned before Dinner Finished Planting Irish Potatoes, Received from Mrs. Horry a Pavillion & from James Guignard $3 Mrs. Burke Visited me.

Thursday, April 14. Rain warm & Cloudy. I began to dig Ground, Sent for the Waggon. Gave Burke 2 Pictures. Waggon came & I went & Dined with Mr. Burke & his Family Returned from thence I met with Mr. Barsdal, who went to house & Supped with me & Lodged thereat at Night it Rained.

Friday, April 15. Barsdale returned to Columbia. I rode with Billy round where fences was to Go, Wind Raised Clouds dispersed, I Sot heaps of Logs on fire, Sent Corn to Taylors Mill & it Returned Meal. I Sent Miss Burke a Pickture Guilded Frame. About 2 OClock P.M. wind was very high & from the westward.

Saturday, April 16. Sot many dry Standing Trees on fire Got to Columbia about 5 OClock found all well.

Sunday, April 17. Fine Weather, Cold, S. Bay gave me 2 blue Letter Cases. No Answer from Bostick. Sot out for our Farm about 3 OClock P.M. Slept at the Farm.

Monday, April 18. Came to Columbia, Scriven & Winstan Visited us also S. Bay.

Tuesday, April 19. I am now at Columbia, Sent Sam & London with Mules to Billy at our Farm. Today fence finished, Visiters Today are Sarah Bay. I paid 4/8 for Bacon. At Night Mrs. Branthwait, & Miss Smythe, William Marrant & William Richardson Visited us. Lidy came home from Farm.

Wednesday, April 20. Yesterday I wrote to North & Webb. Sent for Stephen & William from Farm, Sent my Carriage by Zemo, to Meet Scipio & Assist him with Negroes from Winyaw Visiters today are S. Bay (Paid 1/9 for Beef) Ben Ioor Mr. Harison.

Thursday, April 21. Last Night my Cart Arrived from George Town with Several Negroes, & a Letter & Money from Windham Trapier. I Sent Plenty & Lucy to the Farm & went there myself.

Friday, April 22. Rainey Morning, fitting up Stable Pinning Shingles, Cutting up Logs & burning them, also Plowing for Corn fitted a Door to Stable. Yesterday Dandy Returned to Columbia Sent Sam to Columbia for Ruff Rice, Received half Bushel ditto by Dandy & he returned Directly.

Saturday, April 23. From my Farm I Sent 4 fellows to Mr. Burk (my Neighbour) to Assist him in Rolling up Logs & after Breakfast went myself to his House, & dined with his family, & went to my Family at Columbia, in the Evening a Number of Ladies & Gentlemen Visited us, Mrs. Perault being of the Number in Company with Mrs. Davis & her Daughter, this day Mrs. Caroline Guignard with her two Daughters went off for the high Hills of Santee.

Sunday, April 24. Warm, foggy Morning, I wrote to the following Persons—Captain Bostick, Windham Trapier, Mr. Debose (my Overseer at Dover plantation) Mr. Cheesboro at George Town x' these thus marked, I Sent by my Driver Dandy to George Town I went to Church & heard Mr. Lance & Dined with James S. Guignard received from his plantation a half Bushel Cotton Seed. At Night much Company Visited us.

Monday, April 25. Cloudy Raw Morning, Dandy went Off. Planted a Little Cotton in Garden. I went to the Farm At the Farm Martha Bay with me Burning Logs, Shingling Stable & Planting Rice, Got to Columbia before Sun Set.

Tuesday, April 26. I went to the Farm paid for Milk 100 Cents for Beef $1. 1 ½ dozen Eggs & Wiskey & Molasses Carried to Farm.

Wednesday, April 27; Thursday, April 28; Friday, April 29; Saturday, April 30. At the Farm, fitted up my Stable & Kitchen Cut down, & burt many dry Trees, & Planted Some Rice & 3 Acres Cotton & breakfasted at Columbia Received 2 Letters from Cheesborow & Debose, heard of my Runaways, answered these Letters by Major Carr Paid Mr. Harrison in full for Beef $12 as by receipt. Received a Letter from Mrs. Helin & Answered it by Major Carr, Sent Billy a Plow, a Grind Stone, & 3 falling Axes, by Carriage in Charge of Zemo. S. Bay Visited us. Also Ann & Margaret Bay. Glaze & Prescot, made one of the Said Axes. Tinah Sick in Bed.

Sunday, May 1. A fine Morning, Sarah & Ann Bay Visited us. I went to the State House & Mr. Lance Officiated I dined with Mrs. Bay & her Family. Mrs. Robert Waring & her Daughter Visited us in the Afternoon. Saw in forenoon Judges Waties & Gaillard, Misses Hughes, Hilhouse & other Ladies with Several Colegians.

Monday, May 2. I went to the farm this Morning Negros planting Corn at Farm. Returned Mr. Burk a quart Salt Borrowed. Paid $3 for Bacon, Cut up Logs. Fell dry Trees.

Tuesday, May 3. Rose very Early & Cut Bushes without the Gates. Piled & burnt them, took down 3 pole Houses & Sot them up without the Gate for Negro Houses. Removed Fowl Hous[e], Sot up Grind Stone & Mill Stone for Grinding Corn. Sent Carriage to Columbia for Corn or Pease.

Wednesday, May 4. Planted Corn & Rice at Farm & Cart Logs etc. Received a Letter from North West which Says a Grind Stone & hand Saw are Sent me.

Thursday, May 5 & Friday, May 6. Made Fence & Cleared Land James S. Guignard Visited me the former day. Cleared Land to the Corner of my Fence say South Corner, Sent Mr. Burke 150 Cents to Pay for Potatoe Seed I had of him.

Saturday, May 7. I Got to Columbia about 10 OClock A.M. & Meet Mrs. Horry, her Sister & Sarah Bay in health, the Latter dined with us. Bought 3 Broad Hoes for 3 Dollars Gave Mrs. Horry four Dollars towards House Keeping, Sanders Guignard called on us & at Night a Number of Lassies & Lads Called on us.

Sunday, May 8. Fine Weather finished planting at the farm & began to Hoe. Went to the Methodist Meeting & heard a Sermon by Reverend Mr. Welch. Dined at Home. Mr. Inglisby & Simons & Miss S. Bay dined with us brought a Pig from the Farm. Kept London & Zemo with me all others belonging to the farm went off before Sun Set.

Monday, May 9. I Visited Garden & 2 hands Hoed Corn therein, Mrs. Caroline Guignard with her Daughters returned from the high Hills Santee, I went to Bed Sick at Night.

Tuesday, May 10. Cloudy, & Rain Last Night & this Morning Served out Allowances to Negroes at Farm & Columbia 16 Allowances, Paid for Milk 100 Cents. Paid for homespun for Lucy at the Farm $2. S. Bay Visited us this Morning. At 10 OClock A.M. a hard Shower of Rain fell, took up my Note at the Bank in favour of Mulder for 163 Dollars. Paid for cutting out my Coat 50 Cents. Mrs. Bay Visited us also Huggins & McGill after night.

Wednesday, May 11. Bought & paid Mrs. McGowen for a Cow & Calf $15. Went to the Farm this morning with Mrs. Horry & Martha Bay, & Returned about 2 OClock P.M. Very Windy Weather & Cloudy, Farm Going on Well, Lucy Sick Thereat, Gave Lucy her homespun, Left at Farm William to Hoe Grass.

Thursday, May 12. Cloudy & Cool Changed my Room with Mrs. Horry, went to the Farm, James Guignard Visited us, Last Night Cambell & McGill Visited us.

Friday, May 13. Cut down Warings Hill, went to Colonel Hutchisons He Introduced to his Family, 2 Sons & 2 Daughters, his Lands are Good & his Crops Promising one. It Rained today very much & I Got wet Coming Home. Got a Letter from Dandy.

Saturday, May 14. Cloudy Morning, Mr. Inglisby went with me to the Farm, we Returned in the Afternoon, at Night Mr. Johnston Visited us.

Sunday, May 15. Fair morning Sick Last Night & in the Morning Whipt London for Neglecting me. It Rained before Dinner Francis Robert Shackelford dined with Mrs. Horry, also Did Ann Chivers, Billy came from the Farm & Returned with London & 2 Mules. Isaac & Carlos came to make Window Shutters.

Monday, May 16. Fair Morning. Isaac & Carlos began to make Window Shutters, Scipio & William Howed in the Garden Last Night Several Colegians & young Ladies Visited us, Paid Mrs. McNamara $12 for a Gun which is at the Farm for Killing Crows etc. etc. which destroy Corn Potatoes etc. etc. Visiters today are Sarah Bay, I wrote my Overseer. I Visited my Garden. Mr. Habermont Visited us, bought a quarter Veneson 125 Cents. Visiters, Mrs. Bay, Mrs. Arthur, Miss Harrison & Miss Ferguson.

Tuesday, May 17. Visiters today Mr. James Guignard & Sarah Bay. I went to my Farm & returned in the Afternoon. Found Mrs. James Guignard with Mrs. Horry, Received an Account from Dr. John Wragg.

Wednesday, May 18. Cloudy & warm. Went to the farm fell many dry Trees & burnt thim up, Scipio & Isaac went with me.

Thursday, May 19. Breakfasted at farm. Left Scipio & Carlos, & brought Sam. Finished this morning Planting a Bushel Pease at the Farm Billy Took all hands at the farm to Hoe, he Killed a very large Rabbet, Got to Columbia about 10 OClock A.M. Wrote to Colonel Hutchison & made Return of my Tax amount $140.30 Cents. Paid Dr. Jones for 8 pair Hinges $3. It Rained about 3 OClock P.M. Visiters Mrs. Shutes & Mrs. Cantey & Sa[rah] Bay, wrote to John Cheesborow, & Sent it by young Cuttino.

Friday, May 20. Went to the Farm. Delivered Billy 4 yards homespun, Buttons & thread.

Saturday, May 21. Fair morning I returned from the Farm to Columbia with William & London. Saw Mr. Burk on the Road, met at home the 2 Miss Starks, Sarah Bay & Ann Chivers. Spent the Evening with James Guignard, & family, Mr. Josias Smith of Charles Ton. His Son of the Colledge & Reverend Mr. Montgomery & Several Ladies.

Sunday, May 22. Went to the State House Service performed by Mr. Lance, Saw many Acquaintances Visiters today Sarah Bay, Martha Bay, Mrs. Bay & Billy, Scipio Stephen & Lucy Came from the Farm & returned about 5 Past Maridian.

Monday, May 23. Went to the farm. Canned 3 Bushels Peas which I paid Mr. OHenley 2 ¼ Dollars for.

Tuesday, May 24. Sent for Corn from the Farm & Served out Allowances, Sent Carlos to Columbia Sick.

Wednesday, May 25. Arrived at Columbia before breakfast, Visiters today Sarah Bay James Guignard. Preparing Company for a Parbique at the farm Say Mrs. Bay & her [entry ends abruptly].

Thursday, May 26. Continued. Mrs. Davis's Family, 2 Guignards Messrs. Inglisby, McGill, Winston, Bonneau, Simons, Cambell, Major Cambell & Family, Major Faust Received a Letter from W. Trapier, a Letter from Soloman.

Friday, May 27. At the Farm, Friday Left it in the Morning & in the Evening Returned thereto with Rachel & Abigal & Sundries for Tomorrows dinner at the Farm.

Saturday, May 28. Made a Bower of Bushes at the Farm Killed 2 Hogs & a Turkey & about 10 OClock Company began to Arrive—about 40 in Number. Say 3 Continental Officers, Militia Officers Coligians etc. etc. Colours displayed, Drums, & fife, & before Night a Dance was Struckt up in Farm house & the Evening Concluded with Great Good humour & Joylitry all Returned to Columbia before night.

Sunday, May 29. Excessive warm & dry Weather. Visiters Several. Glorious News Bonapart has defeated the Allied Forces & has Confined at Paris. The Emperor of Russia, & Prinz of Prussia with a Great Many of their Officers & Soldiers Prisoners. A hand Bill from Charles Ton has just Arrived here with this most Important Intelligence. Was I in health & had the Use of my Limbs Oh how I would Go about & Congratulate my fellow Citizens.

Monday, May 30. Pleasant Morning but very dry. I rode to the Farm & Sent Burke an Account of Bonaparts Successes. Cut down & burnt up many Trees.

Tuesday, May 31. Arrived at Columbia, before Dinner, Sarah Bay dined with us. In the Afternoon James S. Guignard & his Mother Called on us. Dry & very warm weather. Inglisby Called on us & as he was tomorrow to Leave this City for Charles Ton took Leave of us.

Wednesday, June 1. Sarah Bay & Mr. Welch & his Wife Visited us, also James S. Guignard I Got to the Farm before night with Trunk Cloaths & Table & Drawers thereto. Brought 3 bags Corn & Sent Carriage back to Columbia, all hands now Hoeing. Sent Carriage with Isaac to Columbia.

Thursday, June 2. Hoed & Lodgd up & burnt Lodgs. About 10 OClock A.M. Carriage arrived with Rachel her Child, & William with Corn & my bed Stead. Scipio & London brought me a Cow & Calf Isaac Came with Some Carpenters Tools. Saw Mr. Burk my Neighbour in the Road. Gave Rachael my Camp bed Stead. Milk Came from Columbia William returned to Columbia.

Friday, June 3. No Rain tho very warm & Cloudy, all hands hoeing, Except 2 Cutting Logs & burning them. Got two Rakes made, took down the Bower & brought all belonging thereto to the House. No Visiters today, yet Several more Oak logs to Cut up & Burn.

Saturday, June 4. Smokeye Weather. I now Consider the Farm as *my* home, & Columbia as Mrs. Horrys Home & Shall Speak of them as Such, I rode round my fields, Breakfasted & went to Columbia, Received a Letter from Mr. Prioleau, & a Letter from Mr. Cheesborow.

Sunday, June 5. I went & heard Mr. Lance Read a Sermon & Saw many Acquaintances. in the Evening the Miss Bays Visited us.

Monday, June 6. James Guignard breakfasted with us I went to the farm & Returned to Columbia to Dinner. Plowing with a Plow. Raking with 2 Rakes hoeing & Thinning of Corn.

Tuesday, June 7. Mrs. Horry & myself Got to the Farm about 10 OClock A.M. Measles brief at Columbia. Negroes hoeing Potatoes, Raking & a Plow Going. Mrs. Horry Returned to Columbia about 4 OClock P.M. Served to Negroes 11 Rations at the Farm. This Evening it Rained, a fine Shower.

Wednesday, June 8. Thick Cloudy & Krisley Morning, Cut up a few Oak Logs & went to Planting Corn & Pease. 2 Plows Going in New Ground. I rode over my New Ground after dinner a Serious Rain Commenced & Continued all the Afternoon, Sent Sam to my Neighbour Burk to hoe, he being Sick London hoed Some Corn near the house. Rachael Washe'd my Dirty Cloaths & Ground Some Coffee, Buiskuit out.

Thursday, June 9. Clear fine Morning, Negroes planting Pease, 2 Plows on New Ground. Repaired my House Chimney. Very Sick Last Night, Pain in my bones, but after rubbing my back it Abated & I Got up & drank chocolate, & Saw from my Piazza my Negroes at work which amused my Mind (The Reader will Observe that I Account the Farm *my home* & will Speak of it as Such & do all my Business thereat) *Columbia* I will Seldom Visit, 'tis *Mrs. Horrys Home.* I must make our Own Provisions. Buying it & Cloathing etc. etc. have nearly Ruined me.

Friday, June 10. Smokey Morning, I was so Sick Last night, that I Sent to Mr. Burke for Sage Tea. It Rubbing with Warm Venegar Gave me Some Ease, & untill day light when I Arose & wrote in this my daily History. Planted Pease & Sot 2 Plows to work. Received by William a Letter from Mr. Ward Postage 17 Cents of North Carolina, a Note from Mrs. Horry & another from S. Bay of Columbia Wrote a Long Letter to Windham Trapier & Sent it to Mrs. Horry.

Saturday, June 11. Sent Carriage to Mrs. Horry with Wood etc. Wrote her a Note. Planting Pease & plowing. This Morning Mrs. Burk Visited me for the first time. Mrs. Bay Horry & Sarah Bay Visited me Dined & Returned to Columbia in the Evening.

Sunday, June 12. I went very Sick with the Rush all over to Columbia & Sent for Doctor Fisher, who Prescribed for me.

Monday, June 13. Yet very Sick at Columbia in Dr. Fishers hands. Grew Better & Slept a Little Last Night.

Tuesday, June 14. Sot out with Sarah & Margaret Bay for the Farm after Breakfast. Served out 7 Rations for Negroes at the Farm, found Negroes there hoeing Corn. About 6 OClock P.M. We returned to Columbia, after Cutting up two Logs & burning them up.

Wednesday, June 15. At Columbia Yesterday Mrs. Bay, Huggins & McGill Visited us. This Morning Miss Ann & Martha Bay rode with me to the Farm where I now write from. 2 Plows Going on New Ground. All other Negroes Hoeing.

Thursday, June 16. Last Evening Got to Columbia with Ann & Martha Bay. A fine Rain fell Yesterday & this morning I Sot out for & Arrived at the Farm & Breakfasted there, 2 Plows Going & fellows Cutting up Logs to Burn, Received by Post a Letter from Dubose 17 Cents, returned to Columbia to Dinner.

Friday, June 17. A fine Rain Last Night, took Rachael to the Farm to wait on me We Got there about 8 OClock A.M. Found Lucy Sick, Negroes Hoeing. 2 Plows Going. Sun is out & 'tis warm. Rolled up & Sot fire to all the Logs in New Ground.

Saturday, June 18. Clear Morning, Sent Carriage to Columbia for Corn & Mrs. Horry (by Scipio) Plows Goes on, Planted Yesterday Some Corn. All other hands Hoeing Corn & Pease. William brought me from Columbia Eggs Milk & Bread; Gave Zemo A Shirt of Homespun Cost 1/6 a yard, which Mrs. Horry, Sent me by William. Carriage about 10 OClock A.M. Arrived at the Farm, Passingers Mr. McGill & Lee. They Dined with me & returned in the Evening to Columbia, where I Sent my Waggon for Storage, or Shelter none being here. Planted more Corn. Say no more to Plant Charles Huggins & another Colegian Visited me after Dinner & Returned to Colledge by Sun Set. Only my Cotton is Grassy.

Sunday, June 19. Fair Morning. Scipio returned from Columbia with Carriage & brought a bag Corn. This Morning I Visited my Neighbour Burk's Family & Dined with them.

Monday, June 20. Cool & Clear Morning Negroes all Hoeing Cotton Corn & Rice, Visiters today (none) Tinah (at Columbia) delivered of a Son (her first Child) Kirbed all the Green Pine Trees in New Field & Cut Bushes before Gate to the Road.

Tuesday, June 21. Sent Scipio to Columbia for Mrs. Horry. Cleaned around fence from Gate to Corner Leading to Columbia. Some Negroes hoeing. I Rode around my Fences. Returned & breakfasted. Served out Allowances. Sarah Bay, Mr. Bossard, Cambell, Habermont Junior, 2 Mr. Guignard & Mrs. Horry Visited me. They all Left me before Sun *down*.

Wednesday, June 22. Clear & fine Weather. All hands hoeing. I rode out around my Plantation & returned to my Farm House about 12 OClock. Black Mule Ran away Last Night to Columbia, brought back with a I Received a Note from Mrs. Horry Answered it by William. Markt my Lines on 2 sides plainer. It went South East further than I thought for & took in more Swamp Land for Rice. Burnt Logs near the Gate.

Thursday, June 23. Dry Smokeye Weather, Lucy hoeing Rice the Rest of the Negroes making up fences from South Corner to Gate. I rode out & Visited Doctor Long bottoms Farm & Returned home about 6 OClock. The Doctor was at home two young men I found with him we Breakfasted &

Dined together, Last night I was very Sick with Cholick Got relief about 12 OClock.

Friday, June 24. Very Cool dry & Clouddy Weather, Negroes finishing making Fences, wind at North, Cleared before my Gate to the Corner on the Road & Corner to the Spring much Smoak around the Farm. Sent London for Milk to Columbia, My Neighbours alarm at so much fire in the woods made by me.

Saturday, June 25. Yesterday I rode to Columbia. Found that Mrs. George Ioor & her Neice had Left it & Gone for Black River & this morning Margaret Bay & myself rode to the Farm & Breakfasted here. Rode Round it & Returned to Columbia before Dinner. Received a Letter by Colonel Huggins from my Overseer Dubose, (nothing new) General Bonapart has Given up his Crown & is to be Allowed a Pention Lewis 18th is restored to his hereditary Rights to Govern the French People. In the Afternoon Visited Mr. & Mrs. Heyward at Mrs. Bays & at Night Slept at our House at Columbia.

Sunday, June 26. Left Columbia Early this Morning & Breakfasted at the Farm, then Rode to the Meeting House near Doctor Long bottoms & heard Preeching by Reverend Mr. Meek, 16 Persons mett. Returned to Farm & Dined & before Night went to Columbia. In the Evening Maurice Simons, McGill, Mr. Heyward & Miss Bays with James Guignard Visited us.

Monday, June 27. I rode to the Farm this Morning Negroes all howing, Vastly dry all Vegitation nearly at an End. May God soon Send us Rain. Removed all Logs & Bushes Leading to Columbia on the Road as far as first Branch, & on Mrs. Burks Side as far as the Spring & Parallel with the Road. I Road in the Evening to Columbia & found Mr. Thurston his Wife & Jane his Daughter with Mrs. Horry, they Slept at our house Last night, Breakfasted & went off for the upper Country.

Tuesday, June 28. Cloudy Morning & Raining. Negroes ditching here & planting Pease at the Farm. Lucy Hoeing & plenty Sick. Read a Letter to Rachael from her Husband. John who is at George Town Served out Allowances to Negroes here Say 18 Allowances. Mrs. Burk Visited me this afternoon before I went for Columbia.

Wednesday, June 29. Frances Huger, Adjutant General in Continental Service Called on me (Last night) at our Columbia House. Also James Guignard, I Received a Letter from Windham Trapier by Post 17 Cents due & I Answered said Letter this day, Mrs. Bay & Margaret Bay her Daughter Dined with me at the Farm & we returned to Columbia before Sun Set, Left Negroes Planting Pease & ditching in Rice Land.

Thursday, June 30. I went with Mrs. Horry & S. Bay to the Colledge where was a Numerous Assembly of People, about 10 Students Spoke on Various Subjects, met with Loud Huzzas etc. Each of them as they Retired from the Stage.

Friday, July 1. I am now at the Farm, Negroes Planting Potatoe Vines. 2 Squaruaring Timber. Went to Columbia, this Evening Met Mrs. Horry, S. Bay James Guignard & Several Collegians.

Saturday, July 2. A Rainey Morning Sot out however Carriage Wheel Gave way & with Great difficulty Got to the farm. Found Negroes at Breakfast. Brought 2 bags Corn & Some Bricks Wrote to North & Web & to Mr. Cheesborow. Brought in Some Timber to House to Enharced it. Doctor Long Bottoms & his Student Mr.   Visited me. I returned by Scipio My Carriage to Columbia to be mended. The Doctor Sent me Some Venison for Dinner. It Rained much today.

Sunday, July 3. Cloudy Morning, I was very Sick Last Night. Pain in my back, by Rubbing with warm Brandy & putting on Flannel, I was Enabled to Rise & Breakfasted Billy went to Columbia this morning. Several Others were absent. About 12 OClock. Warm Sun high Wind at South Zemo brought me from Columbia. A Note from Sarah Bay, She & Mrs. Horry will Come for me Tomorrow in Mrs. Guignards Carriage.

Monday, July 4. I went with Mrs. Horry & S. Bay to Columbia Sick & Sent my Carriage to Mr. Glovers.

Tuesday, July 5; Wednesday, July 6; Thursday, July 7. Remained at Columbia, very Dry. Cloudy, but no Rain.

Friday, July 8. Warm & Cloudy, Doctor Haynsworth Visited us this forenoon. Mrs. Horry Received by the Doctor a Letter from Ann Cheves, her Aunt is better. William is Come from the Farm all are well thereat, Mrs. Bay Also Visited us & Sarah her Daughter.

Saturday, July 9. Rained Last Night & this Morning, Cool & very Cloudy, Doctor Hainsworth Accompanied me to the farm where we Dined & Returned to Columbia before Sun Set. Isaac framing Cills to Add Rooms to the farm house. Plowing Corn done & Negroes hoeing Corn.

Sunday, July 10. It Rained very much Last Night & this morning also Weather Cool & Cloudy. My Carriage Tryed Yesterday & found the Wheels Good, I owe Mr. Glover for the Woodwork & Glaze & prescot for the Tiring & Nails. We hear the Reverend Mr. Travis & his wife from George Town are in Columbia. They are Methodists. After Diner Miss Bay, Bell of Granby & Mr. McGill Visited me also Mrs. Bay.

Monday, July 11. I Left Columbia & Saw Reverend Mr. Travis. Then Called at house of Mrs. Davis & took in Miss Martha Davis & Martha Bay & Arrived at Horrys Farm, about 9 OClock A.M. Mr. Butler not then Breakfasted. Isaac Framing & all the other Negroes planting Potatoe Vines, Lucy Cooking. Soon after we Got to the Farm Mr. Scriven & McGill arrived We dined & about 6 OClock Sot out for Columbia & Arrived thereat before Sun Set. Received a Letter from John Simons Postage 17 Cents a Letter from Mr.

Dubose 17 Cents a Letter from Captain Dent 12 ½ Cents & a Letter from Windham Trapier 17 Cents. My Runaways are Come in Buddy is in Goal. Answered Mr. Dubose Letter. Windham Trapiers & Captian Dent, Colonel Hutchison & Mr. & Mrs. Travis Visited us & Lodged with us. Mrs. Waring & Grafton also came to See us.

BOOK NINE

July 13, 1814–October 31, 1814

Peter Horry's Book   & is as Follows
The following is Peter Horrys daily Journal
or History of his Life.

*W*ednesday, July 13. I rose Early at Columbia, Breakfasted, Took in my Carriage Ann & Margaret Bay, we rode to the Farm, Carpenters Framing, the others hoeing Corn, the Ladies went to Mrs. Smith & bought Butter we then returned to Columbia, this day Mrs. Bay discharged Butler & Paid him $2.

Thursday, July 14. Cold & Cloudy Morning. Mrs. Horry went with me to the Farm, At Waring Farm we bought Vegitables at Farm McGill, Screven & Barksdale Visited us, Sent Mrs. Bay all Butlers Effects from my Farm.

Friday, July 15. S. Bay dined with us I received all my history Books from Mr. Frost.

Saturday, July 16. Miss Goodin & Margaret Bay went with me to the Farm & we returned in the Evening.

Sunday, July 17. I went & heard Mr. Lance Officiate at the State House. 4 Gentlemen dined with us. Sent a Horse & Mule to the Farm.

Monday, July 18. Ann Bay went with me to the Farm where we Breakfasted She & London went to Mrs. Smiths house to Buy Fowls. 2 Plows Going on in New Ground framing Goes on. Cross Cutting Blocks. Others howing Corn. Could Buy no Fowls, Sent London to Mr. Burke. Received a Note from him, that he would Get General Marion's History from Doctor Long Bottoms & Send to my Farm, after Reading it. Cannot Build Mrs. Baye any House. London went after Huckelberries, Scipio & Sam XCut 5 Blocks & brought them to the Farm House. Two Baggs of Corn came thereto from Columbia. We Got to Columbia before Sun Set. James S. Guinard Called on us.

Tuesday, July 19. Cloudy Morning, I went to the Farm & Carried Corn thereto, & Served out Allowances to all the Negroes at the farm Brought a Hog from Columbia, Isaac Framing, Plowing Goes on all others hoeing wrote a Letter to Mr. Dubose (my Overseer) Concerning Negro Carpenter Buddy

Sent it to Mrs. Horry At Columbia to be forwar[d]ed. Sent Mrs. Bay also a Note about her building at my Farm.

Wednesday, July 20. Early this Morning Sent Scipio to Columbia for Waggon & boards. Plowing Goes on. Isaac & Sam Putting Cills on blocks around the House, hoeing also Cloudy, but no Rain as yet. Lucy Sick London Returned from Columbia with Milk, Nails, & a Note from Mrs. Bay. Raising Studs to Enlarge Farm House. Also put up Plates Scipio from Columbia with Straw & 19 Boards. Brought 28 Poles to the Gate. Summoned to work with 5 hands on Road above George Smith 28 Instant. London went to Columbia.

Thursday, July 21. Warm & Cloudy, 2 plows Going 2 Carpenters at work on Farm House, other Negroes Hoeing, London returned from Columbia with Milk, Bread, Beef etc. etc. about 1 OClock P.M. A fine Shower of Rain fell finished Plowing & planted Potatoe Vines, flooring Piazza with Poles, London went to Columbia.

Friday, July 22. Cool & Cloudy Morning, it Rained also, Last Night 2 Carpenters flooring as Yesterday. Waggon with 2 fellows drawing Poles, all others planting Vines London Returned from Columbia with Milk etc. etc. Rain Continies. I Got Eggs & apples from Columbia & brought poles to the House by Carlos & Isaac. About 2 OClock P.M. Sun appeared Remarkable Bright & hot, In the Evening Sent London with Beans & a Cat to Mrs. Horry at Columbia, wrote her a Note Expressing my Wish to See her & Sarah Bay tomorrow brought from Without Gate to Farm House all the Poles. William came from Columbia with a Note from Mrs. Horry to Send her the horse which was done Accordingly. So I Expect her & Sarah Bay Tomorrow Morning.

Saturday, July 23. Cold & Clear Weather Last Evening, Young Davis, McGill & Bardsdale Called on me at the Farm, Sot an hour & went off on Return for Columbia. Three fellows Carpentering, the rest of the Negroes hoeing in New Land. London returned from Columbia with Milk etc. etc., Apples & Tomatis, & says Mrs. Horry & S. Bay will be here after Breakfast, Mrs. Horry came but no S. Bay came. We went to Columbia Saw James S. Guignard & S. Bay.

Sunday, July 24. This morning Cloudy before day James S. Guignard & Mrs. Horry Sot off from Columbia for Camp Meeting about Ten miles off. S. Bay Breakfasted with me. I dined with Mrs. Bay & her Family went to State house & heard Mr. Lance Read Devine Service. After Dinner I Saw the young Players, Bay & Winstan Returned here to their Education. I wrote a Letter to my Overseer at Dover & sent it by Mr.   after Night Mrs. Horry Returned home. S. Bay Visited me.

Monday, July 25. A Thick Foggy Morning, about 11 OClock A.M. I Left Columbia in Company with Sarah & William Bay, we Dined at the Farm, found Carpenters flooring the House, & Negroes hoeing Corn, Sot Waggon to bring Poles from the woods to the Farm House we Got to Columbia about Sun Set.

Tuesday, July 26. I rose Early at Columbia, a Clear Morning, Sot out & Arrived at the Farm. Breakfasted thereat. Brought 3 bags Corn Served out Allowances to Negroes, they are hoeing Corn, Except 2 Carpenters at Work on house, Sam Cutting Poles Waggon fetching in Poles from the woods to farm House. Several Light Showers of Rain fell Today. Carpenters flooring with Boards around 3 sides of the house Intended as 4 Rooms. Went to Columbia & Got there about 6 OClock P.M. Found S. Bay with Mrs. Horry. On my way met Mr. Burk & Waring. Today James Guignard & his Family went to his Farm 4 Miles beyond ours.

Wednesday, July 27. Last night it Rained I Left Columbia Early this morning & breakfasted at my Farm, Sent Neighbour Burk the Columbia Last News Paper Sent Mrs. Horry Some Snap Beans by William, also a few Young Squashes a Rainy day, began to pole up Sides of Rooms.

Thursday, July 28. Rained all Last Night & yet Continues. Sent 4 Negroes to work on High Road near George Smith. Sent to Columbia for boards Sent to Mrs. Horry at Columbia her Horse & Mule. 2 hands bedding for Planting Potatoe Vines. Carlos at work on farm House. Very Unwell Pains all over me Particularly my Neck. Wind at East (high & very Stormy) a Gale at Sea, Vessells on our Coast Reef Sails, & Howl Close to the Wind. Isaac returned with 34 Boards & apples etc. with a Note from Mrs. Horry.

Friday, July 29. Scipio returnd with his party Last Night, I Sent them again on the Road, as the Weather appears better this Morning, Carpenters at Work on Rooms. Billy planting Potatoe Vines, London came from Columbia with Milk, Bread Buiskuit Eggs etc. & returned after Dinner with a Note to Mrs. Horry & a Water Melion & 3 Ears Corn.

Saturday, July 30. Cool & fair Sun Shine Morning, Last Night I was very Sick Indeed, but by Rubbing & drinking Garden Tea with Brandy in it I Got better before day & Got Some Sleep so as to Enable my Getting up to Breakfast. 2 Carpenters at House work all others Hoeing. I went to Columbia this morning & found Mrs. Horry at home. I dined with her, near Night Thomas Waties, Mr. Winstan & Mrs. Bay Visited us. Mrs. Bay & her Family returned home in a Thunder Gush of Wind & Rain. They Sent us Water & Muss Melions & apples.

Sunday, July 31. It Rained all Last Night & is yet Raining before Breakfast. Promiss to be a Wet day about 12 OClock it Cleared up Mrs. Horry went to Meeting. Sarah Bay Called on us & dined with us also Mr. R. Waring. Rain prevented my Going to Church. Mr. McGill, Barksdale William Bay & Thomas Waties also Called on us at Night Miss Bays & Marshal Called on us.

Monday, August 1. A Clear Morning sent Scipio to the Farm for the Waggon, & for Isaac to take up Posts & pailings to Carry to the Farm, Gave Scipio a New Hatt. Cost $1.62 Cents bought of James Patton & Company Merchants Columbia Sarah Bay breakfasted with us. Scipio & Isaac brought the Waggon from the farm about 1 OClock P.M. James S. Guignard & his Family dined with us. After Dinner Miss S. Bay & Miss Marshal Visited us. Measured our Corn in Corn House & found 37 Bushells, James S. Guignards Smoke House took fire, which Caused a Great Alarm.

Tuesday, August 2. A Clear Morning, Isaac Carried a Waggon Load of Posts & Pailings to the Farm. I carried in my Carriage Corn to the Farm. S. Bay & Ann Bay Went thereto, Served out Allowances here Say at the Farm Zemo went to Columbia for another Waggon Load of Posts & Pailings, S. Bay with London went to Mrs. Smith to buy butter & [illegible]. Sent Burk this days Columbia News Paper two Miss Bays went for Columbia in the Afternoon, Carriage Returned after Night.

Wednesday, August 3. A fair Morning Calm but Cool Morning. Carpenters Setting up Posts & Pailings for a Garden between my House & their Kitchen, other Negros hoeing, Lucy Sick. Received a Note from Mrs. Horry, Answered it by Zemo in Waggon for Boards. Zemo brought 16 Boards by Waggon from Columbia, & William returned to Columbia. Received a few 4 dozen Nails from Mrs. Horry.

Thursday, August 4. Clear Morning. Isaac boarding under Pailings Carlos with Billy & other hands Getting Gardon Posts. London & Sam burning Chips in Garden all Posts & Railings being in Garden the Carpenters got to Work to fix them. Mrs. Horry arrived in her Chair at the Farm, brought Beef Peeches etc. etc. Dined with me & returned in my Carriage this Afternoon, This an Excessive hot day.

Friday, August 5. A fair Morning Carpenters finished Garden 'tis Small, but very Convenient for Whites & black, & the Land appears Rich, at Present nothing in it but Mint. After Breakfast Mr. Burke & Miss Marshal, Davis & Martha Bay Visited me & dined with me & After Dinner Mr. McGill, Screven & Bardsdale Visited me the[y] all went off for Columbia, Long before Sun Set. I sent Mrs. Horry by Scipio 1 pound Butter bought of Mrs. Smith for a quarter Dollar Mrs. Horry Sent me some Turnip Seed.

Saturday, August 6. A fair Morning I Sent Sam about the Neighbourhood in Surch of Shingles, Carpenters Pining Garden boards to the Posts & Gitting Rafters. I Examined Marion history Yesterday, & Corrected Errors at bottom of Each Page. Lucy no Better. William with Carriage from Columbia brought Milk, Garden Seeds & 50 pounds 10 dozen Nails had of Habermont, Sam Returned & Says he found Some Shingles at Mr.   beyond Longbottoms he Got me some Butter Milk. I went to Columbia & Got there about 4 OClock

P.M. found Mrs. Horry at home. Saw Sarah Bay & Mr. Barksdale, Received from Post Office 2 Letters paid therefor 1/9—1 from John Cheesborow the other from J. Dubose my Overseer at Dover.

Sunday, August 7. Rained Last Night & this Morning. Answered Mr. Cheesborows Letter. Went to the State house & heard Reading by Doctor Fisher & Mr. Brathwait. Dined with S. Bay & Young Shackelford. In the afternoon Gabriel & Sanders Guignard Visited us. Also a Number of young Ladies & Gentlemen.

Monday, August 8. A fair & Cool Morning I went this morning to my Farm with Rachael, but first breakfasted with Mrs. Horry at Columbia Received J. H. Wicht & Company Account to 27 July 1814 Amounting to $340.29 Cents. Brought 3 bags Corn from Columbia, Sent Sam & Scipio for Shingles after fitting up Waggon therefor, Carpenters working on House, Lucy & Plenty Sick. Other Negroes Hoeing, Had of Habermount 5 pounds 20 dozen Nails & 10 dozen Shingle Nails.

Tuesday, August 9. A fair Morning Scipio after night brought from Mr. Martins 1300 Shingles & went off for another Load. Carpenters putting up Rafters. Other Negroes Cutting & bringing in Poles. Lent Warings Luke a Heaking Froe. Served out weeks Allowanc to Negroes at the Farm. I Sent William to Columbia to Mrs. Horry for Salt & Lathing hammer, Sent her a Basket of Irish Potatoes, this before Dinner. This Afternoon Isaac & Carlos began to Shingle Room Adjoining Chimney. Scipio brought from Mr. Martin by Waggon 1300 Shingles Sent Scipio to Mrs. Horry at Columbia.

Wednesday, August 10. Clear & Cool Morning, Carpenters Shingling. All other Negroes Cutting Poles for Rafters & bringing them in, Shaving them etc. etc. By William from Columbia Received Milk, Garden seed, & a Shingling Hatchet from Luke of Warings Farm also a Columbian Last News Paper, which I Sent to Mr. Burke. A Close hot day.

Thursday, August 11. Clear Sun Shine Morning. I was very Sick Last night. Great pain on my Neck, indeed all over me Carpenters Lathing & Shingling. Gitting more Poles William Came from Columbia with Milk & Peaches. About 10 OClock A.M. Gabriel & James Guignard called on me & Sot about an hour.

Friday, August 12. Last Night Scipio, came from Columbia & brought me a Tongue, Sugar & Eggs & this Morning he went off for a Load of Shingles a fine Shower of Rain fell Last night as Usual my Neck was very painfull. Shingling Goes on & today a Second Room will be done Received by Scipio 543 Shingles of Mr. Martin Sarah & Ann Bay dined today at the Farm & about 5 OClock P.M. Returned to Columbia in my Carriage I also sent Mrs. Horry her Chair.

Saturday, August 13. Yesterday Fell much Rain, this morning very damp & Somewhat Cloudy Carpenters Lathing & Shingling, Zemo Gitting Laths, flatting of Poles. About 10 OClock A.M. Mrs. Horry & Miss Martha Bay arrived here from Columbia, Zemo Got 6 Posts for Doors. Mrs. Horry brought a Hamlet for Negroes, Tomatis & butter Milk for ourselves Got 12 pounds Shingling Nails of Habermont $2.76. Mr. McGill, & Barksdale dined with us at the Farm. We all Sot out for Columbia & Got there about 6 OClock P.M. On the way met Wainstans & Scriven who returned with us to Columbia.

Sunday, August 14. We are now at Columbia a fine Morning, I Road to the State House & heard a Service by Mr. Lance & Saw many Acquaintances of both Sexes. A very hot day. Sent Zemo to farm for the Waggon. William Bay Dined with us. McGill & Gaillard Called on me after night. Waggon Came.

Monday, August 15. A Thick foggy & warm Morning, Loaded Waggon with boards & 1250 Shingles which I Got of James Guignard, I went to the Farm this morning. I wrote a Note to Sarah Bay. Waggon with the above Load Got Safe to the Farm, Got 2 pair Hinges with Staples from Glaze & Prescot at   Returned to Mrs. Horry at Columbia, The Waggon her Horse & Mule by Scipio. Zemo & Sam Getting Laths, Carpenters Lathing & Shingling, Rachael Cooking. Rest of the Negroes hoeing. In the Afternoon Sent William with a Basket of Irish Potatoes to Columbia for Mrs. Horry. Several Showers of Rain fell today.

Tuesday, August 16. Clear Morning. Carpenters Shingling. 3 fellows Getting Shingles. Scipio & William at Columbia with Mrs. Horry. Served out Weeks Allowances to Negroes at the Farm. Finished Shingling Rooms at the Farm. Wrote Mrs. Horry a Note by William & Sent her Some 10 dozen Nails.

Wednesday, August 17. Clear Morning, Sam & Zemo drawing Shingles & Splitting Poles, Carpenters at Work Inner Side of Farm House, all other Negroes hoeing Corn & Pease, Received by William 10 pounds 4 dozen Nails from Habermont Cost $2.30 Cents & from Witch & Company 1/2 pound Gun Powder.

Thursday, August 18. Cool Clear Morning 3 fellows Getting Shingles, Carpenters at Work on Piazza Shed, putting up Rafters, Laths & Shingling thereon. Moved my Bed Stead & other things in the Hal[l].

Friday, August 19. Clear Morning It Rained Last Night, finished Shingling Farm House, Carpenters, at Work on House, Opened Several Doors & Windows. All other Negroes hoeing Corn & Pease. Weather Excessive hot. It now Rains almost every Day, London brought me Milk, Eggs etc. etc. from Columbia. Sent William & London to Columbia to Mrs. Horry & wrote her a Note by them; Put Doors to two side Rooms, on Gabel End of House which makes the Farm House Compleat all but to be plaistered & to have Windows.

Saturday, August 20. Cloudy damp Morning Put out two Fellows to Split Rails. A Wench to Dig Irish Potatoes. Carpenters Putting up Windows & doing other work to Farm house. The other Negroes hoeing Corn & Pease. William & London Returned in my Carriage from Columbia & brought 7 Chairs & a Table & Milk. Sarah & Margaret Bay & Miss Goodwin Visited me & dined with me & in the Evening I Returned in Company with them to Columbia & met Mrs. Horry.

Sunday, August 21. A Clear Morning. I went to the farm, much disgusted with Columbia, being Last Night Robbed from my own bed Room (in which I Slept) my Only Hat, a Tin Cannister with sugar, Coffee, Chocolate etc. etc. & a Gloves, Altho' 4 Huge Negroes Slept in my Room. I wish I had never Seen Columbia & beleave it Contains Every Species of Vileness & Wickedness. I find I have Jumped from the Frying Pan into the Fire from George Town into Columbia Town. I wish my Creditors would take my Houses & Garden therein & Give me a full discharge Oh' Friendship where art thou to be found I have Lived too Long. But Gods Will must be done. I am now at my farm where I hope Ever to be, whether in Life or in Death. I Sent London to Columbia for Milk & wrote Mrs. Horry a Note of my being Robbed Last Night at Columbia.

Monday, August 22. Cloudy Cool Morning. Sent Scipio to Mrs. Horry at Columbia 2 fellows Getting Rails. Carpenters at Work about Farm House. Other Negroes hoeing etc. From Information I am Convinced that Mr. James Guignards Fellow Prince was the Man that Robbed me at Columbia. He was before Whipt publickly at Columbia for Theft now he deserves the Gallows. Isaac & Carlos Claying outward wall of Farm House, which Looks very well Indeed. I wrote James S. Guignard about his man Prince. Before night Mrs. Horry Sent me my Hat which was Stolen.

Tuesday, August 23. Cool & Clear Morning, Carpenters finishing Claying up farm House Walls 2 Rail Spliters. Others Hoeing etc. etc. Billy & London Sent to Columbia for Corn. Brought 12 pecks which was Served out to the People Mr. Cheesborough Visited me at the Farm we dined together & arrived at Columbia about 6 OClock P.M. found Mrs. Horry at Home.

Wednesday, August 24. Clear fine Morning I am at Columbia with Mrs. Horry & Mr. Cheesboro I went for the Farm in my Carriage & took in some Bricks & a board or two, & arrived thereat about 10 OClock A.M. Carpenters Squaring for Gate Posts. Other Negroes Splinting Rails & making up fence for Pasturage on the Public Road.

Thursday, August 25. Cool & Clear Weather Isaac & Sam Making a Large Gate on Public Road Leading to Columbia & Winsborough. Carlos & William Rubbing over plaistering on out Side of Farm House. Billy & Plenty Sick, Stephen & Zemo Splitting Rails.

Friday, August 26. Cloudy Morning, New Gate finished, 2 Splitting Rails, 2 Hoeing. Boys Cutting Poles, Billy Better. Plenty no better, before & After Night fell a Great Deal of Rain.

Saturday, August 27. Cloudy Damp Morning. Broke up work Bench. 2 Rail Splitters. Plenty Growing worse. I Ordered him to Columbia & went There myself, finished Railing my Farm House Piazza, & Claying its flooring & boarded up the Passage Leading into the Garden.

Sunday, August 28. I am at Columbia, a fair Morning, Last Evening a number of my young Acquaintances Visited me. S. Bay breakfasted with us. I went to the State House & Heard Devine Service by young Mr. Lance. Received of Mrs. Horry $15 for [illegible] Oil Sold at $2 per Gallon. Paid for 2 dozen Eggs 1/2. Mr. Winstan & Sarah Bay dined with us. Billy came here & Got a Dog which he carried to the Farm.

Monday, August 29. Rose Early at Columbia & Sent off for the Farm by Scipio, Sent by Waggon Boards & Sundry household Furniture, Soon afterwards I followed & we all Got safe at the Farm, 2 fellows Splitting Rails, Some making up Fences. 2 Carpenters fitting up Stables, Boys Claying Piazza. Scipio Returned with Waggon from Columbia with more boards, Trunks etc. etc. William Took back to Mrs. Horry her Horse & Mule. A Warm Cloudy Morning. London Stripping Blades.

Tuesday, August 30. William with Milk from Columbia. Rained Last Night. A very Cloudy damp Morning. Carpenters at Work on Stable. 2 fellows Getting Long Shingles for Stable. Finished Claying Piazza. Sat up a bed Stead in front South Room. Sent Scipio to Columbia with Waggon for Lumber, Corn & my Desk. Plenty Carrying Rails Sot up Several Pictures in Farm House Hall Mr. Whits refuses Buying my Columbia House. Wrote North & Webb a Letter for Coffee & Sugar. Served out 12 Allowances of Corn to Farm People.

Wednesday, August 31. Thick, Cloudy Morning, Slept in my New Room, 2 fellows Splitting Rails, Carpenters dividing Stable. London from Columbia brought me Milk Tomatis & Pears & a News Paper which I Sent to Mr. Burk. A Note from Mrs. Horry Says She has Received from North & Webb a Barrell Sugar & a Bag Coffee but no Letter or Bill of Cost. Sent London with a quarter Dollar to Mrs. Smith to pay for Butter had of her Saturday Last. Received by Scipio from Columbia 9 Boards, Posts, Wheat & Rye, & 2 Bags Corn. About 12 OClock Misses Gaillard Trescot, & Campbell from Columbia Visited me about sun Set fell 2 heavy Showers of Rain.

Thursday, September 1. Dark Cloudy Morning & warm. I was very Sick Last Night Carpenters Getting Shingles Ready to Cover Stable. Mrs. Horry Dined with me & went off to her Brother's & I went to Columbia, Received a Letter from W. W. Trapier & a Letter from North Webb, Trapier Informed me that the Sheriff at George Town had Seized an Affrican Lad of mine to Pay my Taxes. This hurried me to Columbia, where I now write from & I Consulted with James. S. Guignard who wrote a note to Judge Desaussure.

Friday, September 2. I waited on the Judge Desaussure this Morning & he refered Me to Major Clifton I then went to him & Laid my Compla[i]nt & Papers before him. He then wrote to the Sheriff & Tax Collector of George Town & to Samuel Smith of George Town & warned against Selling my Negro, that if the Sheriff did however Sell he must Abide the Consiquences. I then wrote to Windon Trapier of the Stepts I had taken on this most Extraordinary business & Expressid my Surprized of Their Acting against Law & Justice Scipio went off for George Town about one OClock this day on a Mule & directed if Possible to Get to George Town by Monday next. Mrs. Guignard Senior died Last Night & was buried this Evening on a plantation of her Son about 2 Miles distant from her husbands plantation where She died. A Great Concourse of People Attended & Doctor Montgomery Read or Pronounced an Oration on this Meloncoly Occasion. Mrs. Horry & myself attended the Same & returned home by night.

Saturday, September 3. I Last night was very Sick & this morning Sent for Doctor Fisher who Sent me Some Purging Pills. I took them all by his Directions at once & it was not till the Afternoon they began to Opperate & Violently I then Endeavour to Check the Same but failed.

Sunday, September 4. A Thick warm & Foggy Morning my Lax Seems to be Stopped & I drank warm Coffee being not well I continued at home & did not attend Devine Service. Yesterday Sent a Load of Bricks to our Farm Isaac Sent here, a few of his Tools. Mrs. Bay & Sarah her Daugher Breakfasted with us. Gabriel & Sanders Guignard Visited us. Paid *Monsier my Barber* a Dollars for Shaving me. Billy & Isaac came to me today from the Farm. Sarah Bay Dined with us. Miss Blackburn Lent me a Richmond News Paper Saying General Hill of the British Army with 10,000 Troops had Taken Washington City the Metropolis of the United States had burnt it & taken George Town.*

*Although Horry refers to General Hill as commander of the British at the burning of Washington, Gen. Robert Ross led the British in the attack. Chosen by the Duke of Wellington to command the expedition, Ross sailed with 3,500 of the finest troops of Wellington's army to the Chesapeake, where he was reinforced by 1,000 marines and 100 slaves from neighboring plantations. Ross ascended the Patuxent River and met the Americans under Gen. William H. Winder six miles from the City on the Potomac. Defeating Winder, he went on to burn the capital. Georgetown, in this case, is in the District of Columbia. Johnson, *History of the War of 1812,* 276–86.

It Says Also that General Izard had defeated General Provost of the British & Killed Taken & wounded Nineteen Hundred This is Consolation but do not Ballance against the Loss of Washington. *Now* Virginians Rise & drive the Foe before you & to their Vessells of War. Shame to Congress not to have Guared their House of Meeting with Troops, & not depend on the Melitia which cannot Stand the Bononet.

Monday, September 5. Clear fine Morning Isaac took down boards under Corn House Say 13 & he took down Closet in Rooms next to the Kitchen. I Sent off Rachael with her Child to the Farm. Took down in said Room a Large Looking Glass & Sent it by Isaac to the Farm, went thither myself With Miss Martha Bay & Miss Elizabeth Whitten. Paid Mr. Smith 1/2 for Butter wrote Mr. Burk the News. Sot up Large Glass in my hall at the Farm. Had 30 pounds 4 dozen Nails from Habermont. Before Sun Set the above two Ladies Left the Farm & went in my Carriage for Columbia.

Tuesday, September 6. Cloudy, warm Morning. Isaac Setting up a Closet in my Hall. Plenty Barking Posts for Pailing Fence, Stephen & Zemo Getting Pailings. Lucy Carrying Rails Carlos Getting more Posts for Pailings. Mr. Burk Visited me. I Gave him this days Columbia News Paper it Contains a Confirmation of Washington being taken & burnt. Served 12 Allowances for Negros at the Farm.

Wednesday, September 7. Foggy warm Morning. Carpenters Setting up Pailings. Stephen & Zemo, Splitting Pailings, finished Fencing in Pasture for my Stock, Mules Hogs etc. etc. I wrote a Note to Mrs. Horry & another to James Guignard of Columbia. A very hot day.

Thursday, September 8. A very fine Morning, Carpenters Going on with Pailings Stephen & Zemo Getting Pailings. Plenty & Lucy Making Fence, Sam with Carpenters London from Columbia with Milk, & Tomatis & 2 Hatts Which I Gave to Isaac & Carlos. Paid Patton & Company 3 Dollars as per their Receipt, wrote a Note to Mrs. Horry at Columbia. In the Course of today fell 2 Or more Smart Showers of Rain, Pailing finished as far as the Stable & began 2nd Line, Leading to Stephens House. Finished Digging Irish Potatoes.

Friday, September 9. Cool & Clear Morning, Carpenters Setting up Pailings. Stephen & Zemo, Splitting Pailings, Plenty Cutting Poles, Lucy Stripping Blades.

Saturday, September 10. A very fine Morning. Negroes this day Employed Exactly as Yesterday. William Came from Columbia, Brought me Milk, Bread & Tomatis; Says his Mistress & S. Bay are both Sick & that Mr. Cheesborough is at Columbia & means to Dine with me Today. Mr. Bardsdale Visited me. Also Mr. Cheesborow & McGill dined with me & about 5 OClock P.M. went off for Columbia, finished Pailing to Stephens House & Cleared Avineau to the Same.

Sunday, September 11. A fine Clear Morning I rose Early at the Farm & went to Columbia in time to Breakfast with Mrs. Horry, Miss Margaret Bay & Mr. Cheesborough hearing that Miss S. Bay was very Sick at her Mothers House I went & Visited her (therefore did not attend Devine Service) & found her very Sick in bed received a Note from James Guignard which Says "On Wednesday next Colonel Hutchison & Mr. Heath will Attend to appraise your Property. Mr. Sterling Williamson is a Commissioner & is Expected at the Methodist Meeting Today & you Can Send him the Inclosed Notice." I Sent the said Note to Mrs. Horry at the Methodist Meeting house. I dined with Mrs. Horry, Miss Martha Bay & Mr. Cheesborough. Mrs. H. delivered the Said Note to Mrs. Clifton. At 6 OClock P.M. S. Bay was better. A Smart Shower of Rain fell.

Monday, September 12. I rose Early & had the Corn all Taken out of the Corn House, & flowing boards therein Taken out; I breakfasted with Mrs. Horry & Mr. Cheesborough, Saw James S. Guignard, who Delivered me Captain George Wades Account against me for $329.38 Cents. I rode to the Farm & found the Carpenters Making 2 Gates to the Avinieu. Lucy Cooking & Plenty Cutting Poles & Stephen & Zemo, Getting Pailings. Three bags Corn put in Corn Chest at the Farm where I now are & at 10 OClock A.M. much Rain fell. I rote to Mrs. Horry to Give me in writing what James Guignard had of me & also what Doctor Green had. Rachael Child being Sick I Left it & its Mother with Mrs. Horry at Columbia, Levelled Avineau to Stephens Gate. Billy brought me the Said Boards from Columbia.

Tuesday, September 13. A Rainey wet Morning, Scipio Got here Last night, & returned me Cliftons Papers with a Letter from Mrs. Horry, Clifton, S. Bay & one for me from Samuel Smith, all of which I sent by Scipio to Columbia, with a Note to Clifton for Mrs. Horry & James Guignard to See; Waggon bringing in Poles for Posts, also bringing in Pailings for Carpenters. William from Columbia brought me Some Tripe, Bread & Milk Served out 12 Allowances to Farm Negroes being for a Week. Sent Waggon to Columbia, by William & London wrote Mrs. Horry a Note, Mr. Cheesboro Visited me.

Wednesday, September 14. Cool, Cloudy Morning. Yesterday Received a Sow & 9 Pigs from Columbia Stephen & Zemo Getting Pailings, Plenty Cutting Poles, Carpenters Employed as Yesterday. Sam & William Waggonning Scipio with Carpenter Lucy Pulling up Pea Vine etc. for Mules. London brought me from Columbia Milk, Beef, Biskuit etc. Sent him to Mr. Burke with Columbia Last News Paper, he Returned with some Butter Milk. London Inform me that Sarah Bay is Got much better. I thank God for all his Mercies. Mr. McGill & Cheesborow Dined with me & went off for Columbia about 5 OClock P.M. Finished a Line of Pailings from Stable to the broad

Road near the New Gate, Scipio & London went off for Columbia with a Note from me.

Thursday, September 15. Cool Clear Morning. 2 Splitting Pailings, Carpenters Setting up Last Line of Pailings. Plenty Cutting Poles, Sam & William Waggoning. Pailings & Posts, Lucy Cleaning Avineau, Scipio & London Returned from Columbia with Milk Eggs & Tomatis, Cow & Calf & Horse. Received a Note from James S. Guignard which I Answered today appered Colonel Hutchison Mr. Thomas Heath & Thomas C. Williams on 3 Commissions & Valued my Negroes at this Farm Say 13 Negroes at $4475. This is to Obtain a Loan from the Columbia Bank, Mr. McGill & Edwards Visited me about 5 OClock P.M. for an hour & Returned to Columbia.

Friday, September 16. Clear & Cold Morning, took up 2 Gates, Staked & Ridered Pasture Fence, finished Pailings, Sent Carriage by Scipio, William & London to Columbia for Mrs. Horry. She & Martha Bay Came in Chair. Scipio came in Carriage with Bricks Mortar & Pestle. They Dined with me & about 4 OClock P.M. Returned with Scipio in a Chair. Piazza Inclosed with Pailings & Gate thereto made & hung.

Saturday, September 17. Cloudy Morning. Carpenters Taking down in hall a Large Closet & Setting up two Lesser ones, Plenty Picking Cotton Lucy Sick. Boys Claying Piazza. Stephen & Zemo Cleaning Avineau, Corn in Ears, Thrashed out & Put in Closet in Barrell, Cut up Trees, Stumps etc. in Pasture to Clean it for Planting what may be fenced off. Mr. McGill, Screven, Winstan & Thompson Called on me, About 5 OClock I Sot off from the Farm & arrived at Columbia. Avineau now Looks Clean & Well. Thrashed out my Corn in Ears & Put it in my Corn Chest. Saw James S. Guignard after night, & he Consulted me about a Loan.

Sunday, September 18. I am now At Columbia a Clear Cool Morning James Guignard Sent me a Letter for the Clark of the Court of Common Please at George Town, also one for Richard Shackelford Sheriff of George Town district, both of which I forwarded by Mail. I went to the Chapple & heard Service by Mr. Montgomery Mr. Waring & Wife & Mr. & Mrs. McGill & Samuel Smith & Shackelford Dined *with us*. Mr. Guignard Senior & Junior & Gabriel & Sanders Guignard Called on us after Dinner. I wrote An Advertisment as follows. Of this days date "Prefering a Country Life, I will dispose of my Lot in Columbia, whereon is built a two Strory house, a Kitchen, a Corn House, or Stable, a Poultry House & Negro House. This Lot is nearly Opposite to the Colledge, House & Lands on Elivated brick work, has fine Cellars, & Affords an Extensive Prospect. For terms apply to Messrs. North & Web of Charles Ton, Windham Trapier of George Town, James Sanders Guignard of Columbia, or to me at Horry Farm near Columbia." Signed Peter

Horry wrote & Inclosed the above to North & Web of Charles Ton & Sent it to Post Office.

Monday, September 19. Cool & Clear Morning, Rose Early & Sot out for Farm House arrived there at about 8 OClock A.M. & Breakfasted. Carpenters at Closets in Hall, Stephen & Plenty taking down a Pole House Lucy Sick, Scipio Returned to Columbia with Milk, Cutting up Logs & Cleaning up Certain Part of Pasturage for Planting next Month. Attended yesterday the College Chapple & heard a discourse by Reverend Mr. Montgomery, on the Death of Major Moore, a Valuable Continental Officer My Neighbour Mr. Burk Visited me this Morning, wrote to Windham Trapier of George Town & Inclosed him an Advertisement to Sell my Columbia house & Lot. Finished making 2 Windows to Hall.

Tuesday, September 20. A Cool & Clear Morning. Boys bringing Sand Clay & Bricks to Chimney. Isaac making Chimney Carlos & Zemo Setting up a Pole House in Avineau. Scipio from Columbia with Sundry Letters & papers from Judge Desausure, Lawyer Clifton & James S. Guignard. Served out a Weeks Allowance to Negroes here Some Negroes working in New Inclosed Ground. Scipio returnd to Columbia with a Bundle of Papers & a Letter from me to Windham Trapier & a Note to James S. Guignard.

Wednesday, September 21. Cool & Clear Morning Carriage house finished, took down Stable & Sot it up on the apposite Side, hoeing new Ground, Sent Sam to Columbia for Bricks.

Thursday, September 22. Received Last Evening 250 Bricks from Mr. Willey It Rained Last Night, Clouddy Morning Isaac & Sam worked up in Chimney Said Bricks, Carlos Carriage Stable & Cow House Sent London to Mrs. Horry with Milk & wrote her a Note. Finished Chimney in hall & in Room London returned before Dinner with a Note from Mrs. Horry & a pair of Kid, Flour, & hogs Lard.

Friday, September 23. Clear but very Cold Morning, Isaac Made a Sedan & Cow House. Finished Stable & Cow House, Made a Potatoe House Sent London to Columbia With Milk for Mrs. Horry & wrote her a Note, Mrs. Bay & S. Bay dined with me. I Got Some Sugar from Mrs. Horry.

Saturday, September 24. Very fine Weather Sot up New Gate in Avineau & pailed in the Avineau. Plenty Cutting Poles for Corn House, Waggon bringing in Poles etc. Sent London to Columbia with Milk for Mrs. Horry Lucy Cutting Blades, Scipio brought from Columbia Young Francis Shackelford, who Dined with me & we Returned together to Columbia, Rachel & her 2 Children came with Scipio to Columbia where I now am & met Mrs. Bay & her Daughter Sarah at Mrs. Horrys.

Sunday, September 25. Cool & Clear Morning I rose Early & wrote a Letter to my Overseer Dubose at Dover. Found my Letter to Samuel Smith of

George Town yet at Columbia delivered it & my Overseers Letter to Mr. David Cuttino of George Town. He breakfasted with us. I went to the State House & heard Mr. Lance Officiate. Returned to Mrs. Horry, & S. Bay dined with us After Dinner Mr. Guignard Senior & Junior Called on us also Mrs. Bay & Margaret Bay & Elizabeth & Sarah Guignard.

Monday, September 26. I rose Early, & Sent off Rachael & Sam to the Farm, took in my Carriage Stairs from Corn House & went myself to the Farm & Breakfasted at the Farm, Carpenters at Work on Corn House, Stephen & Zemo splitting Rails, Broke Ears of Corn & beat it into Grains of Corn.

Tuesday, September 27. Clear Morning. Negroes Employed as Yesterday Served out Weeks Allowance of Corn to Negroes here. Sent London to Columbia with Milk for Mrs. Horry He returned with Eggs & Chocolate & Whisky but no Saw.

Wednesday, September 28. Warm Foggy Morning Carpenters Pailing in Potatoe House, Stephen & Zemo Splitting Rails on the back Line. Plenty & Lucy Making up fence from branch to Kitchen, Sent London to Columbia with Milk for Mrs. Horry. Yesterday Billy killed a high Ground Rattle Snake with 11 Rattles. Potatoe House Pailed in. Fence as above finished, & Mules & Cow Admitted into Potatoe Field. Cotton finished Picking. London Returned with Eggs.

Thursday, September 29. Fine Weather 2 fellows Splitting Rails, 2 Picking Cotton, 2 Carpenters at Corn House, Sent London to Columbia with Milk for Mrs. Horry London Returned with a hand Saw Sent me sometime ago by North & Webb which I delivered to Carlos also Received by London Eggs & Tomatis. Sent William to Mrs. Horry before Night, he brought me 10 pounds 6 dozen Nails from Habermont Shop. Sot down Old Gate in Pasture.

Friday, September 30. Fine Weather, Carpenters Shingling Corn House, all other Negroes Carrying Rails to devide between Pasture & New Ground to Plant Small Grains, Such as Rye, Wheat, Barley etc. About Noon my Neighbour Burk Visited me for 3 hands on Monday & Wednesday next Removed Stephens Fowl House to the back of his own House. Miss Sarah & Martha Bay Dined with me today, Colonel Huggins & Mr. McGill called on us & we came in Company to Columbia & met Mrs. Horry at home.

Saturday, October 1. Cool & Cloudy Morning. I rose Early & wrote a Letter by Isaac & Carlos to Mr. Samuel Smith at George Town, & my Overseer at Dover Plantation, Mr. Lance Called on us at Columbia, Margaret Bay went with me to the Farm. I delivered Negro Shoes agreeable to Memorandum Book of this date, brough[t] 3 Whip Saw to the Farm. Dined there & returne'd with Margaret Bay to Columbia by 5 OClock P.M.

Sunday, October 2. I rose Early fine Weather. I wrote a Letter by Isaac & Carlos to Osburn Esquire who Lives on Santee, I went To the Methodist

Meeting House with Mrs. Horry & heard Reverend Mr. Welch Officiate. Saw many Acquaintances, came home & found Francis R. Shackelford at our house. He & Colonel Huggins & his Son Dined with us. In the Evening Mr. McGill & House Called on us.

Monday, October 3. Clear & warm Morning Isaac & Carlos Sot off for my Plantatation Dover by Day light. I went & Breakfasted with James Guignard & Gave him my 2 War Pictures, brought a hen & Chickens to the Farm where I arrived about noon, Sent Plenty & Lucy to help Mr. Burk, Sent my Waggon by Sam to Columbia for a Gate & Long board. Stephen & Zemo Splitting Rails. Sam returned with board & Gate by Night.

Tuesday, October 4. A fair Morning. Send London with Milk to Columbia for Mrs. Horry. Negroes Getting in Blades, Pease & Corn, wrote a Note to James Guignard Respecting the Bank & to pay monies for me. Served a Weeks Allowance Corn to Negroes here Say 10 Allowances, Removed Shingles Sent Sam & William in New Land to Cut Trees, Logs etc. to Clear & Clean the Land better, Colonel Huggins & his Son Visited me & Dined with me & about 5 OClock P.M. went for Columbia.

Wednesday, October 5. Warm & Cloudy Morning. Sent Lucy & Plenty to Mr. Burk, Stephen to Curb Trees the 2 Boys to Burn Rubbish near the Potato House Sent London to Columbia. This morning Mrs. Horry Visited me & dined with me & about five OClock went off for Columbia Received a Letter from John Cheesboro from Statesborough, 2 from Richard Shackelford, & one from Captain Dent of Chareles Town. William brought me from Columbia a Hen & 2 Chickens.

Tuesday, October 6. Fair Morning, Sent London to Mrs. Horry at Columbia with Milk, Two fellows Raking New Ground, 1 hoeing, Sam making Yokes for 9 Piggs, All others Taking in Blades & Corn & Pease. I wrote a Long Letter to Captain Dent of Charles Ton in answer to one Lately Received from him. London Returned with a bottle Venegar, Some Castor Oil & Tincture of Rhubarb 1 Candle & some Coffee.

Friday, October 7. I rose Early a Clear Morning, Miss Smith & her Brother went with me to Columbia I breakfasted & Dined with Mrs. Horry. I Saw about 500 Militia men (Infantry) with 3 pieces of Artill[er]y March off for Chareles Ton. They made a Martial Appearance. I Got to the Farm about 3 OClock P.M. brought with me 5 Ducks a pair New Shoe Boots & a hat. Gave Old Boots & Straw Hatt to William.

Saturday, October 8. Cold & Clear Morning Sent London to Mrs. Horry at Columbia with Milk. Negroes digging Potatoes & falling old Trees in Potatoe Ground. Rachael Cleaning Cotton from the Stem. London Returned from Columbia with a Jacket for Robert & Part of a bottle of Honey wrote a Letter to Richard Shackelford of George Town. Left Cow & Mules in Avineau for the Night 2 Large Trees burnt Entirely out. Sawed 3 13 feet Timber to make Long Troughs.

Sunday, October 9. Rose Early, very Cold (*but no Frost*) Rode to Columbia after Breakfast Got there about 9 OClock A.M. Mrs. Horry not at home. Met with S. Bay & with her rode to the State House, & hea[r]d Mr. Lance Read Pray, Sing Psalms etc. Dined with Mrs. Bay & her Family & Widow Davis & her Daughter Mrs. Scriven & 2 Masters Player. Saw at State House Several Colegians Just Returned to Colledge Say Mr. Bonneau, Johnson, Simons Muller & McGinney. I drank Chocolate at & With Mrs. Horry at Columbia. Present Charles Huggins, Mr. Winstan & 3 Miss Hughs.

Monday, October 10. Clear, Cold Morning. Breakfasted with Mrs. Horry Saw S. Bay & James S. Guignard. Went to the Farm & Got there about 11 OClock A.M. Found the Negroes all digging Potatoes. Buried a Large Troft for Ducks. Sent Sam to Columbia with Waggon for a Troft & Load of Hay. Wrote a note to Mrs. Horry to Enquire for Oats, Rye & Wheat to Plant at the Farm. The Waggon Returned before Night & brough[t] Hay, 2 Bushels Oats from McChanling at 50 Cents per Bushel. Brought also a Large Troft & a Camp Bed Stead.

Tuesday, October 11. All hands Digging Potatoes, Sent London with a Note to Mrs. Horry Requesting Assistance of Lydia & Scipio very Cold Morning, Clear Weather. Buried new Troft along Pailings under Peach Trees. Put 3 Large Logs in Avineau for Troughs for Pease, & Fodder to feed Cows Mules etc. etc. London returned from Columbia, with Greens, News Paper & a Note for me from James Guignard, & a Hoe. I Sent the News Paper to Mr. Burk.

Wednesday, October 12. Clear but very Cold morning. All hands Digging Potatoes, Last Night Mrs. Horry Sent me Scipio & Lydia, & Mrs. Bay Sent me Betty & Rosella so I am 4 hands stronger Today than Yesterday; Sam Finished Pailings round Potatoe House. Dug up & housed all my Potatoes Today & begun Digging Potatoe Slips in Low Ground. Served out Allowances of Potatoes to Negroes Say for a Week. I Long to be at the house of my Cousin Martin at Winyaw, none of my Kindred is more dear to me, her Father brought me up & her Mother my Aunt Trapier was very Partial to me & I once thought the Daughter was so Likewise, but Such Reflections are Vain & Vexsatious.

Thursday, October 13. Clear Moderate Weather all hands Digging Potatoe Slips I Slept Uncommonly well Last Night & felt Religiously Disposed & prayed my Maker for a Reformation in me & I determined to Guard my words & Actions in future & to Set Example of Such to my Acquaintances & Family. Mr. Habermont Called on me & Sot an hour & went off for Columbia.

Friday, October 14. Clear Cold Morning finished digging in all my Potatoes, both Roots & Slips, 5 holes began to Pick Pease Scipio went to Columbia

Last Night digged out two Large Logs in Avineau as Trofts to Put in Pease or Corn etc. etc. Heard firing at Columbia. About 11 OClock A.M. Mrs. Bay & Sarah her Daughter Arrived at the Farm & Dined with me & went too Columbia before night.

Saturday, October 15. William went Yesterday to Columbia with Mrs. Bay & Billy Cut a young Boar at the Farm. Lydia went to her Mistress at Columbia Early this Morning, all hands Picking Pease, Except Sam & Zemo finishing a Troft. Dry, Moderate Weather. Betty & Rosella Returned to Mrs. Bay this Evening, they were 4 days with me. I rode to Columbia this Evening also Rachael & Robert went Likewise. Scipio, Sam, & London went also. We all Arrived about 2 OClock P.M. at Columbia found Mrs. Horry first dined. Billy Sent her 4 Punkins with Mrs. H. Sarah Bay. Saw Margaret Bay, Mr. McGill, James Guignard.

Sunday, October 16. Windy Clear & Cold Morning I went & heard Mr. Lance Read a Sermon etc. etc. then Dined with James Guignard in Company with his Father & their Family, Spent the Evening with Mrs. Bays Family Saw Many Colegians. Slept at our House in Columbia, Got a Charles Ton News Paper wherein was Enserted the Death of Thomas Hall a Revolutionary Officer, of his Services to his Country & his many Virtues, all of which I know to be very Correct, We Served in the 2nd Continental Regiment of South Carolina, were very Intimate & Corresponded untill Death Put an End thereto.

Monday, October 17. A very Clear Cold Morning. I rose Early & Breakfasted with Mrs. Horry & Mr. Mayrant Junior Sot out for Farm & Arrived there with Rachael about 10 OClock A.M. Brought a Bay Glass 8 by 10. Set Scipio with Waggon to Columbia with Milk & Cotton to Mrs. Horry & to the Order of Mrs. Bay. Sent Mr. Burk a Charles Ton News Paper of the Death of Captain Thomas Hall a Revolutionary Officer. Scipio Returned with Waggon from Columbia & brought Oil; Chalk White fence from Mrs. Horry & from Mrs. Bay. Sand paper by Memorandum Book Put up Guineau Corn & Snap Beans. Burk Gave me a Little Butter & Butter Milk.

Tuesday, October 18. A Cold wet Morning, Took in Corn, Sent London with Milk to Mrs. Horry at Columbia, Brought from North Branch 13 Posts for Garden, London returned from Columbia with Eggs, Tomatis & Table Salt, about 2 OClock it began to Rain. News Paper came also before Night Cuggo & Mercury arrived from Dover I received a Letter from Sam Smith & Dubose my Overseer.

Wednesday, October 19. Clear & Cold Morning, Served out Allowances to Negroes both here & at Columbia, Cut down Trees in New Land & branched them off this morning. Raking in Corn & Pease. Sent Waggon to Columbia by Scipio & London with Milk & Allowances & a Little Cotton. It Returned with a Load of Hay & a few things from Mrs. Bay.

Peter Horry's tombstone at
Trinity Episcopal Cathedral in Columbia

Margaret Horry's grave at Prince George Winyah
Episcopal Church in Georgetown

Thursday, October 20. Fair Morning. Sent London to Columbia with Milk for Mrs. Horry. Scipio & Sam & Mercury & Zemo falling Trees & Burning boughs of them, all other Negroes taking in Corn & Pease. Lydia Came from Columbia with a Note from Her Mistress to me & brought me some Ruffs. This morning I went round my Fields; found a good Crop of Pease (all dry) Rice all dry (not much Ears & Grain very Small) not much Corn, Particularly in New Land Going to Columbia; new Ground meant to Plant Small Grain much out of Order [illegible] Particularly where Cotton was Planted But I Live in hopes That the next Crop will be more Productive. London Returned from Columbia with Shirts & 2 pair Shoes from John Brice Price $2 about 11 OClock A.M. all hands went Picking of Pease, all other work must Cease till this is done. Shoes for Cuggo & Mercury. This Night I was very Ill, Winstanly came to See me & as Soon as day I went with him to Columbia. Doctor Fisher came to me & Prescribed for me.

Friday, October 21. I Continued very Sick &

Saturday, October 22. I Got better.

Sunday, October 23. I Got my Bowels Eased. Heard that Colonel Huggins was Elected Senator from Winyaw to State Legislature, & Thomas R. Mitchell, Doctor Blythe, Couchman & Doliessenine Representatives, William Mayrant is Sent to Congress.

Monday, October 24. Yet in Bed Doctor Fisher thinks me much better & Prescribed Allam Nater to [illegible] Sour Part my Room Floor was Drove up. S. Bay has never forsaken me. Carriage brought a Load of wood I write in Bed after Dinner.

Tuesday, October 25. Yet very Sick, Physick oppoiates well.

Wednesday, October 26. Mrs. Horry & Mrs. Bay went to the Farm & Served out a Weeks Provisions of Potatoes Winstan & S. Bay Sot with me all This morning. Changed my Bed Put a hard Mattrass under me. Got up & Sent William & London to the Farm. At Night Ben Ioor Called on us.

Thursday, October 27. Rainy Morning I Got up & Breakfasted on Coffee & Potatoes, my sore is better. Last night Mrs. Bay & Guignard Sot with us a While. About 11 A.M. It [illegible] Raining James Guignard Called on us, also Ben Ioor & S. Bay. After Dinner I Exchanged Rooms with Mrs. Horry. William & London returned from Farm with Waggon Load of Wood & a bottle of Milk, I wish my [illegible] may be for the Better, Sent William with my Mules to the Farm.

Friday, October 28. A fair Morning, Last Evening Charles Huggins & McGill Called on us. William Returned from Farm with Milk & a fine Pigg Sarah Bay Called on us. This morning I Saw our Garden, Mrs. Horry & S. Bay

The Ladies' Benevolent Society.
vs.
Ex'rs of Mr. M. Horry, dec'd.}
Bill for,
Sale of Property

On Monday the first day of March next will be offered for sale, at auction, near the market.

Ten valuable Negroes,
ALSO,

All that valuable LOT of LAND, in Browntown, (adjoining Georgetown,) formerly the residence of General Peter Horry, deceased, together with the *Dwelling House* and numerous *out-buildings* thereon.

Conditions of the Sale ; a *credit* will be given of one, two or *three years*; the purchasers to give Bonds on interest from the date, secured by a Mortgage of the property and approved security; The Deeds to be paid for by the purchasers.
ROBERT HERIOT,
Feb. 10. *Commissioner in Equity,*

DIED, at Georgetown, on the evening of the 15th inst. after a long and most painful illness, Mrs MARY MARGARET HORRY, widow of the late General Peter Horry. Mrs. Horry was a zealous and engaged christian : religion, and that the religion of grace, held the first place in her heart; and in reference to this, the leading objects of her life were chosen, and her steps directed. An ardent and faithful friend, she delighted in those she loved, and they were many : her confidence was entire, as her heart was true. Humane and sympathetic, the cry of the destitute never reached her ear in vain ; and she was literally the Orphan's mother. She fed the hungry, she clothed the naked, she succoured the stranger and relieved the sick. If she had to bless, they were the infirmities of nature; but her wishes were the principles of a Divine religion.

Left: Margaret Horry's executors advertised the sale of ten slaves and the Horry home in Browntown in the *Winyaw Intelligencer* on February 24, 1819, following her death.

Right: The obituary for Margaret Horry published in the *City Gazette and Daily Advertiser* on April 21, 1817

went & heard Revered Mr. Flin at the New Presbetorry Church Ben Ioor & Sarah & Margaret Bay dined with me. I wrote James Guignard Relative to Stamp Paper & to pay Mr. Irlvaine my Mortgage of Zemo & also to pay Taylor the Sheriff my Public Taxes.

Saturday, October 29. A Clear Morning I breakfasted with Mrs. Horry, I Gave J. Guignard a Check on bank & other Transactions with him as by Memorandum Book.

Sunday, October 30. Clear Morning (a Small Frost) Find myself not well Enough to Go to Church. Winstan Visited me Last Evening, This Morning S. Bay & Ben Ioor Visited me.

Monday, October 31. Clear Morning I went to the Farm with Rachael, S. Bay Visited me this morning. [T]ook Some Barley to the Farm.

What follows are Memorandums

December 14, 1814. This day Sold Sambo to Doctor Samuel Green for four hundred Dollars.

December 17, 1814. Delivered F. Delesseline Esquire a Note of Robert Collins for £16.10/9 Payable 1 January 1814.*

*1815.

Appendix A

Horry's Slaves

The following data is taken from Peter Horry's will dated March 3, 1815.

Abigail (Scipio's child)	14	$375
Anthony (Judy's child)	8	$200
August (Bes's child)	2	(Included with the value of Bes)
Beck (Sally's child)	5	$200
Bes	28	$500
Betty (Judy's child)	13	$300
Billy	62	$150
Binah (Judy's child)	15	$350
Bob (Bes's husband)	40	$400
Buddy	50	$450
Candis (Elsey's daughter)	7	$200
Canly	35	$450
Caphina	40	$400
Cariab (Peggy's child)	5	$200
Carlos (Polly's husband)	30	$500
Ceasor	3	$200
Celia	30	$500
Celia (Molly's child)	2	$100
Charlotte (Elsey's daughter)	3	(Included with the value of Elsey)
Cick (Polly's child)	1 ½	(Included with the value of Polly)
Clarinda (Will's child)	10	$250
Cornelia (granddaughter of Plenty)	15	$375
Craimake (Rachell's child)	1 ½	$100
Cudjo	28	$500

Elsey (Griggs's wife)	40	$400
Frank (Molly's child)	5	$200
Frank (Susy's child)		
Glases	3	(Included with the value of Rose)
Grad (Sally's child)	7	$250
Griggs	50	$400
Grippa (Ruta's child)	6 months	(Included with the value of Ruta)
Hardtimes	20	$400
Hercules	25	$400
Ichimy (Judy's child)	2	(included with the value of Judy)
Isaac	40	$450
Jeddo (Caphina's child)	13	$300
Jemmy (an African)	30	$450
Jeremy (Molly's child)	4	$200
Jolin (an African)	30	$50
Jose (Celia's child)	2	(Included with the value of Celia)
Judy (Cudjo's wife)	30	$500
Judy (Prince's wife)	40	$350
Kate (Nanny's child)	13	$250
Libby (Linda's daughter)	4	$400
Linda (Elsey's daughter)	4	$300
Linda (Toby's wife)	60	$5
London (Susy's child)	15	$425
Lucy (Elsey's daughter)	18	$400
Lucy (wife of Plenty)	60	$75
Lydia	10	$300
Lydia	24	$400
Mary	6	$200
Matthias	30	$450
May	2	$100
Mercury	23	$450
Michael (Judy's child)	9	$250
Mingo (Ruta's husband)	25	$400

Molly (Sylvia's child)	1 month	(Included with the value of Sylvia)
Morris (Caphina's child)	1	(Included with the value of Caphina)
Murriah (Buddy's wife)	45	$350
Nancy	12	$175
Nanny (Linda's daughter)	35	$400
Ned		$0 (Ned belonged to someone else)
Nelly (Sally's child)	2	(Included with the value of Sally)
Old Binah/Cinah	70	$1
Old Minda	(Buddy's mother)	$1
Omy (Sylvia's husband)	28	$500
Patty (child of Rose)	13	$300
Peggy	30	$400
Pembrook	25	$450
Peter (Tirah's child)	10 months	(included with the value of Judy)
Peter	4	$200
Phillis	6	$125
Plenty	60	$150
Polly	19	$500
Prince, a cooper	45	$500
Rachell	20	$475
Robert (Peggy's child)	7	$275
Rose	40	$450
Ruta	21	$500
Sally	30	$450
Sally	30	$500
Sam	20	$450
Sampson (child of Rose)	16	$400
Sarah (Stephen's child)	13	$300
Scipio	40	$400
Scrub	22	$400
Sielle	4	$200
Solimny (husband of Rose)	40	$400

Stephen (Lilly's husband)	40	$500
Stephen	60	$200
Subel	9	$150
Sue (Judy's child)	6	$200
Susannah (wife of old Billy)	50	$100
Susy (Mother of Tirah)	40	$375
Susy (Peggy's child)	3	$150
Sylvia	25	$500
Tirah (Susy's child)	16	$450
Toby (Celia's child)	6	$200
Toby	55	$100
Toney	6	$250
Will	45	$350
William (Scipio's child)	16	$500
Young Buddy	14	$350
Zemo	23	$500

Appendix B

Spellings of Names

Peter Horry's Spelling	Correct Spelling
Dr. Allston	William Allston
Joseph Allston	Joseph Alston
Young Allston	Joseph M. Alston
Colonel William Allston	William Alston
Mr. Anderson	Richard O. Anderson
Mr. Asberry	Francis Asbury
Mr. Barksdale/Bardsdale	George or Thomas Barksdale
Mr. Baxter	Francis M. Baxter
Mrs. Bay	Ann Davis Bay
Ann Bay	Anna Isabella Bay
Judge Bay	Elihu Hall Bay
Margaret Bay	Margaret Ransom Bay
Martha Bay, Martha Davis	Martha Davis Bay
Sarah Bay	Sarah Hall Horry Bay
Young Bay	William Bay
Mrs. Allard Belin	Esther Singletary Belin
Mrs. James Belin, Mrs. Belin	Mary Lynch Belin
Mr. Bell	James or William Bell
Captain Bethia	John Bethea
Captain Bingham	Samuel Bigham/Bingham
Miss Blackburn(s)	Georgiana Blackburn
Dr. Blythe	Joseph Blyth
Mrs. Blythe	Elizabeth Frances Allston Blyth
Miss Boone	Catharine Boone
Mr. Bossard	Joseph S. Bossard
Mr. Bostick, Captain Bostick	Benjamin R. Bostick
Mr. Botsworth, Parson Botsworth	Edmund Botsford
Ms. Bowman	Sabina Lynch Bowman

Mr. Boykin	Burwell Boykin
Frank Bremar	Francis Bremar Jr.
Captain Britton	Benjamin Britton
Broughton	Thomas Broughton
Mr. Brown	Joseph Brown
Dr. Brownfield	Robert Brownfield
Mr. Butler	Thomas Butler
Major Cambell/Campbell	James Campbell
Major Capers	William Capers
Reverend Mr. Capers	William Capers
Young Canty, Captain Canty	Charles Cantey Jr.
General Brigade Major Carr	Thomas Carr
Mr. Cassells	John Cassels
Mr. Chapman	Thomas Chapman
Mr. Cheesborough/Cheesboro/ Cheesborow	John Cheesborough
Major Clifton, Lawyer Clifton	Claiborne Clifton
Mrs. Clifton	Mary Cooper Clifton
Mrs. Cogdell	Esther Cogdell
Mr. Cohen/Cowen	Solomon Cohen Jr.
Lieutenant Coker	Thomas C. Coker
Lieutenant Cockley, Young Cockley	William Alexander Colclough
Colonel Conway	Robert Conway
Mr. Course, Mr. Course Junior	Isaac Course
Mr. Croft	Edward Croft
Mrs. Croft	Floride Lydia Gaillard Croft
David Cuttino	David William Cuttino
Young Mr. Cuttino, Mr. Cuttino	Peter Cuttino
Mr. Dalton	Fred W. Dalton
Miss Danford	Eliza Danford
Mrs. Davis, Widow Davis	Martha Cantey Davis
Martha Davis, Maria Davis, Miss Davis	Martha Maria Davis
Warren Davis, Young Davis, Mr. Davis	Warren Ransom Davis
Miss Delesseline, Polly Delesseline	Polly Deliesseline
Captain Dent	John Herbert Dent
Mrs. Desausure	Elizabeth Ford De Saussure
Judge Desaussure, Desassure/Desasure/Desausure	Henry William De Saussure

Mrs. Dinkins	Nancy Smart Dinkins
Mr. Dozer	John Dozier Jr.
Judge Drayton	John Drayton
Mrs. Ellerbe	Anna Maria Wickham Ellerbe
Mrs. Elizabeth Elliot, Mrs. Elliot, Betsey Wayne	Elizabeth Trezevant Wayne Elliott
Eveligh Family, Miss Eveligh	Ann Simmons Eveleigh
Mr. Faust, Major Faust/Faus	Jacob John Faust
Mrs. Faus	Sarah Clarke White Faust
General Fishburn	William Fishburne
Mr. Fleming, Fleming Sr.	George Henry Fleming
Captain Floyd	Charles Floyd
Reverend Mr. Frazer	Hugh Fraser
Mr. Fry	Philip Martin Frey
Gadsden Esquire	John Gadsden
Mrs. Gaillard	Cornelia Marshall Gaillard
Senator Gaillard	John Gaillard
Judge Gaillard, Senator Gaillard	Theodore Gaillard Sr.
Captain Gasqua	Robert Gasque
Mr. Gibs/Gibbs	William Hasell Gibbes
Major Guest	Mordecai Gist
Henretta Glover	Henrietta Bonneau Glover
Mr. Goddard	Thomas Fraser Goddard
Mrs. Goddard	Elizabeth Coon Hutchinson Goddard
Justice Goodwin, Mr. Goodwin	James Goodwyn
Mr. Gourdine, Gourdine Esquire, Theodore Gourdine	Theodore Gourdin II
Mr. Grant	William Grant
Dr. (Samuel) Green/Greens/Greene	Samuel Green
Grier	James Grier
Mrs. James Guignard, Mrs. Guignard Junior	Caroline Richardson Guignard
James Guignards, Mrs. James Guignards Two Daughters	Caroline Elizabeth Guignard, Sarah Slann Guignard
Mrs. Guignard Senior, Mrs. Guignard	Elizabeth Sanders Guignard
James Guignard, J. S. Guignard, Guignards Waggon, Guignard Junior	James Sanders Guignard

Sanders Guignard	James Sanders Guignard II
James Guignards two sons	James Sanders Guignard II, John Gabriel Guignard II
Gabriel Guignard, Guignard Senior, Guignards Office	John Gabriel Guignard I
Gabriel Guignard Junior	John Gabriel Guignard II
Mr. Hails	Robert Hails
A. Hall	Ainsley Hall
Captain Thomas Hall	Thomas Hall
Parson Halling, Reverend Mr. Halling, Doctor Halling	Solomon Halling
Lieutenant Hampton, General Hampton, Hamptons Mill	Wade Hampton II
Mr. Harrell	Lewis Harrell
Old Harrell	Jacob Harrell
Captain Hart	John Hart
General Harrison	James Henry Harrison
Mr. Harvey	John Harvey
Mr. Hassell, Hazzle, Hazle, Captain Hazzle	Andrew Hasell
Doctor Hansworth, Haynsworth, Hainsworth	James Haynesworth
Harbamond/Herbemont/ Hobermount/Habbermont/ Habermount/Habermont	Nicholas Michel Laurent Herbemont
Ben Heriot	Benjamin Heriot
Robert Heriot Esquire and his lady	Maria Eliza Heriot
Mr. Hill, Captain Hill	Joseph Hill
E. Horry	Elias Horry
Mrs. Horry	Margaret Magdalen Guignard Horry
Mr. Hort	Benjamin Simmons Hort
Captain B. Huger, Captain Huger, Ben/Benjamin Huger	Benjamin Huger
Daniel Elliot Huger	Daniel Elliott Huger
Frank/Frances Huger	Francis Huger
Colonel Huggins	Nathan Huggins
Doctor Hughes	John Hughes
Misses Hughes	Sarah Winn Hughes
Mr. Inglesby	William H. Inglesby

Ben Ioor	Benjamin Ioor
Mrs. Elizabeth Ioor, Mrs. E. Ioor	Elizabeth Catherine Guignard Fley Ioor
Sister Ioor, Mrs. Ioor	Emily Richardson Ioor
Miss Richardson	Frances Guignard Ioor
Mr. Ioor	John Ioor
General Izard	George Izard
Judge James	William Dobein James
Mr. Johnson, Captain Johnson, Johnson	Richard Johnson
Widow Thomas Johnson, Mrs. Johnson	Mrs. Thomas Johnson
Joseph	Lizar Joseph
Mrs. Joseph	Sarah Judith Judah
Captain Irvin Keith, Captain Keith	Irvin Keith
Major Keith, Major Commandant Keith	John Keith
Mr. Lance, Lance	Maurice Harvey Lance
Mr. Lartigue	Etienne Lartigue
Mr. Laurens Junior	Henry Laurens Jr.
Captain Lawson	John Lawson
Mrs. Charles Lessesne, Mrs. Lessesne	Binkey Lesesne
Charles, Captain Lessesne, Quarter Master Lessesne	Charles Frederick Lesesne
Joe, Joseph Lessesne, Mr. Lessesne	Joseph Lesene
Joseph Lessesne Junior	Joseph Lesene Jr.
Mr. Lightfoot	Philip Lightfoot
Bowman Lynch, Mr. Lynch	John Bowman Lynch
Miss Lynch	Margaret Lynch
Mr. McGill, Colegian McGill/McGill	John D. Magill
Mrs. Martin, Cousin Martin	Elizabeth Martin
Mr. Marvin Senior, Mr. Marvin, Aron Marvin	Aaron Marvin
Son Charles	Charles Mayrant
Miss Francis, Frances Mayrant	Frances Caroline Mayrant
John Mayrant Esquire and his Lady	Isabella Norvelle Mayrant
Placedia Mayrant	Placidia Mayrant
William/W. Mayrant, Mr. Mayrant, William Mayrant Esquire	William Woodrup Mayrant
Young Mayrant, Mr. Mayrant Son, Mr. Mayrant Junior	William Mayrant Jr.

McCord	David James McCord
Mr. McDufee	George McDuffee/McDuffie
Mr. McFarlin	Andrew McFarlin
McGinney	Albert J. McGinney
Reverend Mr. Meek	Samuel M. Meeks
Messrs. Meyers, The Meyers	Meyers Brothers
G. Mitchell	George Mitchell
Mrs. Mitchell, Colonel William Boone and his Lady	Dorothy Sinkler Richardson Mitchell
Thomas R. Mitchell Esquire, Mr. Mitchell/Mitchell, T. R. Mitchell, Thomas Mitchell, Thomas R. Mitchell	Thomas Rothmahler Mitchell
Colonel Boone Mitchell	William Boone Mitchell
Reverend Mr. Montgomery, Doctor Montgomery	Benjamin Montgomery
John Murrell, Mr. Murrell	John Morrall
Major Motte	Charles Motte
Mr. Mulleger	Albert Arney Muller Jr.
Major Muller	Albert Arney Muller Sr.
Mrs. Murray	Martha McQuillan Murray
Major Murray	William Murray III
Meyers, Meyers Tavern	David Rudolph Myers
Parson, Doctor Norton, Mr. Norton, Reverened Mr. Norton	James Norton
Judge Knot	Abraham Nott
Mr. Ohenlin, OHenry/OHenlin/OHenley	Terence O'Hanlon
Mr. Palmer, John Palmer	John Palmer Sr.
Mr. Pawley	Anthony Pawley
Captain Samuel Perdriau and his wife	Esther Perdriau
General Pickens	Andrew Pickens
Colonel Pickens	Andrew Pickens Jr.
Pinckney's Plantation, Major Pinckney, Pinckney	Thomas Pinckney
Major Player, Player, Young Players, Masters Player	Joshua Player
Samuel Prioleau Junior, Mr. Prioleau	Samuel Prioleau
Mr. Pyatt Junior	John Francis Pyatt

General Jacob Reid	Jacob Read
Mrs. Rees, Mrs. Rees Junior, Mr. Rees and his Lady	Maria Rees
Mr. Rees, Rees Junior	William James Rees
Mr. Read	John Reid
Colonel James Richardson, Colonel Richardson	James Burchell Richardson
John S. Richardson, John Smith (Smyth) Richardson	John Smythe Richardson
Mr. Rouse	William Rouse Sr.
Colegians Mr. Rutledge	Benjamin Huger Rutledge
Mr. Rutledge	Frederick Rutledge
Mrs. Rutledge	Harriott Pinckney Horry Rutledge
Widow of Jonah Horry	Lucretia Sarrazin
Francis R. Shackelford, Young Francis Shackelford	Francis Shackelford
Miss Hannah Shackelford, H. Shackelford	Hannah White Shackelford
Mrs. John Shackelford	Martha Ann Wright Shackelford
Mrs. Francis Shackelford	Rebecca Ballard Shackelford
Dick Shackelford	Richard Shackelford
Robert Shackelford, R. Shackelford, Captain Roger Shackelford	Roger Shackelford
Mrs. William Shackelford	Sarah Collins Withers Shackelford
Young Mr. William Shackelford, William Shackelford Junior	William Cartwright Shackelford Jr.
Captain William Shackelford, Mr. William Shackelford	William Cartwright Shackelford Sr.
Thomas Simons, Simons (colegion)	Thomas Young Simons
Mr. Singletary	Isaac Singletary
Josias Smith	Josiah Smith Jr.
Widow Roger Smith	Mary Rutledge Smith
S. Smith, Sam Smith, Samuel Smith Esquire	Samuel Smith
Captain Smith, Major Smith, Lieutenant Smith, Major Savage Smith, President Savage Smith	Savage Smith
Mr. Solomon	Levy Solomon
Lieutenant Stark	Robert Stark Jr.

General Sumter, Sumpter	Thomas Sumter
Mr. Strebeck	George Strebeck
Engineer Swift	Joseph J. Swift
Mrs. Tom Taylor	Ann Wyche Taylor
John Man Taylor, J. M. Taylor, Man Taylor, Mr. Taylor, John N. Taylor, John M. Taylor, Colonel John Taylor, John Taylor, Taylor's Mill, Captain, Colonel Taylor	John Mann Taylor
Burrington Thomas	Thomas Burrington Thomas
Mrs. Thompson	Elizabeth Sabb Thomson
Samuel Isaac Thurston and his wife	Mary C. Coggeshall Thurston
Mr. Thurston	Samuel Isaac Thurston
Toomer	Anthony Vanderhorst Toomer
Captain Benjamin Trapier, B. Trapier, Captain B. Trapier, Ben Trapier, Ben F. Trapier	Benjamin Fossin/Foissin Trapier
Trapier's Lady, Mrs. B. Trapier, Mrs. Trapier	Hannah Heyward Trapier
Son Horry Trapier, Paul Trapier	Paul Horry Trapier
Windham/Windon Trapier, W. Trapier	William Windham Trapier
Mrs. Travis	Elizabeth Forster Travis
Reverend Mr. Travis, Travis, Mr. Travis	Joseph Travis
Mr. Trezevant	Daniel Heyward Trezevant
Doctor Tucker	Thomas Tudor Tucker
Wades Mill, Captain Wade	George Wade
Mr. Waldo, Waldo	John Waldo
James Ward, Mr. Ward, Major Ward, Ward	James McCall Ward
Mr. Benjamin Waring, Captain Benjamin Waring	Benjamin Waring
Mrs. Robert Waring	Mary H. Taylor Waring
R. Waring, Warings Wagon	Robert Waring
Mrs. Waties	Margaret Ann Glover Waties
Judge Waties	Thomas Waties
Reverend Mr. Wayne, Mr. Wayne Senior	William Wayne
Mrs. Wayne, Mrs. Wayne Senior	Esther Trezevant Wayne
Colonel Otho Williams	Otho Holland Williams
Mr. Sterling Williamson	Sterling C. Williamson

Captain Wilson, John Wilson   John Lyde Wilson

Mr. Wise   Thomas Wise

Withers   John Withers

John Woddrop Esquire   John Woodrop

Doctor Wragg, Dr. John Wragg   John Ashby Wragg

Mrs. Samuel Wragg   Mary Ashby I'On Wragg

Major Wragg, Lieutenant Wragg,   Samuel Wragg
   Mr. Wragg, Wragg

Mr. Youngblood   William Youngblood

Appendix C

Biographical Notes

Alston, Joseph (1779–1816): Joseph Alston, the eldest son of William Alston and Mary Ashe, attended the College of Charleston and entered the junior class at Princeton University in 1795. After studying law with Edward Rutledge and being admitted to the bar in 1799, he left the legal profession to become a rice planter. Alston's estate was valued at £200,000 sterling in 1800. At the death of his grandfather, Joseph Allston, he inherited 100 slaves and the Oaks Plantation, where he resided. In addition to this property, he owned more than 2,000 acres in All Saints Parish and a summer home in Greenville. An 1825 tax return on his estate listed 6,287 acres and 204 slaves in All Saints and 120 acres in Greenville. Alston served in the South Caroline House of Representatives starting in 1802 and, with the exception of 1804, continued to occupy that seat until 1812. He was Speaker of the House from 1805 to 1809. Alston won the hotly contested gubernatorial election of 1812 and served until 1814. From 1812 to 1816, he was brigadier general of the Sixth Brigade of the state militia. Alston represented All Saints in the state senate from 1814 to 1815 and held a number of smaller offices. As an official he was controversial and made bold moves. E. S. Thomas, editor of the *Charleston City Gazette,* was his nemesis and constantly baited him. When Thomas accused Alston of purchasing his seat in the House, Alston sued him for criminal libel. Found guilty and imprisoned, Thomas was later pardoned by Gov. David Rogerson Williams. On February 2, 1801, Alston married Theodosia Burr, daughter of Aaron Burr and Theodosia Bartow. The Alston-Burr alliance was very powerful, and Alston became involved in Burr's attempts to annex the West and conquer Mexico. He invested financially in the plan and even accompanied Burr on an expedition to the western territories. When Burr was arrested for treason, Alston reneged on his support and wrote Gov. Charles Pinckney in 1807 denying his involvement in the plan. No charges were brought against Alston, and Burr was acquitted. Alston's son died of a fever on June 30, 1812, and his wife died at sea in January 1813. He died September 10, 1816, in Charleston and was buried at the family cemetery at the Oaks.

Edgar, *Biographical Directory of the South Carolina House,* 32–35; Devereux, *Rice Princes,* 29–46, 50–73; Groves, *Alston and Allstons,* 51–52, 54, 55; Parton, *Life and*

Times of Aaron Burr, 1:298; Rogers, *History of Georgetown County,* 188–92, 196–97, 207, 221, 232, 261, 265, 267, 315, 376, 522–23; Tomas, *Reminiscences,* 2:69–82.

Alston, Joseph M.: Joseph M. Alston of Georgetown was a sophomore at South Carolina College in 1812. He left the following year.

Moore, *Roll of Students,* 6; Salley, "Journal of General Peter Horry" (1943), 124n.

Alston, William (1756–1839): Nicknamed "King Billy," Col. William Alston was one of the biggest slaveholders in All Saints Parish. The son of Joseph Allston and Charlotte Rothmahler, he was the first of the Allstons to spell his name with one *l,* a change he made in order to distinguish himself from William Allston of Brookgreen. Alston was an extensive property owner in the Carolina lowcountry. By the time of his death, he owned various plantations on the Waccamaw River, including Fairfield (which he inherited from his father), Clifton, Weehawka, Claremont, Midway, Crabhall, and Strawberry Hill. It was Cifton, Alston's main residence, that President George Washington described in 1791 as "large, new, and elegantly furnished." Washington said the rice fields below "looked like fairyland." Clifton was later destroyed by fire, and Alston relocated to Fairfield. At one time he owned Rose Hill and Bellfield Plantations, in addition to land in Georgetown and Charleston. Alston was a captain in Francis Marion's brigade and remained active in the state militia as a major and colonel. In 1788 he represented Prince George Winyah Parish at the state convention for ratification of the federal Constitution. Alston served in the South Carolina House of Representatives for All Saints Parish from 1776 to 1786. He represented both All Saints and Prince George Winyah in the state senate from 1787 to 1790. All Saints continued to elect him intermittently to the state senate until 1815. He acted as tax inquirer and collector for All Saints, was a founding member of the Georgetown Library Society, and a member of the vestry for All Saints. He was also a member and steward of the Jockey Club and helped to organize the fourth South Carolina Jockey Club in 1792. He married Mary Ashe, daughter of Gen. John Baptista Ashe and Rebecca Moore, on February 13, 1777. They had five children: Maria, Joseph, John Ashe, William Algeron, and Charlotte. After Mary's death in 1789, Alston wed Mary Brewton Motte, daughter of Jacob Motte Jr. and Rebecca Brewton. They had at least six children: Rebecca Brewton, Thomas Pinckney, Elizabeth Laura, Charles Cotesworth Pinckney, Jacob Motte, and Mary Motte. Survived by nine children, Alston died June 26, 1839, and is buried at his son Joseph's plantation, the Oaks.

Bailey and Cooper, *Biographical Directory of the South Carolina House,* 35–38; Groves, *Alstons and Allstons,* 51–58; Henderson, *Washington's Southern Tour,* 126; Moss, *Roster of South Carolina Patriots,* 16; Rogers, *History of Georgetown County,*

166, 173; US Department of the Interior, Census Office, First, Second, Third, and Fourth, 1790–1820, All Saints, Georgetown District, S.C.

Allston, William (1772–1848): William Allston was a physician and planter in Georgetown. He received his MD from the University of Pennsylvania on May 15, 1797. Allston purchased Arundel Plantation from John Julius Pringle in 1806 and sold it to Frederick Shaffer in 1841. The family later regained the property when Charles Alston Sr. purchased it for his son Charles Pringle Alston. Allston helped plan and erect Prince Frederick Church on the Black River in 1835. He married Mary Pyatt, daughter of the late John Pyatt, in 1800. They had at least one child, a daughter, who married Dr. Theodore Gourdine. Allston died February 6, 1848, and was buried at Prince George Winyah Episcopal Church.

Groves, *Alstons and Allstons,* 44; "Inscriptions from the Churchyard" (no. 3), 204–5; Lachicotte, *Georgetown Rice Plantations,* 109–11, 277; Rogers, *History of Georgetown County,* 279; *Winyah Observer,* February 9, 1848.

Anderson, Richard O.: Richard O. Anderson was a planter on the Black River. In 1835 he helped plan and erect Prince Frederick Church. Anderson was one of the original members of the Planters Club, an organization comprising plantation owners along Winyah Bay and the Waccamaw, Pee Dee, Black, and Sampit Rivers. In 1850 he owned 284 slaves, and his plantation was valued at $100,000.

Census, Fifth, 1830, Georgetown, S.C.; Rogers, *History of Georgetown County,* 279, 288, 524; *Winyah Observer,* December 22, 1852.

Asbury, Francis (1745–1816): English clergyman Francis Asbury was the founder of American Methodism. At the Bristol Conference of the Methodists in 1771, he volunteered to go to America as a missionary, arriving in Philadelphia later that year. During the American Revolution, Methodist missionaries became suspect due to John Wesley's opposition to American independence. Asbury, the only Methodist missionary who chose to remain in America during the conflict, at war's end became the leader of the Methodist movement. On December 24, 1784, he helped form the Methodist Episcopal Church as a separate denomination and was elected its first bishop. Asbury is best remembered for circuit riding, a practice he encouraged among other Methodist clergy. His ministry started in New York, but he eventually made his way to the South and West. Asbury visited Georgetown frequently through the years and noted his observations in his journal. He deemed Georgetown a "poor place for religion," and in 1794 recorded this impression: "If a man-of-war is a 'floating hell,' these [rice plantations] are standing ones: wicked masters, overseers, and Negroes—cursing, drinking—no sabbaths, no sermons." During his tenure Asbury traveled over more than three hundred thousand miles on horseback, preached 16,500 sermons, ordained four thousand Methodist ministers, and was the driving force in making Methodism the largest and fastest-growing denomination in the United States. Asbury died in Virginia on March 31, 1816.

Asbury, *Methodist Saint;* Clark, Potts, and Payton, *Journals and Letters,* 1:505, 2:7; Ludwig, *Francis Asbury;* Rogers, *History of Georgetown County,* 180–82; Rudolph, *Francis Asbury.*

Barksdale, George (1786/87–1816): George Barksdale was the son of Mary Daniel and George Barksdale. His father was a planter and represented Christ Church Parish in the Third General Assembly from 1779 to 1780. Barksdale owned Greenwich Plantation and resided in Christ Church Parish. His wife was Rebekah B. Barksdale. They had one son, James Edwards, born July 3, 1805, and died February 21, 1812. Barksdale's will is dated February 6, 1814, and he died in 1816.

Bailey and Cooper, *Biographical Directory of the South Carolina House,* 51; Barksdale, *Barksdale Family History,* 470.

Barksdale, Thomas (1780–1850): Thomas Barksdale was the son of Thomas Barksdale and Mary Vanderhorst. He was a planter living in Christ Church Parish and owned Younghall Plantation. Barksdale was a vestryman and secretary-treasurer of Christ Church Parish as well as a commissioner of the public roads. On May 12, 1812, he married Serena Maria Payne in Charleston. They had eight children: Mary Vanderhorst, William Payne, Adelaide, Elizabeth Serena, Emma Julia, Julian Augustus, and infant twins who died in 1834. Barksdale died in his Charleston home in 1850 and was buried at the First Presbyterian Church in Charleston.

Bailey and Cooper, *Biographical Directory of the South Carolina House,* 52; Barksdale, *Barksdale Family History,* 472–73.

Baxter, Francis M.: Francis Baxter was the editor of the *Georgetown Gazette.* He married Mary E. Ervin in St. John's Parish on December 24, 1809.

Jervey, "Marriage and Death Notices" (1933), 40; Rogers, *History of Georgetown County,* 219.

Bay, Andrew (1754?–1838): Andrew Bay was the son of Elihu Hall Bay and Margaret Holmes. He was baptized January 28, 1788. Admitted to the South Carolina bar in 1808, he established a law practice in Charleston. During the War of 1812, he served as a private in the Third Regiment of the state militia. St. Philip and St. Michael Parishes elected him to the Twentieth General Assembly from 1812 to 1813. He was tax inquirer and assessor for St. Philip and

St. Michael from 1818 to 1823, city constable for Charleston's Second Ward in 1821, justice of the quorum for Charleston from 1826 to 1827, 1831, 1834, and 1835, and tax assessor for St. Philip and St. Michael from 1826 to 1834. In 1829 he resided with his father at 16 Logan Street in Charleston. Bay died in 1838.

Bailey, *Biographical Directory of the South Carolina House,* 51; Hagy, *Directories for the City of Charleston,* 137; Smith and Salley, *Register of St. Philip's Parish,* 107.

Bay, Ann Davis (1757–1847): Ann Davis Bay was the sister of Capt. William Ransom Davis, sheriff of Camden District and one of the founders of State-burg. She married William Bay, son of Rev. Andrew Bay and brother of Elihu Hall, Andrew, and John Bay. Ann and William had five children: Anna Isabella, Margaret Ransom, Martha Davis, Sarah Davis, and William. The couple married in 1792 and signed a prenuptial agreement on February 15, 1792. They settled in the High Hills of Santee, in what is now Sumter County, on a plantation given to them in trust by Elihu Hall Bay. The couple separated May 16, 1808, and sold their property. William moved to Warren County, Vicksburg, Mississippi, where he became a cotton planter and died in 1822. Ann and her children moved to Columbia and lived in a house on two acres near Senate, Bull, and Marion Streets. Ann died in 1847 at age ninety.

Bulloch, *Habersham Family,* 128; Maybank and Stockton, *Maybank Family,* 281–82; Moore, *Biographical Directory of the South Carolina House,* 180; Schwab, *Crofts of South Carolina.*

Bay, Anna Isabella: Anna Isabella Bay was the daughter of William Bay and Ann Davis. She married the Reverend P. H. Falker.

Bulloch, *Habersham Family,* 128.

Bay, Elihu Hall (1754–1838): Elihu Hall Bay was the son of Rev. Andrew Bay. He was born in Pennsylvania and spent the early part of his life in Maryland. Bay was educated in New York with the intention of pursuing a career in the ministry. He switched to law, however, due to a speech impediment. In 1772 Bay relocated to Pensacola, Florida, but when the Spanish regained control of the area after the American Revolution, he settled in Charleston and petitioned for citizenship in February 1783. He was admitted to the bar that same year. Bay served at the state constitutional convention in 1790, representing St. Philip and St. Michael Parishes. Both parishes elected him to the house in 1791 in the Ninth General Assembly. On February 16, 1791, Bay was appointed an associate justice of the Court of General Secessions and Common Pleas, continuing in this office until his death. He was excused from some of his judicial duties in 1817, but the state allowed him to retain his salary because of declining health. Bay published two volumes of reports on previous South

Carolina law cases in 1809 and 1811. He also supported nullification in 1832 and was a member of the Charleston Library Society and an ex officio trustee of South Carolina College from 1825 to 1837. Bay wed Margaret Holmes, widow of David Holmes, on September 19, 1781, in Pensacola. They had five children: Andrew, William, Margaret, Eliza, and Maria. The Bays' primary residence was in Charleston, but they also owned a number of summer homes in the High Hills of Santee. Bay died November 10, 1838, at the age of eighty-five.

"An Act to Exempt the Honorable Elihu Hall Bay," in Cooper and McCord, *Statutes at Large*, 6:77; Bailey, *Biographical Directory of the South Carolina House*, 52; Census, Third, Charleston, S.C.; Hagy, *Directories for the City of Charleston*, 137; Hutson, *Journal of the Constitutional Convention*, 3, 7, 8, 9; Lowrie and Clark, *American State Papers*, 1:747, 749, 750, 754; Rogers, *Georgetown*, 315; Schwab, *Crofts of South Carolina*.

Bay, Margaret Ransom (ca. 1803–1831): Margaret Ransom Bay was the daughter of William Bay and Ann Davis. She married Joseph Maybank IV. They had three children: Harriet Hampton, Jacob Bond I'On, and Joseph R. Margaret died October 25, 1831, at Grove Plantation in Christ Church Parish and is buried at Trinity Episcopal Cathedral in Columbia.

Bulloch, *Habersham Family*, 128; Stockton, *Maybank Family*, 281–82.

Bay, Martha Davis (1798–1877): Martha Davis Bay was born January 27, 1798, the daughter of William Bay and Ann Davis. She married Alexander Herbermont, the clerk of the Court of Appeals in Columbia and US consul to Genoa, Italy. They had one son, Alexander Herbermont Jr., who died abroad. Martha was left a widow November 24, 1865. She died December 18, 1877, at age seventy-six in Columbia.

Bulloch, *Habersham Family*, 128; Ruffin and Kirby, *Nature's Management*, 352.

Bay, Sarah Hall Horry: Sarah Hall Horry Bay was the daughter of William Bay and Ann Davis. She was probably named after her uncle Elihu Hall Bay. Sarah married William Mayrant Jr., the son of William Woodrup Mayrant and Ann Magdalen Guignard, in 1819. They had four children: Sarah Ann, William Horry, John Richardson, and Mary Charlotte. Mayrant died January 18, 1840, bequeathing a third of his estate to his wife and the rest to his children. Other sources claim Sarah married Edward Croft in 1836 and that they had no issue. This could have been a second marriage for Sarah, in which case the date is incorrect since William Mayrant did not die until 1840. Peter Horry willed his plantation, Prospect Hill, along with twenty slaves to Sarah when he died in 1815. Horry's wife, Margaret, left one of Horry's other plantations, Belle Isle, to her when she died in 1817. Sarah died sometime in the 1840s.

Croft, *Southern Legacy,* 56–67; Lachicotte, *Georgetown Rice Plantations,* 144; Moore, *Biographical Directory of the South Carolina House,* 180–81; Schwab, *Crofts of South Carolina.*

Bay, William: William Bay was the son of William Bay and Ann Davis. He lived in Columbia, but eventually moved west.

Bulloch, *Habersham Family,* 128.

Bay, William (ca. 1790–1812): William Bay was the son of Elihu Hall Bay and Margaret Holmes. On September 29, 1812, Bay fought a duel with Thomas Crafts, occasioned by an argument about Bishop Theodore Dehone in Charleston. Crafts stated that Dehone was too honorable a person and sensible a man to be a Republican, which offended Bay, a Republican himself. Bay followed with a disparaging comment about the Federalist Party, and the two men discussed the qualifications of Langdon Cheves and John Rutledge, candidates for Congress. As their heated debate continued, Crafts accused Bay of being a "tall, ugly, gawky, Yanke looking fellow." Crafts challenged Bay to a duel, and at noon on September 29, 1812, Crafts shot and killed Bay. There were suspicions of foul play on Crafts's part. Some witnesses claimed that he fired early, and he fled the state. Bay's funeral took place at his father's home. He was twenty-two.

Schwab, *Crofts of South Carolina;* Weidner, "Journal of John Blake White," 114–15; Williams, "Code of Honor," 115.

Belin, Esther Singletary (1774–1851): Esther Singletary was born August 23, 1774, the daughter of Michael and Elizabeth Bacheldor Singletary. She married Allard Belin, a successful planter and slaveholder on Sandy Island, on August 9, 1793. They had four children: Margaret Elizabeth, Allard Henry, Esther Martha, and Esther Mary. Esther died in 1851.

Butt, "Belin Genealogy," 62; Moore, *Biographical Directory of the South Carolina House,* 180; Rogers, *History of Georgetown County,* 66, 254.

Belin, Maria/Mariah: Maria/Mariah Belin was the daughter of James Belin and Mary Lynch. She married Louis Laval, son of Col. Jacinth Laval and Rebecca Withers, on May 8, 1817. They had three children: James Belin, Louis, and Mary Elizabeth.

Butt, "Belin Genealogy," 62–63.

Belin, Mary Lynch: Mary Lynch was probably Mary Lynch Horry, cousin of James Belin. She married James Belin (1739–1809) and they had five children: Maria A., James Lynch, Elizabeth, Sarah, and Margaret.

Butt, "Belin Genealogy," 62–63.

Belin, Sarah (d. 1812): Sarah Belin was the daughter of Allard and Margaret Belin. She died unmarried in 1812.

Butt, "Belin Genealogy," 62.

Bell, James or William: The Scots Irish Bell family migrated from Ireland to Charleston. There were a number of Bells living in St. James Santee as well as in York County. The Bell to whom Horry refers is either James or William Bell from St. James Santee.

Bell and Bell, *Sir Robert Bell,* 80–81.

Bethea, John (1740–1821): "Buck Swamp" John Bethea was born in Nansemond County, Virginia, in 1740. He came to South Carolina around 1756 and settled in Buck Swamp, north of the present town of Latta (Dillon County). A planter, he owned a plantation called Elisha Bethea Place. Bethea served in the American Revolution. He married Absala Parker (d. 1811) and had five sons: William, James, Philip, Elisha, and Parker. Bethea died August 12, 1821.

Sass, *Story of the South Carolina Lowcountry,* 377, 715.

Bigham/Bingham, Samuel: Samuel Bigham was sheriff in Marion County from 1829 to 1833. His first wife was Mary Muldrow, daughter of John Muldrow Jr. and Mary Ellison. His second wife was the widow of Adam Cussac. During the War of 1812, he, Lt. John Shackelford, and Ens. James Ford led a company of infantry of a battalion of South Carolina militia representing Florence, Williamsburg, and Marion Counties. Samuel and his family moved to Sumter County, Alabama, in 1836, where they changed their name to Bingham.

Eaddy, "Capt. Samuel Bigham's Company," 3.

Blackburn, Georgiana: Georgiana Blackburn was the daughter of Stanyaryne Wilson and Anna Eliza Blackburn. She married Francis Marion Galbraith; they had one child, Robert Davidson.

Wilson, *Carolina-Virginia Genealogy.*

Blyth, Elizabeth Frances Allston: Elizabeth Frances Allston was the daughter of William Allston Sr. and Sabina Atchison. She was engaged to her first cousin, John Waties, but her father would not give his blessing. Waties died shortly thereafter and willed his estate to Elizabeth. The property included Friendfield Plantation and numerous slaves. Because she could not manage the estate on her own, she married Dr. Joseph Blyth sometime after February 1, 1791. They left no issue, but her niece, Elizabeth Waties Allston Pringle, was named after her.

Edgar, *Biographical Directory of the South Carolina House,* 153; Pringle, *Chronicles of Chicora Wood,* 73–74; Weiner, *Mistresses and Slaves,* 94.

Blyth, Joseph (d. 1818): Joseph Blyth was the son of Samuel Blyth of Mecklenburg County, North Carolina. Blyth studied medicine under Dr. Benjamin Rush of Philadelphia and became a physician and planter. He served as a regimental surgeon of the North Carolina Continental Line in Charleston, South Carolina, and was in the city when it fell to the British in May 1780. When the war ended, he settled in Georgetown. In 1805 he was given a ferry on the south side of Kingston Lake. Blyth represented All Saints Parish in the Eleventh and Twelfth General Assemblies from 1794 to 1797 and in the state senate for the Thirteenth and Fourteenth General Assemblies from 1798–1800. He also represented Prince George Winyah Parish in the house from 1802 to 1815. Blyth held various local offices as well, including sheriff of Georgetown District in 1789, justice of the quorum for All Saints in 1794, commissioner to establish a ferry over Winyah Bay in 1798, presidential elector in 1800 and 1804, commissioner to improve the bar of Georgetown Harbor in 1800, trustee for South Carolina College from 1805 to 1809, commissioner to run a line between Georgetown and Horry Districts in 1807, commissioner to settle the boundary dispute with North Carolina in 1808, and commissioner to report the degree of damage caused by a road in 1809. Blyth was a member of the Georgetown Library Society from 1799 to 1818 and a member of the Society of the Cincinnati. During George Washington's tour, he welcomed the president at the home of Benjamin Allston in 1791 and delivered an oration on the death of Washington to All Saints Parish in 1800. With Charles Brown, Blyth made an addition of ninety lots to Georgetown east of St. James Street and south of Market Street known as Browntown. Sometime after February 1, 1791, he married Elizabeth Frances Allston, daughter of William Allston Sr. and Sabina Atchison. It was through this marriage that Blyth came into the possession of Waties Point, in addition to Oak Grove and Friendfield Plantations. Blyth died January 3, 1818, and was buried at Prince George Winyah Episcopal Church.

Acts of the General Assembly, 2:208; Edgar, *Biographical Directory of the South Carolina House,* 153; *Eulogies on the Life and Death of General George Washington,* 195; Rogers, *History of Georgetown County,* 173; Smith, "Georgetown," 94.

Blythe, Thomas: Thomas Blythe migrated to Georgetown from Yorkshire, England. Owning a popular tavern on Broad Street in Georgetown, he was also the deputy surveyor in 1743, comptroller of customs in 1743, and justice of the peace in 1755. In 1757 he served as lieutenant of the militia in Georgetown.

Edgar, *South Carolina,* 173; "An Ordinance for the Appointing of Receivers, Comptrollers, and Waiters of the Country Duties, for the Ports of Beaufort, Port Royal, and Georgetown, Winyaw," in Cooper and McCord, *Statutes at Large,* 3:598; Raven, *London Booksellers,* 61, 72; Rogers, *History of Georgetown County,* 51–52, 66, 102.

Boone, Catharine: Catharine Boone was the wife of Christopher Jenkins Jr., one of the ten richest men in British North America in 1777.

Edgar, *South Carolina,* 153; Wilkinson, "Huguenots on Laurel Hill," 131n.

Bossard, Joseph S.: Joseph Bossard was a junior at South Carolina College in 1814. In 1828 he wrote an article for the *Southern Agriculturalist* on the cultivation of rice. On July 13, 1858, he received a patent for a machine to help clean and hull rice.

Bossard, "Reflections on Planting of Seed Rice"; Moore, *Roll of Students,* 7; *Report of the Commissioner of Patents,* 1:430; Rogers, *History of Georgetown County,* 195.

Bostick, Benjamin R. (1791–1866): Benjamin Bostick was born October 11, 1791, in Robertville, South Carolina, the son of Richard Bostick and Mary Harriet Robert. One of the wealthiest men in the community, he owned Pipe Creek Plantation, located a few miles east of the Savannah River. Bostick married Ann Robert, daughter of John Hancock and Anne Maner Robert. His second wife was Jane Aseneth Maner. They resided in St. Peter's Parish in Ingleside Plantation and had twelve children. Bostick died in 1866.

Davant, "Appendices to the Davant Family," 212; Peeples, "Memoirs of Benjamin Spicer Stafford" (1977), 102; Peeples, "Memoirs of Benjamin Spicer Stafford" (1979); Peeples and Pinckney, "Jaudon of Carolina," 124.

Botsford, Edmund (1745–1819): Born in England on November 1, 1745, Edmund Botsford grew up in poverty and was orphaned at age seven. As a young man he enlisted in the British army during the Seven Years' War. He left England for Charleston on November 18, 1765. In August 1766 Botsford visited the First Baptist Church of Charleston, and the following year was baptized by the Reverend Oliver Hart. After being freed from a harsh apprenticeship, Botsford dedicated his life to the ministry and for two years studied under Hart and David Williams with funding from the Religious Society of Charleston. Upon completion of his studies, Botsford was licensed to preach in February 1771 and moved to Euhaw to assist the Reverend Francis Pelot. Shortly thereafter the church relocated him to another branch in Tuckasee King, Georgia, outside Savannah. Botsford received his ordination from Hart on March 14, 1773. When the British took Savannah in the spring of 1779, he fled with his family to South Carolina, where he accepted a position as chaplain for Gen. Andrew Williamson's brigade. While he was in the military, the Welsh Neck congregation asked Botsford to be their supply pastor. His time at Welsh Neck, however, was cut short when the British seized Charleston in 1780, forcing him to leave his family and escape, with Hart, to the North. Botsford was later reunited with his wife and children, and the family remained in Virginia until Charleston was liberated. Botsford preached at Welsh Neck until he accepted a call from the Baptist church in Georgetown in 1796. He was the driving force in rejuvenating the Baptist denomination in Georgetown, which had sustained only a nominal presence in the town in the twenty years following the war. During his pastorate the congregation built a new chapel and was granted legal incorporation by the state as the "Antipedo Baptist Church of Georgetown." Botsford was best known for his ministry to slaves, particularly his 1808 pamphlet *Sambo and Toney: A Dialogue between Two Servants,* which he wrote for the religious instruction of enslaved blacks. Botsford was widowed three times, losing his wives Susannah Nunn, Catharine Evans, and Ann Deliesseline. His last wife was Hannah Goff, who survived him by several years. He had twelve children, only four of whom were still living when he died December 25, 1819. Botsford was buried at the Antipedo Baptist Cemetery in Georgetown.

Broome, "Edmund Botsford"; Edmund Botsford Papers, South Carolina Baptist Historical Collection, Furman University; Mallary, *Memoirs of Elder Edmund Botsford.*

Bowman, Sabina Lynch: Sabina Lynch was the daughter of Thomas Lynch and Elizabeth Allston. Her first husband was William Cattell, a lieutenant colonel, who died in 1778. She later married John Bowman in the 1780s. Sabina granted her husband Peach Tree Plantation and other family property on the Santee River. John possessed 293 slaves and commissioned Jonathan Lucas to build the first water mill for rice production at Peach Tree in 1787. In 1797 John and Sabina were involved in an inheritance dispute concerning the Carrell estate, which ended in John's arrest for contempt of court. They had three children: Esther Lynch, Mary A. H., and John Lynch.

Bullard, *Robert Stafford,* 4; Edgar, *Biographical Directory of the South Carolina House,* 168; Hines, *Lynch Families,* 179.

Boykin, Burwell (1752–1817): Burwell Boykin was the son of William Boykin and Elizabeth Bryant of North Carolina. Before 1760 his family relocated to Camden, South Carolina, where Boykin later acquired more than four hundred acres and Hickory Ridge, Swamp, and Stoney Hill Plantations. His family residence was Mount Pleasant, constructed in 1812. During the American Revolution, Boykin supplied the Continental forces with forage and provisions. He represented District Eastward of Wateree River in the Eighth General Assembly from 1789 to 1790. He also served in a number of smaller capacities, including vestryman for St. David Parish from 1774 to 1775, member of the committee of observation for St. David in 1775, road commissioner in 1778 and 1798, and commissioner to approve securities offered by the sheriff of Camden District in 1795. Boykin married Elizabeth Whitaker, daughter of William Whitaker, in 1782. They had three children: Burwell, Francis, and Elizabeth. Elizabeth Whitaker Boykin died October 2, 1787, and Boykin married her sister, Mary Whitaker. They had fourteen children: Stephen Henry, Catherine, Samuel, John, Thomas, Lemuel, Amelia, Mary, Sarah, Elizabeth Tunstall, Burwell, William Whitaker, Alexander Hamilton, and Charlotte. Boykin died August 17, 1817.

Bailey and Cooper, *Biographical Directory of the South Carolina House,* 83–84; Murphy, *Boykin Family,* 42.

Bremar, Francis: Francis Bremar was a merchant associate of Henry Laurens and married Laurens's sister, Martha. The Bremar to whom Horry refers is probably their son, Francis Bremar Jr.

Burke, *General and Heraldic Dictionary,* 2:70; Weir, *"Last of American Freemen,"* 36.

Britton, Benjamin: Benjamin Britton was the son of Moses and Ann Britton. In 1813 he was appointed a commissioner to build a bridge over Black Mingo Creek, and in 1820 served as a commissioner to repair the bridge. One of the first prominent Methodists in Williamsburg, he contributed to the construction of a community church called Union Church and was elected a ruling elder of Indiantown Church in 1827. He married Sarah Grier, and they had at least one daughter, Ann Durant, who inherited Pleasant Grove, a two-thousand-acre tract in Black Mingo that was a part of her father's estate.

Boddie, *History of Williamsburg,* 74, 196, 210, 211, 264; Census, Fourth, 1820, Williamsburg, S.C.; Jenkinson, *Williamsburg District,* 95.

Broughton, Thomas (d. 1829): The Broughton family settled on Mulberry Plantation in Moncks Corner in 1708. The plantation was originally purchased by Col. Thomas Broughton, who was at one time governor of South Carolina. The property passed down from generation to generation until Thomas Broughton inherited it from his father, Cdre. Thomas Broughton, in 1809. The will stipulated that the land be divided between Thomas and his brother Philip Porcher Broughton. According to the 1820 census, Broughton owned 103 slaves and resided in Charleston. He died in 1829.

Census, Fourth, 1820, Christ Church, Charleston, S.C.; Hamilton, "Mulberry."

Brown, Joseph: Joseph Brown was the son of Joseph Brown Sr., a Georgetown merchant affiliated with Henry Laurens. Brown married Harriet Lowndes, daughter of Rawlins Lowndes, on November 29, 1784.

Census, Third, 1820, Charleston, S.C.; Rogers, *History of Georgetown County,* 119, 123; Salley, *Marriage Notices,* 45.

Brown, Major: Major Brown served as a major in the battle at Moncks Corner. From 1779 to 1781, he acted as a lieutenant colonel in the militia.

Moss, *Roster of South Carolina Patriots,* 109.

Brownfield, Robert (d. 1827): Robert Brownfield was a physician in Cheraw, Georgetown, and Sumter Districts. After serving as a surgeon in Francis Marion's brigade, he settled in Georgetown. Brownfield represented St. David Parish at the state convention for the ratification of the Constitution. St. David elected him to the Eighth General Assembly from 1789 to 1790. In Georgetown he managed a lottery for the sick and destitute and headed the Georgetown Library Society from 1799 to 1812. He was also a member of the Medical Society of South Carolina. Brownfield relocated to Sumter District before 1809 and was elected vestryman of Holy Cross Claremont Parish. He served in that capacity intermittently from 1809 to 1827. Brownfield married Susanna Heriot, daughter of Robert Heriot and Mary Ouldfield. They had three children: John William, Susan, and Robert James. Brownfield died around February 5, 1827.

Bailey and Cooper, *Biographical Directory of the South Carolina House,* 100–101; Census, Third, 1810, Claremont, Sumter, S.C.; Thomas and Thomas, *History of Marlboro County,* 126.

Burnet, Andrew: During the American Revolution, Andrew Burnet served with Francis Marion. He married Elizabeth Washington de Saussure, daughter of Daniel de Saussure. They had at least one son, Andrew William, born June 12, 1811, in Charleston.

May and Faunt, *South Carolina Secedes,* 120.

Campbell, Alexander: Alexander Campbell enlisted in the Continental Army on July 18, 1775, in an independent ranger company under Capt. Ezekiel Polk. He later served as a lieutenant under Capt. Philip Walker and was wounded at Hanging Rock.

Moss, *Roster of South Carolina Patriots,* 140.

Campbell, James (d. 1825): James Campbell lived on the south side of the Black River in Williamsburg and also owned property in Marion. He served under Francis Marion in the American Revolution. Elected to the house, Campbell represented Williamsburg in the Twelfth, Fourteenth, and Twenty-Second General Assemblies from 1796 to 1797, 1800 to 1801, and 1816 to 1817. He also sat in the senate, representing Prince George Winyah and Williamsburg in the Eighteenth General Assembly from 1808 to 1809. He continued to serve Williamsburg in the senate in the Nineteenth and Twentieth General Assemblies from 1810 to 1813 but resigned to accept a major's commission in the US Army. He later returned to the senate for the Twenty-Third through Twenty-Sixth General Assemblies from 1818 to 1827. Campbell held various local offices, including road commissioner in 1799, militia captain in 1800, major from 1808 to 1812, commissioner for the town of Williamsburg in 1801, commissioner to take the bond of security for the clerk in 1804, sheriff for Williamsburg District in 1804, and presidential elector in 1812. His first marriage was to Jane Salters, and his second was to Letitia Montgomery, widow of Isaac Nelson. He wrote his will on March 4, 1825, and left his estate to Susanna and Laura Covert, Isaac Nelson, his nephew William Campbell, and his sisters, Agnes Brown, Elizabeth Todd, and Mary Campbell. He was dead by mid-March.

Bailey, Morgan, and Taylor, *Biographical Directory of the South Carolina Senate*, 1:260–61; Boddie, *History of Williamsburg*, 115, 147, 153, 208, 216, 218–19, 244–45, 256; Moss, *Roster of South Carolina Patriots*, 141.

Capers, William (1758–1812): William Capers was born October 13, 1758, in St. Thomas and St. Dennis Parish, the son of Richard Capers and Martha Bordeaux. Capers participated in the Battle of Fort Moultrie in June 1776 and was commissioned a lieutenant in the Second Regiment of the Continental Line on February 24, 1778. He later served as a captain in Francis Marion's brigade. When the war ended, Christ Church Parish elected him to the Fifth General Assembly from 1783 to 1784. He also served Christ Church as tax inquirer and collector in 1785. After marrying Mary Singletary, daughter of John and Sarah Singletary, on September 10, 1783, he moved to Bull's Head Plantation in St. Thomas and St. Dennis. William and Mary had five children: Sarah, Gabriel, Mary Singletary, William, and John Singletary. His wife died February 10, 1792. Before July 1793 Capers moved to Georgetown and purchased Belleview Plantation. He wed Mary Wragg, daughter of Samuel Wragg and Judith Rothmahler, on November 11, 1793. They had four children: Samuel Wragg, Elizabeth, Mary, and Henrietta. Mary died February 7, 1801. Capers married Hannah Coachman, widow of Jehu Postell, on May 15, 1803. They had three children: LeGrand Guerry, Benjamin Huger, and Richard Coachman. While in Georgetown, Capers was inspector of the Sixth Brigade of the South Carolina militia from 1802 to 1806. Moving to Sumter in 1805, he purchased Woodland Plantation. Survived by his wife and nine children, he died December 7, 1812.

Bailey and Cooper, *Biographical Directory of the South Carolina House*, 129–30; MacDowell, *Descendants of William Capers*, viii, 1–7, 32, 86, 89; Moss, *Roster of South Carolina Patriots*, 146; Salley, "Captain William Capers," 277, 279–81.

Capers, William (1790–1855): William Capers was born in St. Thomas Parish on January 26, 1790, the son of William Capers and Mary Singletary. Both his father and his grandfather were Methodists, and his father helped organize the Methodists in Georgetown. Educated in Georgetown and Stateburg, he entered South Carolina College in 1805 as a sophomore. Forced to take a medical leave until 1807, he left the college in 1808 to pursue a career in law. By November of that year, he was a licensed Methodist preacher. Fully admitted to the South Carolina Conference in 1810 and an ordained deacon, in 1812 he became an elder. Capers held various charges throughout the Carolinas and Georgia, including Wilmington, Georgetown, Charleston, Columbia, Milledgeville, Oxford, and Savannah. In Georgetown he helped the Methodists incorporate as the "Methodist Episcopal Church of Georgetown." In addition to these charges, Capers founded the Asbury Mission to the Creek Indians in Alabama in 1821 and served as superintendent of the mission until 1824. While in Charleston, Capers edited the *Wesleyan Journal* from 1825 to 1827. A year later he acted as the American representative to the British Methodist Conference. A slaveholder himself, Capers began his outreach to lowcountry slaves in 1829, and in 1833 he published a catechism for the oral instruction of slaves. He was editor of the *Southern Christian Advocate* from 1837 to 1840. During his tenure as secretary of the Southern Missionary Department from 1840 to 1844, he broadened mission work to the slaves throughout the entire South. When the Methodist Church split over slavery at the General Conference in 1844, Capers championed the proslavery views of white Southern Methodists. Two years later he was elected a bishop of the Methodist Church, South, on May 14, 1846. He married Anna White of Georgetown on January 13, 1813, and had two children. Anna died in childbirth on December 30, 1815. He married Susan McGill of Kershaw on October 31, 1816. Capers died of heart disease on January 29, 1855, and was buried at Washington Street United Methodist Church in Columbia.

A. V. Huff Jr., "William Capers," in Edgar, *South Carolina Encyclopedia*, 130; Matthews, "Methodist Mission"; Moore, *Roll of Students*, 4; Rogers, *History of Georgetown County*, 193, 221, 314–15, 352–53; Wightman, *Life of William Capers*, 11–12, 24–25, 29, 42, 44–46.

Cantey, Charles, Jr.: Charles Cantey was commissioned first lieutenant on August 3, 1813, and honorably discharged on June 15, 1815.

Ames, "Cantey Family."

Carr, Isaac: Isaac Carr and his wife, Sarah, resided in Georgetown. Carr served as an officer for the Georgetown branch of the Bank of the State of South Carolina in 1816. He was also a vestryman for Prince George Winyah Episcopal Church.

Blair, *Historical Sketch of Banking,* 101; Census, Fourth and Fifth, 1810–1820, Georgetown, S.C.; Cook, *Rambles in the Pee Dee Basin,* 135; McCord, *Chancery Cases Argued,* 66; Rogers, *History of Georgetown County,* 348n.

Carr, Thomas (d. 1827): Thomas Carr was a planter of Prince George Winyah who represented that parish in the Twenty-Second, Twenty-Third, Twenty-Fourth, Twenty-Fifth, and Twenty-Seventh General Assemblies from 1816 to 1823 and 1827 to 1828. Carr served as the intendant of Georgetown from 1813 to 1814 and 1824 to 1825. He was major and inspector of the Sixth Brigade in 1809 and from 1811 to 1814 and major general of the Fourth Division in 1821 and from 1824 to 1827. A longtime member of the Georgetown Library Society, Carr died July 6, 1827.

Camden Gazette, June 21, 1821; Census, Third, 1810, Georgetown, S.C.; *City Gazette and Daily Advertiser,* October 21, 1808, October 21, 1816, November 30, 1818; Moore, *Biographical Directory of the South Carolina House,* 44; Rogers, *History of Georgetown County,* 289n, 528; *Winyaw Intelligencer,* June 26, 1819.

Cassels, John (1770–1830): John Cassels was born in 1770, the only son of James Cassels and Susanna Man. James was a Georgetown planter and British militia captain in the American Revolution who had been banished from South Carolina. His estate was seized, and he took refuge in Florida. In 1788 Archibald Taylor, Mary Man Taylor, and Robert Heriot petitioned the legislature on John's behalf in order to thwart the efforts of the commissioners of forfeited estates to take the family's slaves. The case was decided in John's favor. Still a minor when his parents died, his mother's estate was given in trust to Robert Heriot until John became of age. John became a lawyer and was appointed a commissioner to erect a courthouse and jail in Sumter. He later sold the property for £25,000 sterling and left America for Scotland and then London, where he died in 1830.

"An Act for Vesting in Robert Heriot, Esquire, a Certain Sum of Money, for the Use of John Cassels, a Minor," in Cooper and McCord, *Statutes at Large,* 5:84; *Acts of the General Assembly,* 2:248; Cassels, *Records of the Family of Cassels,* 34–35; Census, Second and Third, 1800–1810, Georgetown, S.C.; Rogers, *History of Georgetown County,* 163–64.

Chapman, Thomas (d. 1820): Thomas Chapman was intendant of Georgetown in 1810. In 1812 he was appointed by President James Madison as the collector of the Port of Georgetown and served in that capacity until his death on November 28, 1820.

Census, Third, 1810, Georgetown, S.C.; *City Gazette and Daily Advertiser,* August 28, 1804, August 3, 1812; *Reports of the Committees of the Senate,* 1:146; Rogers, *History of Georgetown County,* 528.

Cheesborough/Cheeseborough, John W. (1790–1845): John W. Cheesborough was born in 1790, the son of John Cheesborough. A well-known Charleston merchant, he served as a director of the State Bank of South Carolina and of the Charleston Bank at various times. He was also a member of the Charleston Library Society from 1813 to 1827 and owned considerable property in the city. He married Elera of Liverpool, with whom he had three daughters and two sons. Cheesborough died in 1845 and was buried at St. Michael's Church in Charleston.

City Gazette and Daily Advertiser, April 24, 1821; "Georgetown Library Society," 99; Lesesne, *Bank of the State of South Carolina,* 188; Raymond, *Southland Writers,* 2:877; Sutherland, "Rise and Fall of Esther B. Cheesborough," 22–23; Wildey, *Descendants of William Chesebrough,* 509.

Clifton, Claiborne/Claiborn/Clairborne/Clayborn: Claiborne Clifton was born in Virginia and relocated to Richland County, South Carolina, around 1790 where he became a teacher. He started a mercantile partnership with Major John McLimose and studied law under Thomas Henry Egan. Admitted to the bar in 1805, he soon became a successful Columbia attorney and owned property throughout South Carolina and Georgia. He represented Richland in the Seventeenth General Assembly from 1806 to 1808. He also held a number of small offices, including commissioner of Columbia in 1807, commissioner to contract and superintend all work on South Carolina College in 1807, intendant of Columbia in 1808, commissioner of free schools for Richland in 1814, and commissioner to superintend repairs to the courthouse in Richland District in 1814. Clifton was captain of the beat company in Columbia and was eventually promoted to major. He married Mary Cooper of Georgia around 1800. They had at least three children: William Cincinnatus Claiborne, Algernon S., and Massellon J. S. Clifton died in October 1826, survived by his wife and children.

Bailey, *Biographical Directory of the South Carolina House,* 118–19; Census, Third and Fourth, 1810–1820, Richland, S.C.; Selby, *Memorabilia and Anecdotal Reminiscences,* 137.

Cogdell/Cogdill/Cogdail, Esther (1746–1840): Esther Cogdell was born January 11, 1746. She was the second wife of John Cogdell, plantation owner and master of the *Good Intent,* a ship in Georgetown. Cogdell died of influenza on November 16, 1807. According to the will, Esther was to receive a house in Georgetown, his pew in Prince George Winyah Episcopal Church, a carriage, horses, cows, seven slaves, his household and kitchen furniture, and £800 garnered from the sale of the estate. Since they had no children, Cogdell requested that when Esther died, if she left no issue, the remainder of the estate be divided among his nephews. Esther lived in Georgetown for the remainder of her life and was an active member of Prince George Winyah Episcopal Church. She died January 4, 1840, and was buried at Prince George.

Bailey and Cooper, *Biographical Directory of the South Carolina House,* 144–45; Census, Third, 1810, Georgetown, S.C.; Dalcho, *Historical Account of the Protestant Episcopal Church,* 309; De Saussure, *Reports of Cases Argued,* 3:389–92; "Inscriptions of the Churchyard" (no. 4); Rogers, *History of Georgetown County,* 41, 51, 150, 161, 166n, 167, 202, 208.

Cohen, Solomon, Jr. (1802–1885): Solomon Cohen was born in Georgetown on August 15, 1802, the son of Solomon Cohen and Bella Moses. Cohen attended South Carolina College, and upon admission to the bar in 1823, he practiced law in Georgetown until 1838. He was one of the original members of the Planters Club and a member of the Georgetown Library Society from 1829 to 1835. He was director of the Georgetown branch of the Bank of South Carolina from 1819 to 1826, represented Prince George Winyah in the legislature from 1831 to 1836, served as commissioner in equity for Georgetown from 1835 to 1837, and was Georgetown's intendant in 1837. Cohen moved to Savannah in 1838, where he continued to practice law and occupied many prominent positions, including postmaster of Savannah during the Civil War and member of the Georgia delegation to the Democratic Convention in Charleston. In 1866 he was elected a member of Congress from the First Congressional District of Georgia but was denied his seat. He was also cashier of the Central Railroad Bank, president of the Union Society, president of the Mickva Israel Congregation, and one of the original directors of the Atlantic and Gulf Railroad. Cohen died August 14, 1885.

Elzas, *Jews of South Carolina,* 189–90, 205, 241; "Georgetown Library Society," 99; Ochenkowski, "Origins of Nullification," 139; Moore, *Roll of Students,* 9; Rogers, *History of Georgetown County,* 241–49, 288–89, 528; Webber, "Marriage and Death Notices" (1919).

Coker, Thomas C. (b. 1750): Thomas Coker was born in South Carolina in 1750, his father having moved the family from Virginia to the Pee Dee area in

1740. In the American Revolution, he soldiered with Francis Marion. He married Mary Prestwood and was a member of Mount Pleasant Baptist Church.

Boddie, *History of Williamsburg,* 115; Census, First, 1790, Prince Georges, Georgetown, S.C.; *Cyclopedia of Eminent and Representative Men of the Carolinas,* 454; Moss, *Roster of South Carolina Patriots,* 184; Townsend, *South Carolina Baptists,* 94.

Colclough/Coclough/Colchlough, William Alexander: William Alexander Colclough was the son of Alexander Colclough. He resided in Sumter, where he owned Bradford Springs Plantation. During the War of 1812, he served as a lieutenant in the Fifth Regiment of the South Carolina militia and was later promoted to colonel. He represented Clarendon in the Twentieth General Assembly from 1812 to 1813. He married Frances Hunter, who died in 1814. His second wife was Leonora Davis, daughter of Benjamin Davis. They had three children: Mary Mucedora, William Alexander, and Augustus. Colclough died August 28, 1830, in Sumter.

Bailey, *Biographical Directory of the South Carolina House,* 124; Census, Second, 1800, Clarendon, Sumter, S.C.

Conway, Robert (d. 1823): Robert Conway, the son of Daniel Conway and Ann Daniell, was a cabinetmaker in Charleston before moving to Georgetown. He owned approximately 3,319 acres in Georgetown and donated a portion of his land for the village of Kingston, later named Conwayborough in his honor. Conway represented Horry District in the Ninth, Tenth, Eleventh, Twelfth, Fourteenth, Sixteenth, and Seventeenth General Assemblies from 1791 to 1797, 1800 to 1801, and 1804 to 1808. Other offices he held included lieutenant colonel of the Twenty-Fifth Regiment from 1794 to 1802, brigadier general of the Sixth Brigade of the state militia from 1803 to 1812, commissioner to erect a courthouse and jail in Horry District in 1801, commissioner of public buildings for Horry District in 1803, coroner for Horry District from 1820 to 1823, justice of the peace for Prince George Winyah Parish in 1821, and manager of elections for Georgetown in 1823. Conway married Juliana Easton on November 26, 1771. They had at least five children: John Bennet, William Hopkins, Amelia, John Baxter, and Mary Baxter. Juliana died November 28, 1811. He married Susannah Beaty Crownson, widow of Thomas Crownson, in 1819. Conway died in December 1823.

Bailey, *Biographical Directory of the South Carolina House,* 127; *Charleston City Gazette and Commercial Advertiser,* December 8, 1823; Lewis, *Horry County,* 93–99; Rogers, *History of Georgetown County,* 207.

Course, Isaac: Isaac Course, a merchant in Charleston, was elected one of the directors of the Charleston Fire and Marine Insurance Company in 1819.

City Gazette and Daily Advertiser, January 12, 1819, January 26, 1821; Hagy, *Charleston, South Carolina City Directories,* 37, 75, 110, 141; Hagy, *People and Professions of Charleston,* 12.

Croft, Edward (1775–1851): Edward Croft was the son of George Croft and Elizabeth Leger. His father, a Georgetown and Charleston merchant, died when Croft was a small child. Elizabeth married Henry Lenud two years later, and Croft lived with them until he went to college in Maryland to pursue a law degree. He joined the law firm of Langdon Chevis and Jean Paul Cotte in Charleston in 1797. Croft later became the partner of Theodore Gaillard and married Gaillard's sister, Floride Lydia Gaillard, on November 12, 1802. The Crofts resided in Charleston but also owned a home on North Island a few houses down from Peter Horry. Between 1804 and 1815, Edward and Floride had seven children: Floride Peyre, Edward G., George, Randell, John, Theodore G. and Elizabeth L. The Crofts relocated to Greenville in 1821, where Edward played an important role in the construction of the First Episcopal Church. Edward was also the warden of Christ Church Parish. He retired from law in 1825. Floride died in 1833, and Edward married Sarah Hall Horry Bay. They had no issue, and Sarah died in the 1840s. Edward died October 2, 1851, and was survived by three children.

Croft, *Southern Legacy,* 59–67; Schwab, *Crofts of South Carolina;* Wilson, *Genealogy of the Croft Family,* 29–35.

Cudworth, Benjamin (1753?–1814): Benjamin Cudworth of Massachusetts was a merchant in Charleston. He also owned a plantation in Lancaster County as well as property in Pendleton District. During the American Revolution, Cudworth served in a regiment commanded by Col. Alexander Moultrie and was present at the siege of Savannah in 1779. He was exiled to St. Augustine when the British took Charleston in 1780, and his family was banished from Charleston the following year. He later returned and represented the District Eastward of Wateree River in the Seventh and Eighth General Assemblies from 1789 to 1790 and represented Lancaster County in the Ninth General Assembly in 1791. He resigned to become inspector of the excise for survey number two in 1791 and held that position until 1801. Cudworth attended the convention to ratify the federal Constitution in 1788 and voted against adoption. He also served as vendue master in 1783 and deputy supervisor for the US Internal Revenue Department in the District of South Carolina from 1799 to 1801. He was active in Charleston as a member of the Charleston Library Society and steward of the orphan house in 1805. Cudworth married Catharine Kelsy, daughter of William and Mary Kelsy, in 1775. She died in 1813, leaving her daughter as well as their adopted children, Charles L. Yancey and Catherine Maria. Cudworth died October 8, 1814, in Lancaster.

Bailey and Cooper, *Biographical Directory of the South Carolina House,* 163–64; Moss, *Roster of South Carolina Patriots,* 222; Hagy, *City Directories for Charleston,* 5, 30, 63, 100, 144; Hagy, *People and Professions of Charleston,* 6, 52.

Cuttino, David William (1789–1820): David William Cuttino was the son of William Cuttino and Mary Elizabeth Coon of Georgetown. He attended South Carolina College and later entered the medical field. Cuttino married Susan Parnice Park, daughter of Thomas and Mary Botsford Park, in 1814. He was an prominent member of the First Baptist Church of Georgetown. Cuttino died April 3, 1820.

Cuttino, "Descendants of William Cuttino," 136; Cuttino, "Further Notes on the History," 31; Cuttino, *History of the Cuttino Family,* 7–17; Haynsworth, *Haynsworth-Furman,* 91–92; Minutes, First Baptist Church of Georgetown, Georgetown Baptist Historical Society Archives, January 1805–November 30, 1821; Moore, *Roll of Students,* 5.

Cuttino, Peter (1786–1833): Peter Cuttino was born July 14, 1786, the son of William Cuttino and Mary Elizabeth Coon of Georgetown. In 1807 Cuttino married Elizabeth Mary Gaillard (1786–1859). Both were active members of the First Baptist Church of Georgetown, Cuttino being a deacon. He was also a director of the Georgetown branch of the Bank of South Carolina. Cuttino died in 1833.

Clark, *History of the Banking Institutions,* 100; Cuttino, "Descendants of William Cuttino," 136; Cuttino, *History of the Cuttino Family,* 7–17; Cuttino, "Notes on the History," 29; Minutes, First Baptist Church of Georgetown, January 1805–May 9, 1818; Rogers, *History of Georgetown County,* 351; *Winyaw Intelligencer,* December 11, 1819.

Dalton, Fred W. (d. 1813): Fred Dalton graduated from South Carolina College in 1813 and died shortly thereafter.

Moore, *Roll of Students,* 6.

Danford, Eliza: Eliza Danford was the daughter of Isaac Danford. She married Stephen Lester of Yorkshire, England, on Thursday, January 10, 1822.

Jervey, "Marriage and Death Notices" (1948), 84.

Davis, Leonora: Leonora Davis was the daughter of Benjamin Davis and the second wife of William Alexander Colclough. They resided in Sumter at Bradford Springs Plantation and had three children: Mary Mucedora, William Alexander, and Augustus.

Bailey, *Biographical Directory of the South Carolina House,* 124; Cooper and McCord, *Statutes at Large,* 9:502.

Davis, Martha Cantey: Martha Cantey was the daughter of Maj. John Cantey and Susannah McDonald Flud. Martha was the second wife of Capt. William Ransom Davis. They had three children: Warren Ransom, Martha Maria, and Henry. William Ransom was a planter on the Santee River and a captain in the Fifth Regiment during the American Revolution. He predeceased her on December 19, 1799.

Ames, "Cantey Family," 234; Bailey and Cooper, *Biographical Directory of the South Carolina House,* 174–75.

Davis, Martha Maria (d. 1853): Martha Maria Davis was the daughter of William Ransom Davis and Martha Cantey. She married Col. John Ewing Calhoun (b. 1791), the brother-in-law of John C. Calhoun, on February 21, 1822, in Charleston. Residing at Keowee, they had nine children: John Ewing (died young), Florence, Warren Davis, Henry Davis, Edward Boiseau, Martha Maria, William Ransom, Susan, and John Ewing. Martha died November 13, 1853.

Ames, "Cantey Family," 234; Bulloch, *Habersham Family,* 131; Mackenzie and Rhoades, *Colonial Families,* 6:126; Rhyne, *Tales from the South Carolina Upstate,* 23.

Davis, Warren Ransom (1793–1834): Warren Ransom Davis was born the son of William Ransom Davis and Martha Cantey in May 1793. He graduated from South Carolina College in 1810 and studied law in Columbia. He was admitted to the bar in Charleston in 1814 and began practicing law in Pendleton. In 1818 Davis succeeded Benjamin H. Saxon as state solicitor of the western circuit, a position he held from 1818 to 1821. He represented Pendleton and Greenville in the US Congress from 1824 until his death in 1834. Davis never married and left no issue. He was buried in the Congressional Cemetery.

Ames, "Cantey Family," 234; O'Neall, *Biographical Sketches of the Bench,* 2:82; *Records of the Columbia Historical Society,* 12:74.

Deliesseline, Polly: Polly Deliesseline was the daughter of Isaac Deliesseline and Elizabeth Mary Drinker. Her real name was Mary Drinker Deliesseline. She married Benjamin Simmons Hort on September 12, 1812. They had at least one son: Benjamin Simmons.

Helffenstein, *Pierre Fauconnier and His Descendants,* 78; Salley, "Journal of General Peter Horry" (1938), 159n.

Dent, John Herbert (1782–1823): John Herbert Dent was born in Maryland in 1782. Dent was appointed midshipman on March 16, 1798, under Capt. Thomas Truxton in the US frigate *Constellation.* He was aboard when it was captured by the French. Appointed lieutenant on July 11, 1799, he was also on the *Constellation* when it took the French ship *La Vengeance*. Dent was commissioned master commander on September 5, 1804, and captain on December 29, 1811. Captain of the *USS Constitution* in 1804 during the war with Tripoli, he became senior officer in charge of naval affairs in Charleston. Dent was married to Ann Horry, Peter Horry's sister. They lived in Walterboro. Dent died in 1823.

Clark and Pierce, *Scenic Driving South Carolina,* 206–7; Lincoln, "Engraved Portraits of American Patriots," 289.

De Saussure, Elizabeth Ford (d. 1822): Elizabeth Ford was the daughter of Col. Jacob Ford and Theodosia Johnes and sister of Lt. Timothy Ford. The Fords were a prominent family from Morristown, New Jersey. They constructed "Ford Mansion," one of the most prestigious homes in Morristown. During the American Revolution, George Washington and some of his men took shelter at their residence. A number of Washington's acquaintances visited, including the Marquis de Lafayette, French minister Chevalier de la Luzerne, Spanish ambassador Don Juan de Miralles (who died there), and Alexander Hamilton. Martha Washington also stayed for a time. Elizabeth married Henry William De Saussure in 1785 and moved to South Carolina. They had twelve children: Daniel Lewis, Sarah Amelia, Charles Alfred, Anna Frances, Mary Caroline, John McPherson, Louis McPherson, William Ford, Eliza Ford, Henry Alexander, Gabriel Edward, and Octavia Theodosia. Elizabeth died in 1822 in South Carolina.

Burstyn, *Past and Promise,* 18–19.

De Saussure, Henry William (1763–1839): Henry William De Saussure was born August 16, 1763, in Beaufort District, the son of Daniel De Saussure and Mary McPherson. He was serving on the defense lines in Charleston when the city fell to the British in 1780. The following year De Saussure was exiled to Philadelphia for refusing British protection. He used his time in Philadelphia to study law and was admitted to the bar in 1784. He returned to South Carolina in 1785 and established a practice in Charleston with his brother-in-law Timothy Ford. De Saussure served as a delegate to the state constitutional convention in 1790 and represented St. Philip and St. Michael Parishes in the Ninth and Tenth General Assemblies from 1791 to 1794. He was appointed director of the US Mint in 1795 and initiated the first coinage of gold. He resigned this position after four months, however, to continue his service in the South Carolina House of Representatives. De Saussure was a prominent member of Charleston society, acting as vice president and president of the Charleston Library Society, interim judge of the Court of General Sessions and Common Pleas, and trustee of the College of Charleston. He was also a member of the

Society of the Cincinnati and a trustee of Columbia Academy. He attended the Independent Church of Charleston and later, when he moved to Columbia, helped incorporate the First Presbyterian Church. De Saussure married Elizabeth Ford, daughter of Col. Jacob Ford, in 1785. They had twelve children: Daniel Lewis, Sarah Amelia, Charles Alfred, Anna Frances, Mary Caroline, John McPherson, Louis McPherson, William Ford, Eliza Ford, Henry Alexander, Gabriel Edward, and Octavia Theodosia. Elizabeth died in 1822. De Saussure died in March 1839 in Charleston and was buried in Columbia.

Bailey, *Biographical Directory of the South Carolina House,* 154–56; Whittemore, *Heroes of the American Revolution,* 79–80.

Dinkins, Nancy Smart: Nancy Smart Dinkins was the second wife of William Dinkins (b. 1746) of Sumter.

Lester, *Old Southern Bible Records,* 105.

Dozier, John, Jr. (1776–1830): John Dozier Jr. was born January 3, 1776, the son of John Dozier and Elizabeth Giles. A planter, he owned China Grove Plantation in Williamsburg and represented Williamsburg in the Sixteenth, Seventeenth, and Eighteenth General Assemblies from 1804 to 1809. He served in the state senate in the Twenty-First and Twenty-Second General Assemblies from 1814 to 1817. He was also the commissioner of bridges and ferries on the Black River and commissioner to open navigation of Black Mingo Creek in 1811, commissioner to build a bridge over Black Mingo Creek in 1813, and commissioner to repair a bridge over Black Mingo Creek in 1820. Dozier attended Prince Frederick Church. On May 16, 1799, he married Lydia White, daughter of Anthony White and Hannah Barton. They had fifteen children, only eight of whom lived beyond adolescence: Anthony White, Benjamin Franklin, Leonard, Susannah Ann, Elizabeth Giles, Richard, Adelaide Pamela, and Thomas Jefferson. Dozier was survived by his wife and eight children and died August 15, 1830. He was buried at Prince Frederick.

Bailey, *Biographical Directory of the South Carolina House,* 162; Boddie, *History of Williamsburg,* 195.

Drayton, John (1766–1822): John Drayton was born June 22, 1766, in St. Andrew Parish, the son of William Henry Drayton and Dorothy Golightly. He received his education from Nassau Grammar School and the College of New Jersey. He then studied abroad in England and returned to Charleston to work in the law office of Charles Cotesworth Pinckney. Drayton was admitted to the bar in the 1780s and opened his own law practice. He was also a rice planter and owned property on the North Santee River. He was active in the legislature, representing St. Philip and St. Michael Parishes in the Tenth,

Eleventh, and Thirteenth General Assemblies from 1792 to 1795 and 1798 to 1799. Drayton resigned from the house when he was elected lieutenant governor of South Carolina in 1798. When Edward Rutledge died in 1800, he took the governorship and was reelected that same year. Drayton returned to the General Assembly for the sixteenth, seventeenth, and eighteenth senate sessions from 1804 to 1809. He left the senate when he was elected governor again in 1808. He received his last appointment on May 7, 1812, as the US district judge, a position he held until his death. Drayton was a member of the Ancient York Masons, captain of the Charleston Cadet Infantry, militia colonel, and member of the Charleston Library Society. Writing was a passion of Drayton's, and he published several books, including *Letters Written during a Tour through the Northern and Eastern States* and the multivolume work *A View of South Carolina as Respects Her Natural and Civil Concerns*. Another hobby was botany, for which Drayton was recognized by the Royal Society of Sciences at Göttingen, Germany. He received an honorary doctor of laws from South Carolina College in 1807. Drayton married Hester Rose Tidyman (d. 1816), daughter of Philip Tidyman and Hester Rose, on November 6, 1794. They had seven children: Rose Butler, Alfred Rose, Harriott, Sarah Butler, Hester Tidyman, Maria Caroline, and Dorothea. Drayton died November 22, 1822.

Bailey, *Biographical Directory of the South Carolina House,* 164–65; Many, *Southern Literature from 1579–1895,* 127.

Ellerbe, Anna Maria Wickham (1803–64): Anna Maria Wickham was born July 21, 1803, the daughter of Dr. Thomas T. Wickham and Anna Eliza Shackelford. Anna was most likely an only child and independently wealthy. She married John Crawford Ellerbe (1803–42), the youngest son of William Ellerbe and Elizabeth Crawford. They resided on her property in Marion County and had eight children: Thomas Wickham, William Shackelford, Johanna Marie, Richard Plantagenet, Edward Benjamin, Sarah, Araminta, and John C. Lucinda. When Ellerbe died in 1842, Anna married former South Carolina governor Barnabas Kelet Henagan. They had no issue. She died April 14, 1864.

Ellerbe, *Ellerbe Family History,* 4–11.

Elliott, Elizabeth Trezevant Wayne: Elizabeth Trezevant Wayne was the daughter of Rev. William Wayne and Esther Trezevant. She married Francis Elliott and had one son, John Francis Abraham. After Elliott's death Elizabeth wed Louis Miles DesChamps. They had five children, including sons Sinclair Capers and Louis Henry.

Bailey, Morgan, and Taylor, *Biographical Directory of the South Carolina Senate,* 1:386; Trezevant, *Trezevant Family,* 57.

Eveleigh, Thomas (1747–1816): Thomas Eveleigh was born in 1747, the son of George Eveleigh. A lawyer by trade, he married Ann Simmons (d. 1828) on March 23, 1773, in St. Phillips Parish. She bore him nine children: Elizabeth, Samuel, Harriet Ann, Thomas, George, Ann, William, Henry S., and Thomas. When the British captured Charleston in 1780, Eveleigh was arrested and taken prisoner. On December 31, 1781, he and his family were banned from Charleston and moved to Jamestown, Virginia. The Eveleighs returned to South Carolina after the war and settled in Sumter. Eveleigh died in 1816.

Mears, *History of the Heverly Family,* 88, 90–92, 93, 99, 105–6.

Faust, Daniel (d. 1836): Daniel Faust and his brother Jacob John Faust, sons of Jacob Faust, were for many years publishers of the *South-Carolina State Gazette and Columbian Advertiser.* They were also the official state printers, responsible for printing legislative journals and reports. Faust eventually took control of the paper and was the editor and publisher for more than thirty-six years before selling it to S. J. McMorris. He served as intendant of Columbia in 1808 and from 1812 to 1814. He married Sarah Milling, daughter of John Milling. Faust died in 1836.

Bailey, *Biographical Directory of the South Carolina House,* 198; Bailey and Cooper, *Biographical Directory of the South Carolina House,* 500; Boozer, "Bethany Church," 18; *Columbia: Capital City,* 225–26, 239–40; Moore, *Columbia and Richland County,* 466.

Faust, Jacob John (b. 1772): Jacob John Faust was born in 1772 in Orangeburg, the son of Jacob Faust and brother of Daniel Faust. In 1808 he became a captain in the United States Army and was later brigadier general in the South Carolina militia. He represented Richland County in the South Carolina House of Representatives in 1812. Faust and his brother were the official state printers and editors of the *South-Carolina State Gazette and Columbian Advertiser.* He married Sarah Clarke White (1787–1839), daughter of Blake Leay White and Elizabeth Bourquin, at Chapel Hill Plantation on May 6, 1813. She bore him one son, Augustus Brickell.

Journal of the House of Representatives of South Carolina, 780; Oswald, *Printing in the Americas,* 289; Strawn, *Ancestors and Descendants of John White,* 27.

Fishburne, William (1760–1819): William Fishburne was born September 12, 1760, the only child of William and Ann Fishburne. He was raised by his mother and her second husband, Francis Beatty. Fishburne entered the Continental Army at age sixteen. He was appointed a second lieutenant in the First Regiment of the Continental Establishment and promoted to first lieutenant in 1778. Fishburne was wounded at the battle of Stono Ferry on June 20, 1779.

In 1781 he became a captain in the Second Regiment and later a corporal under Francis Marion. He was also in the cavalry under Peter Horry. Fishburne represented St. Bartholomew in the Fifth, Sixth, and Eighth General Assemblies from 1783 to 1786 and 1789 to 1790. After the war he continued his military service as lieutenant colonel of the Twenty-Fourth Regiment, Fifth Brigade, Second Division, and as major general of the Second Division of the state militia. Fishburne married Sarah Snipes, daughter of Maj. William Snipes, by whom he had eight children. After her death in 1804, he married her younger sister Mary Clay Snipes. They had six children. Fishburne died November 3, 1819.

Bailey and Cooper, *Biographical Directory of the South Carolina House*, 233–34; Fishburn, *Fishburns*, 48–49; Moss, *Roster of South Carolina Patriots*, 314–15; Snowden and Cutler, *History of South Carolina*, 3:19.

Fleming, George Henry (1791–1864): George Henry Fleming was born April 20, 1791, the son of James Fleming Sr. and Margaret Durant. Fleming served as a captain in the War of 1812 in the Fifth Regiment of the militia. A planter, in 1822 he was sued by Mark Solomon over an unpaid debt and lost his property in Williamsburg. He left South Carolina in 1845 and relocated to a plantation in Florida. Fleming married Charlotte Mitilda Knox (1799–1857), with whom he had five children: Samuel James, Hannah Elizabeth, George Alexander, Margaret June, and Sarah Agnes. He died in 1864.

Jenkinson, *Williamsburg District*, 24–25; Reese, *John Fleming*, 7, 10.

Floyd, Charles (1747–1820): Charles Floyd was born March 4, 1747, the son of Samuel and Susan Dixon Floyd, in Northampton County, Virginia. Floyd's parents died during his adolescence, and he was sent to live with his uncle, who indentured him as a cabin boy. After fourteen years at sea, he settled in Charleston and managed an indigo plantation. During the American Revolution, Floyd was a member of the first council of safety and helped raise a militia with the St. Helena Guards. Floyd's home was plundered and burned by Tories, and he was captured by the British in Savannah and held prisoner aboard ship. Floyd married Mary Fendin, daughter of John Fendin Jr., in Charleston in 1768. They had one son, John Floyd. The Floyds relocated to McIntosh County, Georgia, in 1795 and settled on adjoining farms called "The Thickets." In 1800 they moved to Camden County, Georgia, and built two plantations, Bellevue and Fairfield. Both he and his wife are interred at the Floyd Family Cemetery near Fairfield Plantation in Camden County. Mary predeceased her husband in 1804. Floyd died at Fairfield on September 9, 1820.

Mathews and Tongue, *Floyd, History and Lineage*, 2–4.

Ford, Timothy (1762–1830): Timothy Ford was born December 4, 1762, the son of Jacob Ford and Theodosia Johnes of Morristown, New Jersey. Ford served in the American Revolution and was wounded in 1780 at the Battle of Springfield. After graduating from Princeton University, he studied law under Robert Morris in New York. He relocated to Charleston in 1785, where he was admitted to the bar in 1786 and established a partnership with his brother-in-law, Henry William De Saussure. Ford owned property in Charleston, Sullivans Island, and Fair Spring Plantation on the Ashley River. He represented St. Philip and St. Michael Parishes in the Tenth, Eleventh, and Twelfth General Assemblies from 1792 to 1797. He also held a number of other offices, including secretary of the American Revolution Society in 1792, commissioner for Charleston to build and repair the jail and courthouse from 1794 to 1814, junior grand warden of the Ancient York Masons in 1794, trustee and secretary treasurer for the College of Charleston from 1796 to 1828 and 1802 to 1813, judge advocate from 1797 to 1800 and lieutenant colonel and judge advocate general from 1801 to 1809 in the state militia, justice of the quorum for St. Philip and St. Michael Parishes, warden for Charleston's Fifth Ward from 1800 to 1801 and the Fourth Ward from 1802 to 1803, vice president and president of the Charleston Library Society from 1816 to 1823 and 1826 to 1830, commissioner of the Charleston Workhouse in 1803, vice president in 1817 and president in 1830 of the Literary and Philosophical Society, director of the Santee Canal Company from 1819 to 1824, member of a committee for the Independent Congregational Church of Charleston in 1819, director of the South Carolina Insurance Company from 1819 to 1823 and 1826 to 1829, warden for Moultrieville, Sullivans Island, in 1823, commissioner to combine all laws in any given subject into a general act in 1825, and commissioner for Charleston to open subscriptions for stock of a company constructing railroads or canals in 1828. Ford married Sarah Amelia De Saussure, daughter of Daniel De Saussure and Mary McPherson, in 1793. She bore him one daughter, Charlotte Matilda. Sarah died in 1799, and Ford married Mary Magdalen Prioleau, daughter of Samuel Prioleau Jr. and Catherine Cores, on November 20, 1800. They had two children: Louisa Catherine and Mary Theodosia. Ford died December 7, 1830.

Bailey, *Biographical Directory of the South Carolina House,* 208–9.

Fraser, Hugh (1763–1838): Hugh Fraser was born in Scotland in 1763 and migrated to South Carolina in 1793. As of 1796 he owned 1,600 acres on the Waccamaw Neck known as "Calais." The point of land jutting into Winyah Bay was named "Fraser's Point" in his honor. Fraser served as rector of Prince Frederick's Parish until his resignation in 1810, after which he became rector of All Saints' Church, serving until 1817. Fraser died in All Saints Parish in 1838.

Bull, *All Saints' Church,* 14–15.

Frey, Philip Martin (ca. 1754–1833): Philip Martin Frey served in the Second Regiment of the South Carolina Continentals commanded by Col. William Moultrie and was one of the earliest recruits in Capt. Peter Horry's company. During his service he acted as a drummer. He was wounded in the leg at the Battle of Fort Moultrie. After the war Frey became a farmer. He and his wife, Nancy, had five children: Michael, Abraham, George M., Andrew, and John T. Frey died in June 1833.

Moss, *Roster of South Carolina Patriots,* 333; Reese, *John Fleming,* 77–79.

Gadsden, John: John Gadsden was born March 4, 1787, the son of Philip Gadsden and Catherine Edwards. Gadsden attended the Associated Academy in Charleston and Yale University, where he graduated in 1804. Admitted to the bar in 1808, he represented St. Philip and St. Michael in the Twenty-Third General Assembly from 1818 to 1819. He was reelected but had to relinquish his seat due to his appointment as US district attorney for Charleston. Gadsden served Charleston in a number of other capacities: intendant pro tempore from 1819 to 1829, major and deputy judge advocate general of the Seventeenth and Fourth Brigades of the militia from 1820 to 1821, commissioner of the Charleston orphan house in 1827, and director of the Office of Discount and Deposit in Charleston in 1828. He was also a member of the Charleston Library Society, Agricultural Society of South Carolina, and the Philomathean Society. On April 29, 1818, Gadsden married Ann M. Edwards, by whom he had one son, Christopher Philip. Gadsden died January 24, 1831, and was buried at St. Philip's Churchyard in Charleston.

Catalogue of the Officers and Graduates of Yale, 93; Holcomb, *South Carolina Marriages,* 42; Moore, *Biographical Directory of the South Carolina House,* 98–99; O'Neall, *Biographical Sketches of the Bench,* 2:51–56.

Gaillard, Cornelia Marshall: Cornelia Marshall, daughter of William Marshall of Florida and Charleston, married Judge Theodore Gaillard Sr. on November 8, 1799. They had nine children: Jane Marshall, Elizabeth Peyre, Cornelia Marshall, Theodore, Floride Judith, Eleanor Mary, William Warren, John Randell, and John. Theodore Gaillard died March 24, 1829. According to the 1830 census, there was a Cornelia Marshall living in Charleston, most likely the widow of Theodore.

Bailey, *Biographical Directory of the South Carolina House,* 221; Burns and Burkette, "Peyre Records" (1975), 142; Census, Fifth and Sixth, 1830–1840, Charleston, S.C.

Gaillard, John (1765–1826): John Gaillard was born September 5, 1765, in St. Stephen Parish, the son of John Gaillard and Judith Peyre. He was accepted to the Middle Temple in London to study law but decided to focus on planting and politics instead. Gaillard resided at Windsor Plantation in St. Stephen but also owned property in St. James Santee and Pendleton District. He represented St. Stephen in the Eleventh General Assembly from 1794 to 1795 and in the state senate for the Twelfth through the Sixteenth General Assemblies from 1796 to 1805. He was president of the Fifteenth and Sixteenth General Assemblies but was forced to vacate that office when he took Pierce Butler's place in the US Senate in 1805. He returned to the South Caroline Senate for the Ninth through the Nineteenth General Assemblies from 1805 to 1827. Gaillard married Mary Lord, daughter of Andrew Lord and Ann Gascoigne, on November 22, 1792. They had three children: Edwin, Theodore Samuel, and Anna. Mary died unexpectedly in 1799. Gaillard died February 26, 1826, and was buried in the Congressional Cemetery in Washington, DC.

Bailey, Morgan, and Taylor, *Biographical Directory of the South Carolina Senate,* 1:539–40.

Gaillard, Theodore, Sr. (1766–1829): Theodore Gaillard Sr. was born November 6, 1766, the son of John Gaillard and Judith Peyre. Gaillard studied law at the Middle Temple in London and was admitted to the bar in South Carolina in 1788. He owned Mon Repos Plantation on the Cooper River as well as a home in Charleston. St. Stephen elected Gaillard to the Thirteenth, Fourteenth, and Fifteenth General Assemblies from 1798 to 1804. He represented Christ Church Parish in the Seventeenth and Eighteenth General Assemblies from 1806 to 1808. During the Fourteenth and Eighteenth General Assemblies, he served as Speaker of the house. When Gaillard was elected a judge of the Court of Equity in 1808, he resigned his house seat and served in that capacity until 1824. He was an associate judge of the Court of General Sessions and Common Pleas until his death. Gaillard was also presidential elector in 1800, director of the State Bank in 1808 and 1811, founder and vestryman for Trinity Episcopal Cathedral in Columbia from 1812 to 1813, member of the Charleston Library Society from 1818 to 1829, and first orator of the '76 Association. Gaillard married Cornelia Marshall, daughter of William Marshall, on November 8, 1799. She bore him nine children: Jane Marshall, Elizabeth Peyre, Cornelia Marshall, Theodore, Floride Judith, Eleanor Mary, William Warren, John Randell, and John. Gaillard died March 24, 1829, in Darlington.

Bailey, *Biographical Directory of the South Carolina House,* 220–21; MacDowell, *Gaillard Genealogy,* 1–3, 6–7, 10–11, 75, 312; "Notices of Conspicuous Members," 91–95; O'Neall, *Biographical Sketches of the Bench,* 1:253–69; Salley, *Marriage Notices,* 100.

Gasque, Robert (b. 1750): Robert Gasque served under Capt. Joseph Hudson, Col. William Baxter, and Gen. Francis Marion during the American

Revolution. As of 1782 he was a lieutenant. According to the census, Gasque lived in Georgetown in 1790.

Census, First, 1810, Prince Georges, Georgetown, S.C.; Moss, *Roster of South Carolina Patriots,* 346, 811.

Gibbes, William Hasell/Hasel/Hassell/Hazell/Hazle (1754–1834): William Hasell Gibbes was born March 16, 1754, in Charleston, the son of William Gibbes and Elizabeth Hassel. Educated in London, he returned to South Carolina to read law under John Rutledge. He went back to London, however, to attend the Inner Temple in 1771. At the start of the American Revolution, Gibbes once again put his studies on hold and was in Charleston by 1778. Commissioned a captain-lieutenant in the Ancient Battalion of Artillery, he witnessed the Battle of Port Royal, the siege of Savannah, and the fall of Charleston. The British arrested Gibbes for disloyalty and exiled him to St. Augustine, where he lived until 1781. When hostilities waned Gibbes was admitted to the bar in South Carolina. He represented St. John Colleton Parish in the Second and Third General Assemblies from 1776 to 1780, and St. Philip and St. Michael Parishes elected him to the Fourth and Fifth General Assemblies from 1782 to 1784. He was a member of the Privy Council in 1783, which appointed him master in chancery in 1783. Gibbes faced impeachment charges by Thomas Lehre in 1811 on grounds he had misused his office. He was impeached by the house but acquitted by the senate. Gibbes was a member of the Fellowship Society in 1773, commissioner for stamping and issuing currency in 1778, member and senior warden of the South Carolina Society from 1789 to 1790, member of the Mount Sion Society in 1779, recorder of the city court of Charleston from 1783 to 1786, vestryman of St. Philip Parish from 1783 to 1787 and St. Michael Parish from 1805 to 1806 and 1823 to 1827, director of the Charleston Mutual Insurance Company from 1811 to 1813, director of the South Carolina Insurance Company from 1823 to 1834, director of the Bank of South Carolina from 1806 to 1808, delegate from St. Andrew Parish to the Episcopal Church convention in 1807, and director of the Santee Canal Company from 1826 to 1834. Gibbes also continued to practice law in Charleston until his death. He married Elizabeth Allston, daughter of William Allston and Ann Simons. She bore him twelve children: Anne, William Allston, Eliza, Harriet, William, Allston, Washington, Henry, William Hasell, Edwin, Benjamin, and Sarah Postell. Elizabeth died February 1, 1806, and Gibbes married Mary Philip Wilson, daughter of Robert and Ann Wilson in 1808. They had four children: Robert Wilson, Ann Isabel, Samuel Wilson, and James Wilson. Gibbes died February 13, 1834.

Bailey and Cooper, *Biographical Directory of the South Carolina House,* 258–61; Burke, *Prominent Families,* 477; Census, First, Second, Third, Fourth, and Fifth,

1790–1820, Charleston, S.C.; *Columbian Herald,* July 6, 1785; William Hasell Gibbes Papers, South Caroliniana Library, Columbia.

Glover, Henrietta Bonneau (1796–1821): Henrietta Bonneau Glover was the daughter of Moses Glover and Anne Wilson of Georgetown and Charleston. She married her cousin, John Waties, by whom she had one son, Thomas. Henrietta died June 2, 1821, at Stateburg and was buried at Holy Cross Church.

Bailey, *Biographical Directory of the South Carolina House,* 236; Glover, *Colonel Joseph Glover,* 13, 36, 81.

Goddard, Thomas Fraser (ca. 1794–1830): Thomas Fraser Goddard was born November 8, 1794, the only child of William Goddard and Mary A. Almond. Goddard was a junior at South Carolina College in 1813. He attended the First Baptist Church of Georgetown and married Elizabeth Coon Hutchinson, daughter of Mary Cuttino and Thomas Hutchinson. They had four children: William, Peter, Mary Elizabeth, and Francis. Goddard died December 25, 1830, and was buried at the First Baptist Church of Georgetown.

Cuttino, "Cuttino Inscriptions," 58; Cuttino, "Descendants of William Cuttino," 136, 139–40; Cuttino, "Further Notes on the History," 29–30; "Goddard's Heirs vs. Urquhart," in Miller and Curry, *Reports of Cases,* 6:659–75; Minutes, First Baptist Church of Georgetown, January 1805–November 30, 1821; Moore, *Roll of Students,* 7; Rogers, *History of Georgetown County,* 195, 236.

Goodwyn/Goodwin, James (d. 1826): James Goodwyn lived in various places in South Carolina, including Camden, Richland, and Fairfield Districts. He represented Richland in the Eleventh, Twelfth, and Eighteenth General Assemblies from 1794 to 1797 and 1808 to 1809. He was also a justice of the peace in Richland in 1798, sheriff for Camden District from 1799 to 1800, major of the Sixth Regiment of cavalry of the state militia from 1808 to 1826, and commissioner to superintend the printing of acts and resolutions in 1809. Goodwyn married Jane Green, widow of John Green, on May 9, 1802. They had at least two children: Eliza Howell and James Harris. Jane died before November 24, 1814. His second wife was Lucy Ann. Goodwyn died sometime before September 18, 1826.

Bailey, *Biographical Directory of the South Carolina House,* 239–40; Census, First and Fourth, 1790–1820, Richland, S.C., Columbia and Fairfield, S.C..

Gourdin/Gourdine/Gurdin/Gardine, Theodore, II (1764–1826): Theodore Gourdin II was born March 20, 1764, the son of Theodore Gourdin and Esther Newman. Gourdin was a wealthy planter, owning thousands of acres in Williamsburg, Georgetown, Sumter, and Charleston. He owned at least four plantations: Richmond, Bluehouse, Washington, and Mount Moriah. He also controlled several ferries, including Murray's, Skrine's, Nelson's, Lenud's, and Hickson's. He is said to have been the wealthiest man in Williamsburg before 1830, owning so much property that he could walk from the Clarendon-Williamsburg line to Georgetown's town clock, about a seventy-five-mile distance, without leaving his property. Gourdin represented St. John Berkeley Parish in the Seventh General Assembly from 1787 to 1788. He served Prince George Winyah Parish and Williamsburg in the state senate in the Twelfth and Thirteenth General Assemblies from 1796 to 1799. He returned to the senate for the Seventeenth and Eighteenth General Assemblies from 1806 to 1809 to represent St. John Berkeley. Gourdin was elected to the US House of Representatives on the Democratic ticket for the Thirteenth Congress from 1813 to 1815. After his stint in Congress, he once again held a state senate seat, this time for St. Stephen Parish in the Twenty-Fourth and Twenty-Fifth General Assemblies from 1820 to 1823. Gourdin also served as commissioner of the high roads for St. John Berkeley from 1785 to 1790, tax inquirer and collector for St. John Berkeley from 1786 to 1787, road commissioner for the area between the Santee and Black Rivers from 1795 to 1796, 1799, 1808, and 1810, trustee of Williamsburg Academy in 1795, committee member to inquire into the practicality of the establishment of a turnpike road from St. Philip Parish to Biggin Church in St. John Berkeley in 1808, commissioner to receive subscriptions for establishment of a company to carry the turnpike system into operation in 1810, delegate from St. Mark Parish to the Episcopal Church convention in 1814, tax collector for St. John Berkeley in 1817, and bridge commissioner over Eutaw Creek at the juncture with Santee River in 1819. Gourdin married Elizabeth Gaillard, daughter of Theodore Gaillard Jr. and Ellinor Cordes, on October 20, 1785. They had ten children: Elizabeth, Ellinor, Theodore Louis, Esther, Henrietta, Peter Gaillard, Samuel Thomas, Robert Marion, John Gaillard Keith, and Hamilton Couturier. Gourdin died January 17, 1826, and was buried at St. Stephen Churchyard.

Bailey, Morgan, and Taylor, *Biographical Directory of the South Carolina Senate,* 1:588–89; Boddie, *History of Williamsburg,* 248; Gourdin, *Gourdin Family,* 8, 19, 26–73, 83–84, 89, 107, 111–12, 124, 134, 135, 139, 141, 148–49, 158, 165–67, 169–71, 173–81, 186–89, 190, 222, 223, 302, 310, 312, 319, 322, 330, 332, 347, 351, 364, 366, 368, 377, 383, 412, 417, 423, 428, 434, 436, 438.

Grant, William (d. 1812): William Grant was an attorney in Georgetown and Charleston and a member of the First Baptist Church of Georgetown. According to Horry he died in 1812, leaving behind a widow and six children.

Census, 1810, Third, Georgetown, S.C.; General Assembly Petitions, no. 180 and 181, 342–47, South Carolina Department of Archives and History; General Assembly Petitions, no. 124, 106–11, South Carolina Department of Archives and History;

Minutes, First Baptist Church of Georgetown, January 12, 1805–February 24, 1812; O'Neall, *Biographical Sketches of the Bench,* 2:459, 601.

Green, Samuel: Dr. Samuel Green, originally from Massachusetts, owned a drugstore at the corner of Main and Lady Streets in Columbia. A prominent citizen, he also owned a hotel, tavern, and a post office. In 1794 he was a county court justice for Richland County. Green's plantation was located above Columbia on the old Winnsboro Road. He married Elizabeth Tillinghast, the widow of Dr. H. H. Tillinghast, in 1795. When she died he married Selina Waring, who survived him. Green died in 1837 and was buried at Washington Street United Methodist Church in Columbia.

Carolina Gazette, February 26, 1808; Census, Third and Fifth, 1810–1830, Columbia, S.C.; *Columbia: Capital City,* 376; Graydon, *Tales of Columbia,* 236; Green, *History of Richland County,* 136–37, 177–78, 200, 231, 308.

Grier/Greer, James: James Grier was the son of Patrick Grier. He resided in Prince George Winyah Parish, where in 1778 he served on the grand and petit juries. He owned at least 1,100 acres on the Great Pee Dee River and more than 3,000 acres in Prince George Winyah, along with numerous slaves. Grier represented Prince Frederick Parish in the Eighth General Assembly from 1789 to 1790. He was also commissioner for clearing the Great Pee Dee and Little Pee Dee Rivers in 1785, tax inquirer and collector for Prince George Winyah in 1785, and commissioner on the lower board of commissioners for the improvement of navigation of the Great Pee Dee River in 1791.

Bailey and Cooper, *Biographical Directory of the South Carolina House,* 288; Census, First, Third, and Fourth, 1790–1820, Prince Georges, Georgetown, S.C..

Gist, Mordecai (1742–1792): Mordecai Gist was born the son of Capt. Thomas Gist and Susannah Cockey on February 22, 1742, in Baltimore. Gist spent his childhood at the family home, Stone Hall, and received his education at St. Paul's Seminary. Gist was a member of the Baltimore Town Non-Importation Committee in 1774, and that year was appointed captain of the first military company raised in Maryland, the Baltimore Independent Company. Commissioned second major of Gen. William Smallwood's battalion by the Maryland Convention on January 1, 1776, he saw combat at the Battle of Long Island later that year. In January 1779 the Continental Congress promoted Gist to brigadier general in the Continental Army, and he commanded the Second Maryland Brigade. During the southern campaign, Congress sent the Maryland and Delaware lines to the South under the command of Maj. Johann de Kalb. At the Battle of Camden in 1780, Gist escaped and was present for the surrender of Lord Cornwallis at Yorktown the following year. He joined the southern army under Nathanael Greene and was victorious over the British at Combahee. Gist spent the remainder of his life in Charleston. He married Cecil Carnan, daughter of Charles and Prudence Carnan, in 1769. She died during the birth of their daughter, Cecil Carnan. Gist married Mary Sterrett on January 23, 1778. They had one son, Independent. Mary died within the first two years of their marriage. His third wife was Mary Cattell, widow of Capt. B. Cattell and daughter of George McCall. She bore him two children: States and Susannah. Gist died in Charleston on September 12, 1792, and was buried at St. Michael's Church.

Boyle, *Biographical Sketches of Distinguished Marylanders*, 147–48, 150–56; Gee, *Gist Family of South Carolina*, 2, 6, 8, 12–16, 18–19; Gratz, "Generals of the Continental Line," 402; Hayden, *Washington and His Masonic Compeers*, 390–95; Lynch, "Brigadier General Mordecai Gist"; "Partial Roster of Officers," 68; Reno, *Maryland 400*, 48–50; Whittemore, *Heroes of the American Revolution*, 6, 40–42.

Guignard, Caroline Elizabeth (1811–65): Caroline Elizabeth Guignard was born in 1811, the daughter of James Sanders I and Caroline Richardson. She married Robert Wilson Gibbes (1809–66) on December 20, 1827. Gibbes was twice mayor of Columbia and surgeon general of South Carolina during the Civil War. They had five children: Ann Isabel, Robert Wilson, Mary How, Elizabeth, and Susan Wilson. Caroline died in 1865.

Mackenzie and Rhoades, *Colonial Families*, 6:232; Meriwether, *Planters and Business Men*, 149.

Guignard, Caroline Richardson (1779–1816): Caroline Richardson was born in 1779, the daughter of William Richardson and Anne Magdalen Guignard. She married James Sanders Guignard I in 1801. They had eight children: John Gabriel II, James Sanders II, Anna Magdalen, William Maynard, Caroline Elizabeth, Sarah Slann, Frances Ann Margaret Horry, and Mary Susan Poinsett. Caroline died in 1816.

Dominick, "Poinsett Genealogy," 68.

Guignard, Elizabeth Sanders (1763–1814): Elizabeth Sanders was born in 1763, the daughter of James and Sarah Slann Sanders. The Sanders were successful planters and owned large plantations in Berkeley and Dorchester Counties. Elizabeth married Gabriel Guignard, with whom she had one son, James Sanders, born in 1780. Elizabeth died in 1814.

Meriwether, *Planters and Business Men*, 4, 149.

Guignard, James Sanders (1780–1856): James Sanders Guignard was born January 14, 1780, the only child of John Gabriel Guignard and Elizabeth Sanders. He served as his father's clerk during his tenure as treasurer of the Upper Division of South Carolina and continued in the position under his father's successor, Robert Witherspoon. Guignard was postmaster of Columbia in 1798 and became treasurer in his own right in 1800, serving for four years. When his term ended, he was selected surveyor general of South Carolina in 1801. He was named commissioner to sell certain lots in Columbia in 1805 and the following year was commissioned ordinary and register of mesne conveyance for Richland District. In 1806 Guignard became clerk of court of Richland County and eventually probate judge, a position he held until his death. Additionally he was a notary and clerk of the Court of Common Pleas and an active member of Trinity Episcopal Cathedral in Columbia, a church he and his father helped establish. He was also captain of the Columbia Artillery, one of the first militia companies organized in Columbia. Guignard's passion, however, was buying and selling land. He owned property starting at age eight and continued to purchase land in and outside of South Carolina until his death. His home in Columbia was bounded by Gervais, Bull, Senate, and Marion Streets. Guignard manufactured bricks on his Lexington County plantation from 1801 to 1805, and by 1850 he had a thriving business under the name Guignard Brick Works. Guignard's first wife was Caroline Richardson (1779–1816), whom he married in 1801. They had eight children: John Gabriel II, James Sanders II, Anna Magdalen, William Maynard, Caroline Elizabeth, Sarah Slann, Frances Ann Margaret Horry, and Mary Susan Poinsett. When Caroline died, he married Eliza Sanders in 1818 and had one daughter, Parthenia Juliana. Guignard died in 1856.

Childs, *Planters and Businessmen*, 15–19, 149; *Columbia: Capital City*, 144–45, 290, 374–75; *Columbia Examiner*, November 8, 1856; Green, *History of Richland County*, 182; James Guignard, "Guignard Brick Works," in Edgar, *South Carolina Encyclopedia*, 411; Jervey, "Marriage and Death Notices" (1944).

Guignard, James Sanders, Jr. (II) (1803–68): James Sanders Guignard Jr. was born October 1, 1803, the son of James Sanders Guignard and Caroline Richardson. He managed Chance Plantation in Edgefield, bequeathed to him by his father along with Still Hopes Plantation in Lexington and the family home on Senate Street in Columbia. James Sanders, his brother John Gabriel II, and their father, John Gabriel I, operated cooperatively. While James Sanders managed the Edgefield estate, his brother took Edisto and his father Lexington. Guignard served as ordinary and clerk of court for Richland County and alderman for the First Ward in Columbia. In 1865 he operated a ferry after the burning of the bridge from Lexington to Columbia. He helped develop his father's brick-making endeavor into a profitable business, Guignard Brick Works. Guginard married his cousin, Elizabeth Richardson, with whom he had nine children: James Sanders III, John Gabriel III, Frances Caroline, Sarah Slann, Susan, Laura, Emma Slann, William, and Benjamin. When Elizabeth died in 1852, he married Anna Edwards, also his cousin. She left no issue. Guignard died suddenly on February 19, 1868.

Childs, *Planters and Businessmen*, 38–41, 149; Taylor, Matthews, and Power, *Leverett Letters*, 477.

Guignard, John Gabriel, I (1751–1822): John Gabriel Guignard was the son of Gabriel Guignard and Frances Deliesseline and the brother of Peter Horry's wife, Margaret Guignard. Guignard spent his adolescence in Charleston with his mother. His several partnerships included Guignard and Freneau, Postell and Guignard, Slann and Guignard, and J. G. Guignard and Co. He also operated a general store at 81 Tradd Street. Guignard relocated to the High Hills of Santee near Stateburg before 1779. He was one of the founders of the Claremont Episcopal Church there and served as warden from 1788 to 1794. The Guignards moved to Columbia in 1790, where he acted as treasurer of the Upper Division of South Carolina, continuing in that capacity until 1798, when he was elected surveyor general. The Guignards' home stood at the corner of Senate and Pickens Streets. They also owned two plantations on the Congaree River: Still Hopes and Rising Hopes. Guignard married Elizabeth Sanders, daughter of James and Sarah Slann Sanders, in 1779. She bore him one child, James Sanders. Elizabeth predeceased her husband on September 1, 1814. Guignard died January 9, 1822. They are both interred in the Guignard family plot at Trinity Episcopal Cathedral in Columbia, a church Guignard helped establish.

Columbia: Capital City, 144–45; Green, *History of Richland County*, 182; Mazyck, "Wills of South Carolina Huguenots"; Meriwether, *Planters and Business Men*, 3–5; Salsi and Simms, *Columbia*, 30.

Guignard, John Gabriel, II: John Gabriel Guignard II earned his medical degree from the College of Physicians and Surgeons of the State of New York in 1823. He was a member of the Medical Societies of New York in 1823 and of Mississippi in 1826. He opened a practice in Woodville, Mississippi, but returned to South Carolina in 1828, where he established himself on Evergreen Plantation in Edisto and in Orangeburg and Barnwell Districts. He represented Orangeburg in the South Carolina House of Representatives in 1840 and was an officer in the state militia. Guignard, his brother James Sanders II, and their father, John Gabriel I, ran the family's plantations. Guignard died in December 1857.

Meriwether, *Planters and Business Men*, 35–38.

Guignard, Sarah Slaun/Slann (1813–44): Sarah Slaun/Slann Guignard was born April 1, 1813, the daughter of James Sanders Guignard II and Caroline

Richardson. She married John Alexander Scott, son of Gov. Abram Marshall Scott and Susan Gray, on February 25, 1830. They had eight children: James Sanders Guignard, Abram Marshall Guignard, Caroline Susan, John Alexander, Sarah Slaun, Maynard Richardson, Calhoun, and Elizabeth Frances. Sarah died in 1844 and was buried in Woodville, Mississippi.

Meriwether, *Planters and Business Men,* 149; Stafford, *General Leroy Augustus Stafford,* 436.

Hails, Robert (b. 1753): Robert Hails was born October 28, 1753, the son of Thomas and Eleanor Hails. Hails owned property in Orangeburg, Camden, and Richland District and around one hundred slaves. He served as a captain in the American Revolution under Light Horse Harry Lee. Hails represented St. Matthews Parish in the Ninth General Assembly in 1791 but resigned when he became sheriff of Orangeburg. He returned to the house from 1801 to 1805 and in 1808 served as treasurer for the upper division of the state. He also served as road commissioner, militia captain, justice of the peace for Lewisburgh County, vestryman and church warden for St. Matthews, representative of St. Matthews in the state constitutional convention, and commissioner to examine the records of the commissioners of Columbia. His first wife was Susannah Richardson. They had three children: Sarah (Susannah), Harriet, and Eleanor. His second wife was Sarah Bozier, by whom he had one son, Thomas Jefferson.

Bailey, *Biographical Directory of the South Carolina House,* 254–55; Census, Third, Columbia, S.C.; Cory, *Ladies' Memorial Association,* 14–15; Dubose, *Notable Men of Alabama,* 1:72–73; Owen and Owen, *History of Alabama,* 3:131.

Hall, Ainsley: Ainsley Hall, a merchant and cotton broker in Columbia, built an extravagant home in Columbia in 1818 known as the Hampton Preston House, which he later sold to Wade Hampton. He married Sarah Cooke Goodwyn. Hall died during the construction of their new home. Upon the mansion's completion, his widow sold it to the Theological Seminary of the Presbyterian Synod of South Carolina and Georgia.

Bacon, *But One Race,* 10; Salsi and Simms, *Columbia,* 34.

Hall, Thomas (1750–1814): Thomas Hall was born June 9, 1750. The Council of Safety commissioned him a second lieutenant in the Second South Carolina Provincial Regiment on June 24, 1775. Wounded at the Battle of Fort Moultrie in June 1776, he was promoted to captain at the siege of Savannah in 1779. He was captured with the fall of Charleston in 1780 and exiled to St. Augustine. Upon his exchange he served as an aide-de-camp to General St. Clair and was present at the surrender of Cornwallis. After the American

Revolution, he became postmaster of Charleston in 1783 and served until 1794. He was also clerk of the US District Court of South Carolina. In November 1785 Hall married Mary Newton, who died in Nassau the following year. His second wife was Sabina Vander Horst Toomer, widow of Joshua Toomer and the only daughter of William Vander Horst. Hall died August 28, 1814, and was buried at a plantation in Christ Church Parish.

Census, Third, 1810, Charleston, S.C.; Trezevant, *Trezevant Family,* 55–56.

Halling, Solomon (d. 1812): Solomon Halling was born in Pennsylvania and studied medicine in Philadelphia. He was appointed senior surgeon in the general hospitals of the Middle and Southern Departments in the American Revolution. After the war Halling began practicing medicine in New Bern, North Carolina, but decided to leave the field for the ministry. In 1792 he was ordained by the Reverend James Madison, bishop of Virginia, and appointed rector of Christ Church at New Bern. Three years later he resigned and was appointed to Saint James' Church in Wilmington. The Diocese of South Carolina appointed him rector of Prince George's Parish in 1809. Halling married three times. His first wife bore him two daughters: Francinia Greenway and Ann Dorothea. She died September 18, 1793, and he remarried on February 8, 1794, to Eunice Kelly, by whom he had two children. After her death he wed Sarah Moore Jones, widow of Frederick Jones Jr. and daughter of George and Mary Ashe Moore. They had four children. Halling died December 24, 1812.

Cheshire, *Sketches of Church History,* 261; Hobart, *Archives of the General Convention,* 5:288.

Hampton, Wade, II (1791–1858): Wade Hampton II was born in 1791, the son of Wade Hampton I and Harriet Flud Hampton. He attended preparatory school in Connecticut and South Carolina College, although he did not graduate. Hampton was lieutenant of the light dragoons during the War of 1812 but resigned his commission in 1814 to go to Mississippi on business. He was in New Orleans during Andrew Jackson's defense of the city and rejoined the military, carrying the news to Washington regarding the victory. He was known throughout South Carolina as Colonel Hampton from his appointment as deputy inspector general of the state troops in 1816. When his military service ended, he managed Millwood Plantation near Columbia. He married Ann Fitzsimons in 1817. Hampton died in 1858.

Ackerman, *Wade Hampton III,* 5–6; Smith, *Slavery, Race,* 205.

Harrell, Jacob: Jacob Harrell and his wife were from Anson County, North Carolina. Harrell served in the American Revolution, and by 1790 had relocated to South Carolina, receiving numerous grants in Georgetown, Williamsburg, Horry, and Marion Counties. Harrell's children included Levi, Leacy, Selah, Ann, Martha, Mary, Jasper, and Lewis.

Smallwood, *Burch, Harrell and Allied Families,* 1:130–35.

Harrell, Lewis (1787–1822): Lewis Harrell was born in Marion, South Carolina, in 1787, the son of Jacob Harrell. As of 1790 he resided with his family in Georgetown. He took an appointment as commissioner to clean out Lynches Creek and served in the War of 1812. Harrell married at least twice. Five of his children were still living at the time of his death in 1822: Josiah, Mary Anderson, Matthew M., Hosiah T., and Lewis.

Census, First, 1790, Georgetown, S.C.; Smallwood, *Burch, Harrell and Allied Families,* 1:130–35.

Hart, John (1758–1814): John Hart was born March 6, 1758. Hart was appointed captain in the Second Regiment of South Carolina on August 18, 1779, but resigned his position when he became second lieutenant in 1780. He was taken prisoner at the fall of Charleston in 1780. When exchanged he rose to the rank of first lieutenant in 1781 and served in that capacity until the end of the war. He married Mary Screven (1767–1845), daughter of Gen. James Screven and Mary Odingsell, on June 17, 1784. Hart died in 1814.

Bulloch, *Habersham Family,* 171; Heitman, *Historical Register of Officers,* 277; Moss, *Roster of South Carolina Patriots,* 422.

Harvey, Francis/Frances (1774–1847): Francis Harvey was born in Edgefield, South Carolina, on August 14, 1774, the daughter of James Harvey and Sarah Clark. She married Holman Eastes (1763–1847), son of Obediah Eastes, on February 9, 1792. Francis died February 19, 1847, in Mount Comfort, Indiana.

Eastes, *Eastes Family of Indiana,* 39.

Harvey, John (ca. 1750–1823): John Harvey was born about 1750, the son of Thomas and Rachel Harvey. Harvey moved to South Carolina with his parents, who had been living in Virginia. In South Carolina he served in the American Revolution under Gen. Elijah Clarke. Harvey received land grants in Georgia for his military service and later relocated there, where he became a Baptist minister. Harvey married twice. After his first wife, Margaret, died, he married a woman named Patsy. His children included Mary, Ruth, James, Rachel, Sally, John, Isaac, Willis, Elijah, Israel, Willis, and Claremond. Harvey died in Clarke County, Georgia, in 1823.

Boddie, *Historical Southern Families,* 1:150–54; Moss, *Roster of South Carolina Patriots,* 424.

Hasell/Hasel/Hazell, Andrew (d. 1821): Andrew Hasell was the son of Andrew Hasell and Mary Milner. A planter in St. Thomas and St. Dennis Parishes, he owned Mount Pleasant and Dog Swamp Plantations on the Cooper River. Hasell represented St. Thomas and St. Dennis in the Twenty-First General Assembly from 1814 to 1815. He was also a major in the South Carolina militia. Hasell was a delegate to the state Episcopal convention in 1821 for St. Paul's Church in Radcliffeborough, warden for Charleston's Fourth Ward from 1820 to 1821, and a member of the Charleston Library Society from 1815 to 1818. He married Hanna Cochran Ash of Charleston around February 1810. They had at least three children: Eliza, Harriet, and Georgiana. Hasell died in the fall of 1821.

Bailey, *Biographical Directory of the South Carolina House,* 269–70.

Haynesworth/Haynsworth/Hansworth, James (1784–1848): James Haynesworth was born October 31, 1784, the son of Henry Haynesworth and Sarah Furman. Haynesworth studied medicine under the direction of Benjamin Rush at the University of Pennsylvania, graduating in 1808. One of the earliest settlers in Sumterville, he married Susan Cox Porter of Charleston, daughter of Capt. John Porter and Polly Cox, in 1810. They had eight children: Susan C., Elizabeth, Thomas B., Joseph Cox, Eleanor Mary, Mary Eleanor, Hortensia, and Amanda. Haynesworth died in 1848.

Haynsworth, *Haynsworth-Furman,* 91–92.

Herbemont/Habermount/Harbemont/Hebermont, Nicholas Michel Laurent (1771–1839): Nicholas Michel Laurent Herbemont was born in France in 1771. He taught French at South Carolina College and was recognized as the finest practicing vintner or winemaker in the early United States. Herbemont's passion was agriculture, and he tested the most popular methods of growing, processing, and fermentation to discover those that best suited the southern climate. He owned a large garden in Columbia and a vineyard at Palmyra, his plantation in Richland County. Herbemont organized and chaired the Agricultural Society of South Carolina, was president of the Board of Regents of the South Carolina "lunatic asylum," and a spokesman for the Society for the Advancement of Learning at Columbia. He died in 1839.

Herbemont, *Pioneering American Wine,* 2–4; Pinney, *History of Wine,* 1:151–52; Sanders and Anderson, *Natural History Investigations,* 36.

Heriot, Benjamin: Benjamin Heriot was a sophomore at South Carolina College in 1807. He served as a second lieutenant in the Third Infantry and established the first federal garrison at Fort Winyah in 1810. He was promoted to first lieutenant in 1811 and ordered to march to Charleston in the fall of 1812 to prepare for a potential Spanish invasion. In his absence from North Island, Peter Horry commanded a battalion of militia to replace Heriot's garrison. Heriot later served in the navy as an agent for the port of Charleston.

Journal of the Executive Proceedings of the Senate, 8:4; La Borde, *History of the South Carolina College,* 450; Wade, "Fort Winyaw at Georgetown," 214–49, 231–32, 235–36, 238.

Heriot/Herriot/Heriott/Herriott/Harriott/Harriot, Robert (1773–1846): Robert Heriot was born May 1, 1773, in Charleston, the son of Robert Heriot and Mary Oulfield. His parents settled in Georgetown, Robert Heriot Sr. being a merchant and planter. Heriot graduated from Princeton University in 1792. In 1827 he organized the Bible Society and held regular meetings. His wife, Maria Eliza (1785–1855), began a Ladies Benevolent Society. They had one son, James LaRoche, born in Georgetown in January 1810. Heriot died March 12, 1846.

Bailey, *Biographical Directory of the South Carolina House,* 254–55; "De La Roche," *Huguenot Society of South Carolina* 80 (1975): 44; Rogers, *History of Georgetown County,* 204, 309, 363.

Hill, Joseph: Joseph Hill served as a captain in the militia under General Marion for ninety-five days.

Moss, *Roster of South Carolina Patriots,* 446.

Horry, Elias (1773–1834): Elias Horry was born June 21, 1773, in Charleston, the son of Thomas Horry and Anne Bradford and first cousin of Peter Horry. He received his education in Charleston and read law under the direction of Charles Cotesworth Pinckney before being admitted to the bar in 1793. Horry owned a number of plantations: Milldam, Camp Main, Newland, Camp Island, Midland, Jutland, Millbrook, the Bluff, Wattahan, Drake's, Edgells Bluff, the Point, and Fairfield. In addition to this property, he owned three houses and lots in Charleston and almost eight hundred slaves. St. James Santee elected Horry to the Eleventh through Fifteenth General Assemblies from 1794 to 1804. He represented St. Philip and St. Michael Parishes in the Thirteenth and Twenty-Ninth General Assemblies from 1798 to 1799 and 1830 to 1831. Horry also held a number of local positions, including justice of the quorum in 1798, trustee from 1813 to 1834, secretary and treasurer from 1813 to 1817, vice president from 1828 to 1833 and president of the College of Charleston from 1833 to 1834, vestryman for St. James Santee from 1813 to 1814, director and president of the State Bank from 1814 to 1821, 1826 to 1828, 1834, and 1822 to 1823, commissioner of the poor in 1814, commissioner of the Charleston Orphan House from 1814 to 1834, warden for Charleston's First Ward from 1814 to 1815, commissioner to regulate weights and measures in 1815, intendant for Charleston from 1815 to 1817 and 1821, vestryman for St. Michael Parish from 1817 to 1819, commissioner for improving and cutting a canal or causeway over Lynch's Island in 1823 and 1825 to 1826, delegate for the North Santee Church to the state Episcopal convention in 1823, commissioner of free schools for St. Philip and St. Michael Parishes from 1829 to 1834, president of the South Carolina Canal and Railroad Company from 1831 to 1834, and trustee of the Medical College of South Carolina from 1832 to 1834. He held memberships in the Charleston Library Society (president from 1831 to 1834), Agricultural Society of South Carolina, Literary and Philosophical Society, South Carolina Society, South Carolina Association, American Revolution, and St. Cecilia Society and was founder and president of the Horticultural Society. Horry married Harriet Vanderhorst, daughter of Arnoldus Vanderhorst and Elizabeth Raven, on October 30, 1797. She died August 6, 1815, and Horry married Mary Rutledge Shubrick, daughter of Thomas Shubrick and Mary Branford, on October 23, 1817. He had at least thirteen children: William Branford, Thomas Lynch, Harriet Vanderhorst, Ann Branford, William Branford Shubrick, Alicia, Richard, Julia Elizabeth, Edward Shubrick, Paul Trapier, Elias, and two others. Horry died September 17, 1834, and was buried in St. Paul's Churchyard in Radcliffeborough.

Bailey, *Biographical Directory of the South Carolina House,* 286–88.

Horry, Jonah (1747–1812): Jonah Horry was born in 1747, the son of John Horry and brother of Peter Horry. He married Sarah Burnet in Charleston on November 5, 1788, who died when their two daughters, Mary Lynch and Ann, were very young. His second wife was Lucretia Sarazen, who survived him when he died in 1812 of a fever. By the time of his death in 1812, he owned approximately fifteen thousand acres in South Carolina and three hundred slaves. Horry was buried in the Huguenot Churchyard in Charleston.

McCormick, *Carson-McCormick Family Memorials,* 39; Schieffelin, "Birth-Date of General Peter Horry," 63.

Horry, Thomas (1748–1820): Thomas Horry was born January 13, 1748, in Prince George Winyah Parish, the son of Elias Horry and Margaret Lynch. Horry owned numerous plantations, including Fairfield, Waltahan, Milldam, Camp Main, Camp Island, the Bluff, and several in Prince George. He also owned a home in Charleston. Horry represented St. James in the last four royal assemblies and on the Committee of Ninety-Nine, in addition to being a member of the first and second provincial congresses and the First, Second, and Third General Assemblies from 1775 to1780. He was in Charleston when the city fell to the British 1780 and swore allegiance to the Crown. He later changed his mind, and Gov. John Rutledge pardoned him. He was elected to the Fifth and Sixth General Assemblies but refused to serve. He was again elected to the house for the Seventh General Assembly from 1787 to 1788 and to the senate for the Eighth General Assembly from 1789 to 1790. Horry also served as commissioner of the high roads, commissioner for the parish church, and road commissioner for St. James Santee. He represented St. James in the convention to ratify the US Constitution and in the state constitutional convention. Horry married Ann Branford, daughter of William Branford and Mary Bryan, on February 13, 1772. They had two children: a daughter and a son, Elias. Horry died January 5, 1820, and was buried at St. Paul's Radcliffeborough.

Edgar and Taylor, *Biographical Directory of the South Carolina House,* 333–34.

Hort, Benjamin Simmons (1791–1825): Benjamin Simmons Hort was born April 6, 1791, in Barbados, the son of William Hort and Catharine Simons of Charleston. He graduated from Yale University in 1808 and returned to Charleston. Hort married Mary Drinker (Polly) Deliesseline, daughter of Isaac Deliesseline and Elizabeth Mary Drinker, on September 12, 1812. They had one daughter, who died in infancy, and three sons. Elizabeth died in Charleston on March 9, 1821, and Hort followed on September 8, 1825.

Dexter, *Biographical Sketches of the Graduates of Yale,* 6:209–10; Salley, "Journal of General Peter Horry" (1938), 159n.

Huger, Benjamin (1768–1823): Benjamin Huger was born in 1768, the son of Maj. Benjamin Huger and Mary Golightly. Huger owned Prospect Hill Plantation on the Waccamaw and was interested in state and national politics. He represented Prince George Winyah Parish in the Twelfth General Assembly from 1796 to 1797 and in the US Congress for the sixth, seventh, eighth, and fourteenth sessions from 1799 to 1805 and 1815 to 1817. When he returned to South Carolina, he was again elected to the South Carolina House of Representatives by Prince George for the Seventeenth through Nineteenth General Assemblies from 1806 to 1812 and the Twentieth General Assembly from 1812 to 1813. He was elected to the Fourteenth Congress in 1815 and served in the South Carolina Senate for the Twenty-Third, Twenty-Fourth, and Twenty-Fifth General Assemblies from 1818 to 1823. In 1819 he was chosen president of the senate, serving through the Twenty-Fourth General Assembly. Huger was also justice of the peace for Georgetown District in 1798, commissioner to establish a ferry over Winyah Bay in 1798, member of the Georgetown Library Society from 1799 to 1823, commissioner to examine and establish a ferry across the Waccamaw and Pee Dee Rivers in 1806, road commissioner in 1807, commissioner to locate and survey land for the erection of forts in 1808, vestryman for Prince George Winyah from 1819 to 1820, director of the Georgetown branch of the Bank of the State of South Carolina in 1819, and ex officio trustee of South Carolina College from 1819 to 1821. Huger married Mary Allston, daughter of John Allston and Mary Faucheraud, on February 18, 1796. They had no children. Huger died July 7, 1828, on Pawleys Island.

Bailey, *Biographical Directory of the South Carolina House,* 290–92; Brown, *Cyclopædia of American Biographies,* 4:219; Rogers, *History of Georgetown County,* 176–77, 179, 185.

Huger, Daniel Elliott (1779–1854): Daniel Elliott Huger was born January 28, 1779, the son of Daniel Huger and Sabine Elliott. Huger attended Princeton University, graduating in 1798. When he returned to South Carolina, he read law under Henry William De Saussure, was admitted to the bar in 1811, and became an associate of Benjamin Cudworth Yancey and James Louis Petigru in Beaufort. Huger was a planter and owned property throughout South Carolina, including Goodwill Plantation in Richland. He represented St. Andrew Parish from the Fifteenth through Twenty-Third General Assemblies from 1802 to 1819. During the War of 1812, he was appointed brigadier general. In 1819 he became an associate judge of the Court of General Sessions and Common Pleas, a position he held until 1830. Huger was again elected to the house for the Twenty-Ninth General Assembly from 1830 to 1831 and served as a delegate for Kingston at the Nullification Convention. After leaving the political scene for a time, he took his senate seat to represent St. Philip and St. Michael in the Thirty-Third and Thirty-Fourth General Assemblies from 1838 to 1841. He was elected to the US Senate in December 1842 but resigned in 1845. Huger was also commissioner to examine the possibility of building new roads leading from Moncks Corner in 1806, member of the Society of the Cincinnati in 1806, trustee of the College of Charleston from 1813 to 1823, elective and ex officio trustee of South Carolina College for many years, director of the State Bank from 1813 to 1834, member of the Charleston Library Society in 1815, commissioner of the Charleston Orphan House in 1815, commissioner of the Charleston Board of Health for the Fourth Ward from 1823 to 1827, member of the South Carolina Society in 1828, commissioner to inquire into a toll road in St. Peter in 1833, member of the Conversation Club in 1848, and honorary member of the Pendleton Farmers' Society. Huger married Isabella Johannes Middleton, daughter of Arthur Middleton and Mary Izard, on November 26, 1800. They had ten children: Mary Middleton, William Elliott, Daniel Elliott Jr., John Middleton, Emma Middleton, Sabina Elliott, Sarah Elliott, Joseph Alston, Arthur Middleton, and Eliza Caroline Middleton. Huger predeceased his wife on August 21, 1854, and was buried at Magnolia Cemetery in Charleston.

Bailey, *Biographical Directory of the South Carolina House,* 292–93.

Huger, Francis (Frank) Kinloch (1773–1855): Francis Kinloch Huger was born September 17, 1773, the son of Benjamin Huger and Mary Esther Kinloch. Huger studied medicine at the University of Edinburgh from 1790 to 1792 and in 1794 went to Flanders and joined the medical staff of the British Army. Within a few months, he moved to Vienna to continue his education. He was imprisoned for eight months after involving himself in a plot to rescue the Marquis de Lafayette from Olmutz Prison. Upon his release he returned to the United States, where he entered the University of Pennsylvania, receiving his medical degree on May 15, 1797. He abandoned medicine for planting and purchased Alderly Plantation in All Saints Parish and a summer home near Stateburg. Huger was appointed a captain on June 1, 1798, and served in the Second Artillery of the US Army. He resigned his post in 1801 but rejoined in 1813 during the War of 1812 as a lieutenant colonel. He was promoted to colonel and was adjutant general from 1813 to 1815 before being honorably discharged in 1815. Huger represented All Saints in the Twenty-Second General Assembly from 1816 to 1817. He was also a member of the Society of the Cincinnati, an elective trustee for South Carolina College, a member of the Pendleton Farmer's Society, and a trustee for Pendleton Academy. Huger married Harriott Lucas Pinckney, daughter of Thomas Pinckney and Elizabeth Motte, on January 14, 1802. They had eight children: Elizabeth Pinckney, Benjamin, Anne Isabella, Francis, Thomas Pinckney, Cleland Kinloch, Mary Esther, and Harriott Horry. Huger died in Charleston on February 14, 1855.

Brown, *Cyclopædia of American Biographies,* 4:514; Edgar and Taylor, *Biographical Directory of the South Carolina House,* 773.

Huger, John (d. 1853): John Huger was the son of John Huger and Ann Broun. A planter who owned Hagan and Island Plantations in St. Thomas and St. Dennis Parishes and Lauren Hill Plantation in St. Luke Parish, he represented St. Thomas and St. Dennis in the Nineteenth and Twentieth General Assemblies from 1810 to 1813. St. Philip and St Michael elected him to the Thirty-First through Thirty-Fourth General Assemblies from 1834 to 1841. He served in the state senate for St. Thomas and St. Dennis in the Thirty-Seventh and Thirty-Eighth General Assemblies from 1846 to 1849. Huger was also commissioner to superintend the building of a church in St. Luke in 1811, commissioner of free schools for St. Thomas and St. Dennis in 1814 and 1841, road commissioner for St. Thomas and St. Dennis in 1844 and 1850, and militia major. In addition to these offices, Huger held memberships in the South Carolina Society and Charleston Library Society. Huger married Ann Heyward Glover, daughter of Wilson Glover and Margaret Heyward, on November 11,

1812. They had six children: Margaret, John, Anna, Alfred, Elizabeth, and Cleland. Huger died April 9, 1853, and was buried at Limerick Plantation.

Bailey, Morgan, and Taylor, *Biographical Directory of the South Carolina Senate,* 2:777.

Huggins, Charles (1792?–1849): Charles Huggins was the son of Nathan Huggins and Mary Vareen. He graduated from South Carolina College in 1814 and subsequently studied law under Gov. John Lyde Wilson. A planter in Georgetown, he owned almost a hundred slaves by 1840. He represented Prince George Winyah in the Twenty-Third and Twenty-Fourth General Assemblies from 1818 to 1822. Locally he was deputy adjutant general of the Fourth Division of the militia in 1821 and from 1824 to 1825, major of the First Brigade in 1822, director of the Georgetown branch of the Bank of State of South Carolina in 1824, and sheriff of Georgetown District in 1824. He also held a membership in the Georgetown Library Society from 1816 to 1832. Huggins's first wife was Louisa Blake Steedman, daughter of Charles John Steedman. They married December 22, 1823. When she died, Huggins wed Harriet Darby, with whom he had three children: C. J., Mary Louisa, and Nathan. Huggins died June 5, 1849.

Census, Fourth, Fifth, and Sixth, 1820–1840, Georgetown; Moore, *Biographical Directory of the South Carolina House,* 131.

Huggins, Nathan (1755–1815): Nathan Huggins was born in 1755, the son of Mark Huggins Sr. and Anna Guerrard of Prince George Winyah Parish. Huggins served as sheriff for Georgetown District from 1791 to 1795 and 1808 to 1812. He represented Prince George in the South Carolina House of Representatives for the Twentieth General Assembly from 1812 to 1813 and in the South Carolina Senate for the Twenty-First General Assembly from 1814 to 1815. Active in the military, he served in the American Revolution and as a lieutenant colonel of the Twenty-Sixth Regiment of the militia from 1808 to 1815. Huggins married Mary Vareen, daughter of William Vareen and Elizabeth Lewis. They had eight children: Martha, Frances, Charles, Maria, Julia, Charlotte, Elizabeth, and Mary Keziah. Huggins died December 17, 1815.

Bailey, Morgan, and Taylor, *Biographical Directory of the South Carolina Senate,* 2:778; Census, Third, 1810, Georgetown, S.C.; Moss, *Roster of South Carolina Patriots,* 17.

Hughes, John (d. 1835): John Hughes was an Englishman by birth and resided in Columbia. He married Sarah Winn, daughter of William Winn and Rosamond Hampton, on May 19, 1792. They had eight children. Hughes died in 1835.

Census, Third, 1810, Columbia, S.C.; Draper, "Genealogical Department," 346; Dorman, *Adventures of Purse and Person,* 257.

Inglesby, William H. (1750–1835): William Inglesby was born in 1750 in Petersborough, England. He immigrated to Charleston in 1784, where he became an active member and deacon of the First Baptist Church of Charleston. Inglesby was a supporter of Baptist ministerial education, an officer of the General Committee in the Charleston Baptist Association, and one of the founders of the Bible Society of Charleston. When Basil Manly wrote the history of the Charleston Church in 1830, Inglesby helped compile information for the project. He donated money to the First Baptist Church of Georgetown and was the inspiration for Rev. Edmund Botsford's pamphlet *Sambo and Toney: A Dialogue between Two Servants.* In addition to his service to the church, Inglesby owned a mercantile business in Charleston, William and Henry Inglesby, with his son. He had a home on Sullivans Island as well as a plantation on Goose Creek. He married three times; his first wife was Mary Blanford of England. They had at least two children, Henry and Rebecca. When Mary died in 1792, Inglesby married Martha Screven in Georgetown in 1794. They had at least two children, Joseph Screven and Elizabeth. Martha died May 26, 1805. His third wife was Mary Hatfield of Elizabethtown, New Jersey, whom he married in 1809. Inglesby died in 1835.

Baker and Craven, *Adventure in Faith,* 23, 216, 255–56; Boddie, *Historical Southern Families,* 1:60; Census, First, Second, Third, Fifth, 1790–1830, Charleston, S.C.; *City Gazette and Daily Advertiser,* July 17, 1806, and May 27, 1807; *Connecticut Journal,* August 2, 1810; Feight, "Edmund Botsford and Richard Furman," 15; Jervey, "Marriage and Death Notices" (1932), 301; Mallary, *Memoirs of Elder Edmund Botsford,* 91; Minutes, First Baptist Church of Georgetown, Georgetown Baptist Historical Society Archives, April 9, 1805; *State Gazette of South-Carolina,* June 12, 1793; Townsend, *South Carolina Baptists,* 23, 74, 212, 223; Webber, "Marriage and Death Notices" (1920), 131; Webber, "Marriage and Death Notices" (1921), 72; Webber, "Marriage and Death Notices" (1922), 154; Webber, "Marriage and Death Notices" (1923), 33.

Ioor/Joor, Benjamin: Benjamin Ioor was a descendant of French Huguenots who fled France and immigrated to South Carolina, where they became a prominent family. Ioor married Sarah Cantey Walter on November 1, 1810.

Burns and Burkette, "Peyre Records" (1975), 138; Hugh Davis, "William Ioor," in Edgar, *South Carolina Encyclopedia,* 482–83.

Ioor, Elizabeth Catherine Guignard Fley: Elizabeth Catherine Fley was the daughter of Frances Deliesseline Guignard and widow of Gabriel Guignard and Col. Samuel Fley. Elizabeth lived in Sumter and married George Ioor, who had first married her sister Frances Guignard. They had no children. She was left a widow when George died in 1809 shortly after their marriage. Elizabeth's will was recorded March 17, 1815.

Richardson, *Genealogical Record,* 13, 16, 134.

Ioor/Joor, Emily Richardson (1782–1864): Emily Richardson, a niece of Peter Horry, was born August 7, 1782, the daughter of William Richardson and Anne Magdalen Guignard. Emily married John Ioor in Georgetown in 1804 and moved with him to Mississippi in 1810, where they established the Hills Plantation. She died there on June 26, 1864.

Dominick, "Poinsett Genealogy," 68; "Marriage and Death Notices" (1926), 180; *Register of the General Society,* 213.

Ioor/Joor, Frances Guignard: Frances Guignard was the daughter of Gabriel Guignard and Frances Deliesseline. Her sister was Margaret, wife of Peter Horry. Frances married George Ioor (Joor) in 1779, with whom she had at least two children, John and Benjamin.

Hinton, "John DuBose Family," 163; "Records Kept by Colonel Isaac Hayne," 169; Richardson and Richardson, "Letters of William Richardson," 3; "Tablets Entered in Huguenot Memoir Book," 80–81.

Ioor/Joor, John (1780–1836): John Ioor was born in South Carolina in 1780. He married Emily Richardson, daughter of William Richardson and Anne Magdalen Guignard, in Georgetown in 1804. He and his family moved to Mississippi in 1810, where he established the Hills Plantation near Woodville in Wilkinson County. Ioor served as a captain in Colonel Neilson's detachment of the Mississippi Militia and fought under Gen. Andrew Jackson at the Battle of New Orleans. Ioor was made commander of the state forces with the rank of general. He was later a member of the Constitutional Convention in 1817, where the Mississippi government was formed. Ioor died at his plantation in Mississippi on May 16, 1836.

Biographical and Historical Memoirs of Mississippi, 348; Boddie, *Historical Southern Families,* 2:29–30; Dominick, "Poinsett Genealogy," 68; *Register of the General Society,* 213; Rowland, *History of Mississippi,* 1:489; Rowland, *Mississippi Territory,* 159, 226, 228.

Izard, George (1776–1828): George Izard was born in London on October 21, 1776, the son of Ralph Izard and Alice DeLancey. Izard's father was a native of South Carolina but acted as a diplomat in Europe. When hostilities between America and England increased, the family relocated to Paris, where Izard attended the Collège de Navarre. In 1780 the Izards returned to Charleston before moving to New York while Izard's father served in Congress. It was during this time that Izard enrolled at Columbia University, although he completed his degree at the College of Philadelphia in 1792. That year Izard left for England with Maj. Thomas Pinckney to attend the Prince of Wales Royal Military Academy but withdrew after a few months to travel Europe and visit the Beauchlair Academy at Marburg. During Izard's travels, South Carolina governor William Moultrie commissioned him as captain of the militia. Izard subsequently entered the École du Génie at Metz, France, where he trained in military engineering and was appointed lieutenant in the US Corps of Artillerists and Engineers. In 1797 Izard once again returned to Charleston, where he oversaw the construction of Fort Pinckney and commanded a regiment of artillerists and engineers before accepting a position as aide-de-camp to Gen. Alexander Hamilton in 1800. Izard served in this position only a short time due to an offer from his brother-in-law, then minister plenipotentiary to the Court of Lisbon, to be his secretary. Izard served in that capacity until 1801 and went to Fort Mifflin near Philadelphia. He then commanded a post at West Point but resigned from the military shortly thereafter. When the War of 1812 began, Izard commanded the Second Regiment of Artillery from 1811 to 1812 and was promoted to brigadier general in New York in 1813. He joined Gen. Wade Hampton's division at Plattsburg in August of that year. He was appointed major general in 1814, commanding the Northern Army on Lake Champlain and reinforcing the Army of Niagara. Izard retired in 1814 and went back to Philadelphia, where he published his wartime correspondence. President James Monroe offered Izard the position of Arkansas's second territorial governor in March 1825. He effectively reorganized the Arkansas government, making it more efficient and establishing a militia. Izard had married Elizabeth Carter Farley Banister Shippen of Philadelphia on June 6, 1803, with whom he had three sons. During Izard's tenure as governor, Elizabeth stayed in Philadelphia until her death in 1826. Izard was forced to leave Arkansas for a time to settle her estate, and President John Quincy Adams reappointed him as governor in 1828. He served until his death on November 22, 1828. Izard was interred near the Peabody School in Little Rock. When Mount Holly Cemetery was constructed in 1843, his remains were moved there.

Eno, "Territorial Governors"; Goodner, "George Izard"; Heidler and Heidler, *Encyclopedia of the War of 1812*, s.v. "George Izard," 258; "Izard of South Carolina"; Manigault, *Military Career of General George Izard*, 462–78.

James, William Dobein (1764–1830): William Dobein James was born December 20, 1764, the son of John James and Jean Dobein. James served under Francis Marion in the American Revolution and published his reminiscences in *A Sketch of the Life of Brig. Gen. Francis Marion, and a History of his Brigade.* Originally from Georgetown, James later relocated to Sumter and owned Brookland Plantation near Stateburg. He represented Prince George Winyah in the Tenth General Assembly from 1792 to 1794, after which he became solicitor of the northern circuit until 1802, when he was elected chancellor of the Court of Equity. In 1824 James became associate judge of the Court of General Sessions and Common Pleas but was impeached by the house in 1827 for alcoholism and found guilty by the senate. James was later elected to the senate for the Twenty-Eighth General Assembly but was denied his seat. He was also a member of the Claremont Society, delegate to the state constitutional convention, ex officio trustee of South Carolina College, and vestryman for the Church of the Holy Cross. James married Sarah Ford on January 22, 1793. They had six children: William Huger, John, James, Sarah Jane, Elizabeth S., and George. Sarah died October 6, 1825, and James died June 4, 1830.

Bailey, Morgan, and Taylor, *Biographical Directory of the South Carolina Senate,* 2:803–4; O'Neall, *Biographical Sketches of the Bench,* 1:236; Woody and Thigpen, *South Carolina Postcards,* 10:23.

Johnson, Richard (1758–1815): Richard Johnson was born in Virginia in 1758, the son of Richard Johnson Sr. and Charity Baker. His family later relocated to Ninety Six District in South Carolina. During the American Revolution, Johnson served as a captain in the militia under Colonel LeRoy and Col. Samuel Hammond and saw combat at the Battle of Eutaw Springs. He represented Edgefield in the Fourteenth through the Twentieth General Assemblies from 1800 to 1813. He married Mary Bugg of Augusta. They had no issue. Johnson died in 1815.

Bailey, *Biographical Directory of the South Carolina House,* 321; Johnson, *Traditions and Reminiscences,* 504–6; Moss, *Roster of South Carolina Patriots,* 503.

Johnson, Mrs. Thomas: Mrs. Thomas Johnson was the widow of Thomas Johnson, a Charleston merchant and South Carolina representative from St. George Dorchester Parish.

Edgar and Taylor, *Biographical Directory of the South Carolina House,* 2:370.

Joseph, Lizar: Lizar Joseph was born in Mannheim, Germany. He became a salt merchant in 1762 and owned a wharf in Georgetown. Part of the Jewish business class in Georgetown, he was appointed clerk of the market, inspector of customs, warden, and coroner. He was also a member and secretary of the Winyah Indigo Society. Joseph married Sarah Judith Judah of Philadelphia, with whom he had eight children.

Census, Second, 1800, Georgetown, S.C.; Elzas, *Jews of South Carolina,* 205, 242–43, 142; Rosengarten and Rosengarten, *Portion of the People,* 107.

Keith, John: John Keith was the son of Dr. William Keith and Anne Cordes. He was a planter in Georgetown and owned Keithfield Plantation on the Black River. Keith represented Prince George Winyah and Williamsburg in the Sixteenth and Seventeenth General Assemblies from 1804 to 1808. He represented Prince George in the senate for the Twenty-Second General Assembly from 1818 to 1819. He was also commissioner to study the placement of Wragg's ferry, commissioner to approve the security offered by the sheriff for Georgetown District, member and president of the Georgetown Library Society, major in the Fifth Regiment of the state militia, commissioner to examine and establish a ferry across the Waccamaw and Pee Dee Rivers, intendant for Georgetown, commissioner for North Island canals, commissioner to locate and survey land in regard to federal forts, elective trustee for South Carolina College, director of the Georgetown branch of the Bank of the State of South Carolina, and commissioner of the public buildings of Georgetown District. Keith married Magdalene Elizabeth Trapier, daughter of Paul Trapier Jr. and Elizabeth Foissin, on January 5, 1793. They had at least three children: James Cordes, John Alexander, and Paul Trapier. Keith died before December 8, 1823.

Edgar and Taylor, *Biographical Directory of the South Carolina House,* 854–55.

Keith, Matthew Irvine (1788?–1857): Matthew Irvine Keith was orphaned at a young age and raised by his uncle, Dr. Matthew Irvine. He studied law and established himself as an attorney in Charleston before serving in the War of 1812. He acted as a colonel and adjutant general of the Second Division and captain of the United Blues, a battalion of the Sixteenth Regiment of the South Carolina militia. St. Philip and St. Michael Parishes elected him to the Twenty-Second through the Twenty-Sixth General Assemblies from 1816 to 1824. When he became master in equity in Charleston in 1824, he resigned his house seat. Keith was once again elected to the house for the Twenty-Ninth and Thirtieth General Assemblies from 1830 to 1833. He was also register of mesne conveyance for Charleston, commissioner in equity for Charleston District, magistrate of St. Philip and St. Michael, master in equity, member of the board of health for the First and Second Wards, commissioner of streets and lamps, and justice of the quorum of St. James Goose Creek Parish. In addition to these offices, he held memberships in the Charleston Library Society and the South Carolina Association. Keith moved to Abbeville in 1848, where he was elected register of mesne conveyance. He married Susan Simmons Heyward on April 8, 1825. They left no issue. Keith died June 19, 1857, in Charleston.

Moore, *Biographical Directory of the South Carolina House,* 145–46.

Kinloch, Cleland (1759–1823): Cleland Kinloch was born in 1759, the son of Francis Kinloch and Anna Isabella Cleland. He studied at Eton College and in Rotterdam, Holland, before returning to Charleston after 1782. His father bequeathed him Weehaw Plantation on the Black River, which he increased to five thousand acres. He also owned Acton, his residence in the High Hills of Santee. Kinloch represented Prince George Winyah at the state convention to ratify the Constitution and in the Eighth, Ninth, Tenth, and Thirteenth General Assemblies from 1789 to 1794 and 1798 to 1799. He was also a member of the Georgetown Library Society and served on the vestry for St. Mark Parish. He married Harriett Simmons, daughter of Ebenezer Simmons Jr. and Jane Stanyarne, in April 1786. They had four children: Anne Isabella, Francis, Cleland, and Harriet. Kinloch died September 12, 1823, and was buried at the Church of the Holy Cross at Stateburg.

Bailey and Cooper, *Biographical Directory of the South Carolina House,* 401–2; Rogers, *History of Georgetown County,* 94, 160–61, 166, 176, 284–85.

Kinloch, Francis (1755–1826): Francis Kinloch was born March 7, 1755, in Charleston, the son of Francis Kinloch and Anna Isabella Cleland. Kinloch attended Eton College in England and Lincoln's Inn to pursue a law degree. After studying in Geneva and Rome, he returned to Charleston in 1778 to protect his estate. He served in the Continental Army as a lieutenant and captain as the confidential officer of William Moultrie and aide-de-camp to Isaac Huger. He was taken prisoner when Charleston fell, released, and recaptured in Albemarle, Virginia, in 1781. He represented Prince George Winyah in the Third General Assembly from 1779 to 1780 and St. Philip and St. Michael in the Seventh, Eighth, and Ninth General Assemblies from 1787 to 1791. Kinloch also served in the Continental Congress, the state convention to ratify the federal Constitution, and the state constitutional convention in 1790, in addition to being Charleston warden, justice of the peace, and member of the Privy Council. Kinloch held memberships in the South Carolina Society, St. Cecilia Society, Charleston Library Society, and Georgetown Library Society. He owned Kensington Plantation on the Black River and Avineau Plantation in Georgetown. He was forced to sell his property due to debt accrued from years spent traveling abroad with his family. He wrote *Eulogy on George Washington* in 1800 and *Letters from Geneva and France Written during a Residence of between Two and Three Years, in Different Parts of Those Countries and Addressed to a Lady in Virginia* in 1819. Kinloch married Mildred Walker, daughter of John Walker, on February 22, 1781. They had one daughter, Elizabeth. Mildred died in October 1784, and Kinloch married Martha Rutledge, daughter of John Rutledge and Elizabeth Grimke, on December 8, 1785. They had three children: Anne Cleland, Frederick Rutledge, and Caroline. Martha died in March 1816. Kinloch died February 8, 1826.

Bailey and Cooper, *Biographical Directory of the South Carolina House,* 402–4; Bull, "Kinloch of South Carolina," 65–67, 69, 159, 162; Rogers, *History of Georgetown County,* 94, 161, 166, 177–78, 195–96.

Lance, Maurice Harvey (1792–1870): Maurice Harvey Lance was born in 1792, the son of Lambert Lance of Charleston. He attended South Carolina College and, while a student, helped found Trinity Episcopal Cathedral, acting as a lay reader. On February 21, 1815, he was ordained and shortly thereafter appointed rector of Prince George Winyah. He was the first minister to study under the Society for the Advancement of Christianity in South Carolina. Lance married Anna Maria Taylor Allston, daughter of Archibald and Mary Taylor, in 1816. They had two children, Francis Simmons Parker and Esther Jane. After Anna's death Lance married Sarah Laura Smith in 1854. He died in 1870.

Nord, "George Whiting Flagg," 231; Thomas, *Historical Account of the Protestant Episcopal Church,* 315, 537.

Lartigue, Etienne: Etienne Lartigue was a trustee of Blackville Academy in Barnwell District. He married Elizabeth Adrianna Bull Stewart. They had at least one son, Gerard Bull, born April 10, 1829, in Barnwell. When Elizabeth died, five children survived her. It is not clear, however, if all of those children belonged to Lartigue or a different husband.

Cooper and McCord, *Statutes at Large,* 8:383; Edgar and Taylor, *Biographical Directory of the South Carolina House,* 888–89; Jones, "Georgia Marriages and Deaths," 393.

Laurens, Henry, Jr. (1763–1821): Henry Laurens Jr. was born August 25, 1763, the son of Henry Laurens and Eleanor Ball. He received his education at Rev. Richard Clarke's school at Islington, England, and then in Geneva, Switzerland. He began attending Westminster in London in 1774 and stayed in Europe for more than a decade before returning to Charleston in 1785. Laurens owned Mepkin Plantation on the Cooper River as well as property in St. John Berkeley, St. Thomas, and St. Dennis Parishes. St. Philip and St. Michael Parishes elected him to the Sixth General Assembly from 1785 to 1786 and again to the Seventh General Assembly, but he refused his seat. He returned to the house to represent St. John Berkeley in the Twelfth, Thirteenth, and Fourteenth General Assemblies from 1796 to 1801. He also served as investor and director of the Santee Canal Company from 1786 to 1821, commissioner of the high roads for St. John Berkeley in 1789 and from 1791 to 1792, delegate for St. John Berkeley at the state constitutional convention in 1790, and vestryman and delegate to the Episcopal Church state convention for St. John Berkeley in 1807. He held memberships in the Charleston Library Society, South Carolina Society, and the Society of the Cincinnati. Laurens married Elizabeth Rutledge, daughter of John Rutledge and Elizabeth Grimke, on May 26, 1792. They had nine children: Eliza Rutledge, Eleanor, John Ball, Martha Rutledge, Frederick, Edward Rutledge, Henry, Harriett Horry, and Keating Simons. Laurens died May 27, 1821.

Bailey and Cooper, *Biographical Directory of the South Carolina House,* 416–17; Census, Third, 1810, Charleston, S.C..

Lawson, John: John Lawson served as a captain in the militia under Col. Benjamin Roebuck in the American Revolution.

Moss, *Roster of South Carolina Patriots,* 557.

Lesesne, Charles Frederick (d. 1821): Charles Frederick Lesesne was the son of Francis Lesesne Jr. and Christina Cantey. He served as a private and lieutenant under Francis Marion in the American Revolution. Lesesne resided in St. Frederick's Parish, where he owned a substantial amount of property. He married Binkey McDonald, with whom he had two children, Charles and William. Lesesne died in 1821.

Owings and Owings, "Lesesne Genealogy," 155.

Lesesne, Joseph: Joseph Lesesne, a butcher, resided on North Island in Georgetown. He married Ann Flowler in the Circular Church in Charleston on July 28, 1804. They lost three children: Josephine, Peter, and Mary Caroline. Only one son, Joseph Jr., survived.

Owings and Owings, "Lesesne Genealogy," 161.

Lesesne, Joseph, Jr.: Joseph Lesesne Jr. was the only surviving child of Joseph Lesesne and Ann Flowler.

Owings and Owings, "Lesesne Genealogy," 161.

Lightfoot, Philip (1784–1865): Philip Lightfoot was born September 24, 1785, the only child of Philip Lightfoot and Mary Warner Lewis. Lightfoot resided in Port Royal, Carolina County, Virginia. He inherited the family's estate, Sandy Point, from his father. Lightfoot married Sally Sevigne Bernard (1790–1859), daughter of William Bernard II of Spotsylvania County, Virginia. They had seven children: Philip Lewis, William Bernard, John Bernard, Edgar Vivian, Fannie Bernard, Ellen Bankhead, and Mary Lewis. Lightfoot died July 22, 1865.

Sorley, *Lewis of Warner Hall,* 278; Tyler, "Lightfoot Family."

Lynch, John Bowman: John Bowman was the son of John Bowman and Sabina Lynch. He changed his name in 1812 to John Bowman Lynch in order to preserve his mother's maiden name. Lynch married a Miss Campbell of Baltimore, who bore him seven children.

Edgar, *Biographical Directory of the South Carolina House,* 168; Groves, *Alstons and Allstons,* 73.

Lynch, Margaret: Margaret Lynch was the first cousin of Thomas Lynch. She married Elias Horry II, son of Elias Horry and Mary Rutledge Shubrick. They were the parents of Elias Horry Jr.

Bailey, Morgan, and Taylor, *Biographical Directory of the South Carolina Senate,* 2:751; Rogers, *History of Georgetown County,* 99.

Magill, John D. (1795–1864): John D. Magill was born in 1795. He graduated from South Carolina College in 1815 and attended medical school at the University of Pennsylvania, earning his degree in 1818. Magill owned Richmond Hill and Oregon Plantations in addition to almost two hundred slaves. He earned a reputation for being the worst master in All Saints Parish. As a direct result of Magill's harsh tactics, his crop yield was well below that of other rice plantations on the Waccamaw, and runaway notices for his slaves filled Georgetown's newspapers regularly. Magill was a delegate to the Southern Rights Association in Charleston in 1851, where he represented All Saints Parish. He was also a member of the Hot and Hot Fish Club in Georgetown. Magill married Mary Eliza Vareen, daughter of Capt. William Vareen, on January 27, 1825. They had nine children, including John D. and William Joseph. Only four survived to adulthood. Magill died in 1864 and left his plantations to his two sons.

Joyner, *Down by the Riverside,* 19, 27–28, 97, 104, 216; Michie, *Richmond Hill Plantation,* 38–39; Moore, *Roll of Students,* 7; Rogers, *History of Georgetown County,* 195, 257, 270, 289, 310, 373; Savage, *African American Historic Places,* 440; Waring, *History of Medicine,* 391.

Manigault, Joseph (1763–1843): Joseph Manigault was born October 19, 1763, the son of Peter Manigault and Elizabeth Wragg. His parents died when he was young, and he and his siblings were raised by their grandparents, Gabriel Manigault and Ann Ashby. Manigault left for Europe in 1781 to pursue his education and enrolled in the Middle Temple. He then studied in Geneva for a time before returning to England to pursue a law degree. He withdrew, however, due to medical problems and came back to South Carolina. Manigault inherited a substantial amount of property from his father and grandfather and became a successful planter. He owned approximately 22,813 acres, including numerous plantations and a mansion on Meeting Street in Charleston. During his southern tour in 1791, George Washington visited his Awendaw residence. Manigault represented Christ Church Parish in the Seventh through the Tenth General Assemblies from 1787 to 1794. He returned to the house for the Thirteenth General Assembly from 1798 to 1799 to represent St. James Santee Parish. He acted as a delegate for Christ Church to the state convention, where he voted in favor of ratification of the Constitution in 1788, and he attended the state constitutional convention in 1790. Manigault was also commissioner for improving the navigation of Goose Creek in 1786, commissioner of the Charleston Orphan House from 1811 to 1820, vestryman for St. Philip Parish from 1823 to 1837, vice president of the South Carolina Association from 1826 to 1835, trustee of the College of Charleston from 1829 to 1830, and a member of the South Carolina Society and Charleston Library Society. Manigault wed Maria Henrietta Middleton, daughter of Arthur Middleton and Mary Izard, on November 25, 1788. Maria died giving birth to their first child, who did not survive. His second wife was Charlotte Drayton, daughter of Charles Drayton and Esther Middleton, whom he married May 27, 1800. They had eight children: Joseph, Ann, twins Peter and Charles Drayton, Gabriel, Henry Middleton, Edward, and Arthur Middleton. Manigault died June 5, 1843, leaving a wife and six children.

Bailey and Cooper, *Biographical Directory of the South Carolina House,* 473–75; Manigault and Manigualt, "Manigault Family of South Carolina," 81–82; Rogers, *History of Georgetown County,* 172, 296–97; Simmons, "Recorded Burials," 49–50.

Martin, Elizabeth Trapier (1745–1817): Elizabeth Trapier was the daughter of Georgetown merchant Paul Trapier and his wife, Magdalen Horry. Elizabeth married Edward Martin on September 17, 1788. They resided at Belvoir Plantation (later Friendfield) on the Waccamaw. A relative is said to have described Elizabeth as "one of the most remarkable women he had ever known for strength of natural understanding, highly cultivated especially with historic lore, & of piety fervent and cheerful, an earnest and enlightened member of the Protestant Episcopal Church and withal a zealous patriot, taking with entire approval and self sacrifice the side of her country in its effort to throw off the British yoke." She was an invalid for the last few years of her life and died June 10, 1817.

Bailey and Cooper, *Biographical Directory of the South Carolina House,* 482–83; Rogers, *History of Georgetown County,* 284n, 350; Trapier, "Notices of Ancestors and Relatives," 31–32.

Marvin, Aaron: Aaron Marvin, a resident of Georgetown, was a director of the Georgetown branch of the Bank of South Carolina, commissioner to approve of public securities, member of the Georgetown Library Society from 1799 to 1809, agent for the American Seamen's Friend Society, and commissioner to receive subscriptions to establish a bank in the town of Hamburg. Marvin attended the First Baptist Church of Georgetown, where he served as secretary, warden, and treasurer. He married Eliza B. Prior, daughter of David and Elizabeth Prior. They had at least two children. Eliza died April 3, 1828, and was buried in the Baptist cemetery.

"An Act to Establish a Bank in the Town of Hamburg, and to Incorporate the Same," in Cooper and McCord, *Statutes at Large,* 40; *Acts and Joint Resolutions of the General Assembly, 1823,* 125; Census, Third, 1810, Georgetown, S.C.; Clark, *History of the Banking Institutions,* 100; "Constitution of the American Seamen's Friend Society," 34; "Georgetown Library Society," 100; Minutes, First Baptist Church of Georgetown, January 1805–November 30, 1821.

Mayrant, Charles (1792–1834): Charles Mayrant was born May 18, 1792, the son of William Woodrup Mayrant and Ann Richardson Guignard. He graduated from South Carolina College in 1811. Admitted to the bar at Charleston in 1814, Mayrant represented Marion District in the Twenty-Fifth General Assembly from 1822 to 1823. He was also a member of Holy Cross Episcopal Church in Stateburg and a trustee of Marion Academy. Mayrant married Caroline Kinloch (1806–1842), daughter of Francis Kinloch and Martha Rutledge. They had five children: Francis Kinloch, Ann Henrietta, Charles, Frances Caroline, and Eliza Nelson. Mayrant died in March 1834 in Sumter and was buried at the family cemetery at Bloom Hill Plantation.

MacDowell, *Gaillard Genealogy,* 205; Moore, *Biographical Directory of the South Carolina House,* 180; Moore, *Roll of Students,* 5; O'Neall, *Biographical Sketches of the Bench,* 2:602, 610; Richardson, *Genealogical Record,* 43; Webber, "Mayrant Family," 87, 89.

Mayrant, Frances Caroline (1795–1883): Frances Caroline Mayrant was born at the High Hills of Santee near Stateburg on October 10, 1795, the daughter of William Woodrup Mayrant and Ann Magdalen Guignard. In 1819 she married Robert Bentham of Charleston, where they owned a mansion. They had two children, Charles Mayrant and Mary Ann. Frances died in 1883.

MacDowell, *Gaillard Genealogy,* 204; Richardson, *Genealogical Record,* 44; Webber, "Mayrant Family," 87.

Mayrant, Isabella Norvelle (1763–1833): Isabella Norvelle Mayrant was born in 1763, the daughter of James Norvelle and Isabella Nelson. Her uncle, Matthew Neilson, paid for her expenses to attend school in Charleston. She married John Mayrant (1762–1836), son of John Mayrant and Ann Woodruff, on

November 19, 1783. They had four children: John, James Norvelle, Ann Isabella, and Mary Eleanora. She died near Stateburg on January 3, 1833.

Bailey and Cooper, *Biographical Directory of the South Carolina House,* 489; Webber, "Marriage and Death Notices" (1917), 144; Webber, "Mayrant Family," 85–86.

Mayrant, John (1762–1836): John Mayrant was born in 1762, the son of John Mayrant and Ann Woodruff. He was orphaned at a young age and raised by his aunt, Judith Mayrant Pringle, wife of Robert Pringle. Appointed midshipman in the South Carolina navy in 1778, he went to Havana, Cuba, and Nantes, France. While in France John Paul Jones commissioned him as midshipman and aide. In 1779 he sailed on the *Bon Homme Richard* and was wounded in a sea battle. After his three-month recovery, he was promoted to lieutenant on the frigate *South Carolina.* After sailing around Europe and the Caribbean, he went to Charleston, where he was appointed fifth lieutenant in 1781 and received prisoners. He was discharged in 1783 at the end of the American Revolution. The following year he investigated the loss of the *South Carolina,* and in 1794 he was given the title of naval captain. St. James Santee elected Mayrant to the Seventh and Eighth General Assemblies, and he served from 1788 to 1790. He attended the state convention to ratify the federal Constitution in 1788 as a delegate for St. James Santee, and he attended the state constitutional convention in 1790. Mayrant relocated to the High Hills of Santee in the 1780s, where he served as justice of the peace for Claremont County in 1788 and vestryman for St. Mark Parish intermittently from 1803 to 1830. He also held memberships in St. George's Jockey Club and Stateburg Jockey Club. Mayrant turned his interest to cotton planting and purchased Ruins Plantation in Sumter District in 1802. He married Isabella Norvelle, daughter of James Norvelle and Isabella Nelson, on November 19, 1783. They had four children: John, James Norvelle, Ann Isabella, and Mary Eleanora. Isabella died January 3, 1833. Mayrant died in Tennessee in August 1836.

Bailey and Cooper, *Biographical Directory of the South Carolina House,* 488–89; Buell, *Paul Jones,* 2:79, 139–40, 345; Garden, *Anecdotes of the American Revolution,* 103–7; MacDowell, *Gaillard Genealogy,* 203; Richardson, *Genealogical Record,* 40; Sumter, *Stateburg and Its People,* 7–8, 99; Webber, "Marriage and Death Notices," 144; Webber, "Mayrant Family," 81–90.

Mayrant, Placidia (1797–ca. 1876): Placidia Mayrant was born at the High Hills of Santee on September 11, 1797. She was the second wife of Rev. J. Jasper Adams (d. 1841). They had five children: Ann, Elizabeth, Caroline, Joseph, and Fannie.

MacDowell, *Gaillard Genealogy,* 204; Richardson, *Genealogical Record,* 45; *Semi-Centennial Historical and Biographical Record,* 1; Webber, "Mayrant Family," 87.

Mayrant, Rufus: Rufus Mayrant attended South Carolina College. He was a junior from 1807 to 1808.

Moore, *Roll of Students,* 4.

Mayrant, Samuel (1806–ca. 1872): Samuel Mayrant was born on Sullivans Island on August 13, 1806. He was an attorney and lived in Sumter, where he died around 1872. He bequeathed his estate to his adopted son, Charles W. Mayrant. Charles was his nephew and son of Charles Mayrant and Caroline Kinloch.

MacDowell, *Gaillard Genealogy,* 204; Richardson, *Genealogical Record,* 46; Webber, "Mayrant Family," 87.

Mayrant, William, Jr. (1792–1840): William Mayrant Jr. was born May 18, 1792, the son of William Woodrup Mayrant and Ann Magdalen Guignard. He graduated from South Carolina College in 1811 and began studying law. He was admitted to the bar in Charleston in 1814. His law practice became so successful that his father left him out of his will. Claremont District elected Mayrant to the Twenty-Third and Twenty-Fourth General Assemblies from 1818 to 1821. He married Sarah Hall Horry Bay, daughter of William and Ann Davis Bay, on April 15, 1819. They had four children: Sarah Ann Mayrant, William Horry Mayrant, John Richardson Mayrant, and Mary Charlotte Mayrant. He died January 18, 1840, and was buried at Holy Cross Episcopal Church in Stateburg.

Jervey, "Marriage and Death Notices" (1945), 16; MacDowell, *Gaillard Genealogy,* 205–6; Moore, *Biographical Directory of the South Carolina House,* 180–81; Moore, *Roll of Students,* 5; Richardson, *Genealogical Record,* 42; Webber, "Mayrant Family," 87, 89.

Mayrant, William Woodrup (d. ca. 1840): William Mayrant, born in South Carolina, was a planter, lawyer, and member of the Fourteenth Congress, serving from 1815 to 1816. He owned the mansion High Hills near Stateburg, as well as one of the first cotton mills in South Carolina. Mayrant married Ann Richardson (b. 1771), daughter of William Richardson and Ann Magdalen Guignard, on May 17, 1787, at Bloom Hill Plantation. They had thirteen children: a daughter, a son, twins William and Charles, Ann, Frances Caroline, Placidia, John W., Woodruff, Emily, Samuel, Robert P., and Charlotte. Mayrant died around 1840.

Abridgment of the Debates of Congress, 5:480–81; MacDowell, *Gaillard Genealogy,* 203–4; Mayrant and Lander, "Two Letters," 1; Richardson, *Genealogical Record,* 39–41; Treese, *Biographical Directory,* 1518; Webber, "Mayrant Family," 86.

McCord, David James (1797–1855): David James McCord was born in Fort Motte, South Carolina, in January 1797. A student at South Carolina College in 1814, he dropped out to study law and was admitted to the bar in 1818. He had a partnership with Henry J. Nott in Columbia from 1818 to 1821 and with Col. W. C. Preston from 1822 to 1824. He was a state reporter from 1824 to 1827, while serving as intendant of Columbia in 1825. After traveling Europe for two years, McCord came back to South Carolina in time to enter the legislature for the Nullification Crisis. He was a trustee for South Carolina College from 1829 to 1837. After retiring from the bar in 1836, he served as president of the State Bank in Columbia and helped start the *South Carolina Law Journal.* He then became compiler and editor of the *Statutes at Large of South Carolina,* initiated by Thomas Cooper. After 1840 he shifted his focus to cotton planting, all the while contributing essays to the *Southern Review* and *De Bow's Review* and editing large volumes. His publications include *Reports of Cases Determined in the Constitutional Convention of South Carolina* and *Chancery Cases in the Court of Appeals of South Carolina.* McCord's first wife was a Miss Wagner of Charleston. He married Louisa Susannah Cheeves (1810–80), daughter of Langdon Cheves, in 1840. She was a poet and headed the slave hospital on their plantation, Langayne, on the Congaree. McCord died in Columbia on May 12, 1855.

Brown, *Cyclopaedia of American Biography,* 212; Moore, *Roll of Students,* 6; O'Neall, *Biographical Sketches of the Bench,* 2:509–11; Wilson and Friske, *Appleton's Cyclopædia,* 4:94.

McDuffee/McDuffie, George (1790–1851): George McDuffee was born in Columbia County, Georgia, the son of John and Jane McDuffie, on August 10, 1790. He graduated from South Carolina College in 1813 and was admitted to the bar. Finding his practice unsuccessful, McDuffee entered the political arena, serving in the US Congress from 1821 to 1834 and as governor of South Carolina from 1834 to 1836. When his term ended, he retired, only to be elected to the US Senate in 1842. He resigned from the Senate in 1842 due to complications from a wound he received in a duel. McDuffee owned Cherry Hill Plantation in Abbeville. He married Rebecca Singleton, daughter of Col. Richard Singleton, in 1829. Rebecca died the following year, leaving him one daughter. McDuffee spent the remainder of his life at the home of his father-in-law. He died March 11, 1851, and was buried in Sumter.

Alderman, *Library of Southern Literature,* 8:3547–48; Wauchope, *Writers of South Carolina,* 278.

McFarlan, Andrew: Andrew McFarlan was at one time the editor of the *Georgetown Gazette,* Georgetown's primary newspaper from 1798 to 1817.

Rogers, *History of Georgetown County,* 219.

McGinney, Albert J.: Albert J. McGinney of Charleston graduated from South Carolina College in 1812.

Moore, *Roll of Students,* 5.

Meeks, Samuel M. (1786–1846): Samuel M. Meeks was born in Laurens "District on August 20, 1786, the son of John and Eleanor Meeks of Ireland. Meeks was a physician and Methodist minister in Columbia, Georgia, and Charleston. He moved to Tuscaloosa, Alabama, in 1819, where he became a druggist and physician. He remained active in the ministry, however, and helped organize the Annual Conference of the Methodist Associated Churches of the Alabama District in 1830. Meeks withdrew from the Methodist Episcopal Church in Tuscaloosa in 1828 and organized the Alabama Conference of the Methodist Protestant Church in 1845. He married Anne Aradella McDowell (d. 1853) on May 19, 1813, by whom he had five sons. Meeks died in Tuscaloosa on May 27, 1846.

Metcalf, *Library of Southern Literature,* 3599; Owen, "Necrology," 25; Owen and Owen, *History of Alabama and Dictionary of Alabama Biography,* 2:983; West, *History of Methodism in Alabama,* 309–10, 420, 740.

Meyers, Mordecai: Georgetown had a large Jewish community, and one of the progenitors of that community was Mordecai Meyers. Meyers had four sons: Moses, Jacob, Abraham, and Levi. Moses was the first Jewish lawyer in South Carolina, admitted to the bar in 1793. He was an active citizen of Georgetown, holding memberships in the Georgetown Library Society and Winyah Indigo Society and serving as clerk of court of the General Assembly and Common Pleas from 1798 to 1817. Jacob took over Abraham Cohen's blacksmith shop and was a member of the Georgetown Library Society, postmaster, and captain in the Winyah Artillery Company. Abraham was admitted to the South Carolina bar in 1796 and served as intendant of Georgetown from 1826 to 1827. Levi earned a medical degree from the University of Glasgow in 1787 and was the first Jewish doctor to hold a membership in the Medical Society of South Carolina. He owned a medical practice in Georgetown and in Charleston. Levi was also active in the legislature, serving in the Ninth General Assembly in 1791. He was commissioner to approve of the bond and security for various public offices, apothecary general of the state militia from 1797 to 1817, and member of the Winyah Indigo Society and Royal Medical Society of Edinburgh.

Bailey, *Biographical Directory of the South Carolina House,* 420–21; Elzas, *Jews of South Carolina,* 45, 100, 128, 141–42, 205, 241–43; Joyner, *Shared Traditions,* 180.

Mitchell, George (d. 1825): George Mitchell was born a slave in Georgetown but purchased his freedom. As a young man, Mitchell was a sailor and built ships in Marion County. He was master of the schooners *Liberty* and *Mitchell.* For many years he was sexton of Prince George Winyah Episcopal Church. The *Georgetown Gazette* published his obituary notice on October 21, 1825, and said of him, "He was no citizen—he shared no civil rights—yet no man contributed more to the general wealth."

Census, Fourth, 1820, Georgetown, S.C.; *Georgetown Gazette,* October 21, 1825; Olsberg, "Ship Registers," 241, 247; Rogers, *History of Georgetown County,* 359–60; Withrow, *Carolina Genesis,* 100, 103–4.

Mitchell, Thomas Rothmahler (1783–1837): Thomas R. Mitchell was born in Georgetown in May 1783, the son of Thomas Mitchell and Anne E. Rothmahler. He attended Harvard University and graduated in 1802. After earning his law degree, he returned to South Carolina and was admitted to the bar in 1808, establishing a law practice in Georgetown. In 1809 he was elected by the Horry District to the Eighth General Assembly. Prince George Winyah Parish elected him to the Twentieth General Assembly, but he was disqualified. He returned to the house to represent Prince George in the Twenty-First, Twenty-Second, and Twenty-Third General Assemblies from 1814 to 1819. Locally he was a member of the Georgetown Library Society from 1799 to 1828, a member of the First Baptist Church of Georgetown, and commissioner to conduct a lottery in Georgetown in 1815. In 1819 he published *Thoughts on the Constitution of the State of South-Carolina.* Mitchell served in the US House of Representatives and in the Seventeenth, Nineteenth, Twentieth, and Twenty-Second Congresses. Mitchell died November 2, 1837.

Colcok, "Marion Family," 47; Houston, *Critical Study of Nullification,* 34–35, 53–56, 100–101; Minutes, First Baptist Church of Georgetown, February 1, 1812; Rogers, *History of Georgetown County,* 191n, 221, 226, 229n, 231–32, 235n, 241, 243; Snowden and Cutler, *History of South Carolina,* 2:580.

Mitchell, William Boone (d. 1814): William Boone Mitchell was the son of John Mitchell and Sarah Boone. He was a planter and owned property in St. Paul and St. George Parishes. Mitchell served in the South Carolina House of Representatives from 1792 to 1804, representing St. Paul in the Tenth, Eleventh, Thirteenth, and Fifteenth General Assemblies, and St. George Dorchester in the Twelfth General Assembly. St. Paul elected Mitchell to the state senate for the Sixteenth through Twentieth General Assemblies from 1804 to 1813. He was also a member of the South Carolina Society, commissioner to fix on a central place for the erection of a courthouse and jail for Colleton District in 1798, justice of the quorum in 1798, trustee to apply escheated property in Colleton District in 1799, commissioner to approve bonds and security for various public offices intermittently from 1800 to 1812, commissioner of free schools for St. Paul in 1811, and commissioner for repairing and completing the courthouse and jail for Colleton District in 1813. In the military he served as captain, lieutenant colonel, and quartermaster general of the state militia from about 1802 to 1814. Mitchell married Dorothy Sinkler Richardson, daughter of James Burchell Richardson and Anne Cantey Sinkler, on June 12, 1810. They had at least one son, William M. B. Richardson. Mitchell died in 1814.

Bailey, Morgan, and Taylor, *Biographical Directory of the South Carolina Senate,* 2:1122–23; *City Gazette and Daily Advertiser,* November 24, 1797, April 30, 1801.

Montgomery, Benjamin: Benjamin Montgomery was a Presbyterian minister. He preached in various places throughout South Carolina, including Camden, Abbeville, Laurens District, and finally Columbia. Professor of logic and moral philosophy at South Carolina College from 1811 to 1818, Montgomery was chosen pastor in 1812 of what became the First Presbyterian Church of Columbia. He married Anne Geddes (d. 1807), sister of Robert Geddes and Gov. John Geddes and the widow of John Dunlap.

Howe, *History of the Presbyterian Church,* 2:127, 138, 149–50, 255–56, 282, 756; Jervey, "Marriage and Death Notices" (1930), 72; O'Neall, *Biographical Sketches of the Bench,* 2:175.

Morrall, John: John Morrall was probably the son of the John Morrall who settled on Waccamaw Neck in 1750. Murrells Inlet in Georgetown is named for the family. A lieutenant in the American Revolution, he had moved to Georgetown by 1808.

Berry, "Sage of Matthew Dolan Church," 12; Mazyck, "Report of the Historian," 17; Salley, "Journal of General Peter Horry" (1938), 47n.

Motte, Charles: Charles Motte was the son of Jacob Motte and Elizabeth Martin. Appointed captain in the Second Regiment on June 17, 1775, he was present at Fort Moultrie on June 28, 1776, and was promoted to major in 1779. Motte was killed in the Battle at Savannah on October 9, 1779.

Jervey, "Marriage and Death Notices" (1934), 170; Moss, *Roster of South Carolina Patriots,* 707; "Remarkable Application of N. H. R. Dawson," 49.

Mulder, Abel (d. 1822): Abel Mulder lived in Columbia, where he died in 1822.

Census, Fourth, 1820, Richland, S.C.; Jervey, "Marriage and Death Notices" (1948), 214.

Muller, Albert Arney, Jr.: Albert Arney Muller Jr. of Charleston graduated from South Carolina College in 1815. He was ordained deacon on April 25, 1817, by Bishop Dehon and priest on May 16, 1818, by Bishop William White. Elected rector of Christ Church Parish in 1819, he served other churches throughout the state.

Dalcho, *Historical Account of the Protestant Episcopal Church,* 282, 302, 397, 436, 534, 564, 567, 614; Gregorie, "Christ Church, 1706–1959," 76; Moore, *Roll of Students,* 7.

Muller, Albert Arney, Sr.: Albert Arney Muller Sr. was a resident of Charleston. He served as a major in Francis Marion's brigade during the American Revolution. St. Matthew Parish elected him to the Eighth General Assembly from 1789 to 1790. Locally he was powder receiver from 1783 to 1786, warden for the Thirteenth Ward from 1784 to 1785 and for the Ninth Ward from 1786 to 1787, and powder receiver and commissary general of military stores in 1788. He married Johanna Magdelene Martin, daughter of Rev. John Nichols Martin, in 1788. She bore him at least two children, Amelia and Albert Arney. Muller suffered a gunshot wound in the stomach in 1789. He died March 26, 1793, and was survived by his wife and children.

Bailey and Cooper, *Biographical Directory of the South Carolina House,* 519; *City Gazette and Daily Advertiser,* March 18, 1790; Moss, *Roster of South Carolina Patriots,* 709; Webber, "Marriage and Death Notices" (1920), 155.

Murray, William, III (1754–1816): William Murray III was born in 1754. He served in the Continental Army during the American Revolution. He was a private in the South Carolina militia as well as a wagon master and commissary under the command of Col. Levi Casey. He also served as a horse soldier and worked as a blacksmith in Georgetown, making rivets and putting on shackles. A William Murray served in the War of 1812 as a private in the First Regiment and as a lieutenant in the Second Regiment of the South Carolina militia, but it is difficult to determine if this was the father or the son. Murray was an active member of the First Baptist Church of Georgetown, where he was a warden, served on various committees, and signed the incorporation petitions. Murray was master for the fire company in Georgetown in 1793, a commissioner of the streets and market of Georgetown in 1796, and election manager in 1806, 1810, and 1812. Murray married Martha McQuillan (b. 1761) in Orangeburg in 1781. They settled at Murrays Crossroads near the Edisto River. They had eight children: William, Sarah, Mary, John, Isaac, Margaret, Martha, and Archibald. Murray died in 1816 on his plantation and was buried at Murray Cemetery.

Black, *Echoes in Time,* 2–5; Census, First, Second, and Third, 1790–1810, George-town, S.C.; *City Gazette and Daily Advertiser,* February 27, 1793, March 1, 1796, October 4, 1806, October 6, 1810, July 4, 1812; General Assembly Petitions, no. 180 and 181, 342–47, South Carolina Department of Archives and History; General Assembly Petitions, no. 124, 106–11, South Carolina Department of Archives and History; Minutes, First Baptist Church of Georgetown, January 12, 1805–February 1, 1812; Moss, *Roster of South Carolina Patriots,* 714.

Myers, David Rudolph (1768–1835): David Myers was born November 29, 1768, the son of Jacob John Myers and Catherine Von Enfinger. Myers owned Fort Marion Plantation near Columbia, a plantation on the Congaree and Wateree Rivers, and more than two hundred slaves. Myers was known for the tavern and general store he operated on Garner's Ferry Road in Richland District. He represented Richland in the Twenty-Third, Twenty-Fourth, and Twenty-Fifth General Assemblies from 1818 to 1823. He was again elected to the house for the Twenty-Ninth General Assembly from 1830 to 1831. Myers married Phalby Mills, daughter of Maj. William Mills and Eleanor Morris, on December 24, 1798. They had eight children, including John Jacob and William Mills. On March 3, 1835, Myers was murdered by John McLemore over a land dispute.

Miller, *Millers and Millersburg,* 199; Moore, *Biographical Directory of the South Carolina House,* 192–93; Salley, "Journal of General Peter Horry" (1943), 124n.

Norton, James: James Norton was the son of William Norton Jr. Raised in the Green Sea area, he became a Methodist minister. He attended the South Carolina Methodist Conference in 1813, where he was appointed assistant to Francis Asbury. Starting in 1816 he served as the traveling companion to William McKendree. Norton died in 1825 and was buried at Washington Street United Methodist Church.

Paine, *Life and Times of William McKendree,* 215; Sellers, *History of Marion County,* 475–78.

Nott, Abraham (1767–1830): Abraham Nott was born in Saybrook, Connecticut, in 1767. Nott attended Yale University and trained for the ministry. He decided not to pursue a ministerial career, however, and moved to Georgia in 1788, where he was employed as a tutor. After a year he moved to Camden, South Carolina, studied law under Daniel Brown, and was admitted to the bar in Charleston on May 27, 1791. Nott was elected to the US Congress in 1800, and in 1804 moved to Columbia, where he was named a trustee of South Carolina College the following year. He practiced law until he became a judge on December 5, 1810, and served in that capacity until his death in

1830. He married Angelica Mitchell in 1794, by whom he had eight children. Nott died June 19, 1830, in Fairfield District.

O'Neall, *Biographical Sketches of the Bench,* 1:121–24.

O'Hanlon, Terence: Terence O'Hanlon, or "Old Terrible," owned a grocery store on Main Street in Columbia. He fired a blunderbuss every Christmas and Fourth of July, and the children hung a "stuffed paddy" on his door every St. Patrick's Day.

Salley, "Journal of General Peter Horry" (1945), 220n; Scott, *Random Recollections,* 35.

Paisley, Robert (d. 1812): Robert Paisley was the son of Robert and Mary Paisley. He resided in Prince Frederick Parish, which he represented in the Seventh General Assembly from 1787 to 1788. He also served as tax inquirer, assessor, and collector. His first wife was Margaret (d. 1788). He later married Ann, with whom he had two children: Robert Anderson and William. Paisley died December 21, 1812.

Bailey and Cooper, *Biographical Directory of the South Carolina House,* 530; Census, Third, 1810, Georgetown, S.C.

Palmer, John, Sr.: John Palmer was the son of John Palmer and Marianne Gendron. Palmer owned Richmond Plantation in St. Stephen Parish, in addition to property in St. Mark, St. John Berkeley, and St. Matthew Parishes. He served as a captain in Francis Marion's brigade and represented St. Stephen in the Second through Sixth General Assemblies from 1776 to 1786 and again in the Sixteenth General Assembly from 1804 to 1805. He served as a delegate for St. Stephen at the state convention to ratify the federal Constitution in 1788. He was also a church warden and vestryman for St. Stephen from 1772 to 1773, 1776 to 1788, 1784 to 1791, and 1800 to 1802; tax inquirer, assessor, and collector for St. Stephen in 1784, 1785, 1788, 1798, and 1799; commissioner of the high roads for St. Stephen from 1787 to 1791 and 1796 to 1799; trustee of Pineville Academy from 1805 to 1816; and commissioner of the high roads for St. John Berkley from 1807 to 1808 and 1813. Palmer married Ann Cahusac (d. 1803), daughter of John Cahusac. They had four children: Ann, John Jr., Joseph, and Marianne Gendron. Palmer died in December 1816 and was buried at the family cemetery at Gravel Hill Plantation.

Bailey and Cooper, *Biographical Directory of the South Carolina House,* 531–32; Census, Third, 1810, Charleston, S.C.; Moss, *Roster of South Carolina Patriots,* 1782.

Pawley, Anthony: Anthony Pawley was most likely the son of Anthony Pawley. He owned property on the Waccamaw River, including Roseberry Plantation. He also had land in Conwayborough and operated a ferry on Kingston

Lake. He later relocated to Georgetown, where he was a merchant. Horry District elected him to the Sixteenth General Assembly from 1804 to 1805. He served as commissioner authorized to lend principal sums arising from the sale of lots in Conwayborough in 1805.

Bailey, *Biographical Directory of the South Carolina House,* 433–34; Census, Second, 1800, Georgetown, S.C.

Perdriau, Esther (1791–1864): Esther Perdriau was born in 1791. The wife of Samuel Perdriau, she had no children. When Samuel died in 1843, he bequeathed half his estate to her with the other half to be divided among his nieces, nephews, and Ann M. China upon Esther's death. She willed her half of the estate to her friend, Samuel J. Bradford, along with annual donations to the Methodist and Episcopal churches in Sumter for ten years. Her estate was worth $107,182 and included sixty-two slaves. She suffered during the last few years of her life and died March 13, 1864.

Clark, *Lineage of Chovine Richardson Clark,* 46–47; *Southeastern Reporter Blue Book,* 36:1004.

Perdriau, Samuel (1773–1843): Samuel Perdriau was born July 17, 1773, the son of John Perdriau and Anne DePont. He owned land in Williamsburg County and was a trustee for the new Methodist meetinghouse constructed at the "Weeping Fountain." Perdriau also owned a plantation in Sumter. He and his wife, Esther, had no children. Perdriau died August 22, 1843, leaving his estate to his wife. Upon her death it was to be divided among his nieces, nephews, and Ann M. China.

Clark, *Lineage of Chovine Richardson Clark,* 45–47; FitzSimons, "Perdriau," 73, 74, 78; *Southeastern Reporter,* 36:1004.

Pickens, Andrew (1739–1817): Andrew Pickens was born in Pennsylvania September 19, 1739, the son of Andrew Pickens and Ann Davis. His family eventually moved to South Carolina, and Pickens settled in Ninety Six, where he owned almost 1,000 acres on Long Cake Creek, 1,426 acres in Pendleton District, and 573 acres on the Seneca River, where his home, Hopewell, stood. In 1805 he lived at the Red House, his residence in the Blue Ridge Mountains. Pickens owned a store in Hopewell, in addition to another mercantile business in Charleston, Andrew Pickens & Company. He was a Presbyterian and acted as an elder in Hopewell, Bethel, and Old Stone churches. Actively involved in the military and witnessing combat at the Cherokee War in 1761, he served as militia captain in the American Revolution and was eventually promoted to major and colonel. Paroled when the British seized Charleston in 1780, he rejoined American forces later that year. After Pickens's involvement at the

Battle of Cowpens in 1781, Gov. John Rutledge made him brigadier general, and he received a sword from Congress. He was present at the second siege of Ninety Six, the capture of Augusta, and the Battle of Eutaw Springs. Pickens was a mastermind at defeating the Cherokees, who signed a peace treaty with him in October 1782 and nicknamed him "Skyagunsta" (Wizard Owl) and the "Wizard of Tomassee." During his military career and after, Pickens represented Ninety Six District in the Second through Seventh General Assemblies from 1776 to 1788. He served Pendleton in the state senate during the Eighth, Ninth, and Tenth General Assemblies from 1789 to 1794. He resigned from the senate to join the US House of Representatives in the Third Congress from 1793 to 1799. When he returned Pendleton elected him to the house for the Twelfth, Thirteenth, and Twentieth General Assemblies from 1796 to 1799 and 1812 to 1813. As chief commissioner for the federal government from 1785 to 1802, he negotiated various treaties that gained the territory east of the Mississippi River and south of the Ohio River. Pickens was also road commissioner in 1770 and 1795, justice of the peace in 1776 and for Abbeville County in 1785, member of the Mount Sion Society in 1778, commissioner for dividing Ninety Six District into counties in 1783, trustee for a public school at Ninety Six in 1783 and for the College of Cambridge in 1785, commissioner to locate a courthouse for Pendleton County in 1789, delegate for Pendleton County at the state constitutional convention in 1790, commissioner to superintend the building of a jail and courthouse in Washington District in 1791, commissioner to open and improve navigation of the Keowee River in 1791, major general of the state militia in 1794, commissioner to approve of securities offered by sheriffs of Washington District in 1795, Jefferson presidential elector in 1796, and member of the Pendleton Farmer's Society in 1815. Pickens married Rebecca Calhoun, daughter of Ezekiel Calhoun and Jane Ewing, on March 19, 1765. They had twelve children: Mary, Ezekiel, Ann, Jane, Jane Bonneau, Margaret, Andrew Jr., Rebecca, Catherine, Joseph, and two unnamed sons who died in infancy. Rebecca died December 19, 1814, and Pickens died unexpectedly in August 1817.

Bailey and Cooper, *Biographical Directory of the South Carolina House,* 552–55; Hartley, *Life of Gen. Francis Marion,* 269–87; Moss, *Roster of South Carolina Patriots,* 771–72; Pickens, "Life of General Pickens"; Skelton, *General Andrew Pickens;* Waring, *Fighting Elder.*

Pickens, Andrew, Jr. (1779–1838): Andrew Pickens Jr. was born November 13, 1779, the son of Andrew Pickens and Rebecca Calhoun. He graduated from Brown University in 1801 and returned to South Carolina to study law and be a planter. He owned part of his father's plantation, Hopewell, on the Seneca River. Pendleton District elected Pickens to the Nineteenth General Assembly, and he served from 1810 to 1812. During the War of 1812, he was appointed lieutenant colonel in the US Tenth Infantry and in the Forty-Third Infantry. He resigned in 1814 but remained a colonel in the militia. He became governor of South Carolina on December 5, 1816, a position he held until 1818. He also served as commissioner to superintend the building of a courthouse in Pendleton District in 1806, commissioner for the Pendleton Circulating Library Society from 1808 to 1814, acting commissioner to alter the western boundary of the public square in Pendleton in 1813, commissioner to superintend the repairs of the jail in Pendleton District in 1816, and ex officio trustee for South Carolina College from 1816 to 1818. Around 1820 Pickens moved to Dallas County, Alabama, where he purchased Susanville Plantation and was elected president of the Alabama State Bank. He left Alabama in the 1830s and settled in Edgefield, South Carolina, at Oatlands Plantation. Pickens married Susan Smith Wilkinson, daughter of Francis and Susanna Wilkinson, on April 19, 1804. They had two children. Susan died January 28, 1810, and he married Mary Nelson. She had no issue. Pickens died June 24, 1838, in Mississippi.

Bailey, *Biographical Directory of the South Carolina House,* 441–42; Pickens, *Cousin Monroe's History,* 57–61, 68–71; Skelton, *General Andrew Pickens,* 30, 32, 34–36; Waring, *Fighting Elder,* 189–90, 200–201, 203, 204–5.

Pinckney, Charles (1757–1824): Charles Pinckney was born in Charleston on October 26, 1757, the son of Col. Charles Pinckney and Frances Brewton. Educated in Charleston and admitted to the South Carolina bar in 1779, he served as a lieutenant in the Charleston regiment of the militia and was present at the siege of Savannah during the American Revolution. Captured when Charleston fell to the British in 1780, he was imprisoned for a year. During the war and after, Pinckney was involved in South Carolina politics. He represented Christ Church Parish in the Third General Assembly from 1779 to 1780, St. Bartholomew in the Fifth General Assembly in 1784, and Christ Church in the Sixth and Seventh General Assemblies from 1785 to 1788. A delegate for the Confederation Congress from 1784 to 1787, he was at the Constitutional Convention in Philadelphia in 1787. In 1788 he attended the state ratifying convention on behalf of Christ Church, where he voted in favor of the Constitution, and he served as president of the state constitutional convention in 1790. Pinckney returned to the South Carolina House of Representative for the Eighth General Assembly in 1789 but resigned when he was elected governor. When his second term ended in 1792, he represented Christ Church in the Tenth, Eleventh, and Twelfth General Assemblies from 1792 to 1796. Pinckney left the house upon his election as governor for a third term in 1796. Christ Church elected him to the Thirteenth General Assembly in 1798, but he did not take his seat due to his appointment to the US Senate in 1798, serving until 1801, when he became minister plenipotentiary to Spain. When he returned home, Christ Church elected Pinckney to the Seventeenth General Assembly in 1806. Elected as governor again, he resigned his seat. He represented St. Philip and St. Michael Parishes in the Nineteenth and Twentieth General Assemblies from 1810 to 1813. He won a seat in the US House of Representatives and represented Charleston District in the Sixteenth US Congress from 1819 to 1821, after which time he retired from politics. Pinckney was also a member of the Charleston Library Society, South Carolina Society, Fellowship Society, and Mount Sion Society. He was a delegate to the Protestant Episcopal Church convention in 1785, an agent to appoint judges to determine the boundary between South Carolina and Georgia in 1786, member of the Privy Council from 1788 to 1790, trustee of the College of Charleston from 1791 to 1793, and vestryman for Christ Church from 1797 to 1808. Pinckney owned a townhouse on Meeting Street in Charleston, several plantations, and land on the Congaree River. Included in his fortune were more than a hundred slaves and a library of almost two thousand books. Pinckney married Mary Eleanor Laurens, daughter of Henry Laurens and Eleanor Ball, on April 27, 1788. They had three children: Frances Henrietta, Mary Eleanor, and Henry Laurens. His wife predeceased him in October 1794, and Pinckney died October 29, 1824, in Charleston.

Bailey and Cooper, *Biographical Directory of the South Carolina House*, 555–60; *Family Reminiscences of the Pinckney*, 8–12, 16, 19–29.

Pinckney, Thomas (1750–1828): Thomas Pinckney was born in Charleston on October 23, 1750, the son of Charles Pinckney and Elizabeth Lucas. He attended Westminster School and graduated from Oxford University in 1768, after which time he studied law at the Middle Temple. Pinckney spent a year traveling and was trained at the Royal Military Academy at Caen, France, before returning to Charleston. He was admitted to the bar on November 25, 1774, and opened a legal practice in Charleston. During the American Revolution, he was appointed a lieutenant of a company of rangers and a captain in the First South Carolina Regiment. He also worked as an engineer at Fort Johnson at Charleston Harbor and was stationed at Fort Moultrie for two years, while acting as a recruiter. He was promoted to major in May 1778 and was present in the expedition against Florida, the Battle of Stono Ferry, and the siege of Savannah. Pinckney was able to escape Charleston when the British captured the city in 1780, but his plantation, Auckland, was burned and his slaves freed. Serving as aide-de-camp to Horatio Gates in 1780, he was wounded at Camden and taken prisoner. He and his brother were paroled to Philadelphia and exchanged later that year. Pinckney served under the Marquis de Lafayette at the Battle of Yorktown and upon his return to South Carolina published a defense of Gates. During his military service, Pinckney held a seat in the legislature, maintained his law practice, and was elected governor of South Carolina in 1787. He was president of the Constitutional Convention in 1788 and in 1789 turned down George Washington's offer of a federal judgeship. When his second term as governor ended, Washington appointed him minister to Great Britain. On October 27, 1795, he negotiated the Treaty of San Lorenzo el Real with the Spanish, which officially granted free navigation of the Mississippi River and a port of entry at New Orleans. Back in South Carolina in 1796, Pinckney was nominated for vice president and subsequently president on the Federalist ticket but lost the election. He served in the US Congress from 1797 to 1801, after which time he stepped out of the political arena. Pinckney was granted one more military appointment, major general in the War of 1812 in charge of the area extending from North Carolina to the Mississippi River. He also negotiated the treaty at the end of the Creek War. Pinckney married Elizabeth Motte, daughter of Jacob Motte and Rebecca Brewton, on July 22, 1779. They had four children: Thomas, Charles Cotesworth, Elizabeth, and Harriott (Harriotta) Lucas. His wife died while in England on October 19, 1797. Pinckney married her sister, Frances Motte Middleton, the widow of John Middleton. Pinckney died of a long and painful illness in Charleston on November 2, 1828.

Bailey and Cooper, *Biographical Directory of the South Carolina House,* 561–65; Michael Bellesiles, "Thomas Pinckney," in Selesky and Boatner, *Encyclopedia of the American Revolution;* "General Thomas Pinckney"; Moss, *Roster of South Carolina Patriots,* 774; Williams, *Founding Family,* 15, 22, 33, 40–41, 49, 53–54, 63, 68, 78, 87, 96, 98–99, 101–2, 116–20, 123, 126, 128, 133–38, 140–43, 145–46, 149–51, 156, 161, 167–68, 170, 174, 177, 193, 195, 207–8, 211, 216, 286, 290–91, 296–307, 313, 322–37.

Player, Joshua (1777–1833): Joshua Player was born March 11, 1777, the son of Thomas and Elizabeth Player. He owned a plantation in Christ Church Parish and worked as a merchant in Charleston in the firm McFarlane and Player. When the partnership dissolved in 1801, he relocated to Fairfield and turned his interest to planting. Christ Church elected Player to the Fourteenth General Assembly from 1800 to 1801, and he served Fairfield in the Twenty-Second General Assembly from 1816 to 1817. Player was a first lieutenant in the Second Regiment of the state militia during the War of 1812. He later received a promotion to major. He married Charlotte Elizabeth Thomson, daughter of James Hamden Thomson and Elizabeth Martha Trezevant, on December 31, 1801. Charlotte died in 1807, and he married Mary Adger, daughter of William Adger, on June 27, 1820. They had several children. Player died November 21, 1833, in Fairfield.

Bailey, *Biographical Directory of the South Carolina House,* 449; *City Gazette and Daily Advertiser,* December 17, 1802; Census, Second, Third, Fourth, and Fifth, 1800–1830, St. Thomas, Christ Church, and Fairfield, S.C.; *Commercial Advertiser,* January 23, 1802; Salley, "Daniel Trezevant, Huguenot," 35.

Prioleau, Samuel (1784–1840): Samuel Prioleau was born September 4, 1784, the son of Phillip Prioleau and Alice Edith Honeyard. Prioleau attended the University of Pennsylvania but did not complete his program. Instead he studied law under William Drayton in Charleston. He joined the bar in 1808 and later became Drayton's law partner. He represented St. Philip and St. Michael in the Twenty-Third through Twenty-Sixth General Assemblies from 1819 to 1825. He resigned from the house when he was elected city recorder of Charleston in November 1825. He was also director of the Bank of the State of South Carolina from 1820 to 1824, commissioner of the Charleston Orphan House from 1823 to 1826, vestryman of St. Michael's Episcopal Church from 1823 to 1832, warden of Charleston's First Ward in 1824, city recorder from 1825 to 1836, intendant of Charleston in 1825, and trustee of the College of Charleston from 1824 to 1826 and the Medical College of South Carolina in 1836, in addition to holding memberships in the Charleston Library Society and Charleston Literary Club and being a contributor to the *Southern Review.* Prioleau married Hannau Motte Hamilton, daughter of Maj. James Hamilton, on March 4, 1811. They had one son, James Hamilton. When Hannau died, he married her younger sister, Elizabeth Lynch Hamilton. They had four children: Samuel, Charles Kuhn, Hannah Hamilton, and Alice Edith. Prioleau died August 10, 1840, in Anderson District.

Bailey, *Biographical Directory of the South Carolina House,* 449; Ellis, *Some Historic Families,* 42–43; "Historical Sketch of the Prioleau Family," 28–35; O'Neall, *Biographical Sketches of the Bench,* 1:324–28; 2:598, 603.

Pyatt, John Francis (1790–1820): John Francis Pyatt was born in 1790, the son of John Pyatt II and Charlotte Withers. He owned Richmond and Rosemont Plantations near Georgetown and represented All Saints Parish in the Third General Assembly from 1779 to 1780. He married Martha Allston (1789–1869), daughter of Benjamin Allston Sr., in 1812. They had three children. By this marriage Pyatt received Turkey Hill and Oatland Plantations. He died in 1820.

Bailey and Cooper, *Biographical Directory of the South Carolina House,* 590; Groves, *Alstons and Allstons,* 46; Nord, "George Whiting Flagg," 232; Rogers, *History of Georgetown County,* 261–62.

Read/Reed/Reid, Jacob (1752–1816): Jacob Read was born in 1752 at Hobcaw Plantation, the son of the Honorable James Read and Rebecca Bond.

Admitted to the South Carolina bar on March 23, 1773, he studied at Gray's Inn in London. Returning to Charleston in time for the American Revolution, he served as a captain in the Charleston militia and an attorney for the state. When the British seized Charleston, he was exiled to St. Augustine and exchanged a year later. Read represented St. Philip and St. Michael Parishes in the Fourth, Fifth, and Sixth General Assemblies from 1782 to 1786. During his time in the house, he served on the Privy Council and Continental Congress. The city parishes reelected him to the house for the Seventh through Eleventh General Assemblies, where he served from 1787 to 1795. He was chosen Speaker of the house in 1787. Read attended the state convention to ratify the federal Constitution on behalf of Christ Church in 1788. Elected to the US Senate in 1794 on the Federalist ticket, he served until 1801. He was also a member of the Charleston Library Society from 1777 to 1816, a delegate for Christ Church Parish at the General Episcopal Church Convention in 1785, vestryman for St. Michael from 1787 to 1789 and 1810 to 1816, founder and president of the South Carolina Jockey Club from 1792 to 1793, committeeman of the Society for the Relief of Widows and Orphans of the Clergy of the Protestant Episcopal Church of South Carolina in 1793, lieutenant colonel of the Twenty-Ninth Regiment from 1794 to 1801, brigadier general of the Seventh Brigade of the state militia from 1805 to 1816, commissioner to locate sites for the erection of forts in 1805, and military commander of Charleston from 1812 to 1813. Read married Catherine Van Horne, daughter of David Van Horne, on October 13, 1785. They had four children: Jacob, William George, Ann Louisa, and Cornelia Annabella. Read died July 16, 1816, survived by his wife and children.

Bailey and Cooper, *Biographical Directory of the South Carolina House,* 597–99; Moss, *South Carolina Patriots,* 803; O'Neall, *Biographical Sketches of the Bench,* 2:603; Rogers, *Evolution of a Federalist,* 69–70, 115–16, 122, 142–44, 183, 186, 188, 190–92, 234, 239–40, 250–52, 268–69, 276–83, 343, 346–48, 363–64, 383, 386, 388, 399.

Rees, William James (d. 1850): William James Rees was the son of William Rees and Mary Hames. Rees owned Oakley Plantation in Sumter District as well as property in Alabama. Claremont District elected Rees to the Twelfth and Thirteenth General Assemblies from 1796 to 1797. He also served intermittently as a vestryman for the Church of the Holy Cross Claremont from 1801 to 1850 and was a commissioner to contract for and superintend the improvement of the navigation of the Wateree River in 1805. Rees and his wife, Maria, had at least one son, Frederick Wentworth. Maria died May 13, 1836. Rees died in 1850.

Bailey, *Biographical Directory of the South Carolina House,* 469; Census, Second, Third, and Fifth, 1800–1840, Sumter, S.C.; Sumter, *Stateburg and Its People,* 16.

Reid, John: John Reid of North Carolina attended South Carolina College. After graduating in 1812, he remained at the college as a math tutor.

Moore, *Roll of Students,* 5; Salley, "Journal of General Peter Horry" (1943), 124n.

Richardson, Charles (1771–1829): Charles Richardson was born November 20, 1771, the son of Richard Richardson and Dorothy Sinkler. Richardson lived in Clarendon County and owned property throughout South Carolina. He represented Clarendon in the Fifteenth General Assembly from 1802 to 1804. He served as a justice of the peace for Clarendon in 1799, commissioner of the high roads for Clarendon District in 1813, founder and vestryman of the Upper St. Mark's Church, and commissioner to approve the securities for public officers for Sumter District in 1829. Richardson married Elizabeth Eveleigh, daughter of Thomas Eveleigh and Ann Simmons, on February 3, 1801. They had nine children, seven of whom died young. Elizabeth died November 4, 1824. Richardson died May 22, 1829.

Bailey, *Biographical Directory of the South Carolina House,* 473–74; Census, Third and Fourth, 1810–1820, Sumter, S.C.; Singleton, *Captain Richard Singleton,* 18–19.

Richardson, James Burchell (1770–1836): James Burchell Richardson was born October 28, 1770, the son of Gen. Richard Richardson and Dorothy Sinkler. Richardson was a successful planter in Clarendon District, owning property throughout the state, including Fiscal, the Rocks, New Belvedere, and Bush Pond Plantations, other plantations in St. John Berkeley and Sabb's Field, a summer house and race course in the Sand Hills, and almost seven thousand acres from Columbia to Charleston. Richardson represented Clarendon in the Tenth through Fifteenth General Assemblies from 1792 to 1804. Governor from 1802 to 1804, he later returned to the house for the Sixteenth General Assembly from 1804 to 1805. Clarendon and Claremont elected him to the Seventeenth and Eighteenth General Assemblies from 1806 to 1809, and he represented Clarendon in the Nineteenth and Twentieth General Assemblies from 1810 to 1813. His last stint in the South Carolina legislature ran from 1816 to 1817 in the Twenty-Second General Assembly. Richardson was lieutenant colonel of the state militia from 1810 to 1814, director of the Bank of the State of South Carolina in 1812, and founder and vestryman for Upper St. Mark's Church. He married Anne Cantey Sinkler, daughter of James Sinkler and Sarah Cantey, on May 10, 1791. They had twelve children: James Sinkler, James Burchell, John Sinkler, Hermione, Sarah Jame Cidelia, Julia Anna, Floride Ann, William Henry Burchell, Matilda Mary, Dorothy Sinkler, Richard Charles, and Margaret Cantey. Richardson died April 28, 1836.

Burgess, *Chronicles of St. Marks Parish,* 88; Edgar and Taylor, *Biographical Directory of the South Carolina House,* 1361–62; Lathrop, *Historic Houses,* 58.

Richardson, John Smythe (1777–1850): John Smythe Richardson was born April 11, 1777, the son of William Richardson and Ann Magdalen Guignard. After attending the College of Charleston grammar school, he studied law under John Julius Pringle. Admitted to the bar on October 30, 1799, he established a law practice in Claremont District. He lived at Bloom Hill Plantation but also owned property in Orangeburg, Ninety Six, Cheraw, and Camden Districts. Richardson represented Claremont in the Eighteenth and Nineteenth General Assemblies from 1808 to 1812, serving as Speaker in 1810. He was elected attorney general of South Carolina in 1810 but resigned to become an associate judge of the Court of General Sessions and Common Pleas. Later president of the Court of Appeals and the Court of Errors, Richardson served as a delegate for Spartanburg District at the Nullification Convention from 1832 to 1833, where he voted in the negative. He was a churchwarden from 1806 to 1807, vestryman from 1809 to 1811, and delegate at state conventions in 1818 and 1821 for the Church of the Holy Cross, Claremont, an elective and ex officio trustee of South Carolina College from 1809 to 1813 and 1818 to 1850, and director of the Santee Canal Company intermittently from 1819 to 1835. Richardson also held memberships in the South Carolina Society, the '76 Association, and the Charleston Library Society. He was later accused of being mentally and physically unfit, but the charges were dropped. He married Elizabeth Lucretia Buford, daughter of William Buford and Frances June, in 1802. They had ten children: Thomas Couturier, John Smythe, Elizabeth Frances, Susan William Ann, David Evans, Maynard Davis, Eleanor Lucretia, William Buford, Langdon Cheves, and Francis Deliesseline. Richardson died in Charleston on May 8, 1850, and was buried at Bloom Hill Plantation.

Bailey, *Biographical Directory of the South Carolina House,* 478–79; *Cyclopedia of Eminent and Representative Men of the Carolinas,* 271–73; Richardson, *Genealogical Record,* 9–11, 17, 19–30, 33, 36–38, 81–114.

Richardson, William Guignard (1773–1849): William Guignard Richardson was born April 16, 1773, the son of William Richardson and Ann Magdalen Guignard. Richardson received his education in Europe and returned to South Carolina to be a planter. He lived at Bloom Hill Plantation in Claremont County and owned property in other areas of South Carolina. Richardson served in the state senate for Claremont in the Twenty-First and Twenty-Second General Assemblies from 1814 to 1817. He was also a militia officer of the Thirty-Second Regiment in 1812, trustee for Lodebar Academy in 1817, and sheriff of Sumter District from 1832 to 1836 and 1840 to 1844. Richardson lost his property in the 1830s after using his estate as security for a friend's loan. His brother, John Smythe Richardson, purchased his plantation, and he moved to Sumter but later came back to Bloom Hill. He married Harriet Ann Eveleigh, daughter of Thomas Eveleigh and Ann Simmons, on February 26, 1798. They had four children: Evelina Ann, William Eveleigh, Laura, and Harriet. Harriet Ann died February 25, 1804. He married Emma Corbett Buford, daughter of William and Frances June Buford, on March 5, 1809. They had twelve children: Julian, Joseph Johnson, Elinor Frances, James Sanders Guignard, Elizabeth Ann, Hugh Fraser, Mary Caroline, Lydia Clegg Buford, Susan Emma, Samuel Clegg Chovine, John Manly, and a stillborn son. Emma died February 25, 1843. Richardson followed on September 8, 1849.

Bailey, Morgan, and Taylor, *Biographical Directory of the South Carolina Senate,* 2:1373.

Roberts, Lynch (d. ca. 1812): Lynch Roberts was one of the seven children of Pierre Robert III and Mary Lynch. Her aunt, Margaret Lynch, married Elias Horry and her sister Nancy married John Horry. She died unmarried between 1810 and 1812.

Burns and Burkette, "Peyre Records" (1974).

Rouse, William, Sr. (1756–1829): William Rouse was born January 30, 1756, in England, the son of Eli Rouse and Martha Asquith. By the time the American Revolution started, Rouse was living in America and served in the Whig forces throughout the South before being taken prisoner by the British. He was granted citizenship in 1783 and moved to Charleston. Rouse was appointed an officer in the state militia on July 4, 1794, and captain of the cavalry in 1797. He was later promoted to major and eventually lieutenant colonel. He was court-marshaled and suspended for six months, however, for refusing to take orders from Jacob Drayton on the grounds that he had been overlooked for a promotion. Rouse represented St. Philip and St. Michael Parishes in the Seventeenth and Eighteenth General Assemblies from 1806 to 1809. He served in the senate for the Twentieth and Twenty-First General Assemblies from 1812 to 1815 and in the house for the Twenty-Fourth, Twenty-Fifth, and Twenty-Sixth General Assemblies from 1820 to 1825. Rouse was also commissioner of tobacco inspection in Charleston in 1801, intendant for Charleston from 1808 to 1810, commissioner of the streets and lamps for Charleston from 1811 to 1813, commissioner of markets from 1812 to 1813 and of the center market in 1824, commissioner to make repairs to the Charleston jail in 1817, assistant to the commissioner and trustee of the Charleston Dispensary from 1820 to 1826, commissioner to superintend construction of the Fireproof Building from 1822 to 1823, warden for Charleston's Fourth Ward from 1823 to 1824, commissioner of the Marine Hospital in Charleston from 1823 to 1824, and commissioner to execute repairs to the Charleston courthouse in 1823. He was a member of the First Baptist Church of Charleston and the Fellowship Society and served as president of the Charleston Mechanic Society in 1803. Rouse married Mary Martha Stuart in 1775. They had six children: Martha Mary, James W., Joshua, John, William Jr., and Christopher Elias. Rouse died in Charleston on June 15, 1829, and was buried at Magnolia Cemetery.

Edgar and Taylor, *Biographical Directory of the South Carolina House*, 1394–96; Tupper, *Two Centuries of the First Baptist Church*, 308.

Rutledge, Benjamin Huger (ca. 1798–1832): Benjamin Huger Rutledge was born around 1798, the son of Hugh Rutledge and Mary Golightly Huger. He was baptized March 10, 1798. Rutledge married Alice Ann Weston in February 1824. He died April 26, 1832, and was buried at the Church of the Holy Cross in Stateburg.

Webber, "Dr. John Rutledge," 21.

Rutledge, Frederick (1769–1824): Frederick Rutledge was born March 1, 1769, the son of John Rutledge and Elizabeth Grimke. Admitted to the bar in 1793, he owned Hampton, Harriott's Villa, Elmwood, Eli, and Waterhorn Plantations as well as property in Georgetown and Charleston. Rutledge represented St. Philip and St. Michael Parishes in the Thirteenth General Assembly from 1798 to 1799. He was also commissioner of streets on Sullivans Island in 1799, trustee for the College of Charleston from 1800 to 1824, warden for Charleston's Tenth Ward from 1803 to 1804, a member of the Charleston Library Society from 1815 to 1824, and member and vice president of the Agricultural Society of South Carolina from 1818 to 1824. Rutledge married Harriott Pinckney Horry, daughter of Daniel Horry Jr. and Harriott Pinckney. They had eight children: Edward Cotesworth, Frederick, Elizabeth Pinckney, Harriett Pinckney, Maria, Thomas Pinckney, John Henry, and Eliza Lucas. Rutledge died April 12, 1824, when he fell from a ferry boat and drowned.

Bailey, *Biographical Directory of the South Carolina House*, 497–98; Rogers, *History of Georgetown County*, 295.

Rutledge, Harriott Horry (ca. 1770–1858): Harriott Horry was the daughter of Daniel Horry Jr. and Harriott Pinckney and the granddaughter of Eliza Lucas Pinckney. Harriott married Frederick Rutledge on October 11, 1797. They had eight children: Edward Cotesworth, Frederick, Elizabeth Pinckney, Harriett Pinckney, Maria, Thomas Pinckney, John Henry, and Eliza Lucas. The Rutledges resided at Hampton Plantation. Rutledge died in 1821, leaving Harriott a widow. She maintained the plantation until her death in 1858.

Bailey, *Biographical Directory of the South Carolina House*, 497–98, Schulz, "Pinckney and Horry," 1:103.

Sarrazin, Lucretia: Lucretia Sarrazin was the second wife of Jonah Horry, brother of Peter Horry. They married in 1793, six months after the death of his first wife. Lucretia had no children but was the stepmother of Horry's two daughters, Anne and Mary. By his will she received their home, a lot in Charleston, and a tract in St. Bartholomew's Parish, along with slaves, carriages, horses, and household and kitchen furniture.

Mathis, *John Horry Dent*, 7; McCormick, *Carson-McCormick Family Memorials*, 39.

Shackelford, Francis (1739–1823): Francis Shackelford was born in 1739, the son of John and Ann Shackelford. He served in the American Revolution and later moved to Marion, where he settled near Godfrey's Ferry on the Great Pee Dee River. He married Rebecca Ballard, with whom he had six children: Willouhby, Francis, Sarah, George, Daniel, and Mary. Shackelford died in 1823.

Harllee, *Kinfolks*, 1:835.

Shackelford, Hannah White: Hannah White Shackelford was the daughter of James and Sarah Shackelford. She married Charles L. Munnerlyn.

Hines, *Hines and Allied Families*, 99.

Shackelford, John (1741–1824): John Shackelford was born in 1741, the son of William Shackelford and Hester Seré. Shackelford resided in Georgetown and was a member of the Winyah Indigo Society. He married Martha Ann Wright in 1780 in Bermuda. They had at least one son, William Frederick. Shackelford died in 1824 and was buried in Georgetown.

Harllee, *Kinfolks*, 1:834.

Shackelford, Martha Ann Wright (1761–1818): Martha Ann Wright was born in 1761. She married John Shackelford (1741–1824). Martha died in 1818 and was buried in Georgetown.

Harllee, *Kinfolks*, 1:834.

Shackelford, Richard (ca. 1772–1808): Richard Shackelford lived in St. James Santee Parish and owned Sewee and Buck Hall Plantations. Shackelford represented St. James Santee in the Fourteenth, Fifteenth, and Sixteenth General Assemblies from 1800 to 1805. He married Mary, with whom he had at least three children: Winthrop, Sarah Ann, and Jonah Collins. Shackelford died September 20, 1808.

Bailey, *Biographical Directory of the South Carolina House*, 514.

Shackelford, Roger (1773–1814): Roger Shackelford was born in 1773, the son of James Shackelford Jr. He died in 1814.

Johnston, *Little Acorns*, 273.

Shackelford, Sarah Collins Withers Vanderhorst (1768–1845): Sarah Collins Withers was born March 16, 1768, the daughter of Richard Withers and Elizabeth Parris. She married Elias Vanderhorst on April 1, 1784. They had two children: Richard Withers and Elias. Vanderhorst died, leaving Sarah a widow at age twenty-two. Her second husband was William Cartwright Shackelford Sr. They married November 23, 1790, and had four children: William Cartwright Jr., James, Hugh, and Mary Lupton. Shackelford predeceased her. Sarah died in November 1845.

Strawn, *Ancestors and Descendants of John White,* 200A–200B.

Shackelford, William Cartwright, Jr. (d. 1827): Born after 1790 in Prince George Winyah Parish, William Cartwright Shackelford Jr. was the son of William Cartwright Shackelford Sr. and Sarah Collins Withers. He and his wife, Mary, had at least three children: Richard Withers, R. F. W., and Susan. Shackelford died in Withersville on September 7, 1827.

Strawn, *Ancestors and Descendants of John White,* 200B–200C.

Shackelford, William Cartwright, Sr.: William Cartwright Shackelford was the son of William Shackelford Jr. He owned around 1,600 acres in St. James Santee and Prince George Winyah Parishes, in addition to more than one hundred slaves. Shackelford represented St. James Santee in the house in the Eleventh and Twelfth General Assemblies from 1794 to 1797 and in the senate in the Twentieth and Twenty-First General Assemblies from 1812 to 1815. Shackelford was also a captain in the militia. He married Sarah Collins Withers (1768–1845), daughter of Richard Withers and widow of Elias Vanderhorst, on November 23, 1790. They had four children: William Cartwright Jr., James, Hugh, and Mary Lupton. Shackelford died before 1845.

Bailey, *Biographical Directory of the South Carolina House,* 514–15; Strawn, *Ancestors and Descendants of John White,* 200A–200B.

Simons, John: John Simons was the son of Eleanor Allston and Peter Simons. He married Elizabeth Lepear, and they had nine children: Peter, Martha Young, Paul, John A., Sarah, Ellen, Rachel, Catharine, and James.

Simms, "Marion Family," 52–53.

Simons, Thomas Young (1797–1857): Thomas Young Simons was born in 1797 and graduated from South Carolina College in 1815. He later graduated from Edinburgh and returned to Charleston, where he became a member of the Medical Society of South Carolina in 1821 and received an appointment as port physician. Simons published the first scientific journal in South Carolina in 1824 and was president of the Medical Society from 1829 to 1830. He was

professor of theory at South Carolina College in 1832, while practicing medicine at the Medical College of South Carolina. Later chosen dean, he was
active in the South Carolina Medical Association and as the Charleston delegate to the American Medical Association from the Charleston Society. Simons
died in 1857.

Moore, *Roll of Students*, 7; Waring, *History of Medicine*, 295–96.

Singletary, Isaac: Isaac Singletary was a Georgetown tailor. He married Elizabeth Attmore, daughter of Ralph Attmore, on April 20, 1786.

Burns, "Vincent Guerin," 43; Census, Third, 1810, Georgetown, S.C.

Skrine, John: John Skrine was the son of Jonathan Skrine and Elizabeth Gaillard of South Carolina. Little is known about Skrine, except that he was born
in St. James Santee Parish.

Edgar and Taylor, *Biographical Directory of the South Carolina House*, 623–24.

Smith, George: George Smith was the son of George Smith and Elizabeth
Waring. Smith and his brother Savage were co-owners of 2,195 acres and more
than two hundred slaves. He was a successful merchant in Charleston and
partnered in the firm of the House of Smiths, De Saussure and Darrell. Smith
married in 1783.

Bailey and Cooper, *Biographical Directory of the South Carolina House*, 665–67.

Smith, Josiah, Jr. (1731–1826): Josiah Smith Jr. was born September 15, 1731,
the son of Rev. Josiah Smith and Elizabeth Darrell. Smith was a Charleston
merchant and owned the sloop *Carolina* as well as the brigantine *Carolina
Society*. He organized the firm the House of Smiths, De Saussure and Darrell,
which became a successful business. Smith owned a home on Meeting Street
and two homes on Broad Street. He qualified for the First General Assembly
in 1776, but the election was voided. He represented St. Philip and St. Michael
Parishes in the Second and Third General Assemblies from 1776 to 1780.
Smith was arrested by the British during the fall of Charleston in 1780 and
exiled to St. Augustine until 1781. He returned to Charleston in 1783. After the
war he represented St. Philip and St. Michael in the Fifth and Sixth General
Assemblies from 1783 to 1786. He was also commissioner of fortifications for
Charleston in 1768 and 1774, a member of the Privy Council from 1783 to
1784, commissioner to ascertain boundaries of forts and low water lots in
Charleston in 1784, a delegate for St. Philip and St. Michael at the state convention to ratify the federal Constitution in 1788, commissioner to purchase
land for warehouses and for having tobacco inspected in Charleston in 1789,
and first cashier of the Charleston branch of the Bank of the United States

until its dissolution in 1810. Smith was a supporter of the Federalist Party and an active member of the Meeting Street Congregation. He married Mary Stevens, daughter of Dr. Samuel Stevens and Mary Smith, on April 15, 1758. They had eight children: Elizabeth, Samuel, Mary, Elizabeth, Josiah, William Stevens, Edward Darrell, and Ann Martha. Smith died in Charleston on February 12, 1826, and was buried in the Independent Churchyard.

Bailey and Cooper, *Biographical Directory of the South Carolina House,* 665–67, 5:253; Smith, *Dwelling Houses,* 177.

Smith, Mary Rutledge: Mary Rutledge was the daughter of Dr. John Rutledge and Sarah Hext. She married Roger Smith (1745–1805). They had twelve children: Thomas Rhett, Roger Moore, Sarah Rutledge, Mary Rutledge, Carolina, John Rutledge, Benjamin Burgh, Hugh Rutledge, Andrew, Anna Maria, Mary Sabina, and Edward Nutt. Mary was left a widow on July 29, 1805.

Edgar and Taylor, *Biographical Directory of the South Carolina House,* 635–36.

Smith, Samuel: Samuel Smith was a Georgetown merchant. He served on the Council of Safety for Georgetown and was an inspector of rice and flour in 1775. He represented Prince Frederick Parish in the state senate in the Fourth and Fifth General Assemblies from 1781 to 1784. He also served on the Privy Council from 1782 to 1783, was a delegate at the state convention to ratify the federal Constitution in 1788 and the state constitutional convention in 1790, commissioner for rebuilding and repairing the courthouse and jail in Georgetown in 1783, commissioner of the pilotage for the port of Georgetown in 1784, commissioner for the inspection and exportation of tobacco from Georgetown in 1796, and ordinary for Georgetown District from 1805 to 1816. Smith was a delegate for Prince George Winyah at the state convention of the Protestant Episcopal Church in 1813 and a longtime member of the Georgetown Library Society.

Bailey, Morgan, and Taylor, *Biographical Directory of the South Carolina Senate,* 3:1509–10.

Smith, Savage (1765–1817): Savage Smith was born December 16, 1765, the son of George Smith and Elizabeth Waring. He worked as a successful merchant and planter in Georgetown. He and his brother George co-owned 2,195 acres and more than two hundred slaves. Smith represented Prince George Winyah Parish in the Sixteenth General Assembly from 1804 to 1805 and in the senate for the Nineteenth and Twentieth General Assemblies from 1810 to 1813. He was chosen president of the senate in 1813. He was also the commissioner for Georgetown to prevent the exportation of nonmerchantable bread and flour in 1796, member of the Georgetown Library Society from 1799 to

1817, firemaster for Georgetown in 1801, commissioner to view and report the repairs necessary to the Georgetown District jail in 1804, militia major from 1804 to 1812, commissioner to locate sites for the erection of forts in 1805 and 1808, commissioner to superintend the cutting of a canal in 1805, commissioner to determine the site of a ferry in Georgetown District in 1807, commissioner to approve the bond and security of the sheriff for Georgetown in 1808, intendant for Georgetown in 1808, commissioner to open a subscription for the Sampit and St. James Santee Canal Company in 1809, commissioner to open a subscription in Georgetown for the Planters' and Mechanics' Bank of South Carolina in 1810, commissioner to superintend the building of a jail in Georgetown in 1810, commissioner of free schools for Prince George Winyah in 1811 and 1813, ex officio trustee for South Carolina College from 1813 to 1814, president of the Winyah Indigo Society from 1814 to 1816, and commissioner to approve the securities given for public offices in Georgetown District in 1817. Smith attended the First Baptist Church of Georgetown and was one of the incorporators. He married Margaret Dill, daughter of Joseph Dill Sr., on November 7, 1793. They had no children. He married Elizabeth Cuttino, daughter of William Cuttino, on May 5, 1795. They had ten children: George Savage, Elizabeth Mary (died in infancy), Elizabeth Mary, William Cuttino, Sarah Edith, Archar Benjamin, Susan Ann, Mary Elizabeth, Thomas Peter, and David Henry. Smith died April 7, 1817.

Bailey and Cooper, *Biographical Directory of the South Carolina House,* 1510–11; General Assembly Petitions, no. 180 and 181, 342–47, South Carolina Department of Archives and History; General Assembly Petitions, no. 124, 106–11, South Carolina Department of Archives and History; Minutes, First Baptist Church of Georgetown, January 1805–February1, 1812.

Solomon, Levy: Levy Solomon was a Jewish shopkeeper and merchant in Charleston who participated in the slave trade from 1809 to 1828.

Census, First, 1810, Charleston, S.C.; Friedman, *Jews and the American Slave Trade,* 153.

Stark, Robert, Jr. (1762–1830): Robert Stark was born January 10, 1762, in Virginia, the son of Col. Robert Stark and Mary Hall. He and his family later moved to Ninety Six District. Stark served in the American Revolution as an adjutant in Samuel Hammond's regiment and saw combat at the battles of Blackstock's, Cowpens, and Eutaw Springs. He was a lawyer and was admitted to the bar in South Carolina on October 22, 1787. Stark was also a prominent landowner, having some 43,470 acres near the Saluda and Edisto Rivers. He moved to Columbia at the turn of the century and represented Saxe Gotha in the Eleventh through Fifteenth General Assemblies from 1794 to 1804.

Chosen Speaker of the house for the Fifteenth General Assembly, he took his senate seat for Saxe Gotha in the Sixteenth General Assembly in 1804 and served one term. He also served as secretary of state for South Carolina from 1826 to 1830, tobacco inspector for the north fork of the Edisto River in 1785, trustee for establishing public schools in Orangeburg District in 1798, commissioner of roads in 1798, justice of the quorum in 1798, commissioner to superintend and contract for the opening of the Broad and Pacolet Rivers in 1801, ex officio and elective trustee for South Carolina College, commissioner to make improvements to the House of Representatives in 1802, trustee for Columbia Academy, commissioner to superintend the rebuilding of the courthouse for Richland District in 1817, and director of the Columbia branch of the Bank of the State of South Carolina from 1826 to 1830. He also helped to organize Trinity Episcopal Cathedral in Columbia. Stark married Mary Winn, daughter of William Winn and Rosamond Hampton, on September 11, 1785. They had nine children. Mary died December 10, 1801, and he married Mary Hay on July 18, 1802. He was again left a widower in 1819. His third wife was Grace Baker, whom he wed in 1825. She bore him eleven children. Stark died September 4, 1830, and was buried at Trinity Episcopal Cathedral in Columbia.

Bailey, *Biographical Directory of the South Carolina House,* 536–37; Dorman, *Adventures of Purse and Person,* 257.

Strebeck, George: George Strebeck joined the Methodist Conference in 1792 but left the denomination within a few years and became a Lutheran minister. He was the pastor of a large church on Mott Street in New York, a congregation that eventually switched to the Protestant-Episcopalian denomination. Strebeck preached at St. Stephen's Church before moving to Charleston. In 1813 he was elected rector of the Protestant Episcopal Church of South Carolina.

Burgess, *Chronicles of St. Mark's Parish,* 39; Wakeley, *Lost Chapters,* 386–87.

Sumter/Sumpter, Thomas (1734–1832): Thomas Sumter was born August 14, 1734, in Virginia, the son of William and Patience Sumter. He enlisted in the provincial militia and was a sergeant in the French and Indian War. In 1761 he played a role in a mission to the Cherokee Nation, after which he left for London with Indian chiefs. When he returned to Virginia, he was arrested for unpaid debts but escaped to Charleston and settled in Orangeburg. He then relocated with his family to Camden District, where he worked as a storekeeper and ran a sawmill and gristmill. During the American Revolution, Sumter served as captain of a volunteer militia company from St. Mark Parish and as adjutant general in the Snow Campaign under Col. Richard Richardson. He became lieutenant colonel of the Second Regiment of Riflemen in 1776 and saw combat at the Battle of Fort Moultrie. By the end of 1777, he had been promoted to full colonel. When the Revolution ended, he purchased a plantation in the High Hills of Santee, in addition to owning Bradford Springs and South Mount Plantations. He resigned his commission in 1778 but was elected brigadier general in 1780. Sumter organized units into "Sumter's Brigade" and earned the nickname "Gamecock." He led forces at Rocky Mount, Hanging Rock, Fishing Creek, Fishdam Ford, and Blackstock's. Upon his final resignation in 1782, the South Carolina legislature gave him a gold medal and named Sumter District in his honor. Sumter represented the District Eastward of Wateree River in the First and Second Provincial Congresses as well as the First, Second, and Third General Assemblies from 1776 to 1780. He served in the state senate in the Fourth General Assembly from 1781 to 1782 and returned to the house for the Fifth, Seventh, and Eight General Assemblies from 1783 to 1784 and 1787 to 1790. Sumter represented the District Eastward of Wateree River at the state constitutional convention and was a vestryman for the Church of the Holy Cross in St. Mark's Parish. Camden District elected him to the US House of Representatives, and he held a seat in the First through Seventh Congresses. He served in the US Senate until 1810, when he retired from politics. Sumter married Mary Cantey, daughter of Joseph Cantey, in 1767. They had two children, Thomas and Mary. They also adopted the illegitimate children of their son. Mary died October 24, 1817. Sumter died June 1, 1832, and was buried at South Mount Plantation.

Bailey and Cooper, *Biographical Directory of the South Carolina House,* 693–96.

Swift, Joseph J.: Joseph Swift, an officer in the Corps of Engineers, undertook an inspection of fortifications from Norfolk to Savannah in 1812, after which he was assigned to Charleston as engineer for the Southern Department. A senior officer of the corps, he was called to Washington to become chief engineer. He was also ex officio superintendent of the Military Academy. In 1814 he was again called to Washington and promoted to brigadier general to direct the defense of the Atlantic Coast.

Wade, "Fort Winyaw at Georgetown," 236, 238, 241, 244, 246.

Taylor, Archibald: Archibald Taylor was a resident of Georgetown. He married Mary Mann, with whom he had two children, John Mann and Anne Marie Taylor. Taylor was chosen joint commissioner for clearing and making navigable Green's Creek in Georgetown in 1798.

Acts of the General Assembly, 198; Bailey, *Biographical Directory of the South Carolina House,* 554; Census, Third, 1810, Georgetown, S.C.

Taylor, John (d. 1821): John Taylor was the son of Samuel Taylor and Eleanor Cannon. He lived in Pendleton District and was admitted to the

South Carolina bar in 1798. Pendleton elected him to the Fifteenth and Sixteenth General Assemblies from 1802 to 1805. He resigned from the house
when he was chosen solicitor of the western circuit on December 2, 1805. Taylor was elected to US House of Representatives for the Fourteenth Congress
from 1815 to 1817. Locally he served as inspector and major of the Fourth
Brigade from 1810 to 1815 and colonel of the state militia in 1821, justice of the
quorum for Pendleton District in 1802, trustee for South Carolina College
from 1802 to 1805, commissioner to superintend the building of the Pendleton
courthouse in 1805, and commissioner to establish the Pendleton circulating
library society from 1808 to 1814. Taylor married Mary Margaret Smith,
daughter of William Smith and Margaret Duff, on December 10, 1804. They
had one daughter, Mary Smith. His second wife was Fanny Owens of Baltimore. Around 1820 Taylor relocated to Alabama, where he died July 12, 1821.

Bailey, *Biographical Directory of the South Carolina House,* 553.

Taylor, John, Sr. (1770–1832): John Taylor was born May 4, 1770, the son of
Thomas Taylor and Ann Wyche. He attended the Mount Sion Institute in
Winnsboro and in 1788 was a sophomore at Princeton University, where he
graduated with honors in 1790. After graduation Taylor returned to South
Carolina to study law under Charles Cotesworth Pinckney in Charleston.
Admitted to the South Carolina bar on June 1, 1793, he practiced law in
Columbia for several years and became a planter, owning several plantations,
including Tickleberry and Pine Tree. His main residence was in Columbia at
Hill House or Arsenal Hill. Saxe Gotha Parish elected Taylor to the Tenth
General Assembly from 1792 to 1794, and he represented Richland in the
Eleventh through Fourteenth General Assemblies from 1794 to 1801. He was
again elected to the General Assembly for the sixteenth session from 1804
to 1805 to represent Saxe Gotha. From 1806 to 1811, Taylor served in the
US House of Representatives for the Tenth and Eleventh Congresses. In 1810
he was elected to the US Senate to complete Thomas Sumter's term. He
remained there through the Fourteenth Congress and resigned in 1816. Richland elected Taylor to the state senate for the Twenty-Third through Twenty-
Six General Assemblies from 1818 to 1825. Governor of South Carolina from
1826 to 1828, he held various other offices, including commissioner for Columbia to prevent the exportation of nonmerchantable bread and flour in 1796,
commissioner of the streets and markets for Columbia in 1797, commissioner
for building a vault in the office of the treasurer in Columbia in 1799, justice
of the quorum for Richland in 1799 and 1802, commissioner to contract for
repairs of state buildings in 1805, intendant for Columbia from 1806 to 1807,
elective and ex officio trustee of South Carolina College, commissioner to
superintend repairs to the courthouse in Columbia in 1816, director of the

Columbia branch of the Bank of the State of South Carolina in 1827, director of the Columbia Theological Seminary in 1828, and member, elder, and synod delegate of the First Presbyterian Church of Columbia from 1830 to 1832. Taylor married Sarah Cantey Chesnut, daughter of John Chesnut and Sarah Cantey, on March 17, 1793. They had sixteen children: James Hunt, John Chesnut, Thomas, Rebecca Ann, John Chesnut, Franklin Cantey, Harriet Chesnut, William Henry, William Jesse, Sarah Cantey, George, Alexander Ross, and four others who died in infancy. Taylor died April 16, 1832, in Camden and was buried in the family cemetery in Columbia.

Bailey, Morgan, and Taylor, *Biographical Directory of the South Carolina Senate,* 3:1582–84; Taylor, "John Taylor," 96–99, 106–8, 174–75.

Taylor, John Mann (1786–1823): John Mann Taylor was born in 1786, the son of Archibald Taylor and Mary Mann. He inherited Mansfield Plantation and more than three hundred acres on Sampit Creek. Taylor represented Prince George Winyah in the Nineteenth General Assembly from 1810 to 1812. He was also a member of the Georgetown Library Society, justice of the peace for Prince George Winyah in 1809, incorporator of the Pee Dee Steamboat Company in 1819, director of the Georgetown branch of the Bank of the State of South Carolina from 1820 to 1822, and commissioner of roads for Prince George Winyah in 1823. Taylor died December 19, 1823.

Bailey, *Biographical Directory of the South Carolina House,* 554; Rogers, *History of Georgetown County,* 282–83.

Taylor, Simon (d. 1821): Simon Taylor, the son of John Taylor and Sarah Hirons, lived in Richland District and was a member of the legislature during the Fourteenth General Assembly. He was also commissioner in equity and sheriff in 1811. In 1818 he relocated to Opelousas, Louisiana. Taylor married Mary Tallman of Barbados, with whom he had six children: Sumter, Edward William, Ellen Claudia, Emma, Martha, Henderson, and John James. His second wife was Eliza M. Henderson, daughter of General Henderson. Taylor died in Louisiana in 1821.

Taylor, "John Taylor," 98, 103–4.

Taylor, Thomas (1743–1833): Thomas Taylor was born September 10, 1743, in Virginia, the son of John Taylor. He later moved with his family to South Carolina, where he settled on the Congaree River. Taylor, along with his brother James, owned extensive property in Richland District, where the city of Columbia was established. He also owned other lots and tracts of land in the vicinity as well as several plantations. Taylor served in the American Revolution as a captain in the Third Regiment of the South Carolina Line. He resigned from this post in 1777. When Charleston fell to the British in 1780, he was commissioned captain and subsequently colonel of the militia. While serving under Thomas Sumter, he was wounded and captured at the Battle of Fishing Creek but escaped. While in the military, Taylor remained politically active. The District Between Broad and Catawba Rivers elected him to the First and Second Provincial Congresses, and he held a seat in the First General Assembly. He returned to the house for the Second and Fifth General Assemblies from 1776 to 1778 and 1783 to 1784. The district elected him to the senate for the Seventh General Assembly from 1787 to 1788, and Fairfield, Chester, and Richland chose him for the Ninth, Tenth, Fifteenth, and Sixteenth General Assemblies from 1791 to 1794 and 1802 to 1805. Taylor served as a delegate for Richland County to the state convention to ratify the federal Constitution in 1788 and as a delegate to the state constitutional convention for the District between Broad and Catawba Rivers in 1790. He also held numerous local offices, including justice of the peace for Camden District in 1776 and Richland County in 1785, road commissioner in 1778 and 1791, commissioner for dividing Camden District into counties in 1783, commissioner for inspection and exportation of tobacco at Friday's Ferry on the Congaree River in 1784, 1785, and 1789, commissioner for clearing the Broad River in 1785, commissioner for the establishment and laying out of Columbia in 1786, member of the Privy Council from 1789 to 1790, Richland County court judge from 1791 to 1793, trustee for the free school in 1792 and the academy of Columbia in 1795, commissioner to conduct and manage a lottery to promote manufacture in South Carolina in 1795, Jeffersonian presidential elector in 1796, commissioner for Columbia to prevent the exportation of nonmerchantable bread and flour in 1796, elective trustee of South Carolina College from 1801 to 1809, commissioner to superintend and contract for opening the Broad and Pacolet Rivers in 1801, commissioner for Columbia to open a subscription to the Planters' and Mechanics' Bank of South Carolina in 1810, and commissioner to conduct a lottery for the First Presbyterian Church of Columbia in 1814. Taylor was also a member of the Mount Sion Society and the First Presbyterian Church of Columbia. He married Ann Wyche, daughter of Peter Wyche and Alice Scott, on January 2, 1767. They had twelve children: Sara, John, Rebecca, William, Lucy, Thomas Jr., Anne, Henry Pendleton, James, Jesse Peter, Benjamin Franklin, and George. Taylor died November 16, 1833, and was buried in the family cemetery in Columbia.

Bailey, Morgan, and Taylor, *Biographical Directory of the South Carolina Senate,* 3:1586–87; Taylor, "Col. Thomas Taylor."

Thomas, Thomas Burrington (1790–1829): Thomas Burrington Thomas was born in 1790, the son of Edward Thomas and Elizabeth Burrington.

Thomas graduated from South Carolina College in 1811 and became a planter in Georgetown. He represented All Saints Parish in the Twenty-Fifth General Assembly from 1822 to 1823. Locally he was a member of the Georgetown Library Society from 1812 to 1828 and a free school commissioner of All Saints in 1820. Thomas died unmarried in 1829 and was buried at Northampton in Georgetown.

Moore, *Biographical Directory of the South Carolina House*, 264; Moore, *Roll of Students*, 5.

Thomson/Thompson, Elizabeth Sabb: Elizabeth Sabb was the daughter of William Sabb. She married William Russell Thomson on February 25, 1783. They had nine children: Elizabeth Deborah, William Sabb, Mary Eugenia, Elizabeth Ann, John Linton, Charles Robert, Harriet Deborah, Charlotte Ann, and Caroline Sophia Rebecca. She was left a widow upon Thomson's death on April 7, 1807.

Bailey and Cooper, *Biographical Directory of the South Carolina House*, 714.

Thurston, Samuel Isaac (c. 1756–1820): Samuel Isaac Thurston resided in Georgetown with his wife, Mary C. Coggeshall. They had five children: Mary C., Samuel Isaac, Jane, Robert, and Caroline. Thurston died June 11, 1820.

Census, Second, 1800, Georgetown, S.C.; Thurston, *Descendants of Edward Thurston*, 37.

Toomer, Anthony Vanderhorst (1775–1856): Anthony Vanderhorst Toomer was born November 14, 1775, the son of Joshua Toomer and Mary Vanderhorst. He owned more than two thousand acres in Christ Church Parish and White Hall Plantation, in addition to town lots in St. Philip and St. Michael Parishes. Toomer represented Christ Church in the Fourteenth, Fifteenth, Seventeenth, Eighteenth, Twenty-First, and Twenty-Second General Assemblies from 1800 to 1804, 1806 to 1809, and 1814 to 1817. A member of the Independent Congregational Church at Wappetaw Creek, he married Mary Daniel Legare, with whom he had five children: Joshua, Henry V., A. Legare, Eliza D., and Anthony Jr. Mary died June 1, 1845, and Toomer followed in 1856.

Bailey, *Biographical Directory of the South Carolina House*, 566–67; Census, Third, 1810, Georgetown, S.C.

Trapier, Benjamin Foissin/Fossin: Benjamin Foissin Trapier was the son of Paul Trapier Jr. and Elizabeth Foissin. He attended Harvard University and returned to Georgetown. In the summer of 1798, he served as a captain under Gen. Peter Horry. Trapier resided in Georgetown and was honorably discharged from the Fifth Infantry on June 15, 1800. He married Hannah

Shubrick Heyward (1783–1867) on December 23, 1802. They had at least eight children, including William Heyward, Paul Horry, Benjamin Foissin, and James Heyward.

Bailey and Cooper, *Biographical Directory of the South Carolina House*, 721; Godfrey, "Organization of the Provincial Army," 138; Rogers, *History of Georgetown County*, 183, 205n, 208, 284, 309–11, 320.

Trapier, Hannah Heyward (1783–1867): Hannah Shubrick Heyward was born in November 1783. She married Benjamin Foissin Trapier on December 23, 1802. They had at least eight children, including William Heyward, Paul Horry, Benjamin Foissin, and James Heyward. Hannah was a member of Prince George Winyah Episcopal Church. She died in 1867.

Davidson, *Last Foray*, 256; Rogers, *History of Georgetown County*, 284.

Trapier, William Windham: William Windham Trapier was the son of Elizabeth Foissin and Paul Trapier Jr. He resided in Georgetown. In the summer of 1798, Trapier served as a lieutenant under Gen. Peter Horry. He was honorably discharged on June 15, 1800.

Bailey and Cooper, *Biographical Directory of the South Carolina House*, 721; Godfrey, "Organization of the Provincial Army," 138; Rogers, *History of Georgetown County*, 183.

Travis, Joseph (1786–1868): Joseph Travis was born September 13, 1786, in Maryland, the son of Robert and Phebe Travis. His parents moved to Rockingham County, Virginia, where they were actively involved in the Methodist Church. His family later relocated to South Carolina. Travis was interested in medicine but decided to pursue a career in the ministry. In 1806 he received a recommendation for the Quarterly Methodist Conference for the Annual Conference in Sparta, Georgia. Appointed to the Brunswick Circuit in the Carolinas, he became an itinerant Methodist minister. After serving Broad River in Georgia in 1808, he was appointed to Georgetown in 1809 and Columbia in 1810. Travis's ministry also took him to Alabama, Louisiana, and later Mississippi, where he became a planter. Travis married twice. His first wife was Elizabeth Forster, whom he wed May 1, 1811. She died in 1843, and he married Mary Smith Butler on May 13, 1845. Travis died in Mississippi on September 16, 1868.

Lloyd, *Lives of Mississippi Authors*, 436; Summer, *Autobiography of Reverend Joseph Travis*.

Trezevant, Daniel Heyward (1796–1873): Daniel Heyward Trezevant was born March 18, 1796, in Charleston, the son of Peter Trezevant and Elizabeth

Willoughby Farquhar. Trezevant graduated from South Carolina College in 1813, after which he attended medical school and began practicing medicine in Columbia. Trezevant married Ann Sewell of New York in Charleston on May 3, 1820. They had eight children: James Davis, Ann Sewell, Elizabeth Willoughby, Daniel Heyward, Sarah King, George Sewell, Catherine Elizabeth, and Peter. Ann died August 20, 1838, and Trezevant married Epps Goodwyn Howell on November 15, 1841. They had six children: Jesse Howell, Peter John, Willoughby Farquhar, William Howell, Lucy Mary, and Robert Gilchrist. Trezevant died in 1873.

Trezevant, *Burning of Columbia*, 1–2; Trezevant, *Trezevant Family*, 55–56.

Tucker, Thomas Tudor (1745–1828): Thomas Tudor Tucker was born June 25, 1745, in Port Royal, Bermuda. He trained for medicine in England and worked at St. Bartholomew's Hospital in 1768. Tucker received his medical degree from Edinburgh in 1770. His plans to start a practice in Charleston in 1771 failed, so he relocated to St. George Dorchester Parish. Tucker owned thousands of acres of land throughout South Carolina. During the American Revolution, he served on guard duty at the powder magazine in Dorchester. He was also a surgeon to a grenadier company of militia in 1775. While acting as a physician and surgeon in a Continental Army Hospital, he was taken prisoner by the British and exchanged on June 9, 1781. He accepted a post in Williamsburg, Virginia, but soon after returned to South Carolina. St. George Dorchester elected him to the Second Provincial Congress in 1775, but he refused his seat. He served in the Fourth General Assembly from 1781 to 1782 and was elected to the Fifth General Assembly in 1783 but declined to serve. He returned to the South Carolina House of Representatives for the Sixth General Assembly from 1785 to 1786. Defeated by Ralph Izard for a seat in the Seventh General Assembly, he was later injured in a duel with Izard. While in recovery Tucker won a special election to the Seventh General Assembly and served from 1787 to 1788. He was also elected to the Confederation Congress in 1787 and served in the US House of Representatives for the First and Second Congresses from 1789 to 1793. Other offices he held include warden for Charleston's Third Ward in 1786, privy councilor from 1786 to 1787 and 1787 to 1788, and member of a committee to consider the Jay Treaty in 1795. Tucker was one of the founding members of the South Carolina Medical Society in 1789 and a member of the South Carolina Society of the Cincinnati in 1783. His last appointment was treasurer of the United States in 1801, a post he held until his death. Tucker married Esther Evans, daughter of George Evans, in 1774. They had at least one son, Henry, who died in 1794. Tucker died May 2, 1828, and was buried in the Congressional Cemetery in Washington.

Bailey and Cooper, *Biographical Directory of the South Carolina House*, 725–26.

Wade, George (1747–1823): George Wade was born May 29, 1747, in North Carolina, the son of Thomas Wade. Wade owned property in both North and South Carolina, and in 1797 a Catawba ferry was vested in his name. He resided in both Lancaster County and Richland District. During the American Revolution, Wade served as a lieutenant and captain in the Continental Army and was wounded at the siege of Savannah. The District Eastward of Wateree River elected Wade to the house for the Fifth General Assembly from 1783 to 1784. He also served as tax inquirer and collector for the District Eastward of Wateree River in 1783, trustee for the free school at Columbia in 1792, commissioner for the inspection of tobacco at Columbia in 1797, commissioner of the streets and markets in Columbia in 1797, and commissioner to sell subscriptions for the Columbia Bridge Company in 1818. Wade married Mary McDonald, daughter of Daniel McDonald and Rebecca Middleton, on November 18, 1766. They had five children: Thomas Holden, Daniel, George Jr., Mary, and Rebecca. Mary died August 22, 1779. He married Martha Taylor, daughter of John Taylor, on October 28, 1784. They had one son, James Taylor. Martha died January 13, 1816. Wade died in Columbia on November 24, 1823.

Bailey and Cooper, *Biographical Directory of the South Carolina House,* 733–34; Wright, *Record of the Descendants of Isaac Ross,* 165, 166, 172, 174–80.

Waties, Thomas (1760–1828): Thomas Waties was born February 14, 1760, the son of John Waties and Elizabeth Rothmahler of Georgetown. Waties attended the University of Pennsylvania but left to serve in the American Revolution. In 1776 he was chosen captain in a company comprising Pennsylvania students. He served as midshipman on an expedition to Europe to obtain frigates for the South Carolina navy in 1778. While at sea he was captured by the British and taken to England, where he was released. Waties returned to South Carolina and became a captain in Francis Marion's brigade. After resigning from the militia, Waties studied law under John Julius Pringle and was admitted to the bar on August 16, 1785. He represented Prince George Winyah Parish in the Seventh and Eighth General Assemblies from 1787 to 1790. On January 20, 1789, he was elected associate judge of the Court of Common Pleas and General Sessions, a post he held until December 1811, when he became chancellor of the Court of Equity. Waties was a warden for Charleston's Tenth Ward from 1786 to 1787, member of the Privy Council from 1788 to 1789, delegate for Prince George Winyah to the state convention, where he supported ratification of the federal Constitution in 1788, vestryman for St. Mark Parish Church of the Holy Cross from 1803 to 1828, and a delegate for St. Mark to the state Episcopal Church conventions in 1806, 1807, 1810, 1812, 1815, and 1817. He was also a member of the Mount Sion Society and

Georgetown Library Society. Waties married Margaret Ann Glover, daughter of Joseph Glover and Anne Wilson, on January 19, 1786. They had twelve children: Anna, Elizabeth, Charlotte Alston, John, Thomas, Thomas, Catherine, William, Mary Andrews, Joseph Glover, Wilson Glover, and Julius Pringle. Waties died June 22, 1828, in Columbia and was buried at the Church of the Holy Cross.

Bailey and Cooper, *Biographical Directory of the South Carolina House*, 753–55; Moss, *Roster of South Carolina Patriots*, 970.

Waldo, John (1762–1826): John Waldo was one of the first licentiate ministers to serve the First Baptist Church of Georgetown. He attended Brown University and moved to Georgetown from New York in 1793. Waldo resigned his position shortly after his arrival but remained actively involved in the affairs of the church until his death. He opened a Latin school in Georgetown and co-owned a general store. He was a member of the Winyah Indigo Society, for which he may have been a schoolmaster at one time, and the Georgetown Library Society. Waldo also wrote several nationally acclaimed books, including *Rudiments of English Grammar* (1811), *A Latin Grammar* (1816), and *The Dictionary Spelling Book* (1818). After surviving a stroke in 1816, he died in 1826, leaving a wife and daughter.

Charleston Baptist Association Minutes, November 4, 1826, South Carolina Baptist Historical Collection, James B. Duke Library, Furman University; *Georgetown Gazette and Mercantile Advertiser,* January 1, 1817; "Georgetown Library Society," 98, 100; *Georgetown Times,* March 12 and 26, 1913; Minutes, First Baptist Church of Georgetown, January 12, 1805–November 30, 1821; Rogers, *History of Georgetown County,* 216; Townsend, *South Carolina Baptists,* 59.

Ward, James McCall (d. 1823): James McCall Ward lived in Charleston and was admitted to the South Carolina bar in 1795. He represented St. Philip and St. Michael Parishes in the Seventeenth General Assembly from 1806 to 1808. He was also a member of the South Carolina Society in 1796, member of St. Andrew's Society in 1798, member and senior warden of the Fellowship Society in 1809, warden for Charleston's Eleventh Ward in 1801, the Eighth Ward from 1801 to 1802, the Seventh Ward from 1803 to 1804, the Sixth Ward from 1807 to 1808, and the Fourth Ward from 1814 to 1815, commissioner of the Charleston Workhouse from 1801 to 1806 and 1812 to 1815, commissioner of lamps in 1804 and streets in 1805, captain of Third Beat Company in 1806, major in the state militia from 1806 to 1823, and magistrate for St. Philip and St. Michael Parishes in 1820. He and his wife, Harriet, had at least four children: Joshua, John, Harriet Amanda, and Eliza Ann. Ward died in Charleston on June 3, 1823.

Bailey, *Biographical Directory of the South Carolina House,* 587–88.

Waring, Benjamin: Benjamin Waring was the son of Benjamin and Anne Waring. He was the eldest of four children.

Edgar and Taylor, *Biographical Directory of the South Carolina House,* 698–99.

Waring, Robert H. (1768–1832): Robert H. Waring was the son of Dr. Robert Waring, a surgeon and botanist in the English army. After his father joined the Patriot cause, Waring was adopted by Col. Benjamin Waring. Waring married Mary H. Taylor (b. 1777), daughter of John Taylor and Sarah Hirons and the cousin of Gov. John Taylor. They had thirteen children: Sarah M., Nancy Ann Taylor, John Cannon, Eliza Lavinia, John Partridge, Malachi Howell, Elizabeth Blaun Scott, Benjamin Guignard, Miss Gasway/Gasaway, Mary Caroline, Henry Ware, Eppes Goodwin, and John Carpenter. The Warings resided in Columbia before moving to Florida. Waring died in Florida in 1832 and was buried in Union Cemetery in Miccosukee.

Historical Collections of the Joseph Habersham Chapter, 2:355; Taylor, "John Taylor," 98.

Wayne, William (1734–1818): William Wayne was born in Wilmington, North Carolina, in 1736, the son of Gabriel Wayne. He moved with his father to Pennsylvania, where he received his education. Wayne returned to Charleston as a glazier and painter. After his first wife died, he married Esther Trezevant, daughter of Daniel Trezevant and Anne Sewell, on May 8, 1777. They moved to Georgetown and had five children: Francis Asbury, Jacob, Elizabeth, William, and Gabriel. It was there that Wayne converted to Methodism. He joined the Methodist Society on August 25, 1774, after hearing Bishop Francis Asbury preach in Georgetown. He received his license to preach and was ordained a deacon in 1791. Wayne died in 1818.

Burgess, *Chronicles of St. Marks Parish,* 67; *Methodist Magazine* (1818): 1:455–59; Snowden and Cutler, *History of South Carolina,* 5:219.

Williams, Otho Holland (1749–1794): Otho Holland Williams served in the Continental Army during the American Revolution. In 1775 he was appointed a lieutenant in a company of Maryland riflemen and joined the army near Boston. The following year he was promoted to major and took command of the regiment after the death of the commanding officer. He was wounded and captured at Fort Washington in New York and imprisoned until 1778. While in prison he was promoted to colonel, and after his release he commanded the Sixth Maryland Regiment of the Continental Army and led it into battle at Monmouth on June 28, 1778. He was ordered south in 1780 to form part of Gen. Horatio Gates's army. After the Battle of Camden, he commanded a corps of light troops and fought at the Battle of Guilford Courthouse, after which he returned to South Carolina to avenge his defeat at Camden. When the war ended, he moved to Baltimore and became a merchant. Williams died on his way home from a trip to Barbados in 1794.

Aronson and Wieseman, *Perfect Likeness,* 307; Konstam and Hook, *Guilford Courthouse,* 31.

Williamson, Sterling C. (c. 1766–1841): Sterling C. Williamson was born around 1766. He later moved to South Carolina and served as sheriff of Richland District from 1799 to 1823. He was also a commissioner for free schools in Richland. Williamson had at least one son, Sterling C. Williamson Jr. Williamson died in 1841 in Georgia.

Holcomb, *South Carolina Magazine of Ancestral Research,* nos. 21–23: 178; *Resolutions of the General Assembly, 1823,* 125.

Wilson, John Lyde (1784–1849): John Lyde Wilson was born in May 1784, the son of John Wilson and Mary Lyde. He studied law under Samuel Chase in Baltimore and was admitted to the Maryland bar. He returned to South Carolina and was admitted to the state bar in 1807. Wilson owned property in Prince George Winyah Parish, and he represented Marlboro District in the South Carolina House of Representatives for the Seventeenth General Assembly from 1806 to 1808. He was elected to the Nineteenth General Assembly in 1810 to represent Prince George, but the election was declared null and void. Prince George elected him to the Twentieth and Twenty-Second General Assemblies, and he served from 1812 to 1813 and 1816 to 1817. He sat in the state senate on behalf of Prince George for the Twenty-Third, Twenty-Fourth, and Twenty-Fifth General Assemblies from 1818 to 1823. He was president of the Twenty-Fifth General Assembly. Wilson was elected governor of South Carolina in 1822 and resigned his senate seat. When his term ended, he once again served in the senate for Prince George in the Twenty-Seventh and Twenty-Eighth General Assemblies from 1826 to 1829. He was a delegate for St. Philip and St. Michael Parishes at the Nullification Convention from 1832 to 1833, where he voted in favor of nullification. He was also militia lieutenant in 1809, commissioner to superintend the building of a jail in Georgetown District in 1810, intendant for Georgetown from 1811 to 1812, captain from 1812 to 1833, director of the Bank of the State of South Carolina in 1814, member of the Georgetown Library Society from 1817 to 1820, elective and ex officio trustee for South Carolina College from 1821 to 1824, commissioner to choose a place for and to erect a lunatic asylum and a school for the deaf and dumb in 1821, member of the Charleston Library Society in 1822, grand master and grand high priest of the Grand Lodge of the Ancient Freemasons, assistant quartermaster general in 1833, and member and solicitor of the Liverpool Line Packet

Company in 1835 and the Charleston Steam Packet Company in 1835. Also an author, he coedited a Charleston newspaper during the War of 1812, penned *Code of Honor*, and published a translation of Lucius Apuleius's *Cupid and Psyche*. Accused of slander, Wilson dueled with Gov. Keating Simons in 1819 and shot Simons in the hip. He married Charlotte Alston, daughter of William Alston and Mary Ashe, on December 31, 1809. They had two daughters. Charlotte died November 26, 1817, and Wilson married Rebecca Eden in 1825. They had three children. Wilson died February 13, 1849, in Charleston.

Bailey, Morgan, and Taylor, *Biographical Directory of the South Carolina Senate*, 3:1758–59; Halpern and Dal Lago, *Slavery and Emancipation*, 149; Simons, *Thomas Grange Simons III*, 87.

Wise, Thomas: Thomas Wise served in the cavalry under Capt. Harry Linus and Col. Peter Horry. Before Charleston fell to the British in 1780, he was under the command of Capt. Richard Richardson and subsequently Gen. Francis Marion.

Moss, *Roster of South Carolina Patriots*, 1007.

Withers, John: John Withers was the son of John Withers, who fought in the American Revolution. Withers married Elizabeth Belin, daughter of James Belin.

Butt, "Belin Genealogy," 62–63; O'Kelley, *Unwaried Patience and Fortitude*, 630.

Woodrop, John: John Woodrop was a merchant in Charleston.

Census, Fourth, 1820, Charleston, S.C.; Hagy, *Directories for the City of Charleston*, 30.

Wragg, John Ashby (1805–70): John Ashby Wragg was the son of Maj. Samuel Wragg and Mary Ashby I'On. Wragg graduated from South Carolina College and earned his MD from the University of Pennsylvania in 1828. He attended the Sorbonne in France from 1828 to 1829. When he returned to America, he became a rice planter and purchased land in Savannah. Wragg married Caroline McDowall (1816–1858), daughter of Andrew McDowall and Pamela Cleary, in 1838. They had seven children. Wragg joined the Savannah Medical Society in 1850. In 1861 he was vice chairman of the Board of Health. Wragg died in 1870.

Hain, *Confederate Chronicle*, 3–8.

Wragg, Samuel (1770–1844): Samuel Wragg was born in 1770, the son of Samuel Wragg and Judith Rothmahler. He attended Harvard University and returned to South Carolina to become a planter in Prince George Winyah

Parish. Wragg represented Prince George Winyah in the Eleventh General Assembly from 1794 to 1795. He also served in the Fourteenth and Fifteenth General Assemblies from 1800 to 1804. Wragg was a militia inspector and major from 1797 to 1844, commissioner to erect a magazine and laboratory in or near Georgetown in 1797, member of the Georgetown Library Society from 1823 to 1830, commissioner to determine a site for a ferry over Sampit Creek in 1807, member of the Cooper River Bridge Company in 1810, director of the Georgetown branch of the Bank of the State of South Carolina from 1819 to 1822, member of the Charleston Library Society from 1823 to 1830, cashier of the Charleston branch of the Bank of the State of South Carolina from 1824 to 1843, trustee for the College of Charleston from 1829 to 1839, and commissioner of the poor on Charleston Neck from 1832 to 1836, as well as being an active member of Prince George Winyah Episcopal Church. Wragg married Mary Ashby I'On, daughter of Jacob Bond I'On and Mary Ashby, on February 19, 1801. They had eight children: Samuel, John Ashby, William Thomas, Mary I'On, Sarah Lowndes, Henrietta Susannah, Thomas Lowndes, and Ann Ferguson. Wragg died in 1844.

Bailey, *Biographical Directory of the South Carolina House,* 618–19.

Youngblood, William: William Youngblood was the son of Peter Youngblood. He inherited Fair Spring Plantation in St. Bartholomew Parish from his father. Youngbood represented St. Bartholomew in the Twentieth and Twenty-Second General Assemblies from 1812 to 1817. He also served as lieutenant governor of South Carolina from 1818 to 1820, sheriff for Colleton District from 1804 to 1808, commissioner to contract for and to superintend repairs to the Colleton District jail in 1807, commissioner to open the two branches of the Salkehatchie River, militia captain of the Twenty-Fourth Regiment from 1807 to 1810 and Fifth Brigade from 1812 to 1819, major general of the Second Division from 1819 to 1829, ex officio trustee for South Carolina College from 1818 to 1820, and vestryman and delegate for St. Bartholomew Episcopal Church. Youngblood married Elizabeth Singleton of St. Bartholomew on November 9, 1800. He later married Eliza Bower, widow of Paul Walter Bower, on October 8, 1822. Youngblood was dead by 1830.

Bailey, *Biographical Directory of the South Carolina House,* 52.

Bibliography

MANUSCRIPTS

Charleston Baptist Association. Minutes. South Carolina Baptist Historical Collection, James B. Duke Library, Furman University.

First Baptist Church of Georgetown. Minutes. Georgetown Baptist Historical Society Archives, Georgetown, SC.

General Assembly Petitions. South Carolina Department of Archives and History, Columbia.

South Carolina Wills. South Carolina Department of Archives and History, Columbia.

William Hasell Gibbes Papers. South Caroliniana Library, Columbia.

NEWSPAPERS

Camden Gazette
Carolina Gazette
City Gazette and Daily Advertiser
Columbian Herald/Patriotic Courier of North-America
Commercial Advertiser
Connecticut Journal
State Gazette of South-Carolina
Winyaw Intelligencer

OFFICIAL RECORDS

Acts and Joint Resolutions of the General Assembly of the State of South-Carolina Passed in December, 1823. Charleston: Faust, 1824.

Acts of the General Assembly of the State of South-Carolina. 2 vols. Columbia: Faust, 1808.

Benton, Thomas Hart. *Abridgement of the Debates of Congress, from 1789–1856. From Gales and Seaton's Annals of Congress . . . .* 16 vols. New York: Appleton, 1857–59.

Cooper, Thomas, and David James McCord. *The Statutes at Large of South Carolina: Acts, 1716–1752.* 10 vols. Columbia: Johnston, 1836–98.

De Saussure, Henry William. *Reports of Cases Argued and Determined in the Court of Chancery of the State of South Carolina, from the Revolution to December, 1813, Inclusive.* 4 vols. Columbia: Cline & Hines, 1817–19.

Hutson, Francis M., ed. *Journal of the Constitutional Convention of South Carolina, May 10, 1790–June 3, 1790.* Columbia: Historical Commission of South Carolina, 1946.

Journal of the Executive Proceedings of the Senate of the United States. 18 vols. Washington, D.C.: US Government Printing Office, 1828–87.

Journal of the House of Representatives of the General Assembly of the State of South Carolina, Being the Regular Session Beginning Tuesday, January 9, 1906. Columbia: Gonzales & Bryan, 1906.

Lowrie, Walter, and Matthew St. Clair Clarke, eds. *American State Papers: Documents, Legislative and Executive, of the Congress of the United States . . . .* 38 vols. Washington, D.C.: Gales & Seaton, 1833–61.

McCord, David J., ed. *Chancery Cases Argued and Determined in the Court of Appeals of South Carolina, from January 1825 to May 1826.* Philadelphia: Carey, Lea & Carey, 1827.

Miller, Branch Walthus, and Thomas Curry. *Reports of Cases Argued and Determined in the Supreme Court of the State of Louisiana.* 19 vols. New Orleans: Penniman, 1831–42.

Records of the Columbia Historical Society. Washington, D.C.: Columbia Historical Society, 1909.

Report of the Commissioner of Patents for the Year 1858: Arts and Manufactures in Three Volumes. 3 vols. Washington, D.C.: Steedman, 1859.

Reports of Equity Cases Determined in the Court of Appeals of the State of South Carolina. Columbia: Black & Sweeny, 1825.

The Reports of the Committees of the Senate of the United States for the First Session, Thirty-Third Congress, 1853–'54. Washington, D.C.: Tucker, 1854.

Resolutions of the General Assembly of the State of South Carolina Passed in December 1823. Columbia: Faust, 1824.

Treese, Joel D., ed. *Biographical Directory of the American Congress, 1774–1996.* Alexandria, Va.: CQ Staff Directories, 1997.

United States Coast Pilot Atlantic Coast. Washington, D.C.: Government Printing Office, 1913.

JOURNAL ARTICLES AND BOOK CHAPTERS

Allston, R. F. W. "On Sea Coast Crops." *American Cotton Planter* 2 (1854): 1–381.

Ames, Joseph S. "The Cantey Family." *South Carolina Historical and Genealogical Magazine* 11, no. 4 (1910): 203–58.

Berry, C. B. "The Sage of Matthew Dolan Church." *Names in South Carolina* 14 (1977): 11–12.

Bossard, Joseph S. "Reflections on Planting of Seed Rice." *Southern Agriculturalist* 1 (1828): 115–17.

Boozer, Herman Wyse. "Bethany Church and Related Names in Upper Richland County." *Names in South Carolina* 19 (1972): 1–54.

Bull, H. D. "Kinloch of South Carolina." *South Carolina Historical and Genealogical Magazine* 46, no. 2 (1945): 63–69; no. 3 (1945): 159–65.

Burns, Martha Bailey. "Vincent Guerin of St. Thomas and St. Denis." *Huguenot Society of South Carolina* 69 (1964): 37–46.

Burns, Martha B., and Alice G. Burkette. "Peyre Records." *Huguenot Society of South Carolina* 79 (1974): 164–76.

———. "Peyre Records." *Huguenot Society of South Carolina* 80 (1975): 133–54.

Butt, Mary McLure. "Belin Genealogy." *Huguenot Society of South Carolina* 67 (1962): 61–64.

Colcok, Charles J. "The Marion Family." *Huguenot Society of South Carolina* 22 (1916): 37–49.

"Constitution of the American Seamen's Friend Society." *Sailor's Magazine and Naval Journal* 1 (1829): 32–34.

Côté, Richard N. "South Carolina Methodist Records." *South Carolina Historical Magazine*. 85, no. 1 (1984): 51–57.

Cuttino, G. P. "The Descendants of William Cuttino." *Huguenot Society of South Carolina* 82 (1977): 133–59.

———. "Further Notes on the History of the Cuttino Family, 1687–1932." *Huguenot Society of South Carolina* 65 (1960): 23–34.

———. "Notes on the History of the Cothonneau Family, 1585–1687." *Huguenot Society of South Carolina* 45 (1940): 42–67.

Cuttino, John S. "Cuttino Inscriptions from Tombstones in the 'Old Baptist Church Cemetery in Georgetown.'" *Huguenot Society of South Carolina* 45 (1940): 57–59.

Davant, Richard James. "Appendices to the Davant Family." *Huguenot Society of South Carolina* 75 (1970): 170–230.

Dominick, Ethel Wannamaker. "Poinsett Genealogy: Additions and Corrects also Descendants of Christopher Samuel Lovell." *Huguenot Society of South Carolina* 86 (1981): 68–79.

Draper, Bell Merrill. "Genealogical Department." *Daughters of the American Revolution Magazine* 50, no. 1 (1917): 343–58.

Eaddy, Elaine Y. "Capt. Samuel Bigham's Company War of 1812." *Three Rivers Chronicle* 1, no. 1 (1981): 3.

Eno, Clara B. "Territorial Governors of Arkansas." *Arkansas Historical Quarterly* 4 (1945): 276–84.

Feight, Andrew Lee. "Edmund Botsford and Richard Furman: Slavery in the South Carolina Lowcountry, 1766–1825." *Journal of the South Carolina Baptist Historical Society* 19 (1993): 1–22.

FitzSimons, Mabel Trott. "Perdriau." *Huguenot Society of South Carolina* 68 (1963): 72–86.

"General Thomas Pinckney: A Carolinian." *Sewanee River* 4, no. 1 (1895): 80–86.

"The Georgetown Library Society." *South Carolina Historical and Genealogical Magazine* 25, no. 2 (1924): 94–100.

Gilmore, Janet C. "Flatboats." In *The American Midwest: An Interpretive Encyclopedia,* 414–15. Bloomington: Indiana University Press, 2007.

Godfrey, Carlos E. "Organization of the Provincial Army of the United States in the Anticipated War with France, 1798–1800." *Pennsylvania Magazine of History and Biography* 38, no. 149 (1914): 129–205.

Goodner, Wes. "George Izard." In *The Encyclopedia of Arkansas History and Culture.* Updated May 27, 2009. http://www.encyclopediaofarkansas.net/encyclopedia/entry-detail.aspx?entryID=3662.

Gratz, Simon. "The Generals of the Continental Line in the Revolutionary War." *Pennsylvania Magazine of History and Biography* 27, no. 4 (1903): 385–403.

Gregorie, Anne King. "Christ Church, 1706–1959, a Plantation Parish of the South Carolina Establishment." *Dalcho Historical Society* 15 (1961): 1–169.

Groome, J. R. "Sedan Chair Porches: A Detail of Georgian Architecture in St. George's." *Caribbean Quarterly* 10, no. 3 (1964): 31–33.

Hamilton, Elizabeth Verner. "Mulberry." *Charleston Museum Quarterly* 2, no. 1 (1932): 7–12.

Hinton, John DuBose. "John DuBose Family." *Huguenot Society of South Carolina* 79 (1974): 138–63.

"Historical Sketch of the Prioleau Family in Europe and America." *Huguenot Society of South Carolina* 6 (1899): 5–37.

Ingersoll, Charles J. "The Battle of the Thames." In *The Great Republic by the Master Historians,* edited by Charles Morris and Oliver H. G. Leigh, 3:27–32. 4 vols. New York: Belcher, 1902.

"Inscriptions from the Churchyard of Prince George Winyah Georgetown, South Carolina." *South Carolina Historical and Genealogical Magazine* 31, no. 3 (1930): 184–208; no. 4 (1930): 292–313.

"Izard of South Carolina." *South Carolina Historical and Genealogical Magazine* 2, no. 3 (1901): 205–40.

Jervey, Elizabeth Heyward. "Marriage and Death Notices from the *City Gazette.*" *South Carolina Historical and Genealogical Magazine* 28, no. 4 (1927): 236–45.

———. "Marriage and Death Notices from the *City Gazette.*" *South Carolina Historical and Genealogical Magazine* 31, no. 1 (1930): 67–73.

———. "Marriage and Death Notices from the *City Gazette and Daily Advertiser.*" *South Carolina Historical and Genealogical Magazine* 33, no. 4 (1932): 299–305.

———. "Marriage and Death Notices from the *City Gazette and Daily Advertiser.*" *South Carolina Historical and Genealogical Magazine* 34, no. 1 (1933): 40–46.

———. "Marriage and Death Notices from the *City Gazette and Daily Advertiser.*" *South Carolina Historical and Genealogical Magazine* 35, no. 4 (1934): 166–72.

———. "Marriage and Death Notices from the *City Gazette* of Charleston, S.C." *South Carolina Historical and Genealogical Magazine* 45, no. 1 (1944): 22–29.

———. "Marriage and Death Notices from the *City Gazette* of Charleston, S.C." *South Carolina Historical and Genealogical Magazine* 46, no. 1 (1945): 15–24.

———. "Marriage and Death Notices from the *City Gazette* of Charleston, S.C." *South Carolina Historical and Genealogical Magazine* 49, no. 3 (1948): 155–62.

———. "Marriage and Death Notices from the *City Gazette* of Charleston, S.C." *South Carolina Historical and Genealogical Magazine* 50, no. 1 (1949): 14–18.

Jones, Laura B. "Georgia Marriages and Deaths." *Georgia Genealogical Magazine* 7 (1963): 356–424.

Lincoln, Natalie Sumner. "Engraved Portraits of American Patriots." *Daughters of the American Revolution Magazine* 50 (1917): 286–91.

Lynch, Branford Gist. "Brigadier General Mordecai Gist." *Daughters of the American Revolution Magazine* 15 (1931): 720–34.

Manigault, Louis, and Gabriel E. Manigault. "The Manigault Family of South Carolina from 1685–1886." *Huguenot Society of South Carolina* 4 (1897): 48–84.

"Marriage and Death Notices from the *City Gazette*." *South Carolina Historical and Genealogical Magazine* 27, no. 3 (1926): 172–80.

Mayrant, William, and Ernest M. Lander Jr. "Two Letters by William Mayrant on His Cotton Factory, 1815." *South Carolina Historical Magazine*, no. 1 (1953): 1–5.

Mazyck, Katherine B. "Report of the Historian." *Huguenot Society of South Carolina* 41 (1936): 16–18.

———. "Wills of South Carolina Huguenots." *Huguenot Society of South Carolina* 38 (1933): 87–100.

Matthews, Donald G. "The Methodist Mission to the Slaves, 1829–1844." *Journal of American History* 51, no. 4 (1965): 615–31.

Nord, Barbara K. "George Whiting Flagg and His South Carolina Portraits." *South Carolina Historical Magazine* 83, no. 3 (1982): 214–34.

"Notices of Conspicuous Members of the Gaillard Family." *Huguenot Society of South Carolina* 5 (1897): 91–102.

Ochenkowski, J. P. "The Origins of Nullification in South Carolina." *South Carolina Historical Magazine* 83, no. 2 (1982): 121–53.

Olsberg, R. Nicholas. "Ship Registers in the South Carolina Archives, 1734–1780." *South Carolina Historical and Genealogical Magazine* 74, no. 4 (1973).

Owen, Thomas M. "Necrology." *Transactions of the Alabama Historical Society* 3 (1898–99): 22–26.

Owings, Nettie Smith, and Marvin Alpheus Owings. "Lesesne Genealogy." *Huguenot Society of South Carolina* 84 (1979): 140–62.

"Partial Roster of Officers under Washington, July, 1778." *Pennsylvania Magazine of History and Biography* 18, no. 1 (1894): 64–72.

Peeples, Robert E. H. "The Memoirs of Benjamin Spicer Stafford." *Huguenot Society of South Carolina* 82 (1977): 100–105.

———. "The Memoirs of Benjamin Spicer Stafford." *Huguenot Society of South Carolina* 84 (1979): 105–6

Peeples, Robert E. H., and Sarah Nichols Pinckney. "Jaudon of Carolina." *Huguenot Society of South Carolina* 88 (1983): 136–46.

Pickens, E. B. "Life of General Pickens." *Journal of American History* 18 (1924): 131–36.

"Records Kept by Colonel Isaac Hayne." *South Carolina Historical and Genealogical Magazine* 11, no. 3 (1910): 160–70.

Richardson, William, and Emma B. Richardson. "Letters of William Richardson, 1765–1784." *South Carolina Historical and Genealogical Magazine* 47, no. 1 (1946): 1–20.

Salley, A. S. Jr. "Captain William Capers and Some of His Descendants." *South Carolina Historical and Genealogical Magazine* 2, no. 4 (1901): 273–98.

———. "Daniel Trezevant, Huguenot, and Some of His Descendants." *South Carolina Historical and Genealogical Magazine* 3, no. 1 (1902): 24–56.

———. "Horry's Notes to Weems's 'Life of Marion.'" *South Carolina Historical and Genealogical Magazine* 60, no. 3 (1959): 119–22.

Salley, A. S., ed. "Journal of General Peter Horry." *South Carolina Historical and Genealogical Magazine* 39, no. 1 (1938): 46–49.

———. "Journal of General Peter Horry." *South Carolina Historical and Genealogical Magazine* 39, no. 4 (1938): 157–59.

———. "Journal of General Peter Horry." *South Carolina Historical and Genealogical Magazine* 44, no. 2 (1943): 124–29.

———. "Journal of General Peter Horry." *South Carolina Historical and Genealogical Magazine* 47, no. 2 (1946): 121–23.

———. "Journal of General Peter Horry." *South Carolina Historical and Genealogical Magazine* 47, no. 3 (1946): 181–83.

Schieffelin, Elizabeth Wellborn. "The Birth-Date of General Peter Horry." *Huguenot Society of South Carolina* 85 (1980): 62–63.

Schulz, Constance B. "Pinckney and Horry." In *South Carolina Women: Their Lives and Times*, 2 vols., edited by Marjorie Julian Spruill, Valinda W. Littlefield, and Joan Marie Johnson, 1:79–108. Athens: University of Georgia Press, 2009.

Simmons, Slann Legare Clement, ed. "Recorded Burials in the Huguenot Churchyard of Charleston." *Huguenot Society of South Carolina* 57 (1952): 31–65.

Simms, William Gilmore. "The Marion Family." *Southern and Western Magazine and Review* 2, no. 1 (1845): 50–58.

Smith, Henry A. M. "Georgetown: The Original Plan and Earliest Settlers." *South Carolina Historical and Genealogical Magazine* 9 (1908): 85–101.

Soule, J., and T. Mason, eds. *The Methodist Magazine*. 11 vols. New York: John C. Totten, 1818–1828.

Sutherland, Daniel E. "The Rise and Fall of Esther B. Cheesborough: The Battles of a Literary Lady." *South Carolina Historical Magazine* 84, no. 1 (1983): 22–34.

"Tablets Entered in Huguenot Memoir Book." *Huguenot Society of South Carolina* 75 (1970): 59–90.

Taylor, B. F. "Col. Thomas Taylor." *South Carolina Historical and Genealogical Magazine* 27, no. 4 (1926): 204–11.

———. "John Taylor and His Taylor Descendants." *South Carolina Historical and Genealogical Magazine* 8, no. 2 (1907): 95–119.

"The Remarkable Application of N. H. R. Dawson." *Huguenot Society of South Carolina* 80 (1975): 46–50.

Trapier, Paul. "Notices of Ancestors and Relatives, Paternal and Maternal." *Huguenot Society of South Carolina* 58 (1953): 29–54.

Tyler, Lyon G. "Lightfoot Family." *William and Mary Quarterly* 3, no. 2 (1894): 104–11.

Wade, Arthur P. "Fort Winyaw at Georgetown." *South Carolina Historical Magazine* 84, no. 4 (1983): 214–49.

Wates, Mylma Ann. "Meanderings of a Manuscript: General Peter Horry's Collection of Francis Marion Letters." *South Carolina Historical Magazine* 81, no. 4 (1980): 352–61.

Webber, Mabel L. "Dr. John Rutledge and His Descendants." *South Carolina Historical and Genealogical Magazine* 31, no. 1 (1930): 7–25.

———. "Marriage and Death Notices from the *Charleston Morning Post and Daily Advertiser*." *South Carolina Historical and Genealogical Magazine* 20, no. 1 (1919): 52–56.

———. "Marriage and Death Notices from the *City Gazette*." *South Carolina Historical and Genealogical Magazine* 21, no. 3 (1920): 121–31.

———. "Marriage and Death Notices from the *City Gazette*." *South Carolina Historical and Genealogical Magazine* 22, no. 2 (1921): 65–72.

———. "Marriage and Death Notices from the *City Gazette*." *South Carolina Historical and Genealogical Magazine* 23, no. 3 (1922): 152–57.

———. "Marriage and Death Notices from the *City Gazette*." *South Carolina Historical and Genealogical Magazine* 24, no. 1 (1923): 30–39.

———. "Marriage and Death Notices from the *South Carolina Weekly Gazette*." *South Carolina Historical and Genealogical Magazine* 18, no. 3 (1917): 143–48.

———. "The Mayrant Family." *South Carolina Historical and Genealogical Magazine* 27, no. 2 (1926): 81–90.

Weidner, Paul R., ,ed. "The Journal of John Blake White." *South Carolina Historical and Genealogical Magazine* 42, no. 2 (1941): 55–71.

Wilkinson, Constance Jenkins. "Huguenots on Laurel Hill." *Huguenot Society of South Carolina* 79 (1974): 83–99.

Williams, Jack Kenny. "The Code of Honor in Ante-Bellum South Carolina." *South Carolina Historical Magazine* 54, no. 3 (1953): 113–28.

Books

Abridgment of the Debates of Congress, from 1789–1856, from Gales and Seaton's Annals of Congress . . . . 16 vols. New York: Appleton, 1857–61.

Ackerman, Robert K. *Wade Hampton III*. Columbia: University of South Carolina Press, 2007.

Alderman, Edwin Anderson, ed. *The Library of Southern Literature*. 16 vols. Atlanta: Martin & Hoyt, 1907–13.

Aronson, Julie, and Marjorie E. Wieseman. *Perfect Likeness: European and American Portrait Miniatures from the Cincinnati Art Museum*. New Haven, Conn.: Yale University Press, 2006.

Asbury, Herbert. *A Methodist Saint: The Life of Bishop Asbury.* New York: Knopf, 1927.

Bacon, Margaret Hope. *But One Race: The Life of Robert Purvis*. Albany: State University of New York Press, 2007.

Bailey, L. H. *The Recent Apple Failures of Western New York*. Ithaca, N.Y.: Cornell University Press, 1894.

Bailey, N. Louise. *Biographical Directory of the South Carolina House of Representatives, 1791–1815*. Vol. 4. Columbia: University of South Carolina Press, 1984.

Bailey, N. Louise, and Elizabeth Ivey Cooper. *Biographical Directory of the South Carolina House of Representatives, 1775–1790*. Vol. 3. Columbia: University of South Carolina Press, 1981.

Bailey, N. Louise, Mary L. Morgan, and Carolyn R. Taylor. *Biographical Directory of the South Carolina Senate, 1776–1985*. 3 vols. Columbia: University of South Carolina Press, 1986.

Baker, Robert A., and Paul J. Craven Jr. *Adventure in Faith: The First 300 Years of First Baptist Church, Charleston, South Carolina*. Nashville: Broadman, 1982.

Barefoot, Daniel W. *Touring South Carolina's Revolutionary War Sites*. Winston-Salem, N.C.: Blair, 1999.

Barksdale, John A. *Barksdale Family History and Genealogy*. Richmond, Va.: Byrd, 1940.

Bell, James Elton, and Frances Jean Bell. *Sir Robert Bell and His Early Virginia Colony Descendents*. Tucson, Ariz.: Wheatmark, 2007.

Ben-Yami, M. *Purse-Seining with Small Boats*. Rome: Food and Agricultural Organization of the United Nations, 1967.

Biographical and Historical Memoirs of Mississippi: Embracing an Authentic and Comprehensive Account of the Chief Events in the History of the State and a Record of the Lives of Many of the Most Worthy and Illustrious Families and Individuals. Spartanburg, S.C.: Reprint, 1978.

Black, Monroe. *Echoes in Time: The Murray, Connor, and Moorer Families of South Carolina*. Salem, Mass.: Higginson Book, 1991.

Boddie, John Bennett. *Historical Southern Families*. 2 vols. Redwood City, Cal.: Pacific Coast, 1957.

Boddie, William Willis. *History of Williamsburg: Something about the People of Williamsburg County, South Carolina, from the First Settlement by Europeans about 1705 until 1923*. Columbia: State, 1923.

Boyd, Muff, and James H. Clark. *Georgetown and Winyah Bay*. Charleston: Arcadia, 2010.

Boyle, Esmeralda. *Biographical Sketches of Distinguished Marylanders*. Baltimore: Kelly, Piet, 1877.

Blair, William Allen. *A Historical Sketch of Banking in North Carolina*. New York: Rhodes, 1899.

Broome, James Foster, Jr. "Edmund Botsford: A Model of Regular Baptist Ministry in South Carolina." MA thesis, Southern Baptist Theological Seminary, 1985.

Brown, James. *The Forester*. 2 vols. Edinburgh: Blackwood, 1861.

Brown, John Howard. *The Cyclopædia of American Biographies. Comprising the Men and Women of the United States Who Have Been Identified with the Growth of the Nation*. 7 vols. Boston: Cyclopædia, 1897–1905.

Buell, Augustus C. *Paul Jones, Founder of the American Navy: A History*. 2 vols. New York: Scribner, 1900.

Bull, Henry DeSaussure. *All Saints' Church, Waccamaw*. Georgetown, S.C.: Winyaw, 1968.

Bullard, Mary Ricketson. *Robert Stafford of Cumberland Island: Growth of a Planter*. Athens: University of Georgia Press, 1995.

Bulloch, Joseph Gaston Baillie. *A History and Genealogy of the Habersham Family*. Columbia: Bryan, 1901.

Burgess, James M. *Chronicles of St. Marks Parish: Santee Circuit, and Williamsburg Township*. Columbia: Calvo, 1888.

Burke, Arthur Meredyth, ed. *The Prominent Families of the United States of America*. Baltimore: Genealogical Publishing, 2008.

Burke, John. *A General and Heraldic Dictionary of the Peerage and Baronetage of the British Empire*. 4th ed. 2 vols. London: Colburn & Bentley, 1832.

Burstyn, Joan N. *Past and Promise: Lives of New Jersey Women*. Syracuse: Syracuse University Press, 1997.

Cassels, R., ed. *Records of the Family of Cassels and Connexions*. Edinburgh: Constable, 1870.

Catalogue of the Officers and Graduates of Yale University in New Haven, Connecticut, 1701–1915. New Haven: Yale University, 1916.

The Catalogue of the University of South Carolina, 1909–1910. Columbia: Bryan, 1909.

Cheshire, Joseph Blount. *Sketches of Church History in North Carolina: Addresses and Papers*. Wilmington, N.C.: De Rosset, 1892.

Chisholm, Hugh, ed. *The Encyclopedia Britannica*. 12th ed. 31 vols. New York: Cambridge University Press, 1921–22.

Chreitzberg, Abel McKee. *Early Methodism in the Carolinas*. Nashville: Publishing House of the Methodist Episcopal Church, South, 1897.

Clark, Chovine R. *Lineage of Chovine Richardson Clark, Manning, South Carolina*. Sumter, S.C.: Wilder & Ward, 1969.

Clark, Elmer T., J. Manning Potts, and Jacob S. Payton, eds. *The Journal and Letters of Francis Asbury*. Nashville: Abingdon, 1958.

Clark, John F., and Patricia A. Pierce. *Scenic Driving South Carolina*. Guilford, Conn.: Globe Pequot, 2003.

Clark, Robert C., and Chris Horn. *University of South Carolina: A Portrait*. Columbia: University of South Carolina Press, 2001.

Clark, W. A. *A History of the Banking Institutions Organized in South Carolina Prior to 1860*. Columbia: State, 1922.

Cochrane, K. L., ed. *A Fishery Manager's Guidebook*. Rome: Food and Agricultural Organization of the United Nations, 2002.

Columbia: Capital City of South Carolina, 1786–1936. Columbia: Columbia Sesquicentennial Commission, 1936.

Cook, Harvey Toliver. *Rambles in the Pee Dee Basin South Carolina*. Columbia: State, 1926.

Cory, Marielou Armstrong Cory. *Ladies' Memorial Association of Montgomery Alabama.* Montgomery: Alabama Printing, 1902.

Croft, Robert William. *A Southern Legacy: The House of Croft.* Baltimore: Gateway, 1981.

Cuttino, G. P. *History of the Cuttino Family.* Atlanta: Emory University Office of Publications, 1982.

Cyclopedia of Eminent and Representative Men of the Carolinas of the Nineteenth Century. Madison, Wisc.: Brant & Fuller, 1892.

Dalcho, Frederick. *An Historical Account of the Protestant Episcopal Church, in South-Carolina.* Charleston: Thayer, 1820.

Davidson, Chalmers Gaston. *The Last Foray.* Columbia: University of South Carolina Press, 1971.

Devereux, Anthony Q. *The Rice Princes: A Rice Epoch Revisited.* Columbia: State, 1973.

Dexter, Franklin Bowditch. *Biographical Sketches of the Graduates of Yale College.* 6 vols. New Haven, Conn.: Yale University Press, 1885–1912.

Dorman, John Frederick. *Adventures of Purse and Person: Virginia, 1607–1624/5.* Baltimore: Genealogical Publishing, 2005.

Dubose, Joel Campbell. *Notable Men of Alabama: Personal and Genealogical.* 2 vols. Atlanta: Southern Historical Association, 1904.

Eastes, LeRoy Franklin. *The Eastes Family of Indiana.* Decorah, Iowa: Anundsen, 1994.

Edgar, Walter B. *Biographical Directory of the South Carolina House of Representatives Session Lists, 1692–1973.* Vol. 1. Columbia: University of South Carolina Press, 1974.

———. *South Carolina: A History.* Columbia: University of South Carolina Press, 1998.

———, ed. *The South Carolina Encyclopedia.* Columbia: University of South Carolina Press, 2006.

Edgar, Walter B., and N. Louise Bailey. *Biographical Directory of the South Carolina House of Representatives: The Commons House of Assembly, 1692–1775.* Vol. 2. Columbia: University of South Carolina Press, 1977.

Green, Edwin L. *A History of the University of South Carolina.* Columbia: State, 1916.

Ellerbe, Ronald William. *The Ellerbe Family History.* Baltimore: Gateway, 1986.

Ellis, Frampton E. *Some Historic Families of South Carolina.* Atlanta, 1962.

Elzas, Barnett Abraham. *The Jews of South Carolina: From the Earliest Times to the Present Day.* Philadelphia: Lippincott, 1905.

Eulogies on the Life and Death of General George Washington, First President. Boston: Manning & Loring, 1800.

Family Reminiscences of the Pinckney, Brewton, Elliott, Odingsells, Ramsay, and Laurens Families. Charleston: Walker, Evans, 1859.

Friedman, Saul S. *Jews and the American Slave Trade.* New Brunswick, NJ: Transaction, 2000.

Garden, Alexander. *Anecdotes of the American Revolution, Illustrative of the Talents and Virtues of the Heroes and Patriots, Who Acted the Most Conspicuous Parts Therein.* Charleston: Miller, 1828.

Gee, Wilson. *The Gist Family of South Carolina and Its Maryland Antecedents.* Charlottesville, Va.: Jarmans, 1934.

Gibbes, Robert W. *Documentary History of the American Revolution.* Columbia: Banner Steam Power Press, 1853–57.

Glover, James Bolan V. *Colonel Joseph Glover (1719–1783) and His Descendants: Thirteen Generations of the Glover Family.* Marietta, Ga.: Glover Family Association, 1996.

Gourdin, Peter Gaillard IV. *The Gourdin Family.* Easley, S.C.: Southern Historical, 1980.

Graydon, Nell S. *Tales of Columbia.* Columbia: Bryan, 1964.

Green, Edwin L. *A History of Richland County.* Greenville, S.C.: Southern Historical, 1996.

Groves, Joseph Asbury. *The Alstons and Allstons of North and South Carolina.* Atlanta: Franklin, 1901.

Hagy, James W. *Charleston, South Carolina City Directories for the Years 1816, 1819, 1822, 1825, and 1829.* Baltimore: Clearfield Publishing, 1996.

———. *City Directories for Charleston, South Carolina for the Years 1803, 1806, 1807, 1809, and 1813.* Baltimore: Clearfield, 1995.

———. *Directories for the City of Charleston, South Carolina.* Baltimore: Genealogical Publishing, 1997.

———. *People and Professions of Charleston, South Carolina, 1782–1802.* Baltimore: Clearfield, 1992.

Hain, Pamela Chase. *A Confederate Chronicle: The Life of a Civil War Survivor.* Columbia: University of Missouri Press, 2005.

Halpern, Rich, and Enrico Dal Lago, eds. *Slavery and Emancipation.* Malden, Mass.: Blackwell, 2002.

Harllee, William Curry. *Kinfolks.* 4 vols. New Orleans: Searcy & Pfaff, 1934–37.

Hartley, Cecil B. *Life of Major General Henry Lee.* New York: Derby & Jackson, 1859.

———. *The Life of Gen. Francis Marion: Also, Lives of Generals Moultrie and Pickens, and Governor Rutledge with Sketches of Other Distinguished Heroes and Patriots Who Served in the Revolutionary War in the Southern States.* Philadelphia: Potter, 1867.

Hayden, Sidney. *Washington and His Masonic Compeers.* New York: Masonic Publishing and Manufacturing, 1866.

Haynsworth, Hugh Charles. *Haynsworth-Furman and Allied Families.* Sumter, S.C.: Osteen, 1942.

Heidler, David S., and Jeanne T. Heidler, eds. *Encyclopedia of the War of 1812.* Santa Barbara, Cal.: ABC-CLIO, 1997.

Heitman, Francis Bernard. *Historical Register of Officers of the Continental Army during the War of the Revolution.* Washington, D.C.: Rare Book Shop, 1914.

Helffenstein, Abraham Ernest. *Pierre Fauconnier and His Descendants: With Some Account of the Allied Valleaux.* Philadelphia: Burbank, 1911.

Henderson, Archibald. *Washington's Southern Tour, 1791.* Boston: Houghton Mifflin, 1923.

Herbemont, Nicholas. *Pioneering American Wine.* Edited by David S. Shields. Athens: University of Georgia Press, 2009.

Hines, Benjamin McFarland. *Hines and Allied Families.* Ardmore, Penn.: Dorrance, 1920.

Hines, Lois Davidson. *Lynch Families of the Southern States: Lineages and Court Records.* Naugatuck, Conn.: Wulfeck, 1966.

Historical Collections of the Joseph Habersham Chapter, Daughters of the American Revolution. 2 vols. Atlanta: Blosser, 1902.

Hobart, J. H. *Archives of the General Convention.* 5 vols. New York, 1911.

Holcomb, Brent H. *South Carolina Marriages, 1800–1820.* Baltimore: Genealogical Publishing, 1995.

———, ed. *The South Carolina Magazine of Ancestral Research.* 30 vols. Columbia: Holcomb, 1979–2001.

Houston, David Franklin. *A Critical Study of Nullification in South Carolina.* New York: Longmans, Green, 1896.

Howe, George. *History of the Presbyterian Church in South Carolina.* 2 vols. Columbia: Duffie & Chapman, 1870–1883.

Hunemorder, Markus. *The Society of the Cincinnati: Conspiracy and Distrust in Early America.* New York: Gerghahn Books, 2006.

Jenkinson, Gordon B. *Williamsburg District: A History of its People and Places.* Charleston: History Press, 2007.

Johnson, Joseph. *Traditions and Reminiscences Chiefly of the American Revolution in the South: Including Biographical Sketches, Incidents and Anecdotes.* Charleston: Walker & James, 1851.

Johnson, Rossiter. *A History of the War of 1812.* New York: Dodd, Mead, 1882.

Johnston, Henry Poellnitz. *Little Acorns from the Mighty Oak.* Birmingham: Featon, 1962.

Joyner, Charles. W. *Down by the Riverside: A South Carolina Slave Community.* Urbana: University of Illinois Press, 1985.

———. *Shared Traditions: Southern History and Folk Culture.* Urbana: University of Illinois Press, 1999.

Katz-Hyman, Martha B., and Kym S. Rice, eds. *World of a Slave: Encyclopedia of the Material Life of Slaves in the United States.* Santa Barbara, Cal.: Greenwood, 2011.

Konstam, Angus, and Adam Hook. *Guilford Courthouse, 1781.* Oxford: Osprey, 2002.

La Borde, Maximilian. *History of the South Carolina College.* Columbia: Glass, 1859.

Lachicotte, Alberta Morel. *Georgetown Rice Plantations.* Columbia: State Commercial Printing, 1955.

Lathrop, Elsie. *Historic Houses of Early America.* New York: Tudor, 1927.

Lavery, Brian, and Patrick O'Brian. *Nelson's Navy: The Ships, Men, and Organization, 1793–1815.* London: Conway Maritime, 1989.

Leary, Lewis. *The Book-Peddling Parson, An Account of the Life and Works of Mason Locke Weems, Patriot, Pitchman, Author and Purveyor of Morality to the Citizenry of the Early United States of America.* Chapel Hill, N.C.: Algonquin Books, 1984.

Lennon, Gered. *Living With the South Carolina Coast.* Durham, N.C.: Duke University Press, 1996.

Lesesne, J. Mauldin. *The Bank of the State of South Carolina: A General and Political History.* Columbia: University of South Carolina Press, 1970.

Lester, Memory Lee Alldredge. *Old Southern Bible Records.* Baltimore: Genealogical Publishing, 1974.

Lewis, Catherine Heniford. *Horry County, South Carolina, 1730–1993.* Columbia: University of South Carolina Press, 1998.

Lloyd, James B., ed. *Lives of Mississippi Authors, 1817–1967.* Jackson: University of Mississippi Press, 1981.

Ludwig, Charles. *Francis Asbury: God's Circuit Rider.* Milford, Mich.: Mott Media, 1984.

MacDowell, Dorothy Kelly. *Descendants of William Capers and Richard Capers and Related Families.* Columbia: Bryan, 1973.

———. *Gaillard Genealogy: Descendants of Joachim Gaillard and Esther Paperel.* Columbia: Bryan, 1974.

Mackenzie, George Norbury, and Nelson Osgood Rhoades. *Colonial Families of the United States of America.* 6 vols. Baltimore: Genealogical Publishing, 1907–17.

Mallary, Charles D., ed. *Memoirs of Elder Edmund Botsford.* 1832. Springfield, Miss.: Particular Baptist, 2004.

Manigault, Gabriel E. *The Military Career of General George Izard.* New York, 1888.

Many, Louise. *Southern Literature from 1579–1895.* Richmond, Va.: Johnson, 1895.

Mathews, Marguerite Marrée, and Alice Collar Tongue. *Floyd, History and Lineage: Charles Floyd, John Floyd of Virginia, South Carolina, and Camden County, Georgia.* Raleigh: Mathews, 1998.

Mathis, Gerald Ray. *John Horry Dent, South Carolina Aristocrat on the Alabama Frontier.* Tuscaloosa: University of Alabama Press, 1979.

May, John Amasa, and Joan Reynolds Faunt. *South Carolina Secedes.* Columbia: University of South Carolina Press, 1960.

Maybank, David Jr., and Robert P. Stockton. *The Maybank Family of South Carolina.* Greenville, S.C.: Southern Historical Press, 2004.

McCormick, Thomas Carson. *Carson-McCormick Family Memorials.* Madison, Wisc.: McCormick, 1955.

McDaniel, Rick. *An Irresistible History of Southern Food.* Charleston: History Press, 2011.

Mears, Neal F. *A History of the Heverly Family.* Chicago: Bates, 1945.

Meriwether, Robert L. *Planters and Business Men: The Guignard Family of South Carolina, 1795–1930.* Columbia: University of South Carolina Press, 1957.

Merrill, George P. *A Treatise on Rocks, Rock Weathering and Soils.* New York: Macmillan, 1897.

Metcalf, John Calvin. *Library of Southern Literature: Compiled under the Direct Supervision of Southern Men of Letters.* New Orleans: Martin & Hoyt, 1909.

Michie, James L. *Richmond Hill Plantation, 1810–1868.* Spartanburg, S.C.: Reprint, 1990.

Miller, Gustavus Hindman. *The Millers and Millersburg and Their Descendants.* Nashville: Brandon, 1923.

Moore, Alexander. *Biographical Directory of the South Carolina House of Representatives, 1816–1828.* Vol. 5. Columbia: South Carolina Department of Archives and History, 1992.

Moore, Andrew Charles. *Roll of Students of South Carolina College.* Columbia: University of South Carolina Press, 1905.

Moore, John Hammond. *Columbia and Richland County: A South Carolina Community, 1740–1990.* Columbia: University of South Carolina Press, 1993.

Morris, Charles. *Heroes of the Navy in America.* Philadelphia: Lippincott, 1907.

Moss, Bobby Gilmer. *Roster of South Carolina Patriots in the American Revolution.* Baltimore: Genealogical Publishing, 1994.

Murphy, Anne Jacobs Boykin. *History and Genealogy of the Boykin Family.* Richmond, Va.: Murphy, 1964.

O'Kelley, Patrick, ed. *Unwaried Patience and Fortitude: Francis Marion's Orderly Book.* West Conshohocken, Penn.: Infinity, 2006.

O'Neall, John Belton. *Biographical Sketches of the Bench and Bar of South Carolina.* 2 vols. Charleston: Courtenay, 1859.

Oswald, John Clyde. *Printing in the Americas.* New York: Gregg, 1937.

Owen, Thomas McAdory, and Marie Bankhead Owen. *History of Alabama and Dictionary of Alabama Biography.* Vols. 2–3. Chicago: Clarke, 1921.

Paine, Robert. *Life and Times of William McKendree: Bishop of the Methodist Episcopal Church.* Nashville: Publishing House Methodist Episcopal Church, 1922.

Parton, James. *The Life and Times of Aaron Burr.* 2 vols. New York: Chelsea House, 1864.

Pickens, Monroe. *Cousin Monroe's History of the Pickens Family.* Edited by Kate Pickens Day. Easley, SC, 1951.

Pinney, Thomas. *A History of Wine in America from the Beginnings to Prohibition.* 2 vols. Berkeley: University of California Press, 1989–2005.

Pringle, Elizabeth Waties Allston. *Chronicles of Chicora Wood.* New York: Scribner, 1922.

Raven, James. *London Booksellers and American Customers.* Columbia: University of South Carolina Press, 2002.

Raymond, Ida. *Southland Writers: Biographical and Critical Sketches of the Living Female Writers of the South.* 2 vols. Philadelphia: Claxton, Remsen & Haffelfinger, 1870.

Redmond, D., W. M. N. White, and J. Camak, eds. *Southern Cultivator.* 39 vols. Athens: White, 1843–81.

Reese, Lee Fleming. *John Fleming: Carolina to California.* San Diego, Cal.: Goodway Copy Center, 1972.

Register of the General Society of the War of 1812. Washington, D.C.: Society, 1972.

Reno, Linda Davis. *The Maryland 400 in the Battle of Long Island.* Jefferson, N.C.: McFarland, 2008.

Rhyne, Nancy. *Tales from the South Carolina Upstate: Where the Cotton and Peaches Grow.* Charleston: History Press, 2007.

Richardson, Elizabeth Buford. *A Genealogical Record with Reminiscences of the Richardson and Buford Families.* Macon, Ga.: Burke, 1906.

Ripley, George, and Charles Anderson Dana, eds. *The New American Cyclopúdia.* 16 vols. New York: Appleton, 1883.

Rogers, George Jr. *The Evolution of a Federalist: William Loughton Smith of Charleston, 1758–1812.* Columbia: University of South Carolina Press, 1962.

———. *The History of Georgetown County, South Carolina.* Columbia: University of South Carolina Press, 1970.

Rosengarten, Theodore, and Dale Rosengarten. *A Portion of the People: Three Hundred Years of Southern Jewish Life.* Columbia: University of South Carolina Press, 2002.

Rowland, Dunbar. *History of Mississippi: The Heart of the South.* 2 vols. Chicago: Clarke, 1925.

Rowland, Eron Opha. *Mississippi Territory in the War of 1812.* Baltimore: Genealogical Publishing, 1968.

Rudolph, L. C. *Francis Asbury.* Nashville: Abingdon, 1966.

Ruffin, Edmund, and Jack Temple Kirby. *Nature's Management: Writings on Landscape and Reform, 1822–1859.* Athens: University of Georgia Press, 2006.

Salley, A. S. *Marriage Notices in the South-Carolina Gazette and Its Successors (1732–1801).* Albany, N.Y.: Munsell, 1902.

Salsi, Lynn, and Margaret Simms. *Columbia: A History of a Southern Capital.* Charleston: Arcadia, 2003.

Sanders, Albert E., and William Dewey Anderson. *Natural History Investigations in South Carolina.* Columbia: University of South Carolina Press, 1999.

Sass, Herbert Ravenel. *The Story of the South Carolina Lowcountry.* West Columbia, S.C.: Hyer, 1956.

Savage, Beth L. *African American Historic Places.* New York: Wiley, 1996.

Schwab, William T. *The Crofts of South Carolina.* Mt. Pleasant, S.C.: Schwab, 2004.

Scott, Edwin J. *Random Recollections of a Long Life, 1806 to 1876.* Columbia: Calvo, 1884.

Selby, Julian A. *Memorabilia and Anecdotal Reminiscences of Columbia, S. C. and Incidents Connected Therewith.* Columbia: Bryan, 1970.

Semi-Centennial Historical and Biographical Record of the Class of 1841 in Yale University. New Haven, Conn.: Tuttle, Morehouse & Taylor, 1892.

Simons, Robert Bentham. *Thomas Grange Simons III.* Charleston: Bryan, 1954.

Singleton, Charles Galloway. *Captain Richard Singleton and Some Descendants.* Dallas, 1962.

Skelton, Lynda Worley, ed. *General Andrew Pickens: An Autobiography.* Pendleton, S.C.: Pendleton District Historical and Recreational Commission, 1976.

Smallwood, Marilu Burch. *Burch, Harrell and Allied Families.* 3 vols. Gainesville, Fla.: Storter, 1968–92.

Smith, Daniel Elliott Huger. *The Dwelling Houses of Charleston, South Carolina.* Philadelphia: Lippincott, 1917.

Smith, Daniel Elliott Huger, and Alexander Samuel Salley. *Register of St. Philip's Parish, Charles Town, or Charleston, SC., 1754–1810.* Columbia: University of South Carolina Press, 1971.

Smith, John David. *Slavery, Race, and American History.* Armonk, N.Y.: Sharpe, 1999.

Snowden, Yates, and Harry Gardner Cutler. *History of South Carolina.* Vols. 2, 3, and 5. Chicago: Lewis, 1920.

Sorley, Merrow Egerton. *Lewis of Warner Hall: The History of a Family.* Baltimore: Genealogical Publishing, 2000.

The Southeastern Reporter Blue Book. 200 vols. St. Paul, Minn.: West, 1887–1939.

Sperry, Kip. *Reading Early American Handwriting.* Baltimore: Genealogical Publishing, 1998.

Stafford, G. M. G. *General Leroy Augustus Stafford: His Forebears and Descendants.* New Orleans: Pelican, 1943.

Strawn, Anne White. *The Ancestors and Descendants of John White and Sarah Elizabeth Green.* Salisbury, N.C.: Salisbury Printing, 1984.

Sturgis, Russell, ed. *A Dictionary of Architecture and Building.* 3 vols. New York: Macmillan, 1905.

Summers, Thomas O., ed. *The Autobiography of Reverend Joseph Travis.* Nashville: Stevenson & Owen, 1856.

Sumter, Thomas S. *Stateburg and Its People.* Sumter, S.C.: Sumter Print, 1949.

Talbert, Roy. *So Fine a Beach: Peter Horry's Summer of 1812.* Conway, S.C.: Coastal Carolina University, 1998.

Taylor, Frances Wallace, Catherine Taylor Matthews, and J. Tracy Power, eds. *The Leverett Letters: Correspondence of a South Carolina Family, 1851–1868.* Columbia: University of South Carolina Press, 2000.

Thomas, Albert Sidney. *A Historical Account of the Protestant Episcopal Church, in South Carolina, 1820–1957.* Charleston: Bryan, 1957.

Thomas, John Alexander William, and William Evans Thomas. *A History of Marlboro County with Traditions and Sketches of Numerous Families.* Atlanta: Foote & Davies, 1897.

Thomas, Joseph, and Thomas Baldwin. *A Complete Pronouncing Gazette or Geographical Dictionary of the World.* 2 vols. Philadelphia: Lippincott, 1880.

Thurston, Charles Myrick. *Descendants of Edward Thurston, the First of the Name in the Colony of Rhode Island.* New York: Trow & Smith, 1865.

Tomas, Ebenezer Smith. *Reminiscences of the Last Sixty-Five Years.* 2 vols. Hartford: Privately printed, 1840.

Townsend, Leah. *South Carolina Baptists, 1670–1805.* Baltimore: Genealogical Publishing, 2003.

Trezevant, Daniel Heyward. *The Burning of Columbia.* Columbia: South Carolinian Power, 1866.

Trezevant, John Timothée. *The Trezevant Family.* Columbia: State, 1914.

Tucker, Spencer C. *U.S. Leadership in Wartime Clashes, Controversy, and Compromise.* Santa Barbara, Cal.: ABC-CLIO, 2009.

Tupper, Henry Allen, ed. *Two Centuries of the First Baptist Church of South Carolina, 1683–1883.* Baltimore: Woodward, 1889.

Wakely, Joseph Beaumont. *Lost Chapters Recovered from the Early History of American Methodism.* New York: Carlton & Porter, 1858.

Waring, Alice Noble. *The Fighting Elder: Andrew Pickens, 1739–1817.* Columbia: University of South Carolina Press, 1962.

Waring, Joseph Ioor. *A History of Medicine in South Carolina, 1825–1900.* Columbia: Bryan, 1967.

Wauchope, George Armstrong. *The Writers of South Carolina.* Columbia: State Publishers, 1910.

Weiner, Marli Frances. *Mistresses and Slaves.* Urbana: University of Illinois Press, 1998.

Weir, Robert M. *"The Last of American Freemen": Studies in the Political Culture of the Colonial and Revolutionary South.* Macon, Ga.: Mercer University Press, 1986.

West, Anson. *A History of Methodism in Alabama.* Nashville: Publishing House Methodist Episcopal Church, South & Barbee & Smith, 1893.

Whittemore, Henry. *The Heroes of the American Revolution and Their Descendants: Battle of Long Island.* New York: Heroes of the Revolution, 1897–99.

Wightman, William May. *Life of William Capers, D.D., One of the Bishops of the Methodist Episcopal Church, South; Including an Autobiography.* Nashville: Southern Methodist Publishing House, 1858.

Wildey, Anna Cheesebrough. *Genealogy of the Descendants of William Chesebrough of Boston, Rehoboth, Mass.* New York: Wright, 1903.

Williams, Frances Leigh. *A Founding Family: The Pinckneys of South Carolina.* New York: Harcourt Brace Jovanovich, 1978.

Wilson, James Grant, and John Friske. *Appleton's Cyclopædia of American Biography.* 6 vols. New York: Appleton, 1887–89.

Wilson, Robert. *Genealogy of the Croft Family.* Aiken, S.C.: Palmetto, 1904.

Wilson, York Lowry. *A Carolina-Virginia Genealogy.* Aldershot, U.K.: Gale & Polden, 1962.

Withrow, Scott. *Carolina Genesis: Beyond the Color Line.* Palm Coast, Fla.: Backintyme, 2010.

Woodman, Harold D. *King Cotton and His Retainers.* Washington, D.C.: Beard Books, 2000.

Woody, Howard, and Allan D. Thigpen. *South Carolina Postcards: Sumter County.* 10 vols. Charleston: Arcadia, 1997–2005.

Wright, Annie Julia Mims. *A Record of the Descendants of Isaac Ross and Jean Brown.* Jackson, Miss.: Consumers Stationary and Printing, 1911.

Wyatt, Thomas. *Memoirs of the Generals, Commodores and Other Commanders.* Bedford: Applewood Books, 1848.

Zepke, Terrance. *Coastal South Carolina: Welcome to the Lowcountry.* Sarasota, Fla.: Pineapple, 2006.

Index

About the Editors

Roy Talbert Jr. holds the Lawrence B. and Jane P. Clark Chair of History at Coastal Carolina University in Conway, where he has taught since 1979. Talbert's earlier books include *FDR's Utopian: Arthur Morgan of the TVA,* which led to his appearance on the History Channel, and the award-winning *Negative Intelligence: The Army and the American Left, 1917–1941.*

Meggan A. Farish is a graduate of Coastal Carolina University and a history doctoral candidate at Duke University. Farish was a research assistant for the Waccamaw Center for Cultural and Historical Studies and an archives processor at the South Caroliniana Library at the University of South Carolina. In 2010 she was awarded the Lewis P. Jones Summer Research Fellowship at the South Caroliniana Library.